CHINA'S MUSLIMS & JAPAN'S EMPIRE

ISLAMIC CIVILIZATION AND MUSLIM NETWORKS

Carl W. Ernst and Bruce B. Lawrence, editors

Highlighting themes with historical as well as contemporary significance, Islamic Civilization and Muslim Networks features works that explore Islamic societies and Muslim peoples from a fresh perspective, drawing on new interpretive frameworks or theoretical strategies in a variety of disciplines. Special emphasis is given to systems of exchange that have promoted the creation and development of Islamic identities — cultural, religious, or geopolitical. The series spans all periods and regions of Islamic civilization.

A complete list of titles published in this series appears at the end of the book.

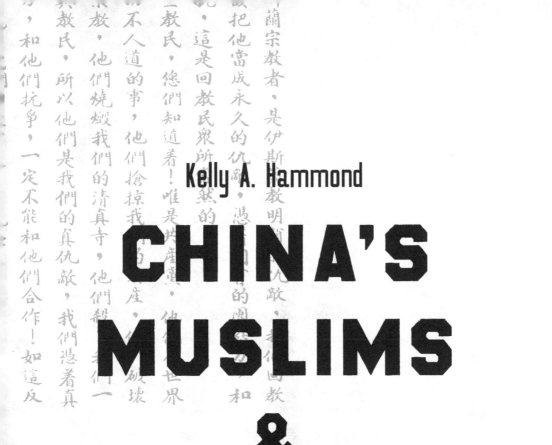

Kelly A. Hammond

CHINA'S MUSLIMS & JAPAN'S EMPIRE

Centering Islam in World War II

THE UNIVERSITY OF NORTH CAROLINA PRESS

Chapel Hill

Publication of this book was aided by the generous support of the
Chiang Ching-kuo Foundation for International Scholarly Exchange.

Designed by Jamison Cockerham
Set in Arno, Scala Sans, Telmoss, and Graveney
by Tseng Information Systems, Inc.

Manufactured in the United States of America

The University of North Carolina Press has been a member
of the Green Press Initiative since 2003.

Front cover background: anticommunist propaganda in Arabic and Chinese
produced by the Hebei Muslim Association, 1939. Courtesy Greater Japan
Muslim League database, Waseda University Library Special Collections.

LIBRARY OF CONGRESS CATALOGING-IN-PUBLICATION DATA
Names: Hammond, Kelly A., author.
Title: China's Muslims and Japan's empire : centering
Islam in World War II / Kelly A. Hammond.
Other titles: Islamic civilization & Muslim networks.
Description: Chapel Hill : University of North Carolina Press, 2020. | Series: Islamic
civilization and Muslim networks | Includes bibliographical references and index.
Identifiers: LCCN 2020010714 | ISBN 9781469659640 (cloth) |
ISBN 9781469659657 (paperback : alk. paper) | ISBN 9781469659664 (ebook)
Subjects: LCSH: World War, 1939–1945—Social aspects—Japan. | World War, 1939–
1945—Japan—Influence. | Muslims—China—Foreign influences. | Muslims—
China—History—20th century. | Japan—Foreign relations—China.
Classification: LCC D744.7.J3 H36 2020 | DDC 940.53088/2970951—dc23
LC record available at https://lccn.loc.gov/2020010714

For my parents

Contents

Figures, Tables, and Maps

Tables

Maps

Acknowledgments

This book has been a long time in the making. Along the way, I have accumulated debts to many people who have offered me their kindness, time, and support. I am also grateful to a number of institutions and agencies for their financial backing over the years. Georgetown University was a fabulous place to pursue my graduate studies in history. The department was encouraging, and my classmates (who have become my colleagues) made the journey less arduous. I was very fortunate to receive funding from the Canadian Social Science and Humanities Research Council, which ensured that I could spend summers in Asia and make ends meet in Washington, D.C. At Georgetown, I was lucky to have James Millward, Carol Benedict, and Jordan Sand as advisors. Beyond the unwavering support from these three individuals, Micah Muscolino, Judith Tucker, and Aviel Roshwald were also thoughtful and generous mentors.

Since I arrived at the University of Arkansas in the fall of 2015, the history department and the Fulbright College of Arts and Sciences have had my back. First and foremost, I need to thank my colleagues in the history department for fostering an atmosphere of collegiality that I never dreamed possible. I reserve a special thank-you for Lynda Coon. She not only watches my dog when I go out of town but has also been an incredibly helpful and encouraging faculty mentor and friend. Beyond my colleagues, the J. William Fulbright College of Arts and Sciences, Ted Swedenburg and the King Fadh Center for Middle East Studies, Ka Zeng and the Asian Studies program, and the Honors College continue to support my research and teaching, both financially and intellectually. I received SEED funding from the vice-provost for research and development, which helped fund a three-month trip to Japan to collect extra sources for this book. The fabulous people who work in the Interlibrary Loan office at the University of Arkansas are also well deserving of a mention: they manage to track down my wackiest requests.

A number of funding agencies have supported the timely completion of this project. Backing from the Henry Luce Foundation/ACLS Program in China Studies in the form of its Early Career Fellowship allowed me to take a year off from teaching and service to complete a draft of the manuscript. A fellowship at the Kluge Center in the Library of Congress provided another extended period where I was able to get the book sent out for review while starting research on my second project. Along the way, I received the Franklin Research Grant from the American Philosophical Society, the Association for Asian Studies Northeast Asia Council Research Grant, and a three-month residency fellowship from the Center for Chinese Studies in the National Library in Taipei. I was also awarded a publication subsidy grant from the Chiang Ching-kuo Foundation. These grants were instrumental for completing the book.

I have made a number of incredible friendships along this journey, and some of them have now become my colleagues. A few deserve special recognition for their support and intellectual curiosity. Micki McCoy and I met teaching English in China in the early 2000s. Kate Merkel-Hess and Denise Ho invited me to join their reading group while I was studying Chinese in Shanghai. Josh Freeman, Eric Schluessel, David Tobin, and I spent way too much time in a "yurt bar" owned by a corrupt Mongolian cop across the street from Xinjiang Normal University in 2007–8. Around that time, Micki McCoy came out to visit me in Xinjiang and we inspected all the Buddhist grottoes we could access in the region before taking a three-day train ride from Urumqi to Shanghai. The five of us seem to have emerged from this period in our lives relatively unscathed, and I value their friendship and support over the years.

Along the way, I have also met a number of people who deserve much more than a shout-out in these acknowledgments. Noriko Yamazaki is a dear friend who read and commented on the entire manuscript. Toni Jensen and Ram Natarajan have become my Fayetteville family. Jeff Wasserstrom has been supportive of my work and career since I wrote a piece for the *China Beat* back in 2008. Abhishek Kaicker is an old friend, going back to our days as master's students in Vancouver. Elise Anderson, David Atwill, Jacob Eyferth, Michael Gibbs Hill, Christine Kim, Jonas Lamn, Fabio Lanza, Diana Lary, Tom Mullaney, Kristian Petersen, Javier Puente, Rian Thum, Aparna Vaidik, Ben Van Overmeire, Stacey Van Vleet, and Elizabeth Williams have all played a role in my journey. Thanks also to Benno Weiner for the encouragement, for the helpful and thoughtful editorial comments, and for always being up to trying new breweries. They are all impressive scholars and great people to be around. I also want to thank the Asian studies "twittersphere" for its collective support and daily laughs throughout this project. There are incredible people working in this field, and I am humbled to call so many of them my friends and colleagues.

Some of the material in the book appeared in a 2017 journal article in the *Journal of Global History*. Thank you to Cambridge University Press for allowing the work to be adapted here with permission. I also need to thank my editor, Elaine Maisner, the Islamic Civilization and Muslim Networks series editors Carl W. Ernst and Bruce B. Lawrence, and the incredible staff at UNC Press for getting behind this project in a serious way. They were all extremely eager about the project from the get-go and have made this process much less painful than I had feared. The blind reviewers also provided helpful feedback, and I hope that one day they will reveal themselves to me so that I can thank them personally. I also wish to thank Mr. Koike in Special Collections at Waseda University Library. He helped secure, at no cost, the copyright for many of the photos in the book that are housed in the Greater Japan Muslim League database.

Finally, a very special thank you to Jonathan Lipman. In 2009, he dug out a stack of Japanese articles from his basement and mailed them to me. These articles were the seeds of this book. He served as the outside reader on my dissertation committee, and selflessly read an entire draft of the manuscript, providing clear and pointed feedback. He is the model of a scholar and mentor that we should all aspire to. My best friend, Rebecca Manley, has also been a constant source of support. We were on a parallel graduate school track—although she is now a veterinary radiologist, not a historian—so we were able to commiserate and celebrate together about the ups and downs of writing, publishing, and working in academia.

I have an incredibly caring family. My mom and stepfather and my dad and stepmom are my biggest cheerleaders. My sister, Brittany, just gets me. She lives in Dubai, and we do not get to see each other frequently, but our sisterly bond is a real and honest one. I am thankful that they have been along for this wild and crazy ride since the beginning. A final thanks is reserved for my dog, Dino. He's a local celebrity in Fayetteville and a constant reminder to get up from my desk and not take life too seriously.

A Note on Romanization

The romanization of Chinese characters uses the pinyin system, with a few notable exceptions such as the names of overseas Chinese and standardized names like Sun Yatsen and Chiang Kai-shek. Japanese translations use the Hepburn romanization system. Korean, Turkish, and Arabic translations were made by the authors who are cited and use the romanization systems of the respective languages at the discretion of the individual authors.

To avoid confusion, I have chosen to keep the name "Beijing" ("northern capital") throughout the book even though the city was technically called "Beiping" ("northern peace") during the Nanjing Decade (1928–37), when the Nationalist capital moved south to "Nanjing" ("southern capital"). After the Japanese occupation of the city in July 1937, most Chinese sources continued to call it "Beiping," while Japanese sources generally use "Beijing." To avoid confusing readers, I decided to stick with "Beijing" throughout the book.

The glossary at the back of the book will be helpful for readers who are familiar with either Chinese or Japanese, or for those who are comfortable with both languages. It includes most of the names and my own translations but omits some common words and phrases in both Chinese and Japanese.

A Brief Note on Sources

This book is the culmination of years of archival research. Overall, the book uses sources in five languages from seven countries to weave together a story about the Japanese Empire's involvement with Muslims from China during World War II. Because of the contentious situation for researchers on the ground in the People's Republic of China, my sources are drawn from a wide variety of repositories. Like many historians and researchers, I have never been granted access to the Number Two Archives in Nanjing, although I did make extensive use of the Beijing Municipal Archives and the National Library in Beijing. I also visited libraries and archives in Dalian and Chengde. The bulk of my research in the People's Republic of China was conducted in 2011–12.

Outside of mainland China, I spent three months at Academia Sinica and Academia Historica in Taipei. As a fellow at the Center for Chinese Studies in the National Library of Taiwan, I had access to many rare Japanese and Chinese books published in the 1930s and 1940s held exclusively in the center's vast collection. In Tokyo, over the course of four trips lasting between two and four months, I worked at the Foreign Ministry Archives, the National Archives of Japan, the Islamic Library at Waseda University, the Oriental Library (J. *tōyō bunko*), and the National Diet Library.

The book also draws on sources from the National Archives and Research Administration (NARA) in College Park, Maryland, the Asian Reading Room at the Library of Congress, and the British Archives at Kew. The materials about tea from the Archives du Maroc were provided by my colleague Graham H. Cornwell. The sources from *Oriente Moderno* came to me through the interlibrary loan staff at the University of Arkansas.

Translations from Chinese, Japanese, French, and Italian are my own, unless otherwise noted.

CHINA'S
MUSLIMS
&
JAPAN'S
EMPIRE

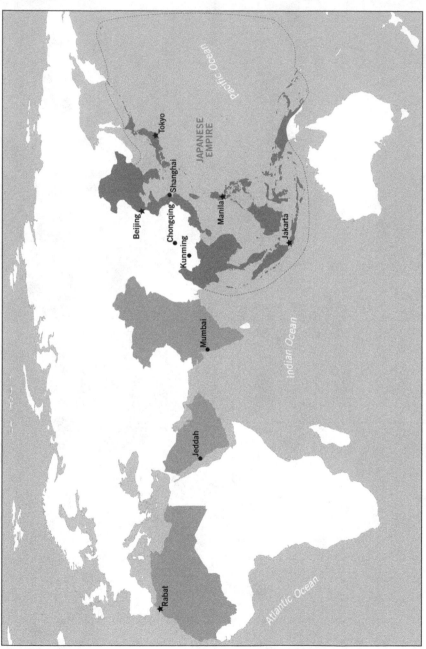

Map 1. Aspirational Islamic spaces beyond what is generally considered the geographic limits of the Japanese Empire. (Data compiled by the author; map by Kristian R. Underwood)

INTRODUCTION

Centering Islam in Japan's Quest for Empire

In 1940, a secret report compiled by the Chinese Foreign Ministry warned the Chinese Nationalist Party (C. *Guomindang*) about "Japan's Near East Conspiracy" to win the support of Muslims around the world.[1] The briefing begins by cautioning that Japanese propaganda made claims like, "Japan is the sun, Islam is the moon, which together emanate enough brightness to shine from East Asia throughout the entire world."[2] These metaphors inspired deep and growing concern among a segment of Chinese Nationalists, who watched as the Japanese government offered incentives, like scholarships to study in Tokyo, or government-sponsored hajj (pilgrimages to Mecca), to Muslims living in occupied China. The report urged the Nationalist government, which by this point in the war had retreated to the inland city of Chongqing, to pay more attention to imperial Japan's campaigns to ingratiate themselves to Muslims throughout Asia, especially with Muslims living in occupied China. The Nationalist concerns were warranted. For their part, Japanese officials hoped their efforts would create a cadre of Muslims who supported their anti-Western, anticommunist agenda, and who were loyal to the Japanese Empire. In turn, both sides were imagining that Muslims, especially those living in occupied China, potentially could be deployed on diplomatic and trade missions around the world in the service of the Japanese Empire.

These gestures by the Japanese government also alarmed many "Sino-Muslims," a diverse community that has been in China for hundreds of years. Sino-Muslims are influenced by Chinese culture, yet they maintain distinct religious and cultural practices associated with their Islamic religious beliefs. The term *Sino-Muslim* distinguishes these communities from

1

non-Chinese speaking Muslim populations in China, such as the Uyghurs, or the Tajiks.[3] As the Nationalists reacted and responded to Japan's attempts to win the support of this vital minority group, Sino-Muslims also debated the upsides and downsides of throwing their support behind the Japanese Empire. Many Sino-Muslims were skeptical of the Japanese Empire's intentions, but others willingly accepted its sponsorship and funding in return for nominal—or even tacit—political support. Sino-Muslim men like Tang Yichen, who became the presiding head of the Japanese-sponsored All China Muslim League and went on a Japanese government-funded hajj in 1938–39, were instrumental in projecting Japan's visions for empire to Muslims around the world. Young Sino-Muslim women like Bai Shufang, who won one of the many Japanese-language speaking contests held across occupied China, were awarded scholarships to study Japanese, and were eventually enlisted as teachers into the service of empire.[4] Tang Yichen and Bai Shufang were just regular people and are not well known, but they were among the ordinary Sino-Muslim men and women who were forced to make difficult decisions while living under occupation in wartime China. These men and women played an important role in Axis diplomacy and Japanese imperial intelligence strategies throughout World War II.

Networking: China's Muslims and Japan's Empire

Scholarship in English has not yet explored this dimension of Japanese imperialism, yet it is clear that the Japanese Empire made concerted and coordinated efforts to win the support of Muslims from China in order to foster broad and far-reaching connections to Muslims, from Damascus to Detroit. Placing Sino-Muslims at the center of Japan's "outreach" to "trans-Islamic" spaces does a number of things.[5] For one, the Japanese Empire had a profound impact on the formation of religious and minority identities on the Chinese mainland in the twentieth century. Beyond this, centering Sino-Muslims and Japan's ambitious Islamic policies helps to reterritorialize the spatial boundaries of the Japanese imperial project. As Sino-Muslims traveled to the Middle East and made connections with Muslims from around the world while studying or working in Tokyo, they helped project Japanese imperial ambitions well beyond what we now consider to be the geographical boundaries of the Greater East Asia Co-Prosperity Sphere. At the same time, the lives of Sino-Muslims and Japanese imperial officials "intersected on a daily basis," and these interactions reveal how Sino-Muslims lived under the "aegis of imperial rule."[6]

Sino-Muslims were supposed to be the proxies for the Japanese Empire to launch purposeful outreach campaigns to Muslims around the world. These were strategic and politicized campaigns devised with the aim of enlarging and expanding Japan's influence in North Africa, Central Asia, South Asia, and the Middle East.[7] In large part, these were also attempts to create new Muslim consumers who could be used to subvert the global capitalist world order based in the North Atlantic and to destabilize Soviet Communism. Through extensive propaganda and outreach, the Japanese government successfully presented Sino-Muslims as important allies in their ongoing efforts to dismantle Western imperialism and Soviet Communism rather than as an integral part of the Chinese nation-state. At the same time, policies dealing with Muslim populations were something that the Japanese Empire had in common with the Nazis and the Italian Fascists. This gave Japanese bureaucrats the opportunity to showcase similarities to their fascist partners and provided an opportunity for inter-Axis cooperation. Through the lens of Sino-Muslims, an examination of the Japanese Empire's long-term plans concerning Muslims around the world foregrounds connections among the Axis powers.

The global war shaped and reshaped discussions about the place of Islam in Asia.[8] Focusing on the ways the Japanese Empire supported networks of Muslims presents the opportunity to think about World War II in East Asia as "a time of unprecedented intellectual and cultural exchange" that was often "complicated but not prevented by military and political turmoil."[9] In some ways, World War II facilitated a period of increased internationalism, and the focus on minority actors traveling around the Japanese Empire expands our visions of what Tessa Morris-Suzuki has termed "the transnational memory of war."[10] Locating the history of World War II in transnational and international experiences dislodges national narratives through the writing of histories that travel beyond national boundaries.[11] With Japanese support, Muslims from China traveled broadly and made connections with Muslims around the world. By examining these "complex webs of multi-directional interactions," beyond the locus of Japanese subjects on the home islands or Sino-Muslim interactions with the Chinese Nationalists and Communists, new imperial formations start to emerge.[12]

Sino-Muslims drew on a wide repository of skills in order to promote and develop networks through the Japanese imperial apparatus. Tokyo was at the "confluence" of these currents, and became a space where educational opportunities, Islamic voices, and anti-imperial sentiments converged.[13] At the same time, the Japanese Empire relied on nonstate actors and their existing networks to help create relationships with Muslims around the world. By tapping into preexisting Muslim networks, the Japanese Empire was able to mitigate uncertainty and limit its own financial investment to create and maintain relationships with Muslims.[14] Through the organizations it supported, such as the Greater Japan Muslim League and the All China Muslim League, the Japanese government facilitated communication and interactions among Muslims who might not have otherwise had the opportunity to meet. Through informal religious networks, members of the Greater Japan Muslim League were also able to devise plans to enter new markets in Islamic spaces and create new Muslim consumers, in an effort to destabilize both the Soviets and European and American commercial interests. Thus, Muslim networks proved an invaluable tool for fostering trade and diplomacy and had an impact on economic development and expansion into new regions where a large proportion of the population was composed of Muslims.[15]

These networks were also more easily able "to reduce, overcome, or circumvent" state structures and institutions. As nonstate actors who were seemingly operating of their own accord even if they had financial backing from the Japanese Empire, Sino-Muslims were presented with "opportunities, resources, partners, and locations" that were not accessible to Japanese subjects and bureaucrats.[16] This is what made Sino-Muslims valuable to the Japanese Empire. These networks provided the opportunity to connect "large structural changes" that were in motion during the war with the daily "experiences of ordinary people in the course of those changes."[17] In turn, this linked Sino-Muslims to larger "patterns of relations among actors that define economic, political and social structures."[18] Focusing on Sino-Muslims and the Japanese Empire, and exploring the interconnectedness between Muslims throughout East Asia and beyond helps to "locate Islam in multiple pasts across several geo-linguistic, socio-cultural frontiers."[19] In short, placing Sino-Muslims at the center of Japan's wartime ambitions presents alternative ways to configure Japanese imperial space.

Muslims from China conceptualized the spatial and temporal boundaries of "Asia" differently than non-Muslims.[20] Opportunities provided to Sino-Muslims by the Japanese Empire widened their understanding of what both "Asia" and the *dar-al-Islam*, or the abode of Islam, meant in this specific wartime moment. The travels of Sino-Muslims and others to Tokyo and around the world helps to reterritorialize the Japanese Empire through the lens of non-Japanese subjects. Examining how Muslims from China were included in or excluded from the hegemonic production of both Asian spaces and Islamic spaces offers an alternative interpretation of how the Japanese Empire projected its wartime visions for a Greater East Asia and how non-Japanese subjects understood the spatial arrangement of the Japanese imperial project on their own terms.[21]

China's Muslims and Japan's Empire complicates the story about the inclusion of Muslims into the Chinese nation-state. The Japanese occupation of North China played a central role in the creation of ethnonationalism on the mainland, where various political actors vied for the loyalty and support of Muslims in China throughout the 1930s and 1940s. This perspective helps account for the diversity of political views within the Sino-Muslim community in China and to establish that there was never a unified Nationalist-supported Muslim resistance against Japan during the war.[22] There are ongoing efforts to demystify war in twentieth-century China, and a number of historians have sparked discussions about the everyday life of civilians and refugees during the war.[23] However, these recent studies focus on Han Chinese, rather than on the lived experiences of non-Han communities in China's vast borderlands. Including the everyday experiences of Muslims living under the shadow of occupation during the war treats the Japanese occupation of the mainland and the wartime experiences of Sino-Muslims as integral parts of modern Chinese history, rather than as a "peripheral story of something that happened over there."[24] Focusing on Japanese policies, Nationalist responses, and Sino-Muslims themselves uncovers hitherto unconsidered political and social outcomes of World War II for minority populations in China. Taken as a whole, the project contributes to understanding the experiences of war in East Asia and to rethinking the place of Sino-Muslims in the broader nexus of Islamic politics in the twentieth century.

Foregrounding the experiences of Sino-Muslims living under Japanese occupation complicates dominant narratives of a cohesive resistance to the Japanese presence on the mainland by drawing attention to the wide variety of experiences Sino-Muslims had during the war. Nationalist assertions of a unified China and the anti-Japanese wartime rhetoric that accompanied these declarations differed wildly from the conditions and situations on the ground experienced by most civilians. In fact, throughout the war close to 200 million people in China were at one time or another under the purview of the Japanese occupying forces.[25] There were certainly segments of Muslim communities that supported the Nationalist government. Yet even within this segment of the population, opinions and backing of the Nationalists were never unwavering and rarely unified. The impression of a united Sino-Muslim resistance reinforces that "forgetting has become official policy" in the current political climate in the People's Republic of China (PRC), where the diversity of wartime voices are muted in the name of national salvation and resistance.[26] Buying into the rhetoric of inclusiveness and resistance to the Japanese during World War II denies agency to Sino-Muslims who were working with the Japanese imperial government throughout the war to articulate their visions of what they believed modern ethnonational sentiments meant within their own communities.[27]

The idea that imperial Japan's attempts to co-opt Muslims from China might have shaped the state-building efforts of Chinese leaders—both Nationalist and Communist—is all but inadmissible in the highly politicized postwar discourses regarding ethnicity and the Chinese state. Postwar scholars and politicians have characterized Japanese imperial attempts to mobilize Muslims as evil and therefore ultimately failed efforts.[28] And yet Nationalist and Japanese policymakers were engaged in a serious and protracted battle to win the hearts and minds of Muslims on the mainland, a battle whose results were never predetermined. During the war, the Nationalists were acutely aware of how vulnerable borderland and non-Han communities were to military and political incursions, and the "degree to which Japanese encouragement of 'ethnic independence' was fostering irredentism among the people of China's periphery."[29]

That the perceived triumphs of the Japanese Empire were quickly overturned and cast as failures is deeply embedded in the wartime historiography, which for a long time cast all Japanese attempts at developing, integrating, and creating a vision for East Asia as "failed ideologies" and policies.[30] It is true that Japan's defeat in August 1945 meant that its ties to Muslims in China and around the world were abruptly severed. It is also true that policies geared to recruiting Muslims were associated with wartime militarism, making them "taboo" topics.[31] However, the fact that these wartime efforts are absent from the postwar historiography should not be taken as an indicator that the policies failed. In fact, throughout the war, the Nationalist government and Allied observers in China were deeply concerned about the ongoing successes of Japan's overtures to Muslims living under occupation in North China and throughout the colonial world.

Although the Japanese imperial government and military's intentions often should be construed as nefarious, their policies and practices also had tangible impacts on Muslims in China and around the world. In saying this, I am not minimizing the horrific violence inflicted on Sino-Muslim civilians and communities by the Japanese Imperial Army; rather, I am underscoring the importance of engaging seriously with Japanese imperial policies that targeted Sino-Muslims on the mainland, and the Chinese Nationalist responses to these policies.[32] In addition, when we focus on Sino-Muslims themselves, we begin to see them more as individuals and involved arbitrators in policy decisions that impacted their own well-being. It is also important to keep in mind that the decisions individuals made to work with the Japanese Empire, the Chinese Nationalists, or other political backers had an impact on their lives long after the war was over.

By the early 1950s, the wartime warning about Japan's "Near East Conspiracy" to lure Muslims over to the Axis side might have read like a relic amid the new Cold War politics in East Asia. But reverberations of the Japanese imperial government's wartime policies continued to ripple through Asia.[33] In 1954, a British consular officer stationed in Karachi sent a number of dispatches to the British office in the Republic of China (Taiwan) requesting information about a group of Muslims from China who were stranded in Pakistan after being denied hajj visas by Saudi Arabia. The officer in Karachi was curious about the relationships and allegiances between Muslims who had fled to Taiwan with the Nationalists, Muslims who had remained on the mainland, and the new Chinese Communist government that was busily consolidating its hold over the mainland. The response from Taipei explained that there were competing groups of Muslims whose loyalties to each other shifted as frequently as their political allegiances and changed regularly depending on who was willing to fund their reform agendas or acquiesce to their political demands.[34] The dispatch clarified that by the late 1940s, the main players with regard to Muslim populations in China were the Nationalists and the Communists, but that the Soviet Union and Japan had exerted considerable influence over Muslims from Xinjiang to Heilongjiang throughout the 1930s and 1940s.[35]

The well-informed British bureaucrat stationed in Taipei also explained that the Japanese government initially had worked with Muslims more successfully than either the Communists or the Nationalists because its strategies and tactics were directed at recruiting lower-level local elites who had remained in the occupied areas. According to the dispatch, this policy appealed to disgruntled Muslims who felt neglected and unsure of their place in either the Nationalist or the Communist visions for the future of China. The report also noted that the Japanese government used Sino-Muslims against the Soviets, the Chinese Communists, and the Nationalists, and as leverage to undermine both British and American political aims in Asia.[36] In the end, the bureaucrat could not provide insights as to why this particular group of Muslims had been denied entry into Saudi Arabia, but he speculated that their wartime affiliation with the Japanese Empire was likely the reason.[37] In this case, wartime alliances and actions continued to have consequences and repercussions for Muslims in Asia long after the Japanese surrender.

Sitting on a Bamboo Fence: Race, Ethnicity, and Sino-Muslims between the Nationalists and the Japanese

The phrase "sitting on a bamboo fence" (C. *zuozai liba shang*) is meant to evoke an uncomfortable and precarious balancing act. This particular idiom was used by an unnamed Sino-Muslim living under Japanese occupation to describe the way he and many of his compatriots felt about their situation during the war.[38] Sino-Muslims often had to make difficult choices that involved taking calculated risks. Evaluating the contested negotiations between the Nationalists, the Japanese, and Sino-Muslims highlights just how disruptive and disorderly this period in modern China was for minorities who ended up being considered a part of the Chinese state but were often "on the fence" about where their political loyalties lay during the war.

In this regard, one of my broader aims is to contribute to the growing body of literature that brings Chinese ethnopolitical history to the forefront of the discussion of the creation of the modern Chinese nation-state.[39] Throughout the first half of the twentieth century, frontier issues were manipulated to serve the needs of all interested parties, and the Nationalists were especially concerned with how to integrate non-Han communities into China's national imagination. The Nationalists expended a great deal of intellectual energy trying to figure out the specific position that groups like Muslims, Tibetans, and Mongolians occupied in their new vision for the nation-state.[40] At the same time, the Japanese Empire paid close attention to the plights and discontent among non-Han populations who were uncertain about their stake in the ever-evolving Nationalist visions of the nation and where they fit into it.

Scholars of borderlands in China are pushing the boundaries of state-making projects in twentieth-century China, demanding the acknowledgment of the non-Chinese elements and influences on the development of ethnonationalist politics.[41] By centering peripheries and peripheral peoples, we see that the state had to work the hardest to make things right on the fringes of the fallen Qing Empire (1636/1644–1911).[42] It was also in these marginal spaces that non-Han communities were the most willing to work with non-Chinese political backers, like the Soviets and the Japanese Empire, to achieve their own reform agendas. When we return agency to these actors in the ongoing struggle about their incorporation into the Chinese state, it becomes clear that simply buying into the narrative about the place of Muslims in China subsumes the myriad ways their story can be told from outside China.[43] These efforts, by myself and others, mark a shift in the scholarship on minorities who now live within the boundaries of the People's Republic of China. We must continue to interrogate non-Chinese elements, processes, and contributions to the creation and development of non-Han identities in late imperial and modern Chinese history.[44]

At the same time, social Darwinism and nineteenth-century racialist ideology played an important role in both the Manchu Qing and Japanese Meiji reformers' conceptualization of race and nation at the end of the nineteenth century. The introduction of Japanese racial neologisms into the Chinese lexicon, especially the notion of *minzu* (J. *minzoku*), contributed to developing ideas about race and racial categorizations in the waning years of the Qing. *Minzu* is a word with a contentious history. It can mean "ethnic group," "nationality," "peoples," "nation," or "race," depending on the context, time period, and political agenda of the writers or publishers using it.[45] The term's malleability provided a space for late Qing and Meiji reformers to formulate how they imagined people to belong in an amorphous and ever-changing iteration of their respective empires. Individuals and groups also internalized the concept and used it to suit their own political agendas vis-à-vis the state.[46]

The vast majority of the people living in China are classified by the state as Han Chinese. The idea of a "Han person" (C. *hanren*) refers to descendants of the Han Dynasty, but the idea of a "Han nationality" (C. *hanzu*) or a "Han people" (C. *hanmin*) is a distinctly modern invention.[47] *Hanren* and *hanzu* are not drastically different, but the racialist connotations embroiled with the concept of *hanzu* make these neologisms distinctly late nineteenth-century ideas steeped in the language of social Darwinism.[48] The identification and categorization of Muslims in China also underwent a similar transformation during the shift from empire to nation-state. Islam in China had long been known as the Hui religion (C. *Huijiao*), and believers were known as disciples of the Hui religion (C. *huijiaotu*).[49] In tandem with the new concept of *hanzu*, Hui nationality (C. *huizu*) emerged as an ethnic moniker in the late nineteenth century.[50] The term is flexible and adaptable, and was deployed in many different ways throughout the first part of the twentieth century.

By the 1930s, there were competing and conflicting ideas of what it meant to be labeled a *huizu* in China. In some cases, it was purely a religious category, while others thought of it as an ethnic one. In some instances, it was even used as a racial category, and others still understood it as a blending of all three.[51] Regardless of the new names and categories, the people now designated by the state as *huizu* had long been part of the social fabric of China. In my own analysis, I favor the use of the term *Sino-Muslim* over *hui* or *huizu* because it also allows us to disengage with the Chinese state's proscribed, defined, and designated term. However, I do use *huizu* as a historical term, as it appears in writings in both Chinese and Japanese throughout the 1930s and 1940s to highlight the specific moment when Sino-Muslim communities in China were working through what these terms meant to them within the context of the ongoing war with Japan.

There are also many instances when Sino-Muslims purposefully used the term *huizu* to describe or talk about themselves. When Sino-Muslims wrote about the Islamic World, they regularly wrote about the *Huijiao shijie*, which quite literally means the "hui-religion world." This term was used to evoke a sense of commonality between themselves and their own ethnoreligious sentiments as Chinese-speaking Muslims in relation to other Muslims around the world. They were not using the term *yisilan shijie*, which would be the literal translation of "Islamic world." This means that there was an effort on the part of Muslims in China to elide their own ethnoreligious sentiment with larger currents of global Islam while coming to terms with their place in the fragmented Chinese state. All of this to say that the term *Sino-Muslim* is imperfect but necessary. Use of the term is in no way meant to detract from the complexity of the experience of Muslims trying simultaneously to come to terms with their place in China and their place in the world.[52]

In the late nineteenth century, revolutionaries trying to overthrow the Qing Dynasty invented the idea that the Han were a cohesive majority.[53] However, this did not mean that the revolutionaries could ignore the other 10 percent of the population who inhabited the vast territories on the peripheries of the crumbling empire. When the Chinese Republic was founded on January 1, 1912, members of the provisional government were conscious of the need to transform the "Inner Asian dependencies of the defunct Qing into integral parts of the Chinese state."[54] As the last Qing emperor abdicated, the new provisional government set out with an ambitious agenda to keep the borders of one of the largest land-based empires in history intact. In order to do this, the new Republican government—which initially was anti-Manchu and often fervently Han-centric—latched onto Qing ethno-political discourses.

As a multiethnic imperial project, the Qing promoted an idea of a peaceful coexistence among the five major groups who lived under its purview: the Han, the Muslims, the Manchus, the Tibetans, and the Mongols. Of course, the reality was much more violent and complicated, but revolutionaries appropriated this ideology. The problem was that the plan rested on the idea that these new citizens of the Republic of China *wanted* to be a part of the revolutionary vision for a new Chinese state. It was in this political milieu that the Japanese, the Russians, and the British tactfully initiated efforts to co-opt non-Han political figures on China's peripheries, thus placing the Nationalist government in a precarious position. Already on the defensive, the Nationalists were forced to work extra hard to try to gain the support of many non-Han communities who were often skeptical of the new Nationalist government.

At the same time, Sino-Muslims had their own ideas regarding their connections to both the Chinese state and to the *dar-al-Islam*. Sino-Muslims were able to connect themselves to an Islamic, non-Chinese past and present in ways that Han Chinese could not. Yet Muslim intellectuals also had to figure out where and how they fit into the *dar-al-Islam* given their "distance and isolation from the Arab heartlands."[55] Sino-Muslims expressed their understanding of their own pasts through genealogical writings that linked them to the Prophet Muhammad.[56] These genealogies and histories, written and compiled by Sino-Muslims, brought together "a vast temporal and spatial expanse" and revealed their need to work "a little harder to situate themselves within an Islamic space" because they lived in a Chinese milieu.[57] This point is useful for thinking about *why* the Japanese were interested in Sino-Muslims. It was these connections to both an Islamic past and to an Islamic present that made Sino-Muslims valuable for Japanese imperial ambitions both within and beyond East Asia.

Aspirational Nationalism and the Fractured Chinese State

The aspirations of the new Republican government regularly fell short of its goals, and throughout the 1920s and 1930s China remained deeply divided:

initially Manchuria was under the control of Zhang Zuolin, succeeded by his son, Zhang Xueliang; Feng Yuxiang's National People's Army controlled most of Henan, Suiyuan, Shaanxi, and part of Gansu; Yan Xishan ruled uncontested in Shanxi and in parts of Hebei; in the Southwest, the Muslim general Bai Chongxi and the "Guangxi faction" ruled the region with relative autonomy; and the Muslim Ma clans held a firm—if oppressive—grasp over large swaths of the Northwest. Beyond this, Central Tibet, Xinjiang, and Outer Mongolia operated "beyond the effective jurisdiction of Nanking," albeit in different ways.[58] Central Tibet and Outer Mongolia had broken away. In Xinjiang, Yang Zengxin continued to pay lip service to the Nationalists while effectively remaining independent until his death in 1928. Following his death, there were a number of tumultuous years in Xinjiang, which included the establishment of the short-lived East Turkestan Republic. The Soviets also installed Sheng Shicai as military governor to rule over the region while brokering for power with other military and political leaders in the region that had previously encompassed Qing Central Asia. This greatly oversimplified snapshot of the fractured political landscape throughout the 1920s and 1930s is a testament to the struggles that the Nationalists encountered while attempting to retain control over Qing territory.

All the while, the increasingly authoritarian Japanese government and military strengthened their foothold in China. By the 1920s, the Japanese government was heavily invested in Manchuria through railroad acquisitions gained as spoils in the Russo-Japanese War (1904–5). Then, in 1931, the Japanese Kwantung Army seized Manchuria in a coordinated military response to a staged bombing of a section of railway along the Japanese-controlled South Manchurian Railway. The Kwantung Army and the Japanese government used the bombing as pretext to establish the Japanese client-state Manchukuo in March 1932. These events culminated in Japan's dramatic departure from the League of Nations in 1933 over the international recognition and sovereignty of Manchukuo.

The establishment of Manchukuo shocked the world. It signaled Japan's "shift from liberal internationalism to Asian regionalism," which had resulted from its complete loss of faith in the post–World War I Wilsonian international world order.[59] Much like the Germans and the Italians, interwar Japanese politicians felt increasingly constrained by the stipulations imposed on them by the Treaty of Versailles. On the other end of the Eurasian continent, Adolf Hitler was consolidating his hold over Germany after the Reichstag Fire, and Benito Mussolini was firmly in control of Fascist Italy. These three powers, feeling maligned by and shunned from global politics, found common enemies in Western liberalism and the increasing threat of Soviet Communism. To combat the growing fear of the Soviet Union, Nazi Germany and the Japanese Empire signed the Anti-Comintern Pact in November 1936. After signing the pact, the Germans recognized Manchukuo, which strengthened the Japanese Empire's perception of its own legitimacy on the Chinese mainland.[60]

The Anti-Comintern Pact realigned the political, economic, and social order in East Asia.[61] From the moment that the Japanese Empire officially associated with Nazi Germany, it ostracized itself from the political and capital centers in the North Atlantic and faced increased economic sanctions from the United States, the Netherlands, and Great Britain. Yet this new bloc simultaneously created and opened new spaces beyond East Asia for Japanese social, cultural, and economic policies. In order to capitalize on these new spaces, Japanese policymakers developed schemes that relied heavily on Muslims from North China, who they imagined would work in the service of empire. The idea was to bring Japanese manufactured goods to Muslims throughout the colonized world in order to create new markets and consumers in Islamic spaces that were opened to them thanks to the impending war in Europe.

The first chapters of this book introduce readers to a number of high-profile Japanese intellectuals who from the end of the nineteenth century were prominent in Japan's burgeoning interest in Islam.[62] However, it was not until the late 1920s that Japanese scholars of Islam were brought into imperial service as efforts to instrumentalize the religion became central to Japanese ambitions in Asia.[63] By the time total war broke out on the Chinese mainland in July 1937, the Japanese Empire was deeply involved with the Muslim populations in Manchukuo. But it was the beginning of the Second Sino-Japanese War that really signaled a shift, as Japanese policymakers and imperialists were able to wield more direct control over Muslim communities under their jurisdiction. The outbreak of war and subsequent occupation also increased the number of Sino-Muslims living under Japanese rule. During this time, the interests of Japanese academics and intellectuals who specialized in Islamic history and theology became more closely aligned with the military's aspirations for the ever-expanding Japanese Empire.

Throughout the 1930s, this convergence between the objectives of Japanese scholars of Islam and Pan-Asianist thinkers provided the ideological support for the Japanese government's increasing backing of Islam and Muslims around the world. Part of the appeal of *Pan-Asianism* was the looseness of the term, which Japanese imperialists manipulated to suit different needs at different times.[64] When defining "Asia," Japanese intellectuals relied on a number of amorphous words to explain commonalities between peoples in the region.[65] The concepts of "cultural unity" (J. *dōbun*; C. *tongwen*) and "racial kinship" (J. *dōshu*; C. *tongzhong*) were fluid enough to be broadly inclusive while appealing to Pan-Asianist sentiments that all Asians were united in a similar struggle.[66] In the late Meiji period, Pan-Asianism morphed from a "vague romantic and idealistic feeling of solidarity into an ideology that could be applied in the sphere of Realpolitik."[67] It was in this political milieu that Japanese intellectuals appropriated this inclusive yet highly malleable term into their official foreign policy as a way to promote "Asia for the Asians" without ever clearly articulating what "Asia" or "the Asians" actually meant. This ideological ambiguity provided the space for Japanese intellectuals who studied Islam and Islamic theology to make Pan-Asian ideas attractive and inclusive for Muslims as well.

The Japanese Empire was intent on presenting itself as a legitimate supporter of Islam. To do this, it invoked Pan-Asianism as a way to highlight connections between itself and Muslims coming into its expansionist imperial visions.[68] However, the military realized that these plans needed the knowledge, research skills, and language skills of intellectuals and academics who had spent years in the field collecting data and who also had deep training in foreign languages.[69] In this regard, Japanese subjects of non-Japanese ancestry who lived beyond the home islands and academics who specialized in religion helped to extend the political and economic aims of the Japanese imperial project through the support and implementation of cultural policies geared to gaining the favor of Muslims.[70] In fact, a number of prominent Japanese Islamic specialists were present in Geneva when the League of Nations debated whether or not to recognize Manchukuo as a sovereign state. Specifically, Wakabayashi Han, a specialist in South Asian Islam who had long advocated for closer ties between Muslims and the Japanese Empire, "witnessed the decision of Japanese diplomats to withdraw from the league upon its refusal to recognize Manchukuo."[71] On the long boat ride back to Japan, he discussed the ways deepening connections to Muslims could benefit the Japanese Empire with Isogai Rensuke, a lieutenant colonel in the Japanese army. These sorts of efforts led to more coordination between academics who studied Islam and the military on matters regarding Muslim civilian populations under imperial Japan's control.[72]

Life under Japanese Rule: Sino-Muslims
and the History of Wartime China

On July 7, 1937, Nationalist China and the Japanese Empire went from being state entities engaged in a protracted conflict to states at war with one another. Without official support from the imperial government back in Tokyo, the Japanese military used the disappearance of a number of Japanese troops stationed on the outskirts of Beijing near the Marco Polo Bridge as an excuse to launch a full-scale invasion of the areas around Manchukuo and the coastal regions of China. Soon after, the world watched in shock and horror as the Japanese army mounted deadly campaigns against Chinese civilians in the southern Jiangsu region during the battle for Shanghai and the subsequent occupation of Nanjing. The early phases of the occupation were disruptive and violent, and, as Chiang Kai-shek's Nationalist government retreated from Nanjing to Wuhan before settling in Chongqing, hundreds of millions of people were forced to make a difficult decision: flee the Japanese forces or stay and take their chances under occupation.

Fleshing out the multiplicity of narratives about the place of Sino-Muslims living under Japanese rule within the broader, global currents of World War II reveals many new complexities of wartime history. After the Nazis invaded Poland on September 1, 1939, events beyond mainland China were always central to how both the Nationalists and the Japanese jockeyed politically vis-à-vis one other and in relation to other international players. At the same time, the diplomatic maneuverings of the European powers regularly overshadowed Nationalist and Japanese ambitions in East Asia. Until the signing of the Cairo Declaration in December 1943, the Chinese Nationalists lacked the manpower or the authority to recover areas occupied by the Japanese.[73] Before that, the Nationalists had become disillusioned with the international situation, especially after the Soviet Union and Japan signed a neutrality pact on April 3, 1941. In this pact, the Japanese Empire agreed to "maintain peaceful and friendly relations between them and mutually respect the territorial integrity and inviolability of the Mongolian People's Republic" in exchange for a Soviet pledge to "respect the territorial integrity and inviolability of Manchukuo."[74] These geopolitical maneuverings were inseparable from the situation on the ground and had direct consequences for the Sino-Muslims who aligned themselves with the Japanese Empire.[75]

Shifting the focus to marginalized peoples caught up in a global war forces us to reconsider how rarely expressions of Sino-Muslim identity during the war were based on a sense of belonging to the Chinese nation-state.

China's Muslims and Japan's Empire restores agency to Sino-Muslims who made decisions to work with their occupiers, and reveals that these men and women were not simply "susceptible" to Japanese propaganda efforts to win their hearts and minds.[76] In fact, certain segments of Sino-Muslims were complicit in Japan's imperial aspirations for a quid pro quo: a better education for their children; a trip to Tokyo; or even a free hajj. Like historian Etsuko Taketani, I am generally "skeptical of the assumption" that Muslims in China fully bought in to Japanese racial and ideological lessons.[77] But this does not mean that they were unreceptive to imperial Japanese overtures. Of course, the exact same thing could be said about Sino-Muslims buying into the racial — and often overtly racist and Islamophobic — Han-centric rhetoric of assimilation promoted by the Nationalists and the Chinese Communists from the 1930s up until this day. In the end, Muslims worked with the Japanese Empire for a variety of reasons, and they did it because they benefited directly.

It is also important to remember that Sino-Muslims were an important part of the Japanese Empire's efforts to undermine "ideological flows" of Western imperialism and Soviet Communism. Sino-Muslims were essential to Japanese visions of promoting "fascist discourse in the Pacific and beyond, and were not only influenced by these discourses but engaged in reshaping them."[78] Sino-Muslims were active brokers in their own fates. Instead of assuming that Sino-Muslims in the 1930s and 1940s were simply correct or incorrect in their political and ideological decisions to align with either the Axis or the Allied powers, by taking a more "dynamic" approach to Sino-Muslim cooperation with Japanese imperial efforts to undermine the Nationalists, the Soviets, and Western imperial powers, we can produce new histories with a different "positionality vis-à-vis imperialism and racism" in the Pacific.[79] These insights provide new perspectives on nation- and state-building in China throughout the war and after it as well.

China was deeply divided during the war, and the Nationalists sought to define their own political platform in opposition to other "wartime alternatives" like the Japanese, the Chinese Communists, or the Soviets, who were all busy making overtures to people living in the borderlands of the former Qing Empire.[80] The Nationalists pointed out that the Japanese Empire was quick to exploit preexisting rifts between Han and Sino-Muslim communities in North China, where Japanese propaganda often emphasized division and difference. For instance, in one smaller community in North China, the Japanese government had apparently donated money to repair a mosque that was destroyed during the war but provided nothing to rebuild the Confucian temple.[81] The response to the "increasing number of overtures made by the Japanese to minorities after the Mukden incident" was that the Nationalists were forced to "produce several suggestions designed to win the minorities over to [their] side."[82] Perhaps the idea of Chinese nationalism was rhetorically strong and appealing for many Han Chinese, but Muslims had different and conflicting goals for what they wanted to achieve in the post-Qing era. For many Sino-Muslims, it was a moment of opportunity.

In 1911, people on the margins were seminal to the idealized Nationalist vision of the state, yet still peripheral in reality.[83] The Nationalists were only really forced to confront the issue of minorities during the Japanese occupation when they were physically pushed away from the Han center of China to the southwestern frontier, where dealing with non-Han communities became an everyday experience for the wartime government in Chongqing.[84] The war with Japan required the Nationalists to rethink frontier policies at a time when these people were no longer simply a theoretical other but a daily presence in the southwestern wartime capital.[85] Nationalist state-building projects during the war were tangible responses to Japanese actions and policies in occupied regions of mainland China and to minorities themselves.[86]

The fractured state, along with the lack of consensus and ambiguity about who belonged to an ever-evolving vision of the Chinese nation-state, became a space where alternate visions and representations of nationhood began to emerge.[87] It was precisely the fragility of nationalist sentiment among large segments of Sino-Muslims that allowed for these feelings to be so easily contested and for the deep insecurities regarding their loyalty to the nation that the Nationalist government held with regards to Muslims living under occupation.[88] For many Sino-Muslims, the idea of the Chinese nation-state and their personal participation in it was vague and distant, and there was a "profound ambivalence" regarding "Japanese imperial presence in the region," leading up to the war.[89] In some of these spaces, Japanese imperial propaganda espousing anti-Western and anti-Soviet sentiments seeped in and trickled down.[90]

Imperial Understories

This is an understory of empire, pieced together from many different sources and archives.[91] It is just one of the tangled narratives that flourish between the mundanities of everyday life on the ground and the canopy of geopolitical superstructures. The main actors are Muslim men and women, as well as Japanese intellectuals and bureaucrats whom most of us have never heard of. Yet their stories are interwoven throughout the subsequent chapters as a way to demonstrate that their voices mattered when making decisions about ethnic policy, domestic policy, and foreign policy for both the Chinese Nationalists and the Japanese Empire during the war. In her most recent work, Louise Edwards argues persuasively that the war created opportunities for women to "seize alternative public roles through participation in the war on many different fronts."[92] This argument hinges on the "transgressive actions" of women during the war, and Edwards demonstrates how the turbulent period "opened up public roles for women."[93] Adopting this notion of "transgressive actions" during wartime brings into focus Sino-Muslims who operated in new spaces and in new places only made available by the circumstances of the war and by their decisions to cooperate with the Japanese Empire.

With all of this in mind, the process through which Sino-Muslims were incorporated into the nation-state in China is of particular importance. It is also especially complex.[94] In the modern era, the nation-state and imperial powers were in constant dialogue with groups who were seen as invaluable to maintaining both the territorial integrity and international legitimacy of the nation or empire.[95] By examining the Japanese interactions with the people that the current party-state now calls *huizu*, Japan's previously unrecognized impact on the construction and definition of "Huiness" as a Chinese state-designated ethnic minority category becomes clear. In their appeals to Muslims, the Japanese used propaganda to help link China's Muslims to anti-imperial movements and as a way to create the semblance of cohesiveness in their growing empire. This provided the space for Sino-Muslims to imagine themselves within the larger community of believers around the world.[96] Yet examinations of these collaborative relationships between Sino-Muslims and the Japanese Empire are all but absent from the Western and Chinese historiography of World War II. Why?

Sino-Muslim Collaborators?

Thus far, I have resisted the urge to use the words *collaboration* or *collaborator*. In the historiography of World War II, these terms carry a particularly pejorative connotation.[97] In the European theater, the breadth of both the theoretical and historical material focusing on collaboration between the Nazis and the Vichy regime is immense, and an assessment of the lessons about their own historical memory imparted on French citizens by academics, journalists, and filmmakers expose the shortcomings of scholarship

Sino-Muslims visit Japan in the late 1930s.
(Greater Japan Muslim League database, Waseda
University Library Special Collections)

on collaboration between the Japanese Empire and people living in China.[98] In fact, nearly fifteen years ago, Timothy Brook pointed out that historians of modern China and Japan were latecomers to the study of collaboration.[99] Yet, in the time since, no works on non-Han communities' collaboration with the Japanese Empire have appeared. *China's Muslims and Japan's Empire* fills this important yet overlooked historiographical void.

Until the early 2000s, examinations of collaborative relationships between populations living under occupation in China and the Japanese Empire were almost entirely absent from Western, Japanese, and Chinese histories of World War II in East Asia.[100] Historians of East Asia faced a number of challenges incorporating the Japanese presence on the mainland into Chinese historical narratives. The inability to access archives on the mainland and the persistence of dominant national narratives that emphasized complete resistance were the most glaring obstacles to a thoughtful reexamination of wartime collaboration. Part of the problem was that after the Japanese surrender, while other countries were rebuilding and reflecting on their wartime experiences, civil war enveloped the Chinese mainland, ultimately dividing the country between Communist China and Chiang's Nationalist government-in-exile in Taiwan. This had important consequences for the ways the Chinese Communist Party (CCP) and the Chinese Nationalists allow their versions of history to be told.[101] However, over the past decade or so, historians of East Asia have started to transcend stories of unified resistance to address questions of what it meant to be a citizen of the Chinese Republic during this tumultuous period. In turn, this research has contributed to new understandings of the processes involved in state-building (and unbuilding) in China in the 1930s and 1940s.[102]

For all of the inroads made by scholars to nuance our understanding of wartime collaboration, the dominant historical narrative in China about the war still centers on complete resistance to the Japanese Empire.[103] In China, those who worked with the Japanese government are simply labeled as traitors, or as "selling out their country" (C. *maiguo*). The term *hanjian*, or "traitor to the Han people" is also frequently used. Being labeled a *hanjian* implies that a person crossed a moral boundary to the point that his or her indiscretions were often associated with chaos and social disorder.[104] Both the historical context and association of *hanjian* with people who transgress boundaries is important: by continuing to refer to collaborators as *hanjian*, the majority of Chinese citizens reject the notion that any sort of accommodation with the occupiers was possible.[105] So why, then, did some Sino-Muslims collaborate with the Japanese Empire? What was in it for them?

Inserting Sino-Muslims into this important conversation about collaboration begins to reveal that their reasons for working with the Japanese Empire were often very different from those of elite Han Chinese collaborators. In turn, these observations shed new light on the historical memory of wartime collaboration with the Japanese Empire.[106] During the war, Muslims in China were in a precarious position, and their loyalties to the Chinese nation were tested in ways different from those experienced by the Han. Nationalism and anti-Japanese sentiment espoused by the Nationalists was a powerful force, but it is important to remember that the nation as envisioned by the Chinese Nationalists often held little appeal for Sino-Muslims.[107] Examining Japanese efforts to win the hearts and minds of Muslims in North China is part of what historian Jonathan Lipman describes as the ongoing and broader challenges to the ethnic and nationalist consciousness of minorities in China, "which are based in a hegemonic ideology that belongs to the nation-state."[108] Only by moving beyond the "black-and-white condemnation of the [Japanese] imperial presence simply as depredation and plunder, and the complacent position that imperialism was essentially a 'helping hand' in bringing China to modernity," can there be a critical assessment of the ways the Japanese presence on the mainland contributed to the understanding of the place of non-Han communities in China.[109]

Serious studies of collaboration in East Asia are still rare, and no monographs or comprehensive studies specifically dealing with ethnic or religious minorities who collaborated with the Japanese imperial project on the mainland exist. Until recently, most scholarship has focused on the Nanjing regime of Wang Jingwei, on the heavily Han populated Jiangnan region, or on the Han populations living in Manchukuo.[110] However, this is slowly changing. For instance, a recent study by John D. Carroll on Hong Kong under Japanese occupation points out that at the local level, people in Hong Kong were quick to forgive political elites for collaboration after the war, understanding that their efforts had ensured the safety of their communities.[111] This observation presents an opportunity to move beyond the idea that colonies are often "imagined as places fraught with tension and failure, where 'cultural clashes' overshadow 'patterns of collaboration and accommodation.'"[112] Furthermore, Yumi Moon's study about collaboration with Japanese officials on the Korean peninsula draws heavily from Fredrick Cooper's work on colonial North Africa to implore readers not to think about colonizers and colonized as "monolithic groups" but instead to understand colonial encounters as "culturally hybridized" spaces where "the colonized did not remain a unified subject of empire—or its passive victim."[113] These observations are useful for incorporating the stories of Sino-Muslims who worked with the Japanese Empire into the history of twentieth-century China.

An emphasis on loyalty to the locality and the strong desire to help Muslims around the world unshackle themselves from the clutches of Western imperialism and Soviet Communism are two themes that resonated with Sino-Muslim collaborators in North China. The Japanese government also provided the potential for alternate visions of how Sino-Muslims could situate themselves in world politics, and gave "local actors" the platform "to pursue opportunity, wealth, or even freedom."[114] The cosmopolitanism of educated Sino-Muslim elites who traveled around East Asia and beyond during the war is regularly juxtaposed with their North China parochialism in ways that may seem contradictory now but obviously made sense at the time. By unraveling these contradictions, it becomes clear that many Sino-Muslim collaborators were not traitors but simply men and women looking out for the best interest of their families, communities, and fellow Muslims.

It is also important to remember that Sino-Muslims were never simply passive agents in their interactions with the Japanese Empire.[115] This is not to say that the Japanese government and army did not monopolize power and avenues for Sino-Muslims to pursue advancement through channels like education. It is, however, necessary to realize that Sino-Muslims were not powerless.[116] By continuing to portray the Japanese occupation as a period of passivity on the part of colonial subjects, or as an active and ongoing wholesale resistance against the Japanese Empire, we miss the nuance as everyone is lumped together as being either "all in" or "all out." In reality, these stories are much more complicated, and the Japanese colonial state was never "monolithic, nor was it omnipotent."[117] This observation encourages us to look through the cracks and fissures to see where minority actors operated on the margins of the colonial state with their own interests at the forefront of their actions.

For most people on mainland China, the options were to pick up and move as the Japanese army approached, or to succumb to life under occupation.[118] There was extreme danger involved in moving during the war. If they stayed, at least people could rely on their local networks to protect them, rather than the less-than-present (and often predatory) Chinese state or strangers.[119] Local and quotidian concerns greatly outweighed national ones as individuals made hard choices based on many circumstances that regularly went far beyond any sort of political loyalties. The war was deeply disruptive, but at the same time civilians were mobile and adaptable, crossing frequently between areas under Japanese control into areas that were not, or from areas firmly under Japanese control into areas that were less tightly monitored.[120] The whole era was one of accommodation and adaptation, and the lives of civilians were often interrupted and sometimes completely displaced by the war.[121]

It should be clear by now that for people living in China during the war, "nationalism was never the exclusive frame of reference" for how they lived their lives.[122] For many Sino-Muslims, identifying with the Chinese nation-state was something they were deeply conflicted about. As Sino-Muslims became "de-localized" because of the increased frequency and ease of travel, and as they gained better access to news and information about Muslims beyond their local communities, their experiences became "shared experiences of hardships, dislocation, bureaucratization, [and] the loss of inherited support networks." In turn, these new experiences were mediated through evolving terms like "class, or the Islamic *umma*" rather than refracted through the narrow Nationalist-imposed vision of the role Sino-Muslims should play in China's future.[123] In many cases, Sino-Muslims chose to hedge their bets and throw their lot in with the Japanese Empire, which provided them with a space to imagine alternative visions for their future as an integral part of East Asia.

Sino-Muslims and the Abode of Islam

This book is also part of the ongoing efforts to disavow myths about Islam and Muslims. Scholars continue to question the idea that a unitary and monolithic "Islam" is constructed in opposition to the equally problematic category of the "West," yet the old paradigm continues to haunt both scholarly and popular approaches to Muslim pasts and presents.[124] Drawing attention to the incredible diversity among Muslim communities and Islamic practices throughout Asia is a step toward a consensus that the oversimplification and reification of the categories "Islam" and the "Muslim world" are not only entirely wrong, they are also reductionist and dangerous. Muslims from Beijing to Batavia may have been brought together by the Japanese Empire during World War II in the pursuit of similar goals and objectives, yet the ways individual communities responded, adapted, and deployed what they learned and observed was always contextual to the local variances of Islamic practices. This book, therefore, is a concerted effort not to use the terms *Muslim world* or *Islamic world* because they reinforce a false notion that there is only one way to practice Islam, while simultaneously flattening Muslims into a homogeneous other.[125] However, at times the terms do appear in both Chinese and Japanese sources from the 1930s and 1940s. Japanese and Chinese intellectuals regularly used the terms *Islamic world* or *Muslim world* to explain how *they* understood Islam and its relationship to the world around them. In these instances, the terms should not be read as a reified category constructed in the present and projected onto the past but rather as historical terms deployed in a specific context at a particular historic moment.

Sino-Muslims helped the Japanese Empire manage its interactions with Muslims in South Asia, Central Asia, Southeast Asia, the Middle East, and North Africa. Japanese policymakers imagined Sino-Muslims as an integral component of their diplomatic and economic engagement with these regions. For their part, Sino-Muslims often saw the Japanese Empire as an important international player that could help them foster connections to broader, transnational networks of Muslim travelers, bureaucrats, and intellectuals. As Sino-Muslims sought political backers and funding to put their own reform agendas into place, the Japanese Empire reciprocated by establishing institutions, associations, and religious schools and mosques in occupied China. These were tangible contributions to the social and built landscape of Islam in China.[126]

By overlaying Japanese imperial ambitions on top of preexisting loyalties to their communities, Sino-Muslims occupied a liminal space where they carefully manipulated their Chinese, Muslim, local, cosmopolitan, and intellectual identities in ways that served their own interests. The Japanese Empire emphasized the inclusion or exclusion of Muslim communities from within China into the Chinese state, East Asia, or the global *umma*. Sino-Muslims did this too, depending on the situations they faced, the people they met, and the ways they wanted others to see them. Sometimes emphasizing their own "backwardness" and "traditionalism" was beneficial, because it got Sino-Muslims what they wanted by exhibiting the transformative powers of the Japanese Empire. Other times, they projected this "backwardness" and "traditionalism" onto others as a way to come to terms with their changing place in the world.[127]

By engaging with the categories and structures of the Japanese imperial state, Sino-Muslims played a role in shaping them. Sino-Muslims provided input during the implementation of Japanese imperial strategies that pertained to Muslims, and they were active agents in the execution of Japanese policies involving Islam. In the same regard, the Japanese Empire regularly presented Sino-Muslims as an aspirational model, and as a positive example of the successes of their developmental policies and support for Islam. The bottom line was that the Japanese imperial project *needed* Muslim communities in North China just as much as, if not more than, Sino-Muslim communities needed the Japanese Empire. This reciprocal relationship was never one of complete equality, but it was never one-sided either.[128] Here examining the connections between the Japanese imperial project and Sino-Muslims offers an opportunity to think critically about the ways an occupying power can shape national discourse. For almost ten years, the Japanese imperial government was the secondary agent — beyond the Sino-Muslims themselves — shaping the ways Muslims from North China understood Islam in relation to the world around them. Japanese imperial rhetoric, much like the Nationalist and Communist rhetoric directed specifically at Muslim populations, thus shaped religious and ethnic nationalisms in China during and after the war.

Imperial Spaces, Imperial Places: Positioning Sino-Muslims

One important characterization of Sino-Muslim collaboration with the Japanese Empire is that it was distinctly transnational.[129] In the wake of the transnational turn, scholars are beginning to appreciate the importance of global networks in the creation and maintenance of imperial and national spaces.[130] However, ethnicity in China is often understood as a hardened category imposed on Chinese people by the nation-state with little to no outside influence. Yet, the constant reconfiguration of the Asia-Pacific region by European, American, and Asian imperial powers in the twentieth century had a lasting impact on the prevailing ethnic classifications within the Chinese nation-state. Paying attention to the global circulations of peoples, ideas, and ideologies foregrounds how the Japanese Empire informed the conversations about the place of Muslims in the Chinese national imagination and about the place of Sino-Muslims within the abode of Islam.

Muslims may not have been central to decision making for government officials in Japan and China, but their role in the periphery of social, cultural, and economic policymaking illuminates new perspectives on the management and operation of the Japanese imperial project.[131] A number of recent works focus on the circulation of Japanese subjects within the boundaries of Japanese imperial space. For instance, Kate McDonald examines "the spatial politics of Japanese imperialism" by exploring just how invested colonial officials were in "territorializing a Japanese national identity on colonized land" throughout East Asia.[132] David Ambaras, in contrast, focuses on the movement of nonstate actors throughout the Japanese Empire to reveal how "mobility simultaneously destabilized and reinforced imperial boundary-making in the South China Sea."[133] *China's Muslims and Japan's Empire* pushes beyond the spatial imagination of the territories that are generally considered to be a part of the Japanese Empire into the aspirational markets and Islamic spaces made available in the context of the war with the help of non-Japanese Muslim actors. This window into the ways Muslims from around Asia experienced the Japanese Empire and the Japanese home islands sheds light on the variations of what Japanese imperial space meant to non-Japanese subjects. Sino-Muslims also traveled all over Asia and the Middle East with financial aid from the Japanese Empire. In dialogue with Japanese imperial officials, Sino-Muslims mediated their relationship to the empire in ways both different from and complementary to that of Japanese subjects from the home islands.[134] In this way, the politics of how imperial space was organized and understood was an endeavor not simply for the colonizer but also for the colonized.[135]

Japanese-occupied China and Nationalist-controlled "Free" China are often treated as separate and distinct entities based on the assumption that the physical and intellectual boundaries between the two spaces were nonporous and rarely traversed. This distinction is a false dichotomy, and in reality, people, goods, and ideas circulated through mainland China, East Asia, and around the world during the war. In this particular case, Japanese-sponsored Sino-Muslims left the occupied areas and traveled around China, to Japan, and throughout East Asia. They traveled around the world on diplomatic missions, on trade missions, and on a Japanese-sponsored hajj to Mecca. Traveling and working in the service of empire, Sino-Muslims encountered groups of Nationalist-supported Muslims who were traveling with the backing of their own benefactors. Nationalist agents also traveled far and wide expounding the virtues of the Allies, and often tried to intervene into the political dealings of the Japanese-sponsored Sino-Muslims.

A number of Nationalist-supported Sino-Muslims also crossed back-and-forth between "Free" and "occupied" China, gathering intelligence to produce detailed reports about Muslim communities living under Japanese occupation. Showcasing the travels and the interactions of different groups of Sino-Muslims with the support of different political backers during the war makes two things clear: just how important Sino-Muslims were to the global war effort and how frequently Sino-Muslims traversed borders during the war. Muslims from North China traveled far and wide on the Japanese dime, forging connections *beyond* the borders of occupied China with other Muslims. These men and women served as the mouthpieces for Japanese imperialism and—whether intentionally or not—helped the Japanese Empire legitimize its claims over Muslims in the region and to an Islamic past simply through their participation in empire-building projects.

Manchukuo was integral to the formation of imperial Japan's wartime identity on the home islands.[136] Likewise, interactions between the Japanese imperial apparatus and Muslims, first from China, and later from other parts of the colonized world, were essential to the projection and maintenance of the Japanese Empire at home and, perhaps more important, abroad.[137] *China's Muslims and Japan's Empire* contributes to the growing body of literature on the Japanese imperial project that aims to "expand the spatial and temporal scope of empire in sometimes unexpected directions," with the hopes of offering new perspectives on the ways Japanese imperialism impacted the daily lives of subjects beyond the home islands during the war and after.[138] In turn, this unveils the "unevenness" of Japan's imperial aspirations to demonstrate how people throughout the Japanese Empire made sense of the empire on their own terms.[139]

The Chinese Communists Take a Page from the Japanese

In their efforts to include Sino-Muslims in their state-building project after 1949, the Chinese Communists took a page from the Japanese Empire's approaches to handling Sino-Muslim minorities living in the People's Republic of China. Not only did they tap into networks of Sino-Muslim elites, academics, and bureaucrats that had been carefully cultivated by the Japanese Empire, but they also repackaged and redeployed much of the anti-imperialist rhetoric and propaganda aimed at Muslims in their own overtures to postcolonial, predominately Muslim countries like Indonesia, Pakistan, and Egypt in the early years of the Cold War.

Previous scholarship contends that the Communists' approach to integrating non-Han communities into their particular vision for the Chinese nation-state was a direct result of their experiences with minorities on the Long March in the Northwest and Southwest.[140] Yet in the 1930s encounters between Muslims and Communists were haphazard, and in the early years of the Shaanxi Soviet, the Communists regularly upset wealthy landowning Muslims with their class struggle programs. However, perhaps more so than land reform, Muslims around the world, including Sino-Muslims, kept a close eye on developments in Soviet Central Asia. Muslim power brokers in China were deeply concerned with the potential loss of *waqf* (mortmain property under Islamic law) endowments and the seizure and redistribution of mosque assets by the Chinese Communists. After all, there was a clear precedent for this in the Soviet Union, where the government had confiscated mosque assets and *waqf* throughout Central Asia in the 1920s.[141]

Overtures to Sino-Muslims by the Communists during the war should be understood not as a Communist recognition of the distinctiveness of Muslims but as an effort to consolidate their own power in the Northwest. By the mid-1930s, the Communists realized that they needed the support of local Muslim power brokers as they regrouped and consolidated their power in Gansu and Shaanxi. Their local policies were not simply efforts to make Muslims into Communists but also were developed with an acute awareness that the support of Muslim communities could make or break the Communists' guerrilla campaigns against the Nationalists and the Japanese in the region.[142] Throughout the war, the Communists adopted two main strategies for managing Muslims: they ceased hostilities with Nationalist-supported Muslim generals in Gansu, and they enlisted Muslims to fight in guerrilla units against the Japanese.

During the war, Mao Zedong also began to shift his approach toward non-Han communities. Initially, the Communists had offered some of these groups the right to self-determination (C. *zizhu*) including the right to secede, based on the Soviet constitutional approach. Yet by 1940 Mao was backpedaling, and these populations were guaranteed autonomy (C. *zizhi*) in return for their help fighting the Japanese.[143] However, it was not until the Communists consolidated power after the establishment of the People's Republic of China that they really began to think seriously about strategies for integrating and incorporating minorities into the new state.[144] It was during this time that they drew on the wartime lessons of the Japanese Empire and the Chinese Nationalists.

Framing China's Muslims and Japan's Empire

Chapter 1 traces the historical development of Japan's interest in Sino-Muslims and is framed within the broader intellectual interest in both Islam and religion that began in the late Meiji period (1868–1912). This discussion provides a sense of the methods and logic behind Japan's increasingly coherent Islamic policy throughout the Taishō Era (1912–26) and the early years of Hirohito's reign until the founding of Manchukuo in March 1932. During this time, the Japanese Empire strengthened its foothold in China and increased its outreach to Muslim communities. All the while, the interests of the Japanese Imperial Army and Japanese scholars of Islam became more closely aligned. The outbreak of war between China and Japan in July 1937 was pivotal for Japanese imperial policy toward Sino-Muslims. In chapter 2, Sino-Muslims who were living under occupation become the departure point for examining Nationalist-supported responses to the Japanese occupation. An examination of widely circulated Nationalist-sponsored Muslim periodicals and internally circulating government reports that covered reconnaissance missions to visit Sino-Muslim communities living under occupation highlights the sense of urgency that this situation merited from the Nationalist government.

Chapter 2 then examines the reactions of Sino-Muslim communities to curriculum changes proposed for Muslim schools by both the Nationalists and the Japanese Empire. These highly contested Chinese- and Japanese-language reforms were implemented in Muslim schools as a way to indoctrinate Muslim youths. They met strong resistance from local Muslim communities, who saw the language reforms as a threat to Arabic-language learning and the local authority of the mosque. In the end, both the Chinese Nationalists and the Japanese Empire had to prove that curricular changes would serve the interests of young Muslims and ended up making concessions to Sino-Muslim communities who resisted these changes to varying degrees.

The next three chapters adopt a widening spatial approach by placing Japan's Islamic policies, Sino-Muslims, and Islam in ever-expanding concentric circles radiating outward from the occupied mainland to East Asia, and then to the Eurasian continent and North Africa. Here it becomes clear that the Japanese government had plans to move into areas with predominantly Muslim populations well beyond what is generally considered to be the geographical limits of the Japanese Empire. In these plans, Sino-Muslims were always central to Japanese imperial outreach to Muslims.

Chapter 3 follows a number of Sino-Muslims who left areas under occupation to visit or study in Tokyo, to travel around East Asia, and to perform hajj with the financial assistance of the Japanese Empire. These policies were first enacted in North China and were then framed out within the larger scope of the management of Muslim populations living throughout the Greater East Asia Co-Prosperity Sphere.[145] Japanese imperial officials regularly cited Sino-Muslims living under occupation as positive or aspirational models in their appeals to Muslims in the Philippines, the occupied Dutch East Indies, and other places throughout the region. Chapter 4 examines plans from the Tokyo-based Greater Japan Muslim League to deploy Sino-Muslims to sell Japanese tea and manufactured goods in new, predominantly Muslim markets throughout South Asia, Central Asia, North Africa, and the Middle East. These plans were central to efforts to create new markets in predominantly Muslim spaces.

The Japanese Empire observed the ways its Axis partners dealt with Muslims in their own empires. Through a close reading of a secret Japanese document called "Italy's Muslim Policy" (J. *Itaria no Kaikyō seisaku*), chapter 5 makes it clear that imperial Japan was both conscious and critical of the way the Italian Fascists and the Nazis handled Muslims under their control. Finally, as I situate imperial Japan's experiences with Muslims in the broader perspective of the global war and Japan's relationship with other Axis powers, the focus shifts to Afghanistan. Afghanistan is not generally discussed in histories of Nazi Germany or imperial Japan's foreign policy during the war. Yet it became a space where Nazi and Japanese imperial objectives and ideologies overlapped and came into conflict. In their attempts to create diplomatic and economic relationships with Afghanistan in the 1930s, both the Nazis and the Japanese Empire had to draw on imagined pre-Islamic connections to the region. The Nazis worked extra hard to fabricate imagined linkages to a mythical Aryan past, while the Japanese associated themselves with pre-Islamic Afghanistan through Buddhism. These efforts were attempts to legitimize wartime claims to a region and people who lived sandwiched between British India and Soviet Central Asia.

The conclusion delves into the legacies of global fascism and offers insights into the connections between Japanese wartime Islamic policy, the ethnic minority policies of the early People's Republic of China, and both the Chinese Nationalists' and Communists' relationships with newly independent postcolonial states with sizable (or majority) Muslim populations in Asia, such as India, Pakistan, Indonesia, Malaysia, and Egypt. With a particular focus on the echoes of anti-Soviet and anti-imperialist rhetoric in postindependence nationalist propaganda produced in Muslim countries by both communist and anticommunist governments around Asia and the Middle East, it argues that the legacies of Japanese fascism persisted into the Cold War.

FROM MEIJI THROUGH MANCHUKUO

Japan's Growing Interest in Sino-Muslims

Recognizing Failure: Assessing Japan's Islamic Policy

By the time World War II broke out in Europe, Japan had a systematic Islamic policy that aimed to integrate Muslims into their empire. These policies started in North China in the 1910s and became more coherent throughout the 1920s, leading up to the establishment of the Japanese client state of Manchukuo in 1932, until the plans were fully realized after war broke out between China and Japan in July 1937.[1] By late January 1938, the *Shanghai Times* was reporting that a member of the Japanese Diet had raised the issue of outreach to Muslims throughout East Asia in parliament. The article followed a conversation in the Lower House of the Japanese Diet, where the speaker acknowledged that Muslims were geographically dispersed and potentially useful as "an effective bulwark against communism." In response to the query, Foreign Minister Koki Hirota reportedly replied, "We are giving full consideration to the problem of co-operation with Mohammedans [*sic*]. Our exchange of ministers with Iran had just that at the back of it. We are also maintaining close contact with Japanese students of Mohammedanism [*sic*]."[2]

The acknowledgment by Japanese members of parliament that there were concerted and coordinated efforts to promote outreach to Muslims throughout Asia is important. Equally important is keeping in mind that many of these policies failed, and that there was no straight line or clearly laid out path from the occupation of North China through to the end of the war. Many policies toward Muslims were tried and tested among Sino-Muslim communities and later adapted throughout the empire. But these plans were always contingent and never predetermined. Their successes *and* failures were dictated by many variables, including access to funds, the international geopolitical situation, and perhaps most important, the necessary buy-in from Muslims themselves.

This never stopped members of the Greater Japan Muslim League from having broad and ambitious goals. The Greater Japan Muslim League's handbook clearly laid out its objectives in three distinct yet interrelated sections.[3] The first stated purpose of the organization was to foster relationships between Muslims from Japan and Muslims around the world, and between Muslims living in the Japanese Empire and non-Muslim Japanese subjects. The handbook stated that this objective could be met by building and providing space for Muslims to meet in cities in Japan, promoting friendly exchanges between Japanese representatives and Muslims, bringing Muslim students to study in Japan, and teaching Japanese to students living in predominantly Muslim regions.[4]

The second purpose of the organization was to further the economic benefits meant to come from these increased interactions. The Greater Japan Muslim League suggested that Japan should increase trade relations and encourage economic exchange with Muslims. The final stated objective of the Greater Japan Muslim League was to promote and sponsor research about Islam and Muslims. This would involve outreach efforts to Japanese subjects who were unfamiliar with Islam, as well as supplying Muslim visitors to the home islands with information and pamphlets about the Japanese Empire to distribute when they returned home.[5]

In addition to the handbook, the Greater Japan Muslim League also published an interview in Japanese with a member to answer common questions about the organization.[6] The interviewee explained that the aims of the Greater Japan Muslim League were different than those of other religious organizations on the home islands because Muslims around the world were oppressed by Western imperialists and Soviet communists, and needed the Greater Japan Muslim League to provide them with technological programs and economic incentives to help them unburden themselves from these oppressive forces.[7] The interviewer then asked about the promotion of foreign trade (J. *gai bōekei*) through the organization, and the respondent made it clear that the Greater Japan Muslim League was tasked with entering new markets outside Japan's current economic bloc (J. *burokku*), which consisted of Manchukuo, Korea, and Taiwan, and into Muslim spaces, such

Japan's Growing Interest in Sino-Muslims

as those in Africa and India.[8] According to the interview, the stated mandate of the Greater Japan Muslim League was to study and research the many different races (J. *iminzoku*) that practiced Islam in order to help Japanese government officials enable trade with these places.[9]

The final section of the interview addressed the costs associated with implementing these types of programs intended for Muslims, such as study abroad and sending Japanese teachers to Islamic spaces to promote Japanese-language learning. The member of the Greater Japan Muslim League responded that the short-term investment would be very small compared to the return in anticipation of the massive increase in economic activity and output that would come from improving relations with Central Asia, South Asia, the Middle East, Africa, and Southeast Asia.[10] For the Greater Japan Muslim League, these plans all hinged on the participation of Sino-Muslims. By presenting Sino-Muslims as a success story of Japanese benevolence to Muslims around the world, the organization anticipated that similar gestures would help to win over Muslims well beyond Japan's imperial reach.[11] However, these plans were ambitious and aspirational, and often did not work out in the ways members of the Greater Japan Muslim League anticipated. Understanding why and how Sino-Muslims were supposed to play such an integral role in the maintenance of Japan's Islamic policy and the expansion of its empire is the purpose of this book.

Meiji through Manchukuo: Japan's Growing Interest in Sino-Muslims

By the mid-1930s, Pan-Asianists, Japanese bureaucrats, and scholars of Islam were embedded in North China, collecting ethnographic and economic data about Sino-Muslim communities that could be used to justify Japanese imperial expansion on the mainland and into new, predominantly Muslim markets. They surveyed Sino-Muslim schools, guilds, and other spaces in order to gauge how the Japanese Empire could promote its support for Islam to Muslims around the world. They also expressed sympathy for the poor living conditions and discrimination faced by Sino-Muslim communities in North China. By tracing the growing attention that a handful of well-educated Japanese academics paid to Sino-Muslims starting in the late Meiji era (1890s) through to the outbreak of war on the Chinese mainland, this chapter provides a sense of the methods and logic behind imperial Japan's increasingly coherent policies toward Islam, which gradually became more coordinated in the years leading up to the founding of the Japanese client-state, Manchukuo. However, it was only after the establishment of Manchukuo that the aims and goals of Japanese intellectuals interested in Islam became more deeply entwined with the Japanese military's expansionist visions for empire. Exploring the Japanese Empire's motivations for becoming involved with Muslims in China makes it clear that both parties hoped to gain something from these interactions.

The history of Japan's involvement with Muslim populations in China is one small part of the story of conflicting loyalties exacerbated by wartime chaos. It is also an important story that has not yet been told. When we acknowledge the deep connections between the Japanese imperial project and Sino-Muslims, a much more complicated and nuanced story about the place of Muslims in the Chinese national imagination begins to unfold. This leads to two conclusions: first, that the Japanese occupation of large swaths of the Chinese mainland between 1937 and 1945 should not be considered a bounded geographic space, and second, that the occupation should not be thought of as a discrete temporal period within the narrative of the past hundred years of modern Chinese history. The Japanese imperial presence on the mainland starting from the end of the First Sino-Japanese War (1894–95) led to engaged discussions and protracted efforts by the Chinese Nationalists to counter imperial Japan's appeal to Sino-Muslim populations. All the while, imperial Japan was developing ambitious global aspirations beyond the mainland, and these plans always required the help and influence of Sino-Muslims.

A brief introduction to the history of Islam in China will familiarize readers with the historical circumstances surrounding imperial Japan's steadily intensifying involvement with Muslims. From there, we will examine the voices of Nationalist-supported Muslims in order to contextualize their concerns and their own reform agendas. Even among Sino-Muslim populations who supported the Nationalists, there was rarely consensus about how to implement reforms or where Sino-Muslims should situate themselves within the emerging Nationalist vision of the Chinese nation-state. Following this, we will analyze the works of Japanese intellectuals and academics who wrote prolifically about Islam in the years leading up to the war, a discussion that will show that Manchukuo's establishment in 1932 provided the Japanese military with the authority to co-opt intellectuals and their networks, while simultaneously supporting a number of Islamic associations on the home islands and on the mainland. Finally, by examining the integration into the Japanese imperial schematic of minority subjects on the home islands — such as the indigenous Ainu, the *burakumin*, and Korean subjects living in Japan — we will assess the useful precedents these groups provided Japanese policymakers trying to make sense of non-Japanese communities and how to include them in their visions for empire.

The Growth and Development of Islamic Studies in Japan

Examining the growth of Islamic studies and popular interest in Islam on the home islands through the lens of Japanese imperial expansion in China provides a starting point for understanding broader policies with respect to Islam. Initially, the study of Islamic history and Islamic theology were niche academic interests for a small number of Japanese intellectuals. However, their expertise was co-opted and used for larger imperial ambitions by bureaucrats and militarists.[12] Many of the academics who had studied Muslims in North China were deeply empathetic toward the low status and poverty that they witnessed among these communities, and they saw the developmentalist agendas to be implemented with the help of Japanese bureaucrats as beneficial for Sino-Muslims and other minorities living in China's vast borderlands.

The would-be Axis powers self-identified as "have-nots" because "they lacked the ideal balance of natural resources, markets and capital to minimize economic instability and provide economic self-sufficiency."[13] Japanese technocrats imagined themselves as fighting "a war on two fronts," one against the domination of the global capitalist world system and another against the threat of worldwide socialist revolution.[14] One tactic in this war was to appeal to Muslims living throughout the colonized world and the Soviet Union with the help of Sino-Muslims. In their plans for Manchukuo and the "state-directed economy" that accompanied their visions, bureaucrats relied heavily on the social science and anthropological research conducted by specialists. The social and cultural policies they promoted, meant to control people and legitimize imperial rule, were also integral to the economic planning for a separate economic bloc in East Asia. In Manchukuo, the men and women Janis Mimura calls "techno-fascists" honed their planning and development skills to "realize a productive, hierarchical, organic, national community based on the cultural and geographic notions of Japanese ethnic superiority."[15] Population surveys and economic data about non-Han populations were gathered and analyzed, and the people living in Manchukuo were ordered and categorized. These data resulted in the publication of hundreds of books, journal articles, pamphlets, and dossiers about Sino-Muslims written and compiled by Japanese scholars of Islam starting in the

1920s. The data also enabled an assessment of the social and cultural landscape of the region and the economic utility of Sino-Muslims in their long-term plans for imperial expansion.

Beyond data collection, Japanese imperialists made important outreach efforts to Muslims on the mainland. Early on, Japanese bureaucrats realized the potential of Sino-Muslims to help Japan destabilize the Chinese Nationalists' nation-building projects. At the same time, Sino-Muslims could help the Japanese Empire create connections to Muslims throughout the colonized world. In a secret report detailing the success of Japanese "penetration" into Sino-Muslim communities, the Nationalists' U.S. allies observed that this had become a "situation custom-made for Japanese infiltration tactics."[16] Manchukuo had become the "base from which Japanese activities among Muslims in other parts of China were directed, and also the testing grounds for organizing techniques later applied on a much larger scale in Occupied China."[17]

As the Japanese government and military exerted more influence in areas with Muslim populations on the Chinese mainland, they focused on recruiting those who had been to Mecca, since they were generally venerated in their communities and able to exert greater influence among their coreligionists. Once again, these efforts did not go unnoticed by the Chinese Nationalists or the United States. In 1928, U.S. sinologist Lyman Hoover claimed that a "Japanese Muslim" appeared in Beijing seeking out the leaders of the important mosques in the city. Hoover reported that the agents gathered information that was "probably made available to the Japanese who later, disguised as Muslim mullahs or pilgrims, entered Sinkiang [Xinjiang] and other Northwestern areas, presumably to investigate and counter Soviet agents there." He went on to say, "At the same time, military agents began the quiet cultivation of some of the Muslim military leaders who they suspected harbored disaffection towards Nanjing."[18] On the ground, Japanese imperialists gathered extremely detailed economic and social data about Sino-Muslim communities in North China as a way to implement and enact policies that would benefit the Japanese economy, and that would appeal to disenfranchised groups. Sino-Muslims became indispensable to Japan's larger ambitions for empire. To understand why, a brief history of the history of Islam in China is needed.

Islam in China

Muslims had a significant presence in the social and political fabric of imperial Chinese history. In the lore, Islam was "introduced" to China in the seventh century, when Muslim envoys in the service of the third caliph Uthman traveled to Guangzhou to discuss trade and diplomacy with the Tang Dynasty (618–907). After the negotiations, Emperor Gaozong erected a mosque in their honor. But more accurately, Islam was not necessarily "introduced" per se, although Arab envoys were dispatched to China on a regular basis throughout the Tang Dynasty. For the next few hundred years, the majority of Muslim sojourners came and went, traveling to and from the Arabian Peninsula and Persia. It was not until the Mongol Yuan Dynasty (1271–1368) that Muslims started to settle permanently in China in large numbers. The Mongols brought in Persians and Central Asians to work as administrators and bureaucrats, and also sent emissaries to places like Bukhara and Samarkand to facilitate trade and diplomatic negotiations. Many of the imperial administrators who came from Central Asia settled and married Chinese women but retained their faith. By the time of the Ming (1368–1644) and the Qing Dynasties (1636/1644–1911), Muslims were an integral part of court politics and foreign diplomatic engagement with the wider world.

Starting in the eighteenth century, the Manchu Qing greatly expanded the territory of the Chinese state, and the region now known as Xinjiang (literally "the new territories"), inhabited by both settled oasis dwellers and nomadic herdsmen, was violently incorporated into the imperial fold.[19] This resulted in resistance and pushback from local power brokers, and throughout the Qing the state brutally suppressed a number of coordinated Muslim rebellions.[20] There were also Muslims who cooperated with the Qing, and their loyalty was rewarded with financial support from Beijing, which was often used to settle old scores. This tension between accommodation and compromise, on the one hand, and violent suppression of Muslim communities, on the other, continues to permeate interactions between the Chinese state and the millions of Muslims who inhabit the vast western territory of the People's Republic of China.

As in other parts of the world, Islam in China is practiced in many ways. Muslims developed their own intellectual traditions, which fused Confucian political and social philosophies with Islamic theology. The intellectual genealogy of this tradition contributed to a corpus of work known as the *Han Kitab*, which produced syncretic thinking about the place of Islam in relation to the Chinese imperial state. The title of this work is telling: *Han* refers to the dominant Han Chinese, and *kitab* is the literal word for book in Arabic. Using Persian, Arabic, and Chinese texts, Muslim thinkers like Wang Daiyu (1570–1660) wrote prolifically in Chinese with the idiom and vocabulary of Confucianism to try to explain the long traditions of Islam to both Muslim and non-Muslim readers.[21]

The particular milieu in which Islam developed in imperial China was also central to the ways Sino-Muslims understood their place vis-à-vis Indian, Persian, Arab, and Southeast Asian Muslims as they began to travel with increasing frequency at the end of the nineteenth century. By the twentieth century, educated Sino-Muslims with a deep knowledge of the *Han Kitab* corpus were seeking religious advice from Muslim scholars beyond China. Part of these efforts, led by scholars like Ma Ruitu, were meant to "make Islam in China less Chinese" by integrating modernist Salafi reformist ideals through correspondence with men such as Egyptian reformer Rashīd Riḍā.[22]

Beyond the specific traits of Islam that took root in China, there are also important variations among the different "schools" of Islamic thought in the region. The majority of Muslims in China are Sunni and adhere to the Hanafi school of Islamic jurisprudence. They are often called the *Gedimu* (from the Arabic *Qadim*, meaning "the old"). The *Gedimu* are further divided into the Wahhabi-centered *Yihewani* (from the Arabic *Ikhwan*), and the *Xidaotang*, which literally translates as "the hall of the western *dao*." Here, the character *dao* is also referenced in both Daoism and one of the seminal texts of Daoism, the *Daodejing*. However, these categories are quite oversimplified and do not account for the intricate and geographically dispersed Sufi networks that are active throughout China.[23] Although adherents of the *Yihewani* are staunchly anti-Sufi, the *Xidaotang* and *Gedimu* are more sympathetic. Among the Sufi orders active in China, the largest are composed of devotees to the *Jahriyya*, *Khuffiya*, and *Qadariyya*. All three orders were imported and adapted to the local context by returned pilgrims and focus on saint and tomb veneration, invocation of the name of god, and chanting.

This is all to say that Muslims in China should never be understood as a collective whole but rather as separated by variances of practices and beliefs that developed in different geographical, social, and political settings.[24] Sino-Muslim communities included various actors with differing political and religious objectives that were often at odds. This is important because it not only unflattens "Sino-Muslims" as a singular category but also returns agency to individual communities in their decisions to work with different political actors in the early years of the twentieth century. Highlighting this diversity recasts Sino-Muslims as active decision makers in the construction of their own ethnoreligious identity vis-à-vis the state, rather than simply as passive agents of Nationalist, Japanese, or Communist policies.

In the late Qing, a rupture occurred in the state-directed narratives about the place of Muslims in China, as Muslims went from being a relatively unproblematic presence to a central problem in the maintenance of empire. Some of this had to do with Qing imperial overreach into areas where indigenous power brokers had traditionally handled local affairs, and some of it had to do with changes in how Muslims saw themselves in relation to the newly emerging Han-centrist racialist nationalist narratives. The result was a number of violent rebellions against the Qing state.[25] After the violence wrought on Muslims throughout the Qing, many young men who were coming of age were ready to bring an end to the antagonistic relationship between their communities and the Qing imperial apparatus. One of these young men was a man named Ma Fuxiang. He was the son of Ma Qianling (1826–1910), who had surrendered to the Qing in 1872 in return for a monetary reward. After surrendering, Ma Qianling pledged his loyalty to the Qing, and promised to help end the violence that plagued China's western borderlands.[26]

Ma Fuxiang was educated in the *Han Kitab* tradition, but he also attended a modern-style military academy. He and his brothers rose to prominence because of their family connections and military prowess, and after his older brother was killed fighting on the side of the Qing government in the Boxer Uprising, he assumed his military post.[27] Like many of his educated predecessors, Ma Fuxiang was interested in the relationship between Confucianism, Chinese culture, and Islam. Through his writings, he tried to rectify the central tenets of Islam with his "lifelong commitment to Muslim participation in the political system of the Qing and then Republican China" as well as with his desire to develop economic opportunities in his native place that would ensure that he and his family members remained wealthy.[28]

For many Muslims in China, the end of the Qing Dynasty signaled a new era, but the failures of the new Republican government to consolidate power also left a vacuum in China's western regions that was filled by the adept and insightful Ma clans, with Ma Fuxiang at the helm. The colloquial moniker applied to them, "Ma Family Warlords," is fitting in some ways and ill-suited in others. Ma Fuxiang and his family definitely ran Gansu, Ningxia, and the surrounding regions with military—and often violent—authoritarianism, but they were also instrumental in deescalating endemic violence, investing in infrastructure projects, and helping develop the region throughout the first two decades of the twentieth century.[29] By the early 1920s, Ma Fuxiang was firmly established as the main power broker in Gansu, far enough from the capital in Beijing to have autonomy in the day-to-day politics of the region.

As Chiang Kai-shek consolidated power during the Northern Expedition, Ma witnessed Chiang's military successes over the Communists and other factions of "warlords" in the south. By 1927, Ma Fuxiang decided that it was in his best interest to align himself with Chiang and support the Chinese Nationalists.[30] Ma Fuxiang was active in helping the Nationalists launch Muslim organizations and continued to sponsor public works and educational development throughout the Gansu-Linxia corridor, where his extended family lived and prospered. His life was cut short by an unexpected illness in 1932, but his family legacy lived on through his son, Ma Hongkui, and his nephew Ma Hongbin. The men quickly took over his role as the pro-Nationalist Muslim wardens of the Northwest.[31] The legacies of Ma Hongkui and Ma Hongbin are fiercely contested, but they did continue to support Chiang in his ongoing fight against the Japanese and the Chinese Communists throughout the 1930s and 1940s.

Ma Hongkui and Ma Hongbin were important allies for the Nationalists, but that does not mean that all Muslims agreed with their agenda, and many were unhappy with their rule. Their opponents forged ahead with their own reform agendas and were always looking for financial backing to try to undermine the Mas'. There were also other Muslim elites who allied themselves with the Nationalists: some did so simply for geopolitical and strategic reasons, whereas others were interested in taking part in the Chinese national project and inserting their own voices into the evolving idea of what the nation should become.[32] When Japanese military encroachment on the mainland culminated in war, the Nationalists were happy to have a number of prominent Sino-Muslims on their side. The Mas and their Nationalist-supported allies, like Muslim general Bai Chongxi and *ahong* (cleric) Hu Songshan, were instrumental in providing support to the Nationalists for the anti-Japanese resistance throughout the 1930s and 1940s.[33]

Bai Chongxi hailed from the southern city of Guilin in Guangxi province, but his family moved to Sichuan province in southwestern China when he was a teenager. He attended a Nationalist-supported military academy and quickly rose through the ranks, becoming a trusted military adviser to the Nationalists. He was heavily involved in Chiang's Northern Expedition and coordinated the purge and murder of Communist cadres in Shanghai in 1927. Throughout the war with Japan, Bai remained a trusted military adviser to Chiang and even retreated with him to Taiwan after the Nationalists were defeated by the Communists in the Chinese Civil War (1945–49). Bai continued to play an important role in politics throughout the 1950s and 1960s as a Sino-Muslim ally in the fight against communism.

Hu Songshan was another prominent Nationalist ally. Hu was from Ningxia and was an important leader of the Wahhabi-based Yihewani sect. After going on hajj in 1925, he returned to China an ardent nationalist because of what he experienced as discrimination being a hajji from China. Although he sometimes advocated for an independent Islamic state for Muslims in China, he allied with the Nationalists to defeat Japan, and he wrote an anti-Japanese prayer for Muslims during the war. These men were key to the Nationalists' efforts to unify the Chinese state, but theirs were not the only Sino-Muslim voices that mattered. In order to understand why and how opposing voices found an unlikely ally in the Japanese Empire, a short introduction to the history of Islam and Japan is necessary.

Islam and Japan

The notion that Islam was a discrete "religion" is a modern invention. The English word *religion* was only introduced to Japan in 1853 by Commodore Matthew Perry and the United States in the letter presented to the Tokugawa Bakufu demanding trade and treaty status. It is made up of two characters imported from Chinese (J. *shūkyō*, C. *zongjiao*), and although *shūkyō* was used before the 1850s, it "loosely" meant the "teaching of a sect" and was often associated with localized Buddhist practices.[34] It only came into popular usage in the 1870s as a way of framing discussions about what are now considered "world religions" or the formalized "global concept rooted in the idea that religion represents a discrete aspect of the human experience."[35]

Defining religion in Japan was a "politically charged, boundary drawing experience," where the concept was "tied directly to the emerging concept of the nation-state."[36] Understanding that Islam and the idea of religion was politicized in Japan from the get-go provides the backdrop for the burgeoning interest in Muslims starting in the 1880s and 1890s. The categories of "Islam" and "Muslim" were formulated and reformulated by encounters between Muslims and the Japanese imperial apparatus, and the changing meaning of Islam in China in the first half of the twentieth century was informed by and in conversation with Japanese imperialists, although both "engaged" with Islam on their own terms.[37]

Historians tend to agree that the study of Islam in Japan and Japanese intellectuals' interest in Islam can be divided into two periods. Although a number of Japanese scholars were interested in Islam before then, the invasion of North China in 1931 marked a turning point in the Japanese Empire's attention to Muslims.[38] Prior to the establishment of Manchukuo in March 1932, the Japanese government hoped it would be able to gain the support of North China's Muslims to create a buffer between colonial Korea and Russian expansion in Siberia, but Japan's approach was haphazard and not well-coordinated. Many of the campaigns to work with Muslims were "unofficial and isolated" efforts. For example, Fukuda Kikuo moved to China and independently opened a school for Muslim youth. There he advocated for the creation of an independent Muslim state in North China and promoted secession to Sino-Muslims.[39]

But as Japan's influence expanded on the mainland, its tactics and approaches to managing Muslims changed as well. After the establishment of Manchukuo, two policies governed Japanese expansion: "advance by sea" (J. *kaiyō seisaku*) and "advance on land" (J. *tairiku seisaku*). The latter had the most direct impact on Muslims in China. Part of the "advance on land" policy advocated enlisting the help of the small number of Japanese scholars who had knowledge about both Islam and Muslims around the world. This expansionist policy was used as leverage to justify the establishment of a number of research institutions and associations, both in Japan and on the Chinese mainland to further the understanding of the different peoples coming under Japanese control. This information helped the Japanese begin to figure out how to best use the mainland's resources—both human and natural—to further the Empire's objectives.

The biggest obstacle to the Japanese Empire in presenting itself as a legitimate and engaged supporter of Islam was that there were only a handful of Japanese Muslims. Few among them could speak Arabic and even fewer had ever been to a predominately Muslim region of the world. This is no indication of their devotion; it is simply a marker of their isolation from what we might consider traditional Islamic cultural centers. There was also very minimal interaction between Japanese subjects on the home islands and Muslims before the late nineteenth century. Although it is likely that individuals from Japan made contact with Muslims from China before the eighteenth century, the first known references to Islam in Japanese sources appear in

Arai Hakuseki's early eighteenth-century tome *Seiyō Kibun* (*The Record of Things about the West*).[40] For the next 250 years, interest in Islam in Japan was nominal. However, after the Meiji Restoration in 1868, knowledge about Islam among Japanese intellectuals burgeoned. On the heels of the Iwakura Mission to the United States and Europe, the Meiji government deployed its first unofficial envoy to the Kajar and Ottoman courts in 1879–80.[41] These missions sent the best and brightest from the new Meiji government to learn from other nations around the world. Career diplomat Yoshida Masaharu, who led the mission, upon his return published a book titled *Expedition to the Islamic World* (J. *Kaikyō tanken*). Historian Selçuk Esenbel notes that Yoshida's mission to Persia and the Ottoman Empire should "be viewed as the beginning of Japanese informal diplomatic contacts with the Muslim politics of west Asia."[42] Although Japanese intellectuals in the twentieth century would try to push their connections to Muslims back in time through the creation of historical myths and narratives, Esenbel is correct that we should limit Japanese diplomatic engagement with Muslim empires and states to the last decades of the nineteenth century.

Qurans and Converts

Beyond the foundations of early diplomatic engagements, biographies of the Prophet translated from European sources began to appear in Japanese, along with books about the Middle East and Central Asia. In 1899, Sakamoto Kenichi recorded his own version of Muhammad's life in Japanese. Twenty years later, Sakamoto made the first translation of the Quran into Japanese using European-language materials.[43] A total of six different Japanese versions of the Quran appeared in the leadup to the war.[44] These translations are a noteworthy outcome of the intensified connections between Islam and Japan, as well as a testament to the skills of the translators who had to make foreign Islamic texts relevant and relatable to Japanese readers. Japanese scholars of Islam often struggled with how to deal with "theologically charged concepts."[45] For instance, the Japanese word *kami*, which literally means "god" or "spirit," is deeply rooted in Japanese animistic traditions, but it was the closest approximation for a translation of "Allah." A 1938 translation of the Quran translated "Allah" as *Ōkami*, which generally refers to the Shinto goddess Amaterasu. These early translations of the Quran into Japanese synthesized Japanese religious expression and Islam.[46] Other notable efforts to translate the Quran were undertaken by Omar Mita (né Ryōchi Mita), who, like so many early Japanese converts to Islam, came to know and understand Islam through his connections to the Chinese mainland.[47] There is healthy academic debate concerning the motives behind the translations of the Quran into Japanese.[48] But, in essence, this engagement relied partly on the increasing knowledge about Islam by Japanese subjects on the home islands who were receiving more news stories about the Nation of Islam in Detroit, Moroccan resistance to French colonialism in North Africa, and Muslim nationalist movements in India and the Dutch East Indies.[49]

One of the first Japanese to convert to Islam is said to be Noda Shōtarō (1868–1904). He lived in Constantinople for many years and accepted Islam during his time teaching Japanese at an Ottoman military academy.[50] Following Noda's conversion in the late nineteenth century, a handful of Japanese military officers also converted, including Ōhara Takeyoshi and Yamaoka Kotaro. Yamaoka somewhat famously holds the title of the first-known Japanese hajji. Among his expressed motives for converting were to better "understand Manchurian Muslims."[51] Both men had served the Japanese military in the Russo-Japanese War and made their way around the Eurasian continent amid rumors that they were spies.

Ōhara and Yamaoka's intentions have been questioned by Japanese scholars, but their religiosity or conviction in their religious beliefs are beyond concern here.[52] What is known is that both men did have connections with the Black Dragon Society (J. *kokuryūkai*) before they converted to Islam. The Black Dragons were an ultranationalist paramilitary organization whose original purpose was to gather intelligence in the Sino-Russian borderlands along the Amur River in the early years of the twentieth century. In English, the name of the organization has a rather ominous orientalist connotation, but the Black Dragons were named for the Heilongjiang River (known as the Amur in Russian), which divides Russia from Manchuria and literally translates as "black dragon river." They are generally remembered for political assassinations, diplomatic machinations, and highly secretive operations, but the Black Dragons also collected valuable intelligence and formed relationships with disgruntled Russian and Qing subjects inhabiting borderland regions. Through the Black Dragons Yamaoka was introduced to Abdürreşid İbrahim, a Volga Tatar seeking exile in Japan because of his resistance to the Russian Communist incursion around the Black Sea.[53] In 1908 Yamaoka invited İbrahim to Japan, where he played a seminal role in the development of a Tatar Muslim community in Tokyo. He also helped fuel a growing interest in supporting anti-Soviet Muslim causes in Japan in

Japan's Growing Interest in Sino-Muslims

the interwar years.[54] Throughout the 1920s and 1930s, Yamaoka and İbrahim remained close and continued to promote Islam throughout Japan.[55] During this time, Yamaoka converted to Islam.

Such conversion stories are perhaps anomalous or atypical in the history of late nineteenth- and early twentieth-century Japan, but they are not inconsequential. These early connections made by Japanese scholars and others interested in Islam paved the way for Japan's growing engagement with Muslims in the 1930s and 1940s. The relationships of men like Yamaoka with Muslims around the world also laid the groundwork for imperial Japan's involvement with Muslims in China. By focusing on the changes in North China from the end of the nineteenth century and on deepening Japanese control over the region, it becomes clear that the Japanese Empire was an important catalyst facilitating changes in local Muslims' increasing interactions with Muslims around the globe.[56]

Expending Intellectual Energy: Japanese Bureaucrats Imagining Connections to an Islamic Past

Because there were so few Muslims in Japan, the Japanese government and intellectuals had to work extra hard to create linkages to an imagined Islamic past and to highlight their munificence to oppressed Muslims around the world. I will examine the historic connections invented during wartime in more depth later in the book, but here, one example from the Meiji era provides sufficient context for us to understand how encounters with Muslims were constructed and manipulated by the Japanese imperial government to suit its imperial objectives. In 1890, an Ottoman frigate, the *Ertuğrul*, was returning to Constantinople after a goodwill mission to Japan when it was caught in a typhoon and sank near Wakayama. Over 550 Ottoman sailors died. The few survivors were housed with local families until they could be returned to Constantinople on two small Japanese warships, the *Kongō* and the *Hiei*. The Ottoman sultan greeted the sailors upon their return to the Sublime Porte and decorated the Japanese officers with medals of honor.[57]

In popular discourse, the shipwreck of the *Ertuğrul* is remembered as the beginning of the diplomatic relationship between the Meiji and Ottoman governments, and the event is commemorated in both Japan and Turkey. Turks generally remember the kindness the Japanese showed the survivors as a testament of the goodwill of the Japanese people. In Japan, the event is remembered as one of the first instances of the newly formed Meiji government participating in a goodwill mission involving Muslims. Clearly, the Meiji government understood the benefits of promoting this as a benevolent act by the Japanese people. As Japan wrestled with how to position itself as a rising power in the Pacific, the shipwreck of the *Ertuğrul* was one of the ways it was able to connect itself to Muslims around the globe.

The *Ertuğrul* disaster occurred during a moment of self-reflection for the Meiji government about the role that religion should play in state politics.[58] Japanese policymakers in the late-Meiji period began to think of religion as a problem that needed to be fixed, mostly because religious expression in Meiji Japan was both amorphous and highly localized. In other words, religion became a "problem" because it defied categorization by the modern state. In their efforts "to develop a secular state," Meiji reformers thus described and created strict categories whereby religion was envisioned "in opposition to" the state.[59] At the same time as the state redefined itself in opposition to newly formed categories of religious identification, Japanese policymakers began to understand the usefulness of religion as a way to include or exclude people from their imperial project.[60] By the late Meiji period, the state had begun to figure out ways to instrumentalize Islam to serve its budding aspirations beyond the home islands. The utility of Sino-Muslims in the diplomatic maneuverings for power in East Asia was not lost on Japanese policymakers.

In the years leading up to the war, religion became a tool that the empire used "in opposition to the new political heresies" of socialism, liberalism, and anarchism, all of which posed real threats to the Japanese imperial apparatus in the interwar period.[61] Religion and religious associations were presented as beacons of morality in opposition to godless communists and anarchists who wrought havoc on urban centers around Japan.[62] At the same time, imperial officials were taking cues about the importance of the international "diplomatic climate" in "shaping the political conversation concerning religion in Japan."[63] This conversation would soon extend to the mainland, where Sino-Muslims were already beginning to question their role vis-à-vis the new Republican government and were searching for alternative political backers in their efforts to bring about their own reform agendas.

Many Sino-Muslim Voices

In the twentieth century, amid the political turmoil throughout East Asia, Sino-Muslims were trying to come to terms with the new political formations in the post-Qing political landscape. Sino-Muslims engaged in healthy and heated debates about their place within China, East Asia, and the broader community of believers. They published their own journals, ran competing organizations, opened competing schools, and debated how they should position themselves in relation to the various political power brokers in the region. These arguments offered alternative voices and regularly drew on the plight of Muslims around the world to try to understand their position in the region.[64]

As the Japanese Empire expanded its influence in China, bureaucrats encountered Muslims who had already started to take a deep and critical look at where they stood in relation to the Chinese Nationalist government or other political backers. Although some Muslims were closely aligned with Nationalist objectives, this group included competing factions with differing views of the future of Sino-Muslims. There never was a unified Sino-Muslim voice in interwar China. This was a problem for the Chinese Nationalists and an advantage, or a point of entry, for the Japanese Empire.

Tensions within the Sino-Muslim community were exhibited in a number of prominent and public ways, with debates and discussions lasting for years. Early on, one of these debates centered on the cutting of the queue (C. *bianfa* or *bianzi*), the mandated Qing men's hairstyle that was seen as a vestige of Manchu imperialism and traditionalism in a rapidly changing world.[65] For most Han Chinese, cutting the queue symbolized ridding themselves of an imperial past. But, as Noriko Yamazaki demonstrates, for many elite Muslims living in and around Beijing in the early twentieth century, cutting off the "pigtail" was a hotly debated theological issue.[66] By framing the cutting of the queue as a theological rather than a national matter, Sino-Muslims were indicating that their allegiances to their religion trumped their loyalty to the new Republican state.

Sino-Muslim writers also regularly emphasized the deep, historical connections between China and the Middle East in order to establish that Muslims had long been integral intermediaries between the two regions. In rhetoric at least, acknowledging the important contributions Islamic culture had made in China allowed Sino-Muslims to connect themselves to broader networks of Muslims while also proving their value to the Chinese nation-state.[67] One of the phrases that nationalistic Sino-Muslim writers frequently used in the years leading up to the war with Japan was "Love Islam, love the nation" (C. *aijiao aiguo*). This slogan was originally used by Arab nationalists in the Middle East and was introduced to China by Sino-Muslim Wang Jing-zhai. However, once the war started, this phrasing was inverted to place loyalty to the nation before loyalty to Islam (C. *aiguo aijiao*).[68] Throughout the war with Japan, Nationalist propaganda regularly reminded Muslims of this message. The message of salvation for both the nation and Islam was clear: in the eyes of the state, Muslims' obedience to the authority of the nation became a question of religious theory and doctrine.[69] Yet, for many Sino-Muslims, inverting their personal loyalty to God and loyalty to the state was never an option. In this regard, Nationalist rhetoric and propaganda did not align with what large segments of Sino-Muslim communities wanted for their own futures.

At the same time, some Nationalist-leaning Sino-Muslims felt that it was the responsibility of Muslims in China to demonstrate to their fellow citizens — both the Han and other groups of people, such as the Tibetans — that they were behind the Nationalist war efforts to defeat Japan.[70] As citizens of a fragmented Republic, the Chinese Nationalists pushed a message that devotion (C. *duxin*) to Islam would allow the country to succeed and prosper as a whole.[71] After the war ended, Muslims who had maintained support for the Nationalists came forward to collect what they felt they were due for their loyalties and support of the *Guomindang*. Thus, "Love Islam, love the nation" evolved yet again after the war to become "Encourage religion, build the nation" (C. *yujiao jianguo*).[72]

Unlike their Han Chinese neighbors, Sino-Muslims were urged to trust that Allah would protect them in the war against the Japanese, while maintaining their faith in the Chinese nation.[73] In this case, religion was the savior of the nation, and a strong faith in Islam was needed before attachment to the nation, though the two were not seen as incompatible. As "Chinese fellow Muslims" (C. *Zhongguo de jiaobaomen*), Muslims living in Free China were also responsible to the larger community of the *dar-al-Islam*.[74] The term "Chinese fellow Muslims" is interesting as in this instance "Chinese" was a type of Muslim, not the other way around. In this case, certain Nationalist-supported Muslims presented Islam as a tool that could be harnessed for the good of the nation and used to defeat the Japanese Empire.

Sino-Muslims also used the Quran to justify the notion that religion and the modern state were not mutually exclusive. For instance, Ma Hongkui frequently combined theological and nationalistic arguments in his writing, buttressing his points with oft-quoted verses from the Quran. Ma felt that in order to defeat the Japanese and set China on its proper course of unity and development, Muslims needed to follow the will of God and help the Nationalists win.[75] Ma's overall point was that faith in Islam would eventually allow Sino-Muslims to take their rightful place in the modern nation-state.[76]

In their efforts to understand their place in the new geopolitical formations in East Asia, Sino-Muslims expressed curiosity about the world beyond their borders. Articles often appeared in popular and widely circulated journals like *Yuehua* about Muslims outside China. Some writers wrote rather favorably about the situation for European Muslims and explained that their condition was similar to their own. Like Sino-Muslims, European Muslims had been living in Europe for centuries, were geographically disbursed throughout the continent, and only made up a small minority of the overall population.[77] Muslims in China read that the French government had provided the funds to build a mosque in Paris after World War I because of the wartime contributions of the large North African Muslim community living in the city. They also learned that the Muslim Brotherhood (*Dixionghui*) had founded a branch in Paris in 1907, and that Muslims from French colonies sometimes had the opportunity to study in France. Some Muslims even used French as their first language, which was in fashion (C. *fengxing-yishi*) among certain circles of North African Muslims.[78]

Yet not all Sino-Muslims presented colonial encounters for Muslims living in Europe in such a positive light, and other Sino-Muslim writers were deeply concerned about their brethren living under French, British, and Dutch colonial oppression.[79] Contrary to the previous portrayal, the *Muslim Student Journal* presented the French not as benevolent supporters of diasporic and cosmopolitan Muslims living in Paris but as colonial oppressors who imposed their language on North Africans and stifled Islam.[80] Differing viewpoints on this single issue demonstrate that Sino-Muslims were concerned with the fate of their brethren beyond China in the years leading up to the war.

Nationalistic Sino-Muslims were also fully aware of the importance of overseas Chinese Muslims in their ongoing propaganda battle with imperial Japan. In their calls to increase resistance to the Japanese military after the invasion and occupation, Nationalist-supported Muslim writers appealed to Sino-Muslims living abroad (C. *zai haiwai*) to disseminate anti-Japanese messages in their host countries.[81] They called on the "overseas *hui*" (C. *hui huaqiao*) to support the resistance, linking their support for the defeat of the Japanese Empire to their unique status as expatriate Muslims *and* Chinese.[82] Enlisting the services of Sino-Muslim students and entrepreneurs living throughout Southeast Asia and the Middle East might seem like small efforts, but from Sino-Muslims' perspective, every ounce of help counted toward the ultimate goal of Japan's defeat.[83]

Nationalist-supported Sino-Muslims made real efforts to resist Japanese imperialism in China and abroad. In their pleas, they directly mentioned the successes of the Japanese Empire in recruiting and supporting

Muslims in China. One suggestion for curtailing Japan's nefarious plans to win over Muslims throughout the colonized world was to promote overseas educational exchanges with places like India, a wartime ally of the Nationalists. In these plans, the Nationalists would rely on students to spread anti-Japanese messages in their host countries. In return, they would also offer scholarships to students from predominantly Muslim regions to study in China. This would allow Indian Muslims and other allies to see for themselves the oppression and suffering inflicted by the Japanese.[84]

A More Coherent Policy: Japanese Organizations, Data Collection, and Publications for Muslims in Occupied China

In this milieu Japanese intellectuals interested in the history of Islam came together with the support of the military to promote their mission to disseminate information about Muslims to subjects on the home islands, and to create closer connections with Sino-Muslim communities on the mainland. In order to facilitate this, the Japanese government established Islamic associations at home and throughout East Asia in the leadup to the war.[85] By the 1930s, it became a priority for imperial Japan to bring as many religious associations and organizations as it could under the direct control of the government.[86] Under these auspices, the goals of many religious organizations were reformulated to "resist Communism and uphold the East Asian new order."[87] The Japanese imperial government presented itself to religious organizations as more tolerant of religion and indigenous religious practices than Western imperial powers. In this regard, for many established religious organizations, collaborating with the Japanese Empire often helped further social and political objectives.[88] During this time, the most important coordinators of Middle Eastern and Islamic studies in Japan, men such as Matsuda Hisao (1903–82), Kobayashi Hajime (c. 1890–1963), and Ōkubo Kōji (1899–1950), saw their own interests in promoting the history of Islam and Islamic theology line up with the Japanese Empire's growing interest in instrumentalizing Islam and Muslims in new ways.[89]

Between 1932 and 1937, there was a dramatic increase in interest in Muslims and a growing understanding among Japanese policymakers of Sino-Muslims' importance to Japan's imperial outreach efforts. As the number of classes on Islam in universities grew throughout the 1930s, so too did the number of associations dedicated to the study of Islam. In 1932, renowned scholar of Islam Kobayashi Hajime founded the Islamic Culture Study Group at Komazawa University in Tokyo. Following this, a number of Islamic academic research institutes were repurposed and renamed for broader appeal, such as the Islamic Society (J. *Isuramu gakkai*) in Tokyo. After 1937, two other major Islamic research institutes were established in Tokyo: the Association of Islamic Culture (J. *Isuramu bunka kyōkai*) and the Islamic Studies Group (J. *Kaikyō han*), which was housed within the Ministry of Foreign Affairs.[90] The following year, the Greater Japan Muslim League (J. *Dai-Nippon Kaikyō kyōkai*) was founded with funding from the Japanese government and military.[91] Later the same year, Kobayashi Hajime was appointed head of the newly formed Greater Japan Muslim League. Starting in 1938, the association published a monthly journal called *Islam* (J. *Kaikyō ken*), followed a few months later by another journal named *Islamic World* (J. *Kaikyō sekai*). The Greater Japan Muslim League also published Chinese-language journals like *Muslim Affairs* on the mainland from May 1938 through to the end of the war.

Beyond this, other larger and influential cultural organizations of the Japanese Empire, such as the umbrella association known as the Greater Asia Association (J. *Dai Ajia Kyōkai*) commissioned Japanese scholars and journalists who had long been interested in Islam to work for the imperial government.[92] Starting in 1933, the Greater Asia Association published a monthly journal called *Greater Asianism* (J. *Dai Ajia shugi*), which frequently featured articles about the relationship between pan-Asianism and Islam, and also covered international events relating to Muslims and the Japanese Empire as well as anticolonial movements among Muslim populations throughout Asia, the Middle East, and Africa.[93]

Through these religious associations, the Japanese imperial project gathered information and data about Muslim populations throughout Asia. Although the stated goals of these organizations was to promote the mutual understanding between Islamic and Japanese cultures, their close ties with high-ranking military officials like Hayashi Senjūrō ensured that the objectives of the organization went far beyond simple research and promotion of cultural understanding to intelligence gathering and military strategy development.[94] For four months in 1937, Hayashi Senjūrō was prime minister of Japan.

In fact, the cultural objectives of the Japanese Empire were always closely linked to its economic and militaristic ambitions on the mainland and beyond. On the home islands, the Greater Japan Muslim League staged exhibits about Muslims for Japanese subjects who knew little about Islam. In 1937 and 1938 it mounted a public exhibition about Islam in Tokyo and Osaka. The Greater Japan Muslim League estimated that somewhere around

150,000 people visited the exhibit in the two cities.[95] It was through concerted and coordinated efforts like these that the Japanese populace learned about the importance of Muslims in the Japanese Empire's quest to rid Asia of Western imperialism and communism.

These efforts expanded to the Chinese mainland, and Japanese-sponsored newspapers published in North China, such as the *Shengjing Times*, regularly included images and stories about Muslims. Historian Thomas DuBois argues that in the case of Japanese-published periodicals in Manchukuo, "the images of religion . . . were inextricably related to both sweeping social trends and particularistic political needs."[96] These combined efforts were meant to make Muslims legible to Japanese subjects and to explain their aspirations regarding Muslim people living throughout the empire. Promoting Muslim religious associations and research groups throughout Asia should be understood as part of imperial Japan's efforts to create an alternate economic and political bloc.

In 1934, the Japanese established the Xinjing Islamic Association (C. *Xinjing yisilan xiehui*) in the capital of Manchukuo with the help of some Japanese Islamic specialists who were working on the mainland, such as Kawamura Kyōdo. They also established the Manchurian Islamic Association (C. *Manzhou yisilan xiehui*) the same year. The stated objectives of these organizations were to support the policies of the new government, to support Islam, and to resist communism.[97] The initial success of these associations led the Japanese government to open more branches in cities throughout Manchukuo. After the occupation of Beijing in July 1937, all of the associations came under the umbrella of the Japanese-sponsored All China Muslim League (C. *Zhongguo Huijiao zonglianhehui*), which was based in Beijing. The Japanese installed Wang Ruilan as chairman and the Japanese Muslim Takagaki Shinzo as general adviser. Wang had long been the cleric at the famous Niujie Mosque in Beijing.[98]

The Beijing branch of the All China Muslim League was originally located near Guang'an Gate but soon moved to a building adjacent to Zhongnanhai, the former imperial gardens next to the Forbidden City that served as the administrative nerve center for the Japanese occupation.[99] The North China (C. *huabei*) branch was also the only "real" branch of the All China Muslim League. The other five branches were hypothetical, or "aspirational" branches that were intended to open throughout the entire mainland as the Japanese Empire spread throughout China to places like the Southwest (C. *xinan*), South China (C. *huanan*) and the Northwest (C. *xibei*).[100] In 1938, the North China branch also had seven subordinate chapters in larger cities throughout occupied China. According to reports circulated among Chinese Nationalists, there were a total of 374 active members in the seven different chapters throughout North China.[101] Each chapter was further subdivided into a research branch to oversee communications and publications, and an educational branch to help administer schools and mosques in the region under its jurisdiction.[102] By the early 1940s, about twelve full-time employees worked at the Beijing chapter of the All China Muslim League, and Zhang Wangmou, a well-known elite Sino-Muslim from Beijing, served as the "spiritual head" of the organization.[103]

The promotion of these organizations through the mouthpiece of Sino-Muslims on the mainland reflected the Japanese government's growing desire to articulate a clearer and more coherent policy regarding Islam. It also highlights the efforts of the Japanese government to bring academic research associations under the control of the army—even if only indirectly.[104] At the same time, Sino-Muslims staked a claim in these organizations and their overtly political agendas. Some even published writings articulating their desire that these new Japanese-sponsored religious organizations would help Muslims in North China gain a higher degree of education and find good jobs.[105]

Fieldwork and the Collection of Data in Sino-Muslim Communities

Beyond the upsurge in the number of associations concerned with understanding Islam and their affiliated publications, the Japanese government also began sending research teams specializing in Islamic studies to document living conditions in Sino-Muslim communities. Kobayashi Hajime led a number of research trips throughout North China and into the Mongolian border areas under Japanese control under the supervision of the Research Branch of the South Manchurian Railway Company. On one trip in 1938, the group visited forty-six mosques, including five women's-only mosques, throughout the region, stopping for extensive research and data collection in Datong and Zhangjiakou.[106]

These research branches also produced reports on the economic output of Muslims living in occupied China. One report relayed detailed information about Muslim guilds in Beijing. The report divided the Beijing Muslim community into specific economic sectors. According to the report, the top six jobs for Muslims in the city in descending order were fruit and vegetable vendor, pack animal trader, camel trader, beef and mutton butcher and vendor, duck vendor, and jade trader.[107] Having perused the extensive details concerning garlic, watermelon, and pumpkin sales by Muslims at markets around Beijing, I can safely conclude that the amount of data collected by Japanese investigators regarding the financial transactions of fruit and vegetable sellers reflected the strategic importance of understanding the economic situation in Beijing's Muslim communities.[108]

The data provided the Japanese imperial apparatus with clear and specific insights into the economic well-being of Sino-Muslim communities. It also provided Japanese imperial officials with the quantifiable data they needed to secure financial backing for their proposed development plans on the mainland. This particular report concluded that in order to create better relationships with Muslim vendors, the Japanese Empire should fund the building of more mosques around the city.[109] This type of deep ethnographic data was collected around the empire and regularly used to justify the implementation of policies directed at certain segments of the population. In this case, highlighting the business acumen of Muslim vendors in Beijing played into Japanese ideas about using Sino-Muslim entrepreneurs in potential business ventures throughout the Middle East and North Africa.

In this regard, it is impossible to disassociate Japan's interest in Islam during this period from its imperial ambitions. Growing appeals to Islam reflected the increasing number of researchers and scholars working to categorize Muslims and problematize their place within the Chinese state for the advantage of the Japanese Empire. Through articles published in journals like *Dai Ajia Shugi* about Muslim communities on the mainland, imperial Japan justified its contributions to the development and "civilization" of Sino-Muslims.[110] The increased attention paid to Islam after 1932 "reflected a change of attitude toward the pan-Asian movement, which came to be increasingly appropriated by the Japanese state in those years, culminating in the declaration of the Greater East Asian Co-Prosperity Sphere in 1940."[111] One of the ways Japanese scholars of Islam aligned their academic objectives more closely with the broader ambitions of the imperial government was by tying Islam to Pan-Asian ideology.

Pan-Asianism and Islam

Until recently, scholars regarded Pan-Asianism as a "defeated ideology."[112] It is certainly true that after the war, Pan-Asianism fell out of favor as people throughout East Asia had been convinced that it was only used to give credibility to Japanese militarism, but "the ideology itself cannot be dismissed merely as disguised imperialism."[113] The assumption that Pan-Asianism failed neglects to take into account the ways it was put into practice through the networks that Japanese imperialists fostered between Sino-Muslims and Muslims around the world for commercial and economic purposes during the war. Imperial Japan paid extra attention to Muslims because they were seminal to projections of visions of East Asia, and Sino-Muslims were expected to become "a showpiece and a microcosm of a racially transcendent pan-Asian unity."[114] Through the promotion of economic development among Muslim communities, the Japanese imperial government attempted to bridge its engagement with Sino-Muslims with Muslim populations around the world in order to build new commercial networks in Islamic spaces opened by the war.[115]

To be certain, these connections with Sino-Muslims were not the only outreach efforts by the Japanese Empire to religious minorities living on the mainland. Many of the structures and institutions were replicated to appeal to Buddhists living in Mongolia and Tibet, as well as throughout Southeast Asia.[116] Transnational Buddhist networks developed throughout the twentieth century largely with the help of Japanese Buddhists.[117] In his work on Tibet, historian Gray Tuttle offers a case for thinking about how "the state can 'use' religion for its ends, such as to divide or unite an ethnic group," and how "religious institutions can also 'use' the state to accomplish certain goals, such as the maintenance of prestige or property."[118] Through expanding connections to the outside world, Tuttle contends that Tibetan Buddhists were deeply involved in the "remaking of religion as a political enterprise," which was "intimately linked to the imagination of a new social and intellectual community," among the global community of Buddhist believers in the late nineteenth and early twentieth century.[119] The Japanese Empire was able to tap into networks that Buddhists and Sino-Muslims on the mainland were already developing by offering them the means to achieve their reform agendas.

However, there were a number of important differences between these Buddhist and Islamic networks. For one, there was a large Buddhist community in Japan, and Buddhism had long been a part of the social and cultural life on the home islands. This meant that the Japanese government did not have to devote as much energy to making Buddhism and Buddhists legible to subjects on the home islands. Another important distinction had to do with the potential to politicize and instrumentalize Islam. Whereas the majority of Buddhists lived in Southeast Asia, South Asia, Central Asia, and East Asia, Muslims also lived in places that we generally consider to be beyond the sphere of Japanese imperial influence during the war, like the Middle East, East Africa, North Africa, the Balkans, the Caucasus, and even North America.

With the help of the Japanese Empire, Muslims from China started "forging international links" that superseded the nation-state through an imagined common religious identity.[120] Sino-Muslims were swept up in currents of globalization that tied them to transnational political movements such as Pan-Asianism, Pan-Islamism, and Pan-Arabism.[121] In this regard, it is not useful to separate Japan's imperial aspirations from the ways it went about securing and maintaining its empire from the ways it represented itself as protector of Muslims around the world.

One person who always understood the importance of Muslim voices was Sun Yat-sen, the leader of the Chinese Revolutionary Alliance (C. *tongmeng-hui*) and the man generally considered to be the father of modern Chinese nationalism. Sun was also an early proponent of Pan-Asianism, influenced by circles of Pan-Asianist thinkers he encountered during his exile from the Qing Empire in Japan.[122] In 1912, he delivered a speech to Muslims in Beijing about how they could incorporate his ideology of the Three Principles of the People (C. *sanmin zhuyi*) into their daily lives. An integral part of Sun's ideological platform for political reform in China, the three principles are often translated as "nationalism" (C. *minzu zhuyi*), "democracy" (C. *minquan zhuyi*), and the "people's livelihood" (C. *minsheng zhuyi*). Together, they formed the political slogan that was supposed to usher China into a new era based on the will of the governed. In this speech, Sun highlighted the connections between Muslims living in the new Republic and those living in the broader abode of Islam.[123] A decade later, he delivered a speech in Tokyo about Pan-Asianism, the Three Principles of the People, and the common cultural heritage shared by East Asians. He called on East Asians to join together and draw on this vague notion of a "common cultural heritage" to defeat Western materialism.[124] For Sun, Pan-Asianism was one way to resist imperialism and allow all the people living in Asia to free themselves from Western oppression.[125]

A number of Japanese Pan-Asian thinkers also wrote extensively about the relationship between Islam and Pan-Asianism. One of the most influential Pan-Asian thinkers of the 1930s, Ōkawa Shūmei (1886–1957), wrote prolifically about Islam and Pan-Asianism, and was especially interested in Wahabi reforms and Pan-Islamism.[126] Like Sun, Ōkawa believed that Islam could be used as another force in the battle against Western imperialism because all "Easterners" were united in solidarity against the West. Politically active throughout his career, he gained notoriety after the war for being the only civilian to be tried by the International Military Tribunal in the Far East. He was declared unfit to stand trial and sentenced to life in a psychiatric facility. During his incarceration, he continued his work on a Japanese translation of the Quran.

Ōkawa read the history of Islam in China refracted through the lens of Pan-Asianism. This allowed ideologues and Pan-Asianists to recast "the relationship between the universality of the Japanese Empire and local national cultures."[127] Ōkawa imagined that the ideological backing of Japan's expansionist visions could align with the religious beliefs of the people who were under their control. In his view, there was a universal — and highly idealized — appeal to Islam that took precedence over the overwhelming diversity among Muslim communities, and ideological movements like Pan-Arabism and Pan-Islamism "could be an inspiration for rethinking the relationship between the empire and the national cultures in the Greater East Asia Co-Prosperity Sphere as well."[128]

Besides Ōkawa, a number of important and influential Japanese Pan-Asianists were also Muslim converts. These included writer Tanaka Ippei (1882–1934) and Ahmad Aruga Humihachirō (1868–1946). Both Tanaka and Aruga were interested in the theological and ideological possibilities of syncretism between Islam and Shinto. In 1899, twenty-something Aruga converted to Christianity and left his post as a high school principal to proselytize. He later joined a trading company and traveled extensively throughout the Indian Ocean. After his retirement in 1932, he converted to Islam.[129] Aruga self-published a number of pamphlets and articles about Islam. Like Ōkawa, he believed that winning the support of Muslims around the world was the only way the Japanese Empire could defeat the Western imperialists.[130]

On a slightly different path, Tanaka Ippei spent many years in China working as an interpreter for the army. After graduating from Takushoku University, Tanaka spent the majority of his time between 1904 and 1920 on the mainland. In China, he met Wakabayashi Han, one of the early pioneers of Islamic studies in Japan. Tanaka converted to Islam in 1923 at a mosque in Jinan after years of learning about Islam and interacting with Muslim communities in China.[131] He was one of the first Japanese hajjis, and the published chronicle of his pilgrimage was instrumental in introducing Islam to Japanese subjects on the home islands.[132] After he converted, Tanaka was eager to proselytize in Japan and imagined that he could convince large num-

bers of Japanese people to accept Islam. When proselytizing, Tanaka emphasized development work among Muslim communities in North China to
highlight the transformative powers of the Japanese Empire. Muslims from
China provided Tanaka with the perfect model to prove Japan's loyalty to
Muslims and the religious tolerance of the Japanese Empire. Tanaka died
suddenly in Mecca on his second hajj and left a number of his works unfin-
ished.[133]

Much like the corpus of the *Han Kitab*, Tanaka Ippei's deep knowledge
of both Islam and Confucianism allowed him to explore the syncretic re-
lationship between Shinto and Islam.[134] Tanaka's views about the spiritual
East in diametric opposition to the materialist West were common among
Pan-Asian thinkers at the time, but his ideas about the relationship between
Islam and Pan-Asianism distinguished him from his peers. In his essay
"Islam and Greater Asianism" (J. *isuramu to dai Ajia shugi*), published in
1925, Tanaka emphasized the importance of Muslims in China to Japan's
Pan-Asian vision.[135] Tanaka developed a particular interest in Liu Zhi, the
late seventeenth-century neo-Confucian Muslim scholar, and he translated
Liu Zhi's biography of the Prophet into Japanese. He was also drawn to the
syncretism of late-Ming Chinese Muslim scholar Wang Daiyu.[136] In his writings, he drew parallels between the Prophet Muhammad and Japanese Buddhist warrior monks (J. *sōhei*), since he believed that both were courageous
fighters devoted to defending their faiths.[137]

Tanaka was so taken with the *Han Kitab* corpus that he even translated
at least one classical Chinese book from the early eighteenth century into
Japanese and provided a short commentary on the work. In 1941, the Greater
Japan Muslim League published his annotated translation of Liu Jielian's
(1670–1724) *Tianfang zhi sheng shi lu nian pu* (J. *Tenpō shisei jitsuroku*).[138]
Tanaka begins the translation with a ten-page introduction to the history
of Islam in China, followed by an introduction to Sino-Muslim intellectual Liu Jielian and his work. Liu's most prominent contribution to the *Han
Kitab* corpus was a history of the Prophet drawn from Arabic and Chinese
sources. Following this, there is a two-page lament (C. *ai*) written in Chinese by Tanaka about the loss of vitality among Sino-Muslims during the
late Qing and Japan's contribution to the revitalization of Islam on the mainland.[139] In the afterword, Tanaka explains that he translated the book to help
Japanese readers deepen their understanding (J. *fukai rikai*) of the history
of Islam in China.[140]

Tanaka never shied away from extoling the benefits of Islam for Japanese imperial objectives, in statements such as the following: "In a period

of decadence such as the present, we urgently need the temper of rigor and vitality found in the moral discipline of our Japanese spirit. . . . I have no hesitation in affirming that the austere message of Islam will not only be very useful in the restoration of our country but will also prove indispensable both to the establishment of Pan-Asianism and to the completion of Japan's imperial mission."[141] His work highlights the importance that certain Pan-Asianists placed on religion and the cultivation of Muslims as a way to secure and broaden the Japanese imperial project.

Suzuki Takeshi was yet another Japanese convert who promoted a Pan-Asianist agenda in his writings. He performed hajj in the early 1930s and published an account of his journey.[142] Suzuki's pilgrimage story begins by justifying Japan's connections with Muslims in China: since there were so few Muslims in Japan, Japanese Muslims had to look outward to Islamic communities on the mainland to help them connect with their "Muslim brothers" around the world.[143] Suzuki lauded the Japanese Empire and explained to his readers in the preface of his hajj journal that being Muslim in Japan was a pleasant experience. He described an atmosphere of religious plurality on the home islands, mandated by Japan's policies of religious freedom enshrined in the 1889 Meiji Constitution. For him, there was no inherent incompatibility with being an observant Muslim and a subject of the Japanese Empire, and he believed that the emperor had a divine duty to protect everyone under his authority.[144] Although it now reads like a rather obvious propaganda tract for religious inclusion in the Japanese imperial project, Suzuki clearly made his own connection to Islam with the help of Muslims from the mainland. In this case, Sino-Muslims are presented as the spiritual middlemen to Islam. The plans of Japanese policymakers almost always relied on Sino-Muslims to act as middlemen to establish and maintain relationships with Muslims around the world. Yet, in order to do this, the Japanese Empire needed to fabricate histories and connections to Muslims in the hopes of being taken seriously.

New Relationships Founded on a Long Historical Memory

Creating historical narratives that tied Muslims to Japan dating as far back as the fifteenth century gave Japanese imperialists the opportunity to legitimize their claims over Muslims throughout Asia. Historical relationships linking Japanese commodities, Muslims from China, and Muslim traders circulating the *dar-al-Islam* also provided justification for forging new relationships with Muslim communities in East Asia and beyond. To Japanese observers,

Muslims from China had already established the networks needed to develop connections to Muslims beyond North China, and it was up to the Japanese strategists to figure out how to tap into them.[145] By drawing on the mythologized connections of Muslims from China to a broadly conceived idea of Asia, Japanese strategists used Islam as a way to validate their incursions into these areas.[146] Through historical narratives and myths, Japanese imperialists presented Muslims in China as culturally and racially distinct from the Han Chinese and closer to Arabs. Origin stories about how Muslims had arrived in China from Arabia were not new, but Japanese scholars used specific vocabulary and framed these narratives in ways that benefited their particular imperial objectives.

Sino-Muslims had long been engaged in genealogical writing that tied their ancestry to Arabia and the Prophet Mohammed, but they always had to "work a little harder" to situate themselves within an Islamic past.[147] If finding a connection to a distant Islamic past centered in the Hejaz was difficult for Muslims living in China, it was almost impossible for the Japanese Empire. Japanese scholars of Islam in the first half of the twentieth century often projected the relationship between Sino-Muslims and Japan as far back as the Ming Dynasty. From here, they imagined links to Sino-Muslims to connect themselves to extensive networks of Muslim traders who circulated prized Japanese goods and porcelains (J. *bijutsu kōgei*) to elite Muslim buyers around Eurasia.[148] In one example, Japanese intellectuals pointed out that the elites of the Mughal Dynasty (J. *mugaru teikoku*) appreciated Japanese craftsmanship and placed enormous value on Japanese pearls and white jade carvings. Since white jade is only mined in Xinjiang, this looped Muslims from China into the stories of early modern interconnectivity based on the exchange of commodities between Mughal India and Japanese craftspeople.[149] For Japanese imperialists, this was a sign that commercial networks had previously existed without the interference of the West, and that they should be reenvisioned for a future Asia free from Western intervention or capital.

Japanese scholars of Islam had other ways to push back their own connection to Muslims from China hundreds of years. Some claimed that Japan's contact with Sino-Muslims could be traced back to traditions of the *Han Kitab* because Chinese works on Islam were widely read and circulated among Japanese scholars during the Tokugawa period.[150] Although some writings by Sino-Muslim scholars like Wang Daiyu surely made their way to Japan in the seventeenth and eighteenth centuries, claims that they were in "heavy circulation" among the Tokugawa elite are likely hyperbolic. Other

Japanese scholars traced the arrival of Persian and Arabic scientific texts in Japan through Chinese translations, a connection that served two purposes. For one, it tied twentieth-century Islamic revival movements in the Middle East to Japanese wartime interests by highlighting that scientific innovation in the early modern Middle East was appreciated by Japanese intellectuals. It also connected Japan to the Middle East going back to the thirteenth and fourteenth centuries through translations by Chinese Muslim intellectuals.

It was true that Muslim traders had arrived in China during the Tang Dynasty from the same regions as the Manicheans (J. *manikyō*).[151] From that point on, Japanese narratives about Islam in China indicated that there had always been problems and divisions between "Chinese people" (J. *shinajin*) and the "Hui nationality" (J. *kai minzoku*).[152] Here, the choice of the word *shinajin* to describe the Chinese people is intentional and important. By not using the Chinese Nationalist term *zhongguoren*, the Japanese were being purposefully pejorative while simultaneously dismantling nationalist rhetoric of the five peoples of the Chinese nation-state (C. *Zhonghua minzu*). In these narratives, the *huizu* (J. *kai minzoku*) had inherent characteristics that both differentiated them from Han Chinese and from other minorities in China. It was these specific qualities that made them exceptional candidates to become loyal subjects of the Japanese Empire.

The perceived business acumen of Sino-Muslims was viewed as an asset for imperial Japan, who hoped to expand their industrial and commercial enterprises throughout Asia and in the Middle East. In these racialized tropes, Sino-Muslims were presented as having an inherent business prowess, unlike Mongolians and Tibetans, who Japanese imperialists claimed lacked entrepreneurial spirit.[153] Japanese scholars introduced Arabs as experienced seamen and great traders who had transported Islam from the Middle East to South Asia and East Asia like a piece of precious cargo. As descendants of Arabs, Sino-Muslims had inherited this entrepreneurial wherewithal. These commercial connections were supposed to help Sino-Muslims and the Japanese Empire forge long-lasting networks that would connect them to South Asia, the Middle East, and Africa. For Japanese observers, "overseas Chinese Muslims" (J. *Kakyō kaikyōto*) were well positioned at trading entrepôts throughout the South Seas (J. *nanyō*), and these networks needed to be harnessed in order to foster trade.[154]

Throughout the war, Nationalist-supported propaganda claimed that the Japanese Empire wanted to exploit an essentialized ideal of a "militant Muslim" to help them conquer the mainland. One again, these racialized narratives drew on Western stereotypes dating back to the Crusades that characterized Muslims as inherently violent. They were readily appropriated by Nationalists writers who tried to vilify Sino-Muslim collaborators. However, many writings by Japanese Islamic scholars expounded the virtues of Islam as a peaceful religion and came to the exact opposite conclusions. Japanese scholars of Islam argued that the history of violent Muslim uprisings in China was due to the oppression Muslims had suffered at the hands of the Qing, and was not due to some inherent characteristic of Islam.[155]

Writing in the Japanese-published Chinese-language journal *Huijiao*, Mei Cun (pseudonym) developed the thesis that Islam was a peaceful religion. They noted that Islam had once thrived in China because a separation of church and state dating back to the Qin Dynasty (221–206 BCE) fostered an atmosphere of religious plurality throughout imperial Chinese history. Thus, when Muslims had arrived during the Tang Dynasty, locals were able to find parallels between the foundational teachings of Islam and "Chinese" religions such as Buddhism. This had allowed Muslims to relate to non-Muslims and enabled people of all different religions to live in harmony throughout imperial history. For Mei, the Muslim rebellions during the Qing were the fault not of the Muslims themselves but of the Qing regime. It was the Qing who had violated the long history of religious plurality and accommodation that Sino-Muslims had grown accustomed to over centuries. For Mei, it was up to the Japanese Empire to restore the balance.[156]

Mei went on to say that Muslims in China had been optimistic after the overthrow of the Qing, but that their hopefulness had soon turned to disappointment. It was only once Manchukuo had become an "independent state" that Muslims in North China were allowed to thrive once again, and they claimed that Sino-Muslims worked with Japan in the hope of bringing about perpetual peace (C. *yongjiu heping*) in East Asia.[157] Once this peace was achieved, Sino-Muslims would be able to return to their natural nonviolence. Mei went on to extend this logic to the larger community of Muslims throughout the world. Only by standing together with their Muslim brothers beyond the borders of Manchukuo would Sino-Muslims be able come to peaceful solutions to problems that plagued all Muslims, like exploitation by Western colonial powers.[158]

This article could simply be dismissed as Japanese wartime propaganda. However, that would overlook the fact that Chinese writers supported by the Japanese Empire were writing about Islam in a way that suited the specific needs and agenda of the empire by making Sino-Muslims integral to the creation of lasting peace throughout East Asia. By disseminating distinct narratives about the place of Islam in Chinese society, and the place of Sino-

Muslims in the project to build a Greater East Asia, the Japanese Empire and Sino-Muslims like Mei actively disavowed the Chinese Nationalists' agenda of including minorities in the national imagination.

Minorities on the Home Islands:
Koreans, *Burakumin*, and Tatars

Imperial Japanese policymakers had a number of specific sources and models to draw on as their interest in Muslims on the mainland deepened. For one, they followed their own familiar precedents for managing non-Japanese subjects, including late Meiji policies regarding Korean émigrés to the home islands and the *burakumin*, a group sometimes called Japan's hidden caste of untouchables, who faced discrimination due to their employment in sectors such as butchery, tanning, undertaking, and other "unclean" professions.[159] They also had another fascinating case study to draw upon. In the early 1920s, the Japanese government naturalized a small group of Muslim Tatar refugees who made their way to Japan after fleeing Bolshevik persecution. This group served as model anti-Soviet Muslims in Japan's increasingly coordinated outreach to the Middle East. Beyond these examples on the home islands, the handling of the "Korea Question" on the Korean peninsula at the turn of the twentieth century, as well as growing interest in other pan-movements, such as Pan-Turanism and Pan-Arabism, provided Japanese policymakers with useful models for thinking about how to incorporate Muslims into the imperial fold.[160]

Recently, historians of Japan have highlighted the need to rethink the prewar treatment of minorities living on the home islands and collaboration with Koreans on the peninsula.[161] These works address how minorities were understood as part of the Japanese imperial project and how they were an integral part of Japan's broader justifications for building an empire in the first place.[162] At the same time, there was always a degree of ambiguity and uncertainty about how to approach those who were not Japanese, or not "Japanese enough." This ambiguity had serious implications for the position of minorities within the "emerging ideal of an emperor-centered, homogeneous Japanese nation-state: the *kokutai*." *Kokutai* (C. *guoti*) is another amorphous term borrowed from Chinese. Although it was around in the 1850s and was used by people like Aizawa Seishisa, the term did not gain real cultural valence in the Japanese lexicon until after the Meiji Restoration, when it came to embody the relationship between the emperor and his subjects. The concept was continuously contested as non-Japanese subjects were incorporated into the empire.[163] How to rectify the relationship between the *kokutai* and non-Japanese subjects living on the home islands and in the colonies closest to the home islands, like Korea (which was annexed by Japan in 1910) and the island of Formosa (which Japan acquired in 1895, when it defeated the Qing in the First Sino-Japanese War), became a central concern for political theorists who needed to legitimize Japan's rule over an ever-increasing number of non-Japanese peoples.[164]

The ongoing conversation about the place of Koreans and *burakumin* within Japanese society permeated the discussion of Japan's ambitions for a better Asia, and by the end of the Meiji period, regular Japanese subjects were conversant in the ways the Japanese government imagined the Koreans and the *burakumin* fitting into society.[165] Like Muslim communities in China, *burakumin* had traditionally occupied sectors of the economy as intermediaries working on the fringes of society. In order to figure out how to integrate these *buraku*-specific sectors into the larger economy, the government conducted extensive ethnographic studies of *burakumin* communities as early as the first decade of the twentieth century. A number of reports put out in the early years of the war detailing specifically Muslim-dominated industries in China, such as jade trading, butchering of nonpork products, and wool trading, resembled earlier studies of the *buraku* economy. Although Japanese bureaucrats who worked with Sino-Muslim communities made no explicit comparisons to the *burakumin* in their reports, the methods used and the type of data collected for their studies were similar.[166]

The Russian Revolution and the March First movement for Korean independence in 1919 forced the Japanese Empire to reexamine how it incorporated non-Japanese subjects into its evolving ideas of the *kokutai*. After World War I, Koreans demanded independence from the Japanese, but the movement was violently suppressed by the Japanese army after several months of revolt against Japanese colonial rule. After 1919, the integration of Koreans became a "problem" (J. *mondai*) that needed to be addressed. This rhetoric of trying to "fix" minority issues in the empire would echo throughout policy reports and folios dealing with Muslims throughout the 1930s and 1940s, such as the 1938 policy reports *The Tatar Problem* (J. *Tataru mondai*) and *The Islamic Problem* (J. *Kaikyō mondai*).[167]

The shift concerning Japanese-controlled Korea happened around the same time as the Tatars fleeing Bolshevik persecution found a welcoming home in the Japanese Empire. The Tatar refugees were resettled in Tokyo and naturalized by the Japanese government. In Tokyo, the government built them a school, and it featured them regularly in propaganda outreach to

١٩٣٦. طوكيودا مكتب اسلاميه شا كردلارينك بالشيؤيزم كه قارشى
يأبون ـ كيرمان اتفاقنه موفقيت تلهب دعأ قيلولارى .
一九三六年日獨防共協定の成功ヲ祈ル東京回教學校生徒

Pupils (Tatar girls) of the Islamic School in Tokyo pray for the success
of the Japanese-German alliance against bolshevism, 1936.
(Greater Japan Muslim League database, Waseda
University Library Special Collections)

Muslims around the world. The Tatar émigré community served two distinct needs for the Japanese imperial government, which cast itself as a protector of Islam *and* as a savior from Soviet Communism. Unlike the Koreans, where the "policy of commonality between Japanese and Koreans left no room for the existence of a distinct Korean culture,"[168] the Japanese needed the Tatar refugees because their religious and cultural differences suited the changing needs of the empire.[169] In 1936, the government assembled young Tatar women studying at the Tokyo Mosque School, established for the Tatar refugees. The caption, written in Japanese and East Turki, explains that they were praying for the success of the Japanese-German alliance against bolshevism after the signing of the Anti-Comintern Pact in 1936. Here, the politicization of Muslims as both different yet integral to the Japanese visions for a Greater East Asia offers the opportunity to think about the ways non-Japanese subjects were used and deployed in the service of empire, likely without their explicit consent.

In the early 1930s, Japanese scholars of Islam suggested circulating propaganda about the flourishing Tatar community in Tokyo to demonstrate to Muslims in China imperial Japan's noble intentions.[170] Through outreach efforts to poorer Muslim communities, Japanese imperialists hoped to attract the attention of Muslims in Gansu and Yunnan, or, as they put it, the places where "the most famous Muslims come from."[171] In this outreach, the Japanese imperial government drew on its experiences with the Tatars in order to highlight the parallels between the poor economic standing and the relative proximity to the Soviet Union of both the Tatars and Sino-Muslims. For Japanese bureaucrats, highlighting the equivalencies between the Tatar Muslims who had fled the Bolsheviks and Muslims resisting the Soviets in the northern Chinese cities of Chengde and Fengtian gave them the chance to present themselves as liberators from Soviet oppression in two distinct and unrelated cases.[172] Japanese scholars of Islam also claimed that through exposure to the Tatar community in Tokyo, Japanese people were learning about Islam and had developed a sense of goodwill toward Muslims.[173]

This continued reliance on the émigré Tatar community as a gauge of Japan's commitment to protecting the religious rights of Muslims was a common trope in the empire's propaganda throughout the 1930s and 1940s. Joseph Stalin's crackdown on Muslims provided Japanese imperialists with an entry into Muslim communities, and they successfully exploited Stalin's harsh policies with promises to rid the region of "red devils" (J. *akaoni*).[174] In this propaganda, Japan represented itself as respecting religious freedom and encouraging religious minorities to flourish and develop in its empire.

Why This All Matters: Commercial Ties and Cultural Policies

During World War I, the Japanese Empire and a number of countries in the Middle East established trade relations as imperial policymakers searched for markets for Japan's cheaply produced manufactured goods and cotton textiles beyond East Asia.[175] This search for new markets helped lay the foundations for Japanese diplomatic engagement with a number of regions that had predominantly Muslim populations. According to one Nationalist source, by the late 1920s the Japanese government was selling arms to the Saud family in Arabia, and helping the Afghans upgrade their army.[176] These ventures did not go unnoticed by the British or the Chinese Nationalists, who often expressed concern about Japanese commercial ties and exports to predominantly Muslim regions.

Hand-in-hand with the expanding commercial networks, the Japanese

Empire also began to foster deeper diplomatic engagement with the Middle East, North Africa, and South Asia. Japanese bureaucrats understood that in order to create commercial relationships with places that were predominantly Muslim, they needed to understand Islamic customs, traditions, and social mores. It is clear that the Japanese Empire was anxious to create markets in predominantly Muslim places to undermine Western imperialism and to disrupt global capital flows. It is also clear that they did not think they could do this without the help of Sino-Muslims.

The Japanese imperial project in North China introduced new institutions and strict modes of governance. However, even in places where expression was as tightly controlled, as in Manchukuo, religion and expressions of religious belief were always up for negotiation.[177] This negotiation took place on a number of different levels: within the community, at the state level, and on a global scale.[178] Institutions, such as civic organizations and schools, promoted Japanese imperial religious and ethnic policy at the community level, and helped to define the meaning of what it meant to be a Muslim living in the Japanese Empire. The institutions that were established or funded by the Japanese Empire also endorsed connections among Muslims. They provided Sino-Muslims with a new vocabulary and space to understand their immediate surroundings as well as their place in relation to Muslims around the world. Using the experiences with minorities on the home islands and with the help of Japanese scholars of Islam, the Japanese Empire transposed new mappings of religious expression onto the Muslim communities that already existed. At the same time, Sino-Muslim men and women used the tools of empire at their disposal to get things they wanted from the Japanese Empire. How all this worked in practice is the focus of the next two chapters.

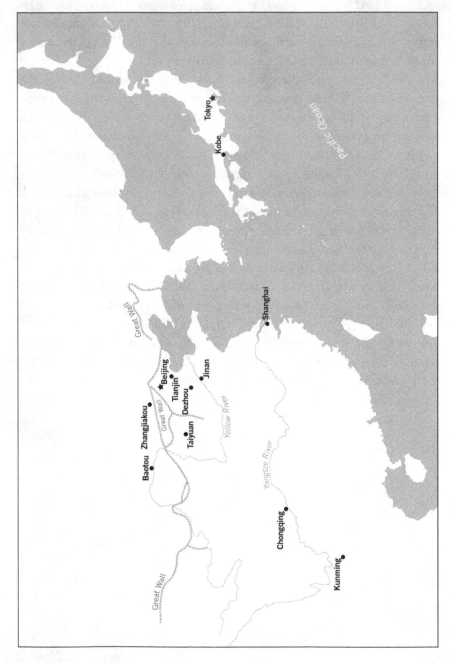

Pacific Ocean

Tokyo

Kobe

Great Wall

Shanghai

Beijing

Jinan

Tianjin

Dezhou

Zhangjiakou

Great Wall

Taiyuan

Baotou

Yellow River

Yangtze River

Chongqing

Great Wall

Kunming

2

SITTING ON A
BAMBOO FENCE

Sino-Muslims between the Chinese
Nationalists and the Japanese Empire

In 1940, Wang Shiming contemplated the fate of Sino-Muslims in the Nationalist-backed journal *Chinese Muslims' National Salvation Monthly*: "What will happen to the more than 200 mosques that have come under Japanese control?"[1] The question highlights the awareness and the deep insecurities of Sino-Muslims living in Free China about the fate of Muslims living under Japanese occupation. The context of these insecurities reveals some of the motives and methods behind imperial Japan's attempts to win the loyalties of Muslim populations throughout China. Japanese policies offered benefits and a general approach to modern life that were genuinely attractive to some Sino-Muslims. The Nationalist government was also acutely aware of Japanese policies and tactics in the occupied areas and responded to Japan's successes in Sino-Muslim communities. Sino-Muslim elites like Bai Chongxi regularly mentioned the efforts of the Japanese Empire in their nationalist appeals to Muslims throughout China. By 1939, Bai warned that "in places like Beijing, Tianjin, Shanghai, and Nanjing, where there are large Muslim communities, not only has the Muslims' National Salvation work not yet taken definite form but a few of our fellow Muslims there have been willing to be used by the enemy."[2] In this rousing speech he made it clear that politics and religion were inseparable, and that the fate of the nation relied on a coordinated effort on the part of Sino-Muslims to resist the Japanese.

Throughout the war, Nationalist-supported Muslims traveled secretly to the occupied regions to report on Japanese activities in Muslim communities. Based on their observations, they offered policy suggestions and directives to the Nationalist government in Chongqing, whose concern about Japanese recruitment tactics among Sino-Muslim communities continued to mount during the war.[3] In this context, schools became central to debates surrounding the future of Sino-Muslims living in both Free and occupied China. The Japanese Empire had long-term plans to teach the Japanese language to Muslim communities in North China that were central to its visions for a Greater Asia. These plans were meant to connect Muslims to Tokyo and to help create expansive networks of Japanese-speaking Muslims.[4] The Chinese Nationalists also had plans to standardize Chinese-language learning for all citizens of the Chinese state. These objectives regularly conflicted with the educational aspirations of Sino-Muslim communities.

For their part, Sino-Muslims wrote prolifically about the pros and cons of working with either the Japanese government or the Chinese Nationalists. For some, the Japanese Empire seemed like the best option, given that the others were the Nationalists, the Chinese Communists, or the Soviets. Others thought that the Japanese government could enable connections with their coreligionists throughout the colonized world. Others still worked with the Japanese Empire out of self-interest and fully understood their utility to the Japanese imperial project. At the same time, Japanese scholars of Islam waxed poetic about green and fragrant spring evenings in Tokyo, meant to symbolize the blossoming relationship between Islam and Japan.[5] Yet Japanese policymakers did not limit their efforts to the realm of the rhetorical and instead committed themselves to tangible projects to demonstrate their support for Islam.[6]

Despite the geographical and cultural distance between East Asia, Southeast Asia, South Asia, the Middle East, and North Africa, the Japanese Empire projected connections between themselves and Muslims living in all of these places. However, in these expansive visions of empire, Japanese bureaucrats needed Sino-Muslims for these tenuous connections to work. Apart from the Tatar émigrés, there was also a handful of Indian Muslim merchants and exiles living in Kobe and Nagoya. The South Asian Muslim community in Nagoya built the first mosque in Japan in 1931 with financial support from South Asian and Arab benefactors. In 1935, the South Asian Muslim community contributed the majority of the funds to build a second mosque in Kobe.[7] However, the third mosque built in Japan—the Tokyo Mosque—was funded almost entirely by the Japanese government

Welcoming ceremony at the Tokyo Mosque for Muslims
visiting from North China and Mongolia, April 1939.
(Greater Japan Muslim League database, Waseda
University Library Special Collections)

and opened in 1938. This shift from externally raised personal donations for the construction of mosque projects to the Japanese government's funding of the Tokyo Mosque as a larger project of empire reflects Japan's deepening interest in presenting itself as a protector of Islam. At the opening of the Tokyo Mosque in 1938, to prove their benevolence toward Islam, Japanese imperialists claimed that their government had built over a hundred mosques in China.[8] In Japan's appeals to Muslims, these efforts were meant both to demonstrate the goodwill of imperial Japan and to undermine the Chinese Nationalists and their allies. In the Japanese imperial imagination, the key to all this posturing was Sino-Muslims.

Postwar scholars and politicians in both Japan and China have characterized Japanese efforts to mobilize Muslims during this period as evil, disingenuous, and ultimately a failure, and therefore not worthy of inquiry.[9] Yet Japanese policies influenced how the Nationalists addressed important issues facing Muslim communities all over China. In this regard, discussing the construction of non-Han identities must consider the Japanese presence in North China. Integrating Muslims into the national imagination was an extremely complicated process where all actors played off of one another for their own benefit. The Japanese Empire's support for Muslims in the occupied areas physically divided Muslim communities, which in turn forced people to make the difficult decision to either stay in their homes and live under Japanese rule or become wartime refugees.[10] Sino-Muslims made pragmatic decisions depending on their family situations that were often in no way informed by any sort of attachment to the Nationalists or the idea of the Chinese nation.[11]

The Japanese Empire also had ambitious plans to use Sino-Muslims in its overtures to anticolonial Muslims around the world. Recovering the ongoing debates about Muslims and Islam between the Chinese Nationalists and the Japanese Empire as they jockeyed for domestic and international legitimacy during the war acknowledges the vigor of these exchanges and their impact on state-building in twentieth-century China. Furthermore, continuing to look at the Japanese occupation as a complete break with the way that Sino-Muslims conceived of their relationships to both the state and society in twentieth-century China diminishes the important anti-imperialist and anti-Soviet intellectual trends fostered by the Japanese Empire, and ignores some of the real changes that they introduced to the physical and cultural landscape of occupied China.[12]

Nationalist Responses to the Japanese Successes
with Muslims Living under Occupation

Chinese state-building during this period was a messy, complicated, dynamic process involving many different actors with just as many different visions for the future of the nation. In 1938, the Nationalist government was in crisis as it retreated in advance of the Japanese army from Nanjing to Wuhan, and then to Chongqing. The precarious situation on the ground partially explains why it was not the Nationalists' top priority to figure out what to do with the dispersed Muslim families from North China who were fleeing the advancing Japanese, and many issues were more immediate than meeting the demands of the elite Sino-Muslims who wanted a say about their place in the postwar national imagination.[13] However, as the wartime situation stabilized, the Nationalists realized that they needed to respond with their own policy initiatives directed specifically at non-Han communities to counter Japanese policies. Throughout the war, the Nationalist government sent students to Egypt to study, and it also sent a number of goodwill missions to Iraq, Iran, Egypt, and Afghanistan, partly in response to what the Nationalists imagined as Japan's successful campaigns to court Muslims.[14] The government even sent to Mecca a hastily organized delegation of students studying at Al-Azhar in Egypt to intercept a group of Sino-Muslims on a Japanese-sponsored hajj.

In addition to their growing concern with the Japanese influence on Muslims from China, the Nationalists also expressed anxiety about the role that Muslims from China played in enabling connections between the Japanese Empire and Muslims around the world. These anxieties manifested in increased diplomatic engagement with Muslim allies and in fostering connections between like-minded Sino-Muslims living in Free China and overseas Sino-Muslims (C. huihuaqiao).[15] The Chinese Nationalists' foreign policy engagement with Muslim communities in places like Southeast Asia, India, and the Middle East was in many ways a direct response to the perception that the Japanese Empire was making successful overtures to Muslims around the world. Distracted at the beginning of the war and unable to see the Japanese successes for what they were, Nationalist policymakers initially fumbled their own wartime policies for integrating Muslims into the nation-state. But, as the war went on, U.S. operatives in China remarked that the Nationalists became highly attuned to Japanese efforts to win over Sino-Muslims. One U.S. operative remarked that, "in recent years, the Chungking [sic] Government has become increasingly aware of the strategic importance of Muslim minorities within its borders, and of Japanese efforts to utilize this minority. This awareness has resulted in increased efforts to win the friendship of Muslims, not only in China but in the wider Islamic world."[16]

Sino-Muslims who were living in Chongqing or Kunming during the war and who supported the Nationalists wrote frequently about Japan's efforts to win over Muslims. At first, the Nationalists argued that the Japanese understood little about the long, sometimes fraught relationship between Muslims and the Chinese state. Nationalist observers considered Japan's relationship with Muslims too new and superficial to lead to any tangible outcomes. In their writings, they invoked clichés that portrayed Japanese imperialists as only interested in Muslims because Islam supposedly glorified war and Muslims were a war-mongering people, much like the Japanese.[17] In truth, Japan's strategy and motivations for reaching out to Sino-Muslims on the mainland were much more complicated than recruiting some sort of Muslim mercenary army. By the early 1940s, the tune had changed, and U.S. observers noted that the Nationalist government appeared to be using all possible channels to "counter Japanese activities and to present her side of the Sino-Japanese War to the Islamic world, hoping to win voluntary Muslim support."[18] The Nationalists had "direct answers" to Japanese-sponsored organizations through the promotion of their own visions for a Sino-Muslim future in China.[19] Yet, at the same time, these observers readily acknowledged that Han Chinese bureaucrats in charge of developing policies in the borderlands demonstrated deep antagonism toward non-Han communities. The knee-jerk responses by the Nationalist bureaucrats to the Japanese Empire indicated two things to U.S. observers in Chongqing: first, that the Japanese Empire was initially quite successful in currying favor with Muslims living under occupation and, second, that the Nationalist government's policy concerning minorities was reactionary and haphazard.[20]

For instance, the Nationalist government founded the Chinese Muslim National Salvation Federation as a "direct response" to the Japanese-sponsored All China Muslim League.[21] In 1938, Chiang Kai-shek invited prominent Muslim leaders to a conference in Hankou to establish the Chinese Muslim National Salvation Federation. The influential Muslim warlords-cum-governors of Ningxia and Qinghai—Ma Hongkui, Ma Bufang, and Ma Buqing—were made honorary chairmen under the leadership of Bai Chongxi.[22] At the conference, General Bai gave an important speech that was later published and widely circulated. He spoke about the relationship between Sino-Muslims and the broader "Islamic world" (C. *Huijiao shijie*).[23] The Japanese presence on the mainland looms heavy over Bai's speech.

By overcoming their differences and working with the Han, he proclaimed, Sino-Muslims could move forward with policies that would save both their country and religion (C. *cejin jiuguo yu jiao gongzuo*) from the Japanese Empire once and for all.[24]

Following this initiative, the Nationalists sponsored the first National Muslim Congress in 1939, where they changed the name of the organization from the Chinese Muslim National Salvation Federation to the Chinese Muslim Association. The stated objectives of the newly formulated association were to create propaganda and policy directed specifically at resisting the Japanese Empire through mechanisms such as traveling troupes who put on plays in Muslim communities. At the congress, the Nationalist government also earmarked funds to rebuild the largest mosque in Chongqing, which had been destroyed by a Japanese air raid. The project enabled the Nationalists both to highlight how Japanese atrocities on the mainland impacted Muslim communities and to emphasize that the Nationalist government was willing to divert funds from the war effort to support Islam.

Their actions were also direct reprisals against Japanese wartime policies regarding Muslims and responses by the Nationalist leadership to the destruction and suffering inflicted on Muslim populations by Japanese aggression. Like the Japanese Empire, the Nationalists tied their aid to propaganda that presented them as bettering the lives of Muslims through wartime reconstruction efforts. These were responses to a real and tangible threat. At the same time, the Japanese-sponsored All China Muslim League was actively distributing anti-Soviet and anti-Nationalist pamphlets. The text in the following figure warns that communists around the world were corrupt and the true enemy of Muslims in China. Printed in both Chinese and Arabic, it was likely distributed in mosques throughout the occupied areas.

Reconnaissance Missions to Occupied China to Observe and Report on Japanese Policies toward Muslims

In response, the Nationalist government sent operatives on missions to collect on-the-ground information about the situation in the occupied regions. In some ways, getting into the occupied areas was not difficult for Sino-Muslims.[25] However, there was a definite risk for Nationalist-sponsored operatives, like Yang Jingzhi, in traveling to areas under Japanese occupation. Originally from Beijing and a graduate of Beijing University, Yang fled south in 1937 to Kunming, then made his way to Chongqing. In 1940, he returned secretly to the occupied areas to collect information on Japanese policies

河北省保定道　　回教聯合大會

قاتلوا الاسلام عدوه المبين فيجب على المسلمين ان يتخذوه
عدوا مبينا وتحب عليهم ان يارجوا الهم بقوة التاليف
الحق يامسلمين اعلموا القوم جلادان يفسدون
فى الارض ويسلمون خراجنا ويهدمون دينا
الاسلام وتحرقون مساجدنا ويقتلون علمائنا
وهم عدونا الحق فيجب علينا ان خاربلهم بقوة
التاليف الحق ولا نصالح لهم البتة نهم الاعاى
ونهم الدين ونهم المسلم

共主義實現，我們回教前途才有光榮。

實團結力，和他們抗爭，一定不能和他們合作！如這反

些教長與教民，他們燒燬我們的清真寺，他們殺了我們一些教民，這是回教民眾所當懲的！他們擄掠我們的財產，他們破壞我們的宗教，他們焚燬我們的清真寺，他們殺了我們一些教長與教民，所以他們是我們的真仇敵，我們憑著真

咳！一切不人道的事，他們撐掠我們的財產，他們破壞我們的宗教，他們焚燬我們的真仇敵，他們憑著真

民眾應誠把他當成永久的仇敵，憑著固有的團結力，和我們回教民眾所當懲的！唯是共產黨，他們在世界

反對伊斯蘭宗教者，是伊斯蘭教明顯的仇敵，我們回教民眾應誠把他當成永久的仇敵，憑著固有的團結力，和

Anticommunist propaganda in Arabic and Chinese produced by
the Japanese-sponsored Hebei Muslim Association, 1939.
(Greater Japan Muslim League database, Waseda
University Library Special Collections)

and speak with Muslims. After returning to Chongqing, he compiled a report, *Japan's Muslim Policy* (C. *Riben zhi Huijiao zhengce*).

Japan's Muslim Policy offers a complicated picture of communities deeply divided by Japanese aggression and genuinely conflicted about where their loyalties lay. The report outlines and analyzes specific successes regarding Muslims in occupied areas while offering suggestions and policy directives based on its conclusions. It also summarizes conversations recollected by Yang with a number of Turkic Muslims (who presumably spoke Chinese or talked to him through a translator) and Sino-Muslims living under Japanese occupation.[26] Upon returning from his reconnaissance mission, Yang deemed Japanese propaganda efforts in the occupied regions to be highly successful. He suggested that the Nationalists needed to devote more attention to getting Muslims to understand their integral role in the Chinese nation (C. *Zhonghua minzu*). He also recommended sending Muslim agents from Free China into the occupied regions to infiltrate mosques for counterintelligence purposes.[27]

Yang's research yielded some interesting, and perhaps surprising, results. He conducted interviews with friends and acquaintances he knew from before the war who had not fled when the Japanese occupied Beijing. He also interviewed Muslims he met while traveling under cover. In these conversations, he asked most people how they justified staying in occupied China. His interview subjects cited economic incentives and family as the two most important factors. In a number of cases, the Japanese government ensured that people's families were well cared for with assistance such as tuition waivers or covering hospital fees for older relatives.[28] This deep connection to locality and family comes up over and over when we examine the experiences of Sino-Muslims during the war, undermining the perceived connection that many in Chongqing assumed that Sino-Muslims felt toward the state. Working with the Japanese was in many instances not ideologically motivated but simply a means of survival.

Yang concluded that among the Muslim populations in Beijing and Tianjin, those most likely to work with the Japanese were shopkeepers and entrepreneurs, since they had the most to gain. He explained that by 1931, the Japanese military apparatus was integrating itself into existing commercial networks in North China, and after 1937 the government either subsidized or bought most of what was produced in Muslim-dominated industries in North China. For instance, the Muslim-dominated butchering industry for nonpork products sold the majority of its meat to the Japanese Imperial Army and Navy at fixed and inflated prices. Likewise, the wool industry — where Muslims occupied the economic niche as middlemen between Mongolian herders and Han Chinese weavers — also profited because the Japanese Imperial Army requisitioned most of the wool at favorable prices. The army purchased upward of 90 percent of the wool coming through large trading entrepôts in border towns like Zhangjiakou.[29]

Another important sector of the economy dominated by Muslims who profited immensely from the Japanese occupation were vendors who hawked barbequed lamb kebabs (C. *kao yangrouchuan*).[30] Yang claimed that *yangrou chuar* vendors sold their skewers at inflated prices to Japanese soldiers in the capital. Yang also claimed that a number of the vendors were willing to "sell out Islam" (C. *maijiao*) by selling the soldiers beer.[31] Yang believed that these public displays of economic collaboration on the streets of Beijing led Han Chinese to suspect that all Muslims willingly worked with the Japanese to make extra money.[32] For Yang, it was evident that economic collaboration was taking place in almost every sector that employed Muslims in large numbers in cities throughout occupied China. This trend concerned him, since it could foster Han Chinese animosity toward Sino-Muslims.[33] Exacerbating existing tensions between long-standing communities is a common tactic used by imperial powers to generate support from disenfranchised minorities. In this case, Yang believed it was working for the Japanese Empire.

Sino-Muslims told Yang that the well-being of their family was the most important factor in their decision to stay. In his travels, Yang met a young Muslim in Jinan who explained that the Japanese had killed both of his brothers. His elderly parents were now his sole responsibility. When Yang probed him further, the man became defensive: not wanting to suffer the same fate as his brothers, he claimed that he was left with no choice but to cooperate with the Japanese in order to care for his aging parents. This was a common theme in collaborators' defenses of their actions after the war, and a valid one in many cases.[34] Back in Beijing, Yang ran into a Sino-Muslim classmate from his days at Beijing University who agreed to talk with him on the condition of anonymity. Before the occupation, the man had been the principal at a school in Dezhou, Shandong. He admitted to Yang that he had few regrets about choosing to stay in North China. Yang asked his friend whether he felt a moral or religious responsibility to resist the Japanese Empire. His classmate explained that Japanese officials had enlisted his services as an educator, moved him and his ailing mother to Beijing, provided her with excellent medical care that she desperately needed, and paid him on time — something his Chinese employers had never done. When pressed further about his decision to stay and work with the Japanese, Yang's classmate replied, "Mei banfa" — there simply was no other way.[35]

Yang was not the only Nationalist-supported Muslim who secretly visited occupied China. Zhu Jianmin also reported on his experiences sneaking into North China. Like Yang, Zhu observed that the Japanese were working to appeal to Muslims in China by presenting themselves as supporters of Islam, including through projects like the Tokyo Mosque.[36] Zhu also found to be astute the Japanese Empire's observations regarding unrest in Western-occupied Muslim regions of the world, and he argued that it supported "Islamism" (C. yisilan zhuyi) in these places.[37] Like Yang, Zhu had a number of suggestions for Nationalist policymakers to counter Japanese overtures to Muslims. First and foremost, he urged the Nationalists to promote reconciliation between Sino-Muslim and Han communities. He also recommended that the Nationalists improve Muslim schools and bolster propaganda efforts directed at Sino-Muslims living in Free China. Finally, he said, the Nationalists needed to work harder to vilify the Japanese imperial ambitions in the eyes of Muslims in Free China, occupied China, and beyond.[38]

In 1938, another Sino-Muslim, Xue Wenbo, secretly returned home after leaving the occupied regions the year before. Xue discovered that resisting Soviet Communism was especially important for Muslims who lived in Xinjiang and North China, and he noted that the Japanese government supported Muslim communities in these efforts. In occupied China, Xue was introduced to a hajji who spoke with him on the condition of anonymity because of his fear of Japanese retribution. This tension between genuine fear of the occupier and appreciation for Japanese support in resisting the Soviets complicated the relationship of many Sino-Muslims with the Japanese occupying forces. When Xue asked the hajji about his choice to remain in occupied China, the man replied that working with the Japanese was like performing a juggling act: there were many things to consider at the same time, and if he dropped one of the "balls," the act would be over.[39]

When pressed further, the hajji became irate and warned Xue that the only aggressors Muslims needed to concern themselves with were the Soviets and the British. For this man, the localized concerns of his community—which he understood as fighting off Soviet Communism and Western imperialism—outweighed concerns about the Japanese Empire. In this regard, it seems that Japanese propaganda geared to resisting the Soviets and the British was effectively filtering down to the level of the community. When Xue probed him further about his feelings regarding the Three People's Principles (C. *sanmin zhuyi*), he was shocked by the hajji's answer: "What does *sanmin zhuyi* do for Islam?"[40] The old man might have known that his stance would appear unorthodox to his interviewer, but it differed little from that of many northwestern Sino-Muslims who lived under both the Qing and the Republic: secular ideology was not a relevant concern; what mattered was the state's behavior toward local Muslim populations rather than its appeals to them.[41]

The observations of Yang, Zhu, and Xue underscore the fractured nature of both nation- and state-building in China throughout the 1930s and 1940s. Beyond the important connection to the native place, local institutions continued to be an important way that people ordered and understood their daily lives during the war.[42] Through its efforts to support Islam on the mainland, the Japanese government elicited direct responses from the Nationalists, who observed the Japanese Empire's management of Sino-Muslims. In this process, schools for Muslim youths became ground zero in the battle between the Japanese government, the Chinese Nationalists, and Muslim communities.

Ground Zero: Muslim Schools and Language Reform

Both the Japanese Empire and the Chinese Nationalists used educational reforms to attempt to influence Sino-Muslims for political purposes. Both parties also received pushback and resistance from local Muslim communities when trying to implement changes to curriculum. In this case, it is clear that Sino-Muslims were not simply passive agents of state-directed reforms, and "the transition from the Qing Empire to the Republic of China gave Muslim modernist reformers a chance to promote an alternate vision of the Chinese nation-state" where they played a larger and more definitive role in policymaking.[43] Sino-Muslim reformers had been actively trying to improve Muslim schools, and had already built "new-style schools" and teacher-training facilities for new-style teachers, such as Chengda Teachers Academy. But these efforts faced resistance from the old guard and often lacked funding.[44] By tapping into insecurities Muslim reformers expressed about outdated learning methods and the challenges graduates faced in the modern world after completing a traditional madrasah education, the Japanese government and the Nationalists offered Muslims the opportunity to remake schools, albeit with input from their respective educational advisers.

Overall, the Nationalist approach to Muslim education in the 1930s and the 1940s appears to be less consistent and cohesive than the Japanese approach. In order to appeal broadly to Sino-Muslims, the Nationalists knew they needed to reform education, but Islamic education was not a top priority for them in the 1930s. There were also competing voices and intellectual trends regarding the place of Sino-Muslims in the Chinese nation-state, which often resulted in incoherent messaging about the place of Muslims in the new national education system. The Japanese Empire projected a more cohesive vision for Islamic education in North China, and this vision was later extended to Muslims throughout the Greater East Asia Co-Prosperity Sphere.

Most of the debates over curriculum for Muslim children during this time centered on one issue: language. Both the Japanese and the Nationalists met the most resistance from Muslim communities in China when they attempted to substitute Chinese- or Japanese-language classes for Arabic-language classes. Muslims focused on Arabic not only because it is the language of the Quran, but also because it allowed them to participate in transnational political and religious communities. This point was not lost on the Japanese or the Nationalists, and, apart from some hardcore Chinese Nationalist assimilationists, there was never much discussion by either party about eradicating Arabic from the curriculum altogether. Both powers understood the value of having a group of Muslims with the cultural capital to converse socially and linguistically with Muslims beyond the mainland. However, the debates about reducing the number of hours spent on Arabic in favor of vernacular Chinese- or Japanese-language and culture classes were often heated.

Educational reforms in Muslim schools in China were an important part of the dialogue in the 1930s and 1940s among Sino-Muslims, the Nationalists, and the Japanese, who were all trying to determine the place that Sino-Muslims should occupy both in China and throughout what Chinese and Japanese observers often termed the "Muslim world" or the "Islamic world." All parties were aware of the role that education played in molding modern citizens and subjects, and they dedicated substantial energy to discussing Islamic educational reforms. Yet, although both governments actively tried to control Muslim populations, the success of educational reforms ultimately lay in the hands of Muslims themselves, who were willing to make concessions, but only to a point. In this regard, schools became "a site where different classes or interest groups regularly engaged in ideological struggles over meaning, values, and principles," and a place where "dominant ideologies" were "thus a product of compromise."[45] This process is exemplified by Nationalist and Japanese imperial efforts to manage educational reforms at Islamic schools while simultaneously responding to pushback from local Sino-Muslim communities.[46] The Japanese Empire's struggle to project its outreach to Muslims around the world while balancing the contradiction of claimed "peaceful coexistence and co-prosperity" with Japan's military occupation of North China provided an avenue for Sino-Muslim communities to negotiate the terms of educational reforms to suit their needs.[47] Here, tracing the tensions, mediations, and frustrations of all the actors involved in language and educational reforms highlights how Japanese imperial ambitions contributed to the process of "making" Muslims in China during the war.[48]

Japanese policymakers debated long and hard in the 1930s about the benefits of teaching Japanese and reducing the number of Arabic classes for Sino-Muslims living under occupation. Learning Japanese was not completely new to young Sino-Muslims. Since the 1910s, Sino-Muslim students had been encouraged to study in Japan.[49] In Tokyo, they published a periodical, *Awake Mohammedans*, which had a small circulation on the mainland. By the 1930s, Japanese authorities sought out Sino-Muslims who with "friendly

Moro (Filipino Muslim minority) foreign students in Tokyo, 1940s.
(Greater Japan Muslim League database, Waseda
University Library Special Collections)

encouragement" might be persuaded to cooperate with imperial Japan. In order to incentivize cooperation, Sino-Muslims were offered scholarships and opportunities to study abroad in the imperial capital. These incentives would have been very difficult for ambitious Sino-Muslim youths to pass up, and one Sino-Muslim reported that within the realm of education, "the Japanese tempt us by giving us much face. They offer to put us over non-Muslims."[50] The Japanese Empire aspired to cultivate a group of Muslims from around Asia who could communicate with each other in Japanese but would also be conversant in Arabic. By 1943, the Japanese Empire were partially able to achieve this goal as Moro, Javanese, Burmese Muslims, Afghans, and Sino-Muslims who were conversant in Japanese studied together in Tokyo.[51] This was no small feat and required years of planning.

By 1938, in and around Nanjing, Catholic schools were quick to fill the

Sino-Muslims between the Chinese Nationalists and the Japanese Empire

vacuum left by Nationalist-supported schools that moved west ahead of the Japanese advance. In smaller urban areas along the coast, Catholic schools were often the only "educational outfits in occupied territories above the lower primary."[52] In a report to the Japanese Education Ministry about the state of Muslim education in China, a Japanese bureaucrat noted a similar pattern at Muslim schools in occupied Beijing. The official was surprised to find that many of the students attending Islamic schools were not Muslim. According to the report, among the nineteen Islamic schools listed in Beijing, fourteen had admitted Han Chinese students. The majority only had a handful of non-Muslim students, but at a couple of schools, such as the Andingmen Mosque School (C. *Andingmen qingzhensi xuexiao*) and the Xizhimen Mosque School (C. *Xizhimen qingzhensi xuexiao*), non-Muslim students outnumbered Muslim students almost four to one.[53] A Japanese report from 1938 also noted that of the 320 students registered at the Oxen Street Elementary School (J. *Gyū gai shōgaku*), apparently only 250 were Muslim.[54] Before the war, it would have been highly unlikely for a Han Chinese student to attend a Muslim school in a cosmopolitan city like Beijing. However, the realities of war blurred ethnic and religious lines, and as people adjusted to life under occupation, they were forced to make choices about their daily routines. For some Han Chinese families who did not leave Beijing, ensuring that their children continued their education seems to have outweighed any misgivings they might have had about sending their children to an Islamic school.

Minorities and Learning Japanese in School: A New Vocabulary of Anti-imperialism

Schools became laboratories for Japanese policies directed specifically toward Islam that were then exported and adapted throughout the growing empire. Japanese policymakers realized that in many places, Muslim schools provided families and communities with tangible connections to state power beyond the madrasah or the local mosque. Muslims collaborated with Japanese educational reforms for a variety of reasons, such as economic incentives and opportunities for social advancement through education.[55] Partly through schools, the Japanese Empire provided Muslim youth with the vocabulary to understand their changing position vis-à-vis their broader interests for Asia, along with information about the situation of Muslims beyond their immediate surroundings, albeit from a Japanese perspective. In schools, the Japanese promoted their imperial agenda in a seemingly innocuous way to a receptive population. In return, young Muslim men and women were given opportunities to learn Japanese, travel to Japan, or study in Tokyo. Some students received from the Japanese Educational Ministry a small stipend that varied depending on their gender, level of proficiency, and area of study.[56] Like public works projects in Manchukuo, educational reforms instituted by the Japanese government were "coordinated attempts to project their presence as a positive force in the areas they had conquered; while they were not entirely convincing, there were elements of their projects that did resonate even with those who resented their presence."[57] Life under occupation was harsh, but Japanese support for Sino-Muslim educational opportunities and reforms were successful enough to elicit a coordinated response from the Chinese Nationalists.

~~~~~~

The Japanese influence on the development of the Chinese education system cannot be underestimated.[58] After their defeat by the Japanese Empire in the first Sino-Japanese War (1894–95), Qing reformers looked to Meiji Japan for educational alternatives to the centuries-old Confucian-style education system. Qing observers were impressed with three aspects of the Meiji education system: it was universalist, it promoted social and intellectual conformity, and it imbued the populace with loyalty to the emperor.[59] At a time when the Qing was facing serious threats to its prestige and power, all three of these features were in line with the government's attempts to maintain sovereignty through fin-de-siècle reforms. The Qing government not only adapted the Japanese educational model to suit its needs but also accepted hundreds of Japanese teachers and educational advisers to help implement reforms. This was not an altruistic gesture but rather "grew out of an increasingly popular belief among Japanese from the 1880s on, that Japan had a special role to play in China's political and economic life," and out of the Japanese government's increasing desire to gain access to the mainland.[60]

The full-scale invasion of Manchuria marked a shift in policy toward education, but given the presence of imperial Japan in the realm of education from the first decades of the twentieth century, Japanese participation in educational reforms was not as abrupt as other works suggest.[61] With regards to Islamic education, Japanese observers in China acknowledged that if they wanted educational reform in newly occupied territories, they needed to address both the economic and political concerns of Sino-Muslims.[62] This inspired the Japanese government and members of the Greater Japan Muslim League to put forth an educational reform program intended to make a lasting impact on Sino-Muslim students who came under their educational purview.[63] Japanese bureaucrats on the mainland began to curry favor with Muslim youths by offering scholarships to study in Tokyo and student loans to pay for university tuition.[64]

Until now, nothing has been written about the concrete ways in which Nationalist educational policies directed at non-Han communities reacted to policies implemented by the Japanese in North China during the war. Calling attention to the Japanese educational policies aimed at non-Han communities helps dispel the notion that China was a unified geopolitical entity at any time throughout the Republican era. It also underscores the ongoing influence of the Japanese Empire on the education of millions of youths — both non-Han and Han Chinese — living under its control. The Nationalists used schools in Free China as places to recruit and mobilize Sino-Muslims; at the same time, Japan was using schools to advance its own imperial ends. Despite these efforts, much of the recent scholarship on nationalism, social networks, and community organizations in Republican China continues to treat the occupation of North China as a break from developments in educational policy on the mainland.[65]

Previous scholarship on education in twentieth-century China also tends to overgeneralize both the spatial and temporal contiguities of the nation-state.[66] These works are useful for thinking about the mediation between government policy and the realities that people faced in understanding their daily lives in the wealthy Jiangnan region. However, these studies fail to take into account the Japanese contributions to this ongoing intellectual discourse in the occupied areas during the war regarding non-Han communities.[67] The debates in which the Japanese government, the Chinese Nationalists, and Sino-Muslims engaged about the place of minorities in schools and the visions for a national curriculum played out in many different ways throughout the war and had little to do with elite Han student activism centered around Jiangnan. In this regard, displacing Han-centric narratives about education reform throughout the 1930s and 1940s brings to light the multitude of voices and visions for the future of the people who now live in the PRC.

Inserting Sino-Muslims into the Discussion about Educational Reforms in Twentieth-Century China

Madrasahs are found wherever there are Muslims, and although the curriculum varies, the teaching style and the objectives are similar. Until the twentieth century, if Muslims in China received any formal education it was likely a madrasah education.[68] In China, madrasahs created a sense of community among Muslims through the teaching of Arabic (or Persian) and Islamic theology. This was similar to the imperial educational model, where students memorized the Confucian canon and Classical Chinese texts from an early age. However, the madrasah was different because it gave Sino-Muslims a connection to the *umma*, or the larger community of believers, beyond imperial China.

By the beginning of the Republican period, educated Muslims were increasingly aware of and concerned about many Sino-Muslims' lack of conversational Arabic skills, which became glaringly obvious as they began to travel more frequently to the Middle East. This "crisis" in Islamic education could even be said to originate in the late Ming and early Qing, as Muslims struggled to find a place for themselves in both the Chinese and Islamic spheres. Madrasahs gave students deep training in theology, but in the eyes of many Islamic reformers they failed to produce Muslims with the skills needed to function in the rapidly changing world at the turn of the twentieth century. Just as the new Republican government was attempting to do, Sino-Muslims began to reenvision the role that education should play in the lives of their children, and in many cases they imagined more direct state intervention in the educational process.[69]

As Sino-Muslims looked critically at the madrasah as an educational model, competing voices emerged about the role language should play in the new curriculum. Numerous Sino-Muslim reformers insisted that learning literary and written Chinese was essential to Muslims' future in China. Some reformers went as far as calling for the compulsory education of Muslim girls.[70] Alternatively, scholars like Ma Wanfu, one of the founders of the Ikhwan (C. *yihewani*) movement in China, advocated maintaining strict theological learning at the madrasah in Arabic. Less conservative Muslim reformers argued that the madrasah model was untenable given the pressures of the modern world and needed to be abandoned completely. Although there was disagreement about how to reform Islamic education in China, there was consensus that changes needed to be made to the current system.

Competing ideologies and pedagogical methodologies went head to head as different interest groups sought to maintain or increase their visibility and ensure that their educational needs were met without compromising their faith in Islam in the process. Part of the problem was trying to figure out how these new strands in Islamic modernist discourses from the Middle

East could be transmitted to young people without the youth losing a sense of a distinct identity in China. Muslim elites acknowledged their need to reconcile their religious beliefs with new ideas like constitutionalism, secularism, and nationalism, and their views were developed and refined through increased efforts to connect with Muslims outside of China who faced similar issues.[71] In essence, both the Japanese and the Nationalists included Muslims in their competing visions for how they could be incorporated into their respective modern educational realms long after Sino-Muslims had started to think critically about these questions within their own communities.

Before the May Fourth Movement in 1919, foreign languages — especially English and Japanese — accounted for more hours per week of secondary school curriculum than any other subjects. This came to an abrupt halt in 1922 as the government tightened control over the national curriculum to devote more hours to learning vernacular Chinese and to "ideological training rather than foreign-language acquisition."[72] This policy also reflected a desire to bring religious schools under state purview and to tighten control over both the curriculum and the students in Christian missionary schools. Although the directive was aimed at curbing the influence of missionary schools, madrasahs fell into the newly created category of "private religious" schools.[73] In practice, the Republican state never had the capacity to enforce these regulations beyond urban centers in the predominantly Han coastal regions. For at least twelve years there was no singular Chinese state, and even after 1928 Jiang's "central government" in Nanjing always had competitors — including the Japanese — who controlled large swaths of territory and thus directed policy in regions under their control.

Beginning in 1928, indoctrination in the Three People's Principles took precedence over everything else, and religious education of all types — Christian, Buddhist, or Islamic — was supposed to be relegated to the waste bins of traditionalism and parochialism. Once again, this policy shift from up top should not be understood as a reflection of the receptiveness or the permeation of these policies at the local level.[74] In reality, local concerns about education diverged from nationally promulgated policies as communities beyond the main urban centers of China adjusted their curriculum needs to meet the changing demands of their own communities with the meager resources they had available to them.[75] By the mid-1930s, Chiang Kai-shek's New Culture Movement envisioned that the spread of a single written language (C. *baihua*) and a single spoken language (C. *putonghua*) would facilitate the creation of an idealized Chinese citizenry by providing a simpler written language and a common vernacular.[76]

The Nationalists linked morality, culture, language, and education to imbue the Sino-Muslim educational experience with meaning and coded political messages. Literacy and education in Chinese were thus central to China's nationalist project of integration, whether developmental or assimilationist, and learning Chinese was presented as a "crucial step in the staged, developmentalist process of nationalization."[77] For the Nationalists, acquiring a level of literacy in Chinese inculcated both language and culture (C. *wenhua*) into Muslims who were supposed to "become" Chinese.[78] But Nationalist-supported Sino-Muslims writing from Kunming and Chongqing after the outbreak of the war broached the topics of educational policy, curriculum development, and citizenship formation differently from their Han Chinese counterparts. Their perspectives on the place that education should occupy in the lives of young Muslims highlights the wide variety of intellectual trends addressing various meanings of citizenship and nationalism circulating among Muslim intellectuals at the time.

One of the ways the Nationalists responded to the Japanese successes educating Muslim youths was simply to claim that everyone on the mainland resisted Japan (C. *quanmin kangzhan*), and that Muslims should follow the lead of their countrymen. Focusing on Japanese aggression, the issue of education was often expressed in terms of anti-Japanese propaganda that emphasized the extreme hardship (C. *chiku*) and suffering of all people during the war.[79] A 1938 article about Muslim schools featured in a pro-Nationalist Muslim journal begins by comparing the "War of Resistance" against the Japanese to the Thirty Years' War and the Hundred Years' War in Europe. The comparison highlights the impact of all three wars on the daily lives of normal people, implying that the "War of Resistance" was all-encompassing and would forever change the social and political landscape of China.[80] By comparing the situation in China to early modern European wars, the author created an ahistorical analogy where early modern Europe was somehow on the same plane as China in the 1930s, perhaps implying China's backwardness.

Beyond this, the author's main point was to draw attention to the precarious lives of Muslims close to the occupied areas. He claimed that part of the problem was a lack of funds and resources for schools, which were being diverted from education to the war effort. The commentary implored the Nationalist government to prioritize supporting Muslim schools along the border (C. *bianjiang jiaoyu*) so that students could be indoctrinated with anti-Japanese messages.[81] The argument makes it clear that in order to successfully resist the Japanese occupation, Sino-Muslims living close to the border needed to devote their energy to learning Chinese rather than Arabic, which would make them more modern, like their Han neighbors. In this instance, Sino-Muslims were presented as liminal actors, occupying a space between the Nationalist visions for the nation and the Japanese Empire's efforts to win them over. Learning vernacular Chinese was framed as a way to resist Japan and as a duty for Sino-Muslims. The author noted that the Han also needed to support the *huizu* because the Muslim community should not be expected to bear the full burden of this formidable task. In the end, it was imagined that this policy would allow Muslims to pass on the messages of resistance to their religious brothers living under occupation (C. *zhanzhu*).[82] The tying of the occupation's proximity to increasing educational efforts to "develop" national sentiment among Muslims in this region indicates a reactive nationalist sentiment that was contingent on Sino-Muslim youths being indoctrinated with anti-Japanese propaganda.

The Centrality of Language—Arabic, Chinese, or Japanese— and Visions of What It Meant to Be a Chinese Muslim

Language acquisition was central to the ways the Japanese Empire, the Nationalists, and Sino-Muslims framed their arguments for and against changes to Islamic educational models in both unoccupied and occupied China. The Japanese government emphasized the importance of learning Japanese so that Sino-Muslims could take part in its ambitious visions for the larger Islamic community living in and around the Japanese Empire. The Nationalists, in contrast, emphasized the values of learning vernacular Chinese so that Muslims could be more easily incorporated into the Chinese nation-state. Finally, Muslims insisted on maintaining a connection to Arabic and often vehemently resisted the substitution of Japanese or vernacular Chinese. The Japanese government and the Nationalists quickly figured out that Arabic was central to the Sino-Muslim identity, and that if they hoped to make any headway inserting themselves into curriculum planning in Muslim schools, the importance of Arabic learning could not be diminished. At the same time, receptiveness to Japanese-language reforms differed by community under occupation: where Sino-Muslims were a small minority within the general population, Japanese bureaucrats found it easier to win approval for curriculum change that promoted Japanese interests. In places with a relatively large and well-established Muslim community, like Beijing, the Japanese faced more direct opposition to their language policies.

Both the Nationalists and the Japanese government faced pushback from local Muslims when they attempted to institute educational reforms, and tensions between the state and local communities led to compromises regarding curriculum changes. Schools created, enforced, and maintained order, and they were supposed to be places where ideas were easily channeled to relatively "uncritical recipients"—that is, children.[83] But it is important to remember that in schools throughout the mainland, language became the vehicle for individuals to reconceive their relationship to the state. By providing students with a new vocabulary in a language they might not otherwise learn, the Japanese Empire and the Chinese Nationalists were able to mold the ways children spoke, the words they used, and how they conceptualized their connections to their religion, their communities, and the state or empire.[84] In the end, even students who did not become politically active or outward supporters of either the Japanese Empire or the Chinese Nationalists were exposed to propaganda in schools, with an intensity that made an impact.[85]

In some instances, the Nationalist reformers framed learning Arabic as an obstacle that prevented Muslims from keeping up with national education standards. In arguing that religion and religious instruction had no place in the classroom, nationalist writers sometimes turned to metaphor. One example compared education to a car: education had many components, which all needed to be maintained in order to operate like a well-oiled machine. However, religious education only had one component, so much like a car, which could not operate with only one working part, an education that focused purely on religious instruction could not drive people into the modern world.[86] The analogy highlights the Nationalists' preoccupation with religious education as a vestige of a bygone era, holding China back from the modern world.

For a number of Han Chinese working on the issue of language reform, resistance to the Japanese and the assimilation of non-Han communities went hand in hand. In an attempt to transcend difference and fulfill their vision of unity, some Nationalists even claimed that Muslim parents would be happy to send their children to national schools with Han children because they realized the value of a "national education."[87] By sticking together as a country and resisting the Japanese, assimilationists claimed, Sino-Muslims could defeat the Japanese Empire and integrate themselves into the dominant Han Chinese community. In this instance, only by assimilating would Muslims be strong enough to contribute to the resistance, and only by learning Chinese would they be able to assimilate properly. Sino-Muslims could thereby emerge from being seen by the rest of the Chinese as poor and ignorant (C. *pinyu*), and only then truly become a part of the nation.[88] These arguments for assimilation, cloaked in the language of development and the notion that all Muslims aspired to fluency in *putonghua*, permeated much of the Nationalist discourse about Sino-Muslim educational reforms.[89]

Less extreme educational models specifically designed with the concerns of Sino-Muslims in mind were devised by reform-minded students like Ding Zaiqin. While attending teachers' college in Kunming, Ding suggested that educational methods and techniques imported from Europe, America, and Japan had all failed to create new consciousness among Muslims in China. He suggested purging all mosque schools of old clerics and starting fresh with young, college-trained Muslim teachers.[90] Ding believed that the greatest problem plaguing Sino-Muslims was that the old guard only knew Arabic or Persian and therefore resisted change, since their positions depended on maintaining the status quo. Ding also suggested that a focus on science, technology, and military training could be achieved while maintaining the religious integrity of Muslim schools. He cited Turkey as a model, where modern reforms had been made to the education system under Mustafa Kemal Ataturk.[91] Ding was perhaps naive to not fully grasp the European roots of Ataturk's reforms and their fundamentally secular goals. Yet his point was clear: in order to reform Muslim schools, the old guard needed to go.

This idea of purging the old guard was a radical suggestion, if perhaps less so than advocating for complete assimilation. However, Ding had a less extreme solution to integrate Sino-Muslims into the Han Chinese vision for the nation-state. His proposal was never implemented, and it likely would have faced insurmountable resistance from cities with large, wealthy, and long-established Muslim communities, such as Kunming or Beijing. However, the public calls by some reform-minded Muslims to wipe the slate clean and rid schools of old clerics attest to the diversity of viewpoints about the best way to reform schools in China in the 1930s and 1940s.

Learning Chinese was presented as a way for Sino-Muslims to become better citizens.[92] For instance, adopting to Nationalist educational standards, Muslims would be able to produce a more accurate translation of the Quran, making Islam more widely accessible.[93] Arabic was presented as an antiquated language, holding Muslims in China back from achieving their full potential. This point was reinforced through a striking comparison with Chinese Buddhists. Buddhist scriptures had long been translated from Sanskrit and adapted and developed within a specifically Chinese milieu, incorporating the language and idioms appropriate to their surroundings. By learning to use and translate texts into Chinese like the Buddhists had done, Muslims would be able to bring a more appropriate translation of the Quran to a wider audience.[94] Chinese-language skills could allow a new generation of Sino-Muslims to grow up as "religious citizens" (C. *gongmin jiaotu*), once again tying religiosity and belief in Islam to the achievement of full citizenship.[95] These competing visions for education, as well as the repeated emphasis on the differences between Muslims living under occupation and those living in Free China, help to emphasize the fact that there was nothing resembling a cohesive Muslim nationalist resistance on the ground in China in the late 1930s and early 1940s.

The multiplicity of visions for Muslim education in China provided many alternatives for integrating Muslims into the Chinese nation-state. On the one hand, Sino-Muslims wanted to modernize their schools and had been attempting to do so on their own terms, giving their communities a chance to participate in the nation-building process on equal footing.[96] On the other hand, Islamic schools were a way of preserving their faith and distinguishing themselves from the Han. In their search for answers to these questions, Nationalist Muslims presented a variety of educational models for making new, nationalist, Muslims in China. By envisioning Muslims who had cultivated both a civic and a religious consciousness, Nationalist-supported writers proposed various scenarios whereby the Han and the *huizu* could learn to work together to improve the nation and defeat the Japanese.[97] The Nationalists seemed to recognize that different groups of Muslims had different priorities when it came to education, but they wanted the changes to take place within a framework where Chinese-language learning took precedence over Arabic.[98]

The Japanese Empire was able to capitalize on these ambiguities and inconsistencies by highlighting the incongruities between the Nationalists' rhetoric about inclusive unity and the reality of the situation on the ground.[99] Nationalist writers also readily acknowledged that the Japanese Empire was successful in its efforts to make schools both free and mandatory in Manchukuo, and was educating young Muslims living under occupation.[100] As the Nationalists and Nationalist-supported Sino-Muslims hashed out arguments about minority education policies, they pointed to the Japanese as either a point of difference or as a model of success. For their part, the Japanese invested heavily in Sino-Muslim educational reforms and wrote extensively about these efforts in field reports and well-documented articles.

Muslim Schools under Occupation:
Receptiveness and Resistance

The maintenance of Japanese imperial legitimacy among Sino-Muslims was partly contingent on an understanding by those living under occupation that the education system could serve the pedagogical needs of their children.[101] The tension between creating a sense of legitimacy by providing a quality education, on the one hand, and advancing the agenda of the Japanese Empire, on the other, shaped educational policies toward Muslims. In territories under Japanese control, the degree of receptiveness to Japanese-language curriculum reform varied among Muslim communities. This receptiveness depended on a number of factors outlined in an important policy document written by reputed Japanese scholar of Islam, Kobayashi Hajime. The report, *The Japanese Language and Muslim Children* (J. *Nihongo to kai-min jidō*), was first printed in 1940 as an internally circulating document and later republished for a general audience.[102] For Kobayashi, Japanese-language skills gave Muslim children a whole new set of possibilities for the future. He proposed that learning Japanese was a way for Muslims from China to distinguish themselves from their Han neighbors and get ahead in the world.[103] Kobayashi's report validated the Japanese Empire's efforts to teach Muslim children Japanese and stressed that the acquisition of Japanese would strengthen the place of Sino-Muslims in the international community.[104]

Although the Japanese had already tried many of these educational policies in Hokkaido with the Ainu and in Korea, their approach to Sino-Muslims in Manchukuo was a little different. For example, in Ainu schools, the Ainu language was banned. But Japanese bureaucrats recognized that Sino-Muslims' ability to speak both Arabic and Japanese was valuable for diplomatic maneuverings and trade dealings with Muslims in the Middle East and North Africa, and they never attempted to ban Arabic outright.[105] In some ways then, it was their difference as Arabic speakers and Muslims that made them valuable to the Japanese Empire rather than their potential to assimilate and become fully Japanese, as was the goal with the Ainu and Koreans. Supporting proficiency in both Arabic and Japanese among Muslim populations was fundamental to Japan's long-term imperial planning from the mid-1930s.

Before the outbreak of war in July 1937, a Japanese journal called *Islam* (J. *Isuramu*) published an article about the state of Islamic education in North China and assessed Muslim schools in the region. The article explained to Japanese readers that throughout the 1910s and 1920s, prominent members of the Beijing Muslim community established new schools after exposure to Islamic modernist movements in the Middle East. These schools were seen as examples of nonmadrasah institutions' success and as models for the more modern Islamic schools that could be established with Japanese funds. The article cited the opening of a Muslim Teaching College (J. *Kaikyō shihan gakugō*) in 1912 on Oxen Street (J. *Gyū gai*) in Beijing by the famous Chinese hajji Wang Haoran. The school was supposed to train teachers under the new guidelines provided by the Nationalists for certifying private school teachers.[106]

According to *Isuramu*, Wang had initially faced resistance for teaching nonreligious subjects like science, and Beijing clerics claimed that studying vernacular Chinese would dilute religious education, causing students to become more secular.[107] However, Wang eventually persuaded Muslim parents that an education beyond Quranic and hadith memorization would be beneficial for the community. The article claimed that Wang had also presented his new educational model as a way for Muslim children to participate in the modern-style education system without having to attend school with Han Chinese students.[108] In this case, Wang's successes were evidence that Japanese officials could convince Muslims in North China to adopt Japanese-language training if they offered subjects like science and technology in schools. Wang's model was also used as evidence that Japanese bureaucrats could convince Muslims that they were not trying to integrate Muslims into Han Chinese schools or assimilate them into the dominant Han culture, as many contemporary Nationalist intellectuals and education reformers were attempting to do. Here, the Japanese commentators had an alternative educational model specifically for Sino-Muslims based on reforms Beijing Muslims had tried to implement in their own communities, which were vastly different from the Nationalist-supported reforms.

The Japanese author also extended these arguments to the education of young Sino-Muslim women. Wang Haoran had opened a school specifically for Muslim girls in Beijing. Before then, there were no such schools in the city. With Wang's backing, the Muslim community donated money and opened the New Moon Women's Middle School (C. *Xinyue nüzhong xuexiao*) with the explicit purpose of training Muslim women to become certified teachers.[109] However, the school had trouble getting off the ground and closed after a few years. This failure was an opportunity for the Japanese Empire, and in 1932 plans were initiated to provide funding for teacher training for Muslim women in North China.[110]

The education of Sino-Muslim women was seen as a point of entry into the large Muslim community in Beijing. Educating Muslim women to speak, read, and write Japanese would allow them to participate more actively in the increasingly interconnected world.[111] Japanese imperialists argued that since many Muslim women did not have the opportunity to go to school at all, their parents would be more open to accepting instruction in Japanese. Projecting this vision for imperial language-learning into the future, the Japanese bureaucrats who devised these plans hoped to send these women out to disseminate Japanese and the imperial curriculum to a larger group of Muslim students throughout the empire. These types of aspirations were not novel among imperial powers, but their long-range goals and the all-encompassing scope of these policies indicate that the Japanese had far-reaching plans for integrating Muslim populations into their empire. In this instance, the Japanese were able to present their educational model as an un-fulfilled vision of Sino-Muslims, and as a way to successfully educate Muslim women, who would then be deployed in the service of the empire.[112]

The Japanese projected their visions for Muslim education in North China beyond what they imagined would be their ultimate victory in the war.[113] These long-range plans also had to do with their visions for the family in North China. Children became a central concern of imperial policy and gave the Japanese a way to socialize the entire family. To publicize the Japanese Empire's position on education and its relationship to the family, a number of weekly columns directed at Muslim families were featured in newspapers that circulated in the occupied areas. *Mengjiang Xinbao* ran an advice column on Islamic social mores that offered commentary on the daily struggles faced by Muslims.[114] The columns centered on the role parents should play educating their children in partnership with the state-sponsored education they received at school.[115] Another regular column in *Mengjiang Xinbao* covered Muslim "taboos" (C. *jinji*) and instructed readers in how to interact with their children at home. The columns emphasized that the family should reinforce what children were learning at school, and that parents must be positive and pious role models for their children. The writers argued that the home should be the headquarters of imparting Islamic norms and values, and that parents needed to lead by example by refraining from haram (forbidden) practices.[116] Mothers and fathers were urged be positive role models by not drinking alcohol, not arguing, and not smoking inside their homes.[117] The message was clear: only through good behavior in the home would Muslim children thrive in school, and only by attending a modern Japanese-sponsored school would children get ahead.

Here, the relationship between parents and the Japanese Empire was supposed to be symbiotic. Even if parents did not speak Japanese, work for the Japanese government, or otherwise support the Japanese imperial project, the fact that their children were learning how to speak Japanese formalized their relationship with the empire and brought them into the imperial fold, tacitly accepting Japanese rule.[118] For their part, Japanese bureaucrats had to ensure that parents were satisfied with the Islamic education their children were receiving to avoid resistance from the parents and the community.

Some of these tensions are exemplified in one striking example. Students from a new Muslim school in Datong wrote a short play in Japanese and performed it for their community. The performance was covered in *Mengjiang Xinbao*. The reviewer remarked on the high level of Japanese proficiency among the students, who had written a play about the "East Asia Liberation War" (C. *dadongya jiefang zhan*) that centered on the importance of resisting Western imperialism in Asia.[119] The editor did not report that the parents and community members in attendance would not have been able to understand the play unless they spoke Japanese. According to the writer, the play was a grand success, praised by everyone who attended. The success was attributed to the communities' support for Japanese-language learning among the young Muslim population. Although this is likely an embellishment by the reviewer, it should not detract from the main point: here were Sino-Muslim students performing a pro-Japanese/anti-Western play in Japanese, using the vocabulary of their occupiers, which the community attended to support. Sino-Muslim schoolchildren acquired Japanese-language skills and learned the Japanese imperial rhetoric of resistance to Western imperialism. Through performance, they transmitted this viewpoint to their communities.[120]

Japanese authorities also encouraged other forms of family participation in Islamic education. Japanese-language speaking competitions specifically for Sino-Muslims were held frequently throughout Manchukuo. Young Muslim women excelled in these competitions, and a number of them, like Bai Shufang, were awarded scholarships to continue studying Japanese. *Mengjiang Xinbao* reported that Bai had placed first in the competition in Datong, and that her parents were in the audience to cheer her on.[121] Although it is unlikely that her parents could understand her speech, they supported her. Once again, this constituted tacit acknowledgment of the Japanese imperial reach into the realm of the family.[122]

Newspapers published in occupied China were peppered with similar stories of Japanese-language plays and competitions held for Muslims, as well as other non-Han communities. For example, at another large Japanese-language speaking competition held in Datong mostly for Mongolian and Muslim students, around 400 community members reportedly attended. The goal of the event was to promote interaction between members of the Muslim and Mongolian communities living in the north China border-lands.[123] Students made short speeches about the "East Asia Liberation War" and emphasized the importance of fighting British and Soviet imperialism in the region. The winner of the competition was a young woman named Ding Shuyuan from the second-level Japanese class at Datong's Muslim elementary school.[124]

The connections between Japanese-language learning, Muslim women's education, and the home went even further in North China. The Japanese-sponsored North China Islamic Women's Association held small seminars on home economics for Muslim women, where they were also introduced to a few words of Japanese.[125] One group of Sino-Muslim women even joined teachers from Japan to celebrate the Japanese children's *matsuri* festival and to learn more about the manners and customs of Japanese women. The students dressed in kimonos, expressed an interest in learning about Japanese culture, and served alcohol (C. *baijiu*) and tea to the community.[126] There is no indication that the Muslim women objected to serving alcohol, but it is noteworthy their participation in a haram ritual would be publicized. According to the news coverage, all the women agreed that Japanese and Muslim women in North China should work together to create a happy and harmonious relationship (C. *hele*) for the sake of Greater East Asia.[127] Although we are left to guess at these Muslim women's motivations for participating in events sponsored by the Japanese Empire (ennui? genuine interest?), the Japanese Empire's efforts to provide a modern education for young Muslim women in North China is a significant part of the story of wartime China and the Japanese impact on the lives of Sino-Muslims.

Although women may have been receptive to learning Japanese, Chinese clerics were opposed to such classes in Muslim schools. Their desire to maintain the status quo can partly be understood as a need to retain control over the education of the youths in their communities, and to uphold their own legitimacy. However, this was not exceptional in occupied China, and Nationalist educational reforms also met resistance from the old guard. Clerics realized that their positions could be marginalized if the number of hours devoted to learning Arabic were reduced in order to teach Japanese and other modern subjects, like science and technology.[128] This ongoing struggle for authority was summed up by a Japanese observer: most clerics had only studied the "Arabian Classics" (C. *yalabiya jingdian*), and their knowledge came from the Quran and hadiths, which were "unsuitable" for modern students. In the end, the biggest threat to Japanese educational aspirations in the region was not the Arabic language per se but the people teaching Arabic, who stood to lose cultural and religious authority.[129]

Methods, Motivations, and Incentives for Educating Young Muslims

Japanese bureaucrats like Kobayashi Hajime made frequent trips to Muslim schools in areas under occupation to report on their status.[130] These reports highlighted the redemptive qualities of the Japanese Empire, and demonstrated that the Japanese were able to intervene in Muslim educational reforms at a moment when relations between Sino-Muslims and the Chinese state were particularly abysmal.[131] They also reiterated common tropes concerning the suppression and devastation of Sino-Muslim communities by the Qing in the late imperial period. In this presentation of the history of Islam in China, Sino-Muslims lagged behind in their economic and social development, which led them to become more conservative and narrow-minded than their Han neighbors.[132] The help of the Japanese Empire gave Muslims from China an opportunity to "unshackle" themselves from oppression.[133] Japanese scholars and bureaucrats depicted a scenario where Muslims were oppressed and neglected by the Chinese state, and left to fend for themselves on the fringes of a rapidly changing world. At this critical juncture in Sino-Muslim/Chinese state relations, the Japanese Empire appointed itself as a savior who would enable Muslims to choose an alternate future.[134]

In addition to historicizing the contemporary situation in Sino-Muslim communities to suit their educational agenda, Japanese officials also regularly attended the opening of new Muslim schools. Always conducted with great fanfare and favorably reported, these events served an obvious propaganda purpose. For instance, when the Zhangjiakou Muslim Middle School (C. *Zhangjiakou qingzhen zhongxuexiao*) opened, the entire Sino-Muslim community, along with a number of Japanese imperial officials, reportedly came out to celebrate. Kobayashi Hajime, who attended, wrote that the

At the opening of a Muslim Elementary School, both the Manchukuo and Japanese flags are prominently displayed. (Greater Japan Muslim League database, Waseda University Library Special Collections)

school was a place where Muslim identity would be fostered while students strove for excellence. The students who graduated from the school, he said, would go on to serve in the army, work for the government, or become teachers. In these capacities, young graduates would act as positive role models and representatives to younger members of their community and to Muslims throughout Asia.[135]

In his report on the opening of the school in Zhangjiakou, Kobayashi makes clear that these were long-term policies, intended to foster a sense of community among Muslims living throughout Asia and the Middle East. Reports on schools often stressed that the main goal of the education system was to prepare Muslim youths for the world they would encounter *after* Japan won the war. Implicit in Kobayashi's argument is that these young Muslims, who would be working in the service of empire, were meant to interact and converse with other Muslims in not Arabic or Chinese but Japanese. Sino-Muslims were urged to learn Japanese because once imperial Japan defeated the Western imperialists, this would help them get ahead in the new world order envisioned by Japan.[136] In retrospect, these plans are a testament to Japan's ambitious outlook and to the way the war was going: at the time, the inevitable outcome was victory, and Japanese bureaucrats needed to prepare for it.

Japanese officials had a variety of experiences trying to convince Sino-Muslims to accept Japanese-language training into the curriculum. In areas where Japanese was most successfully integrated, Sino-Muslims were presented as "less religious" than their counterparts.[137] In his report on Muslim schools in four localities under occupation, Kobayashi Hajime assessed the implementation of Japanese-language programs at schools in Zhangjiakou, Beijing, Datong, and Houhe. Of the four places, he deemed Beijing to be home to the most "backward" (J. *kōshin*) Muslim community. According to Kobayashi, Beijing's Sino-Muslim community was larger, more deeply entrenched, and "more Islamic" (J. *kaikai-shoku*) than in other places, and therefore the schools were less receptive to taking time away from learning Arabic to teach Japanese.[138] Kobayashi's conclusions can be read in a number of ways, but, without questioning the religiosity of Sino-Muslims throughout the occupied regions, it seems clear that in Beijing, which had more Sino-Muslim power brokers with money and connections, they were able to more easily resist and rebuff Japanese offers than were Muslims in smaller, poorer, communities.

This counterintuitive presentation of cosmopolitan Beijingers as "more backward" than their neighbors from smaller localities was likely a strategy by Japanese bureaucrats to subdue the uproar among the city's Sino-Muslims about Japanese-language instruction in their schools. Beijing's large, wealthy, and vibrant Muslim community also may have been more abreast of developments in the war than more isolated communities. When Kobayashi tied the perceived religiosity of Muslims to their receptiveness to Japanese-language pedagogy, he also muted the question of national sentiment that these communities might have felt toward the *Zhonghua minzu*. Muslims' resistance to Japanese policies was about their belief in Islam, not about an attachment to the Chinese nation-state.[139] Kobayashi's argument was that resistance implied religious conservatism and traditionalism, and that only by embracing the Japanese language could Sino-Muslims become modern and liberal.

In contrast, the Muslim school in Zhangjiakou was open and receptive to Japanese-language learning. During his visit to the trading entrepôt north of Beijing, Kobayashi reported that the school received a hefty stipend from the Japanese government. The school administration arranged a special concert on the occasion of his visit to thank the Japanese Empire. The children sang songs in Japanese about Badaling (a famous section of the Great Wall that passes close to Zhangjiakou) and the greatness of imperial Japan. Kobayashi transcribed one song by the children about weaving a red, white, and green braid. This was a rather obvious metaphor for the interwoven relationship between the green Muslim crescent and the Japanese imperial rising sun.[140] The description of the concert provides a segue to the emblematic relationship Kobayashi saw developing between Japan and Muslims throughout Asia.[141] He remarked that Muslim children were an undervalued resource, and said Japanese imperial officials needed to pay more attention to their education because Sino-Muslims had influence within the broader community of Muslims throughout Asia, South Asia, and the Middle East.[142] Sino-Muslim children were seen as a way to leverage Islamic communities, as children became proxies between the Japanese Empire and worldwide Muslim communities. According to Kobayashi, the curriculum was intended both to serve the needs of the local community and to advance the goals of empire.[143]

School schedules were full, and Muslims took Friday afternoons off for prayers, which made finding time for Japanese difficult. The two examples of schedules reproduced below provide insight into the daily rhythms of Sino-Muslim students who attended schools under Japanese occupation.

There was an emphasis on physical education, and students also had free periods and homework periods. At the first school, students attended three Japanese lessons, three Chinese lessons, and six Islamic culture classes per week. At the second school, students had five Chinese classes and only two classes each of Japanese and Arabic per week. These two examples of schedules demonstrate that schools approached the integration of Japanese into their curricula in a variety of ways. They also illustrate that there was no standard curriculum at Muslim schools; courses and their content varied from school to school.[144]

In Beijing, where Japanese bureaucrats faced the most resistance to their language policies, Kobayashi advised presenting the school in Zhangjiakou as a positive model, one showing that Japanese-language classes would not impede Arabic learning.[145] The main mosque on Oxen Street in Beijing was in charge of overseeing some of the smaller Muslim schools around the city. Kobayashi believed that the mosque took this responsibility very seriously. To reduce the mosque's influence over curricular decisions, he proposed shifting the jurisdiction of Muslim schools in Beijing from the private sphere to the public sphere. This would give the Japanese government more autonomy to implement pedagogical changes, since the schools would then be under the direct control of the occupation government. This radical suggestion highlights the resistance that Kobayashi and others faced implementing policies in Beijing. It also reflects the variety in different communities' responses to the Japanese occupation and demonstrates that the Japanese Empire was forced to seek individualized solutions for different communities depending on the reception of the proposed policy.

Among the reasons the Beijing Muslim community gave the Japanese for not wanting to include Japanese-language classes was that it would be too taxing for children to learn three languages. Instead, they needed to focus on learning Arabic, which was indispensable for their religious education.[146] For Kobayashi, this confirmed that Beijing's Muslims were both more Islamic and more backward than those in other parts of occupied China. In places like Zhangjiakou, he said, children had no problems learning three or even four languages in elementary school. For Kobayashi, this indicated that they were both smarter and more progressive than Muslims in Beijing.[147] Kobayashi offered the example of the school established by the Japanese government for the Tatar émigré children naturalized on the home islands after fleeing Bolshevik persecution. According to Kobayashi, the Tatar children were not only integrated into Japanese society but also became model subjects of the Japanese Empire.[148] Kobayashi expressed a great deal of admi-

SCHEDULE 1

		Monday	Tuesday	Wednesday	Thursday	Friday	Saturday
Morning	*Period 1*	Arithmetic	Japanese	Arithmetic	Japanese	Arithmetic	Japanese
	Period 2	Ethics; morality	Arithmetic	Chinese	Arithmetic	Chinese	Arithmetic
	Period 3	Music	Calligraphy	Drawing	Ethics; morality	Calligraphy	Grammar
Afternoon	*Period 4*	Chinese	Free period	Composition	Chinese	Free period	Chinese
	Period 5	Phys ed.	Homework	Music	Homework	Phys. ed.	Homework
	Period 6	Islamic culture	Islamic culture	Islamic culture	Islamic culture	Islamic culture	Islamic culture

SCHEDULE 2

		Monday	Tuesday	Wednesday	Thursday	Friday	Saturday
Morning	*Period 1*	Arithmetic	Japanese	Arithmetic	Chinese	Japanese	Arithmetic
	Period 2	Free period	Chinese	Chinese	Ethics; morality	Arithmetic	Chinese
	Period 3	Chinese	Arabic	Ethics; morality	Free period	Arabic	Ethics; morality
Afternoon	*Period 4*	Penmanship; calligraphy	Gymnastics	Gymnastics	Composition	Technology; crafts	Extracurricular activities
	Period 5	Music	Arithmetic	Free period	Composition	Free period	
	Period 6	Extracurricular activities	Extracurricular activities	Extracurricular activities	Extracurricular activities	Extracurricular activities	

Table 1.

Example of two school schedules where Japanese-language courses were incorporated into the curriculum. (Kobayashi Hajime, "Nihongo to kaimin jidō," *Kaikyōken* 57 [1940]: 39–40)

Table 2.
Reproduction of original schedules from Kobayashi's report.
(Kobayashi Hajime, "Nihongo to kaimin jidō," *Kaikyōken* 57 [1940]: 39–40)

SCHEDULE 1

		月	火	水	木	金	土
上午	第一節	算術	日語	算術	日語	算術	日語
	第二節	修身	算術	國文	算術	國文	算術
	第三節	音樂	書法	圖畫	修身	書法	語法
下午	第四節	國文	自然	作文	國文	自然	國文
	弟五節	體育	作業	音樂	作業	體育	作文
	弟六節	回教文	回教文	回教文	回教文	回教文	回教文

SCHEDULE 2

		月	火	水	木	金	土
上午	第一節	算術	日語	算術	國文	日語	算術
	第二節	自然	國文	國文	修身	算術	國文
	第三節	國文	阿文	修身	自然	阿文	修身
下午	第四節	習字	體操	體操	作文	工藝	課外活動
	弟五節	音樂	美術	自然	作文	自然	
	弟六節	課外活動	課外活動	課外活動	課外活動	課外活動	

Tatar children from the Tokyo Islamic School attend
a meeting of the Greater Islam Muslim League, 1928.
(Greater Japan Muslim League database, Waseda
University Library Special Collections)

ration for the Tatar children, who learned Japanese and Arabic, a language
described as "Tatar" (J. *Tatarugo*), as well as Russian.[149]

The ten-year anniversary of the Tokyo Islamic School was celebrated in a
number of articles in Japan's scholarly journals and popular press. A five-page
article chronicling the school's achievements appeared in the widely circulating *Japan and Japan's People* (J. *Nihon oyo Nihonjin*). The article included
a number of photos of the students and administrators and noted that, in
the presence of dignitaries from Afghanistan and Manchukuo, the speaker
lauded imperial Japan for helping Muslim children.[150] This school was proposed as a model, a place where students learned many different languages,[151]
and a demonstration to Sino-Muslims that they could become subjects of
imperial Japan without compromising their ethnoreligious identities.[152]

Conclusions

Japanese-language policies were a chance for everyone in the empire to
strive toward a common future using the same language.[153] At the same time,
Japanese bureaucrats never failed to acknowledge that their main objective
was to connect with Muslims around the world with the help of Japanese-

speaking Sino-Muslims.[154] To demonstrate how useful Japanese-language learning could be for Sino-Muslims, Kobayashi reported that when a number of Muslims from North China visited Japan and were introduced to the Tatar community in Tokyo, they communicated in Japanese.[155] Finally, Kobayashi explained that if Sino-Muslims spoke Japanese, this could help foster a deeper understanding between Japanese subjects and Muslims throughout the world. This again tied Japanese educational reforms in North China to global objectives. Through a deeper and better understanding of Islam, Japanese subjects on the home islands would be able to comprehend and justify their growing interest in and involvement with the Middle East, South Asia, and Southeast Asia. There seemed to be no downside to teaching Japanese to Sino-Muslim children living under occupation in North China.[156]

The Nationalists, the Japanese Empire, and Sino-Muslims used a lot of ink discussing the different possibilities for educational reforms that would allow Muslims living in China to participate in the modern world. In many ways, the protracted battle for the hearts and minds of Muslims on the mainland gave Sino-Muslims the opportunity to implement changes they had been considering for years before the war started. In the case of Muslims living under occupation, some families witnessed the tangible benefits of their children learning Japanese at school, while others were less convinced that this would be a useful skill in the future. In other words, it was up to the Japanese imperial officials to convince Sino-Muslims of the benefits of learning Japanese. Education was a powerful tool that both the Nationalists and the Japanese Empire tried to use for their own advantage. Sino-Muslims also understood the value of education for their children, and in some ways the war provided the space for animated discussions about topics that had already been taking place within Sino-Muslim communities. In these debates, the benefits and drawbacks of madrasah education versus a modern curriculum came to the top of the political agenda as Japanese bureaucrats attempted to implement changes in Muslim schools throughout occupied China.

The "unevenness" of the implementation of Japanese-language reforms in Muslim schools throughout the occupied regions is also evidence that these policies were never simply implemented from the top down and that they required buy-in from local communities.[157] In the occupied regions, Sino-Muslim communities varied in size and economic standing. These differences had an impact on how Japanese educational policies were accepted and adapted to the local context. Even among ethnic populations in China, Japanese policies for those living under occupation were never evenly applied or accepted. The occupation also opened up new spaces and educational possibilities for Muslim women and for study-abroad programs, which no doubt enriched and enlivened communities while offering Muslims from North China the opportunity to engage more broadly with Muslims around the world.

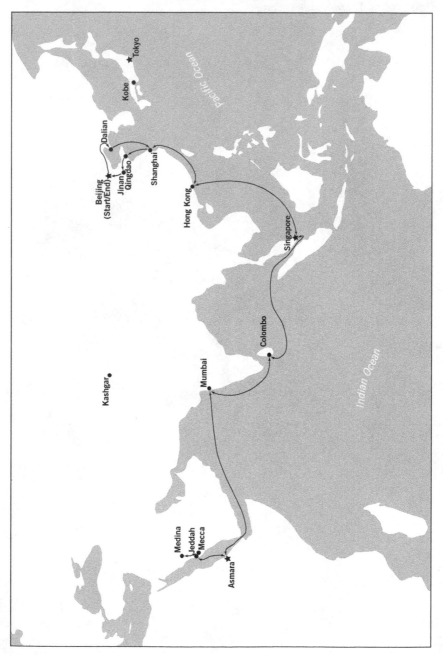

Map 3. The route taken by Tang Yichen and other members of the Japanese-sponsored hajj delegation in 1938–1939. (Data compiled by the author; map by Kristian R. Underwood)

Tokyo

Kobe

Dalian

Beijing
(Start/End)

Jinan
Qingdao

Shanghai

Hong Kong

Singapore

Kashgar

Colombo

Mumbai

Medina
Jeddah
Mecca

Asmara

Pacific Ocean

Indian Ocean

3

SINO-MUSLIMS BEYOND OCCUPIED CHINA

During the war, Sino-Muslims left Japanese-occupied regions to engage with Muslims *beyond* areas under occupation. The Japanese Empire used a number of tactics to recruit and work with Muslims around the world to undermine Soviet Communism and Western imperialism. These included sponsoring Sino-Muslims to study in Japan, inviting Sino-Muslims to attend events on the home islands, deploying Muslims from China to smooth over diplomatic and trade relations throughout Asia and the Middle East, and presenting Sino-Muslims as allies in Japan's efforts to combat Allied propaganda throughout its expanding empire in places like Malaya, Burma, the Dutch East Indies, and the Philippines. A certain segment of Sino-Muslims also traveled far and wide during the war with the help of connections facilitated by Fascist Italy and Nazi Germany. These missions and trips gave Sino-Muslim men and women the opportunity to connect with Muslims they might not have met otherwise. None of these efforts went unnoticed by the Chinese Nationalists, who responded to these overtures with their own propaganda and organized Nationalist-supported Muslims to help spread anti-Japanese messages to Muslims around the world.

Tokyo became a focal point for Muslims during the war, attracting students, businesspeople, and colonial dissidents from all over the world. For the Japanese Empire, Muslims constituted a key link to anti-imperial movements that would also promote a vision of cohesiveness throughout Asia. In Tokyo, Muslims from occupied China were joined by Muslims from places such as Afghanistan, Turkey, Persia, Egypt, West Africa, Yemen, India, Burma, and the Philippines. While visiting or living in the imperial capital, this group of men and women witnessed for themselves how imperial Japan imagined its changing role vis-à-vis Muslims and engaged in conversations and debates about anticolonial and anticommunist struggles.

Transgressing and Traversing Borders: A Variety of Spatial Arrangements for the Japanese Empire

A number of notable books are concerned with territorializing and questioning the spatial arrangements of the Japanese Empire.[1] These works focus on the movement of Japanese subjects from the home islands, and others like Koreans and Taiwanese, throughout the empire. The government's promotion of travel from the home islands to the colonies through government-sponsored efforts helped "legitimate the territorial claims" to what Kate McDonald calls "the spatial politics of Japanese imperialism."[2] Inverting McDonald's framework, I contend that the same could be said for Sino-Muslims who traveled from occupied China to Tokyo and throughout Southeast Asia, South Asia, East Africa, and the Middle East with financial support from the Japanese imperial government. By examining Japanese colonial space through the lens of Japan's Islamic policies and its efforts to bring Muslims to Tokyo or deploy Sino-Muslims to smoothen diplomatic engagement and boost capital ventures, we can reconsider territories generally conceived to be beyond the geographic confines of the Japanese Empire as integral to the maintenance of empire. Sino-Muslims were in dialogue with Japanese subjects, travelers, and imperial officials and mediated their relationship to the Japanese Empire in ways different from yet complementary to those of McDonald's "colonial boosters," who traveled from the metropole to the colonies. The ways Sino-Muslims experienced the Japanese Empire, the metropole, and places beyond Japanese imperial purview provides new ways of conceiving Japanese imperial space. In this regard, the politics of how space was organized and understood was an endeavor not simply for the colonizer but also for the colonized.

When we consider the ways Sino-Muslims experienced the Japanese Empire, we begin to unlock the variations and varieties of what Japanese imperial space meant to non-Japanese people living within the empire. In his examination of the movement of Japanese nonstate actors and "transgressives" throughout the Japanese Empire, David Ambaras demonstrates that "mobility simultaneously destabilized and reinforced imperial boundary-making in the South China Sea."[3] In the same way, carefully curated tours of the home islands showcased how the Japanese government wanted Muslim visitors to understand imperial Japan, and how it wanted Japanese subjects to understand Islam. Along with the Afghans, Javanese, Sumatrans, Yemenites, Moro, and other Muslims who visited Japan, Muslims from China participated in particular programs geared to reinforcing a specific image of Japan, Japanese subjects, and the imperial project vis-à-vis Muslims. Yet Muslims drew their own conclusions about the Japanese Empire and wrote about it on their own terms.

Sino-Muslims might never have been central to decision making for policy and government officials, but their role in the periphery of social, cultural, and economic policymaking offers new perspectives on the management, operation, and long-term vision of the Japanese imperial project. These "side stories" of empire provide a novel take on what the Japanese government wanted to accomplish during the war and who was needed to facilitate these long-term aspirations.[4] Continuing to disentangle the complexities of wartime imperial spaces will enable fuller comprehension of the prolonged impact on people's lives of Japanese imperial policies guided by Japan's wartime ambitions.[5] There were innumerable ways for subjects of the Japanese Empire to configure imperial space, and while McDonald and Ambaras examine the movement of Japanese subjects within the empire as a way to better understand Japanese territory from the perspective of the home islands, perhaps we can learn just as much about Japan's wartime objectives by following Sino-Muslims who traveled to the home islands and throughout Asia and the Middle East with the sponsorship of the Japanese Empire.[6]

The Tokyo Mosque and Sino-Muslims

On Friday, May 11, 1938, the Tokyo Mosque opened with great fanfare. Muslim delegates from all over the world made their way to the capital of imperial Japan to participate in the opening ceremonies. While in Tokyo, participants enjoyed a variety of events meant to highlight imperial Japan's technological and social advancement, as well as its benevolent support for Islam.[7] Included in the guests' all-expenses-paid trip to Tokyo were visits to places such as the zoo at Ueno Park and the Japanese Imperial Naval Academy.[8] The opening ceremonies were presided over by the charismatic cleric Abdürreşid İbrahim, a Tatar exile and important ally of the Japanese government.[9] As the events surrounding the opening of the Tokyo Mosque highlight, histories of the Japanese occupation of China rarely address the importance of transnational actors from the mainland who lived under the shadow of the Japanese occupation but also traveled abroad during the war.

Prayers at the Tokyo Mosque overseen by Imam Abdürreşid İbrahim.
(Greater Japan Muslim League database, Waseda
University Library Special Collections)

In the capital, a group of Sino-Muslim men were able to witness for themselves how imperial Japan imagined its changing role in relation to Islam.

Five Sino-Muslims were invited to take part in the opening ceremonies. The men chosen to accompany Tang Yichen, then the presiding head of the Japanese-sponsored All China Muslim League, were Liu Jinbiao, Li Zongqing, Zhao Yunsheng, and Wang Lianyu. Tang Yichen (1897–1972) is the most important character in this chapter. He was born into a prominent Muslim family in Beijing in the last decade of the nineteenth century. His father, Tang Yutian, and his four brothers were well-known Muslim businessmen in Beijing. His family had extensive holdings in the city's halal butchering industry, and his brother Tang Fuzi was one of the main benefactors of the Tianqiao Mosque (C. *Tianqiao qingzhensi*).[10] His family was politically active and known throughout the Muslim community in Beijing before the war for supporting political initiatives that focused on educational reforms and resisting communism.

When the Japanese occupied Beijing, Tang and his family did not leave. Instead, he worked closely with the Japanese to found the Beijing branch of the All China Muslim League (C. *Zhongguo Huijiao zong lianhehui*) in February 1938.[11] Since 1927, Tang had published a journal, *Zhenzong Monthly*, for which he also wrote most of the articles, and it came under Japanese control after the occupation of the city.[12] *Zhenzong Monthly* had a circulation in the low thousands among Muslims living throughout North China. It covered regional affairs as well as the situation of Muslims worldwide. After 1937, *Zhenzong Monthly* also started publishing articles pertaining to Japanese policies and attitudes toward Islam, and it covered Tang's trip with the four others to attend the opening of the Tokyo Mosque.

In Tokyo, Tang and his companions had the chance to meet and interact with a number of important Muslim dignitaries from around the world. Among the VIPs in attendance at the inaugural Friday prayers were Prince Hussein of Yemen, the Afghan and Egyptian consuls, and high-ranking diplomatic representatives from the Kingdom of Saudi Arabia, the Dutch East Indies, India, and the Philippines. A glaring omission from this list was the Turkish consul or any other representative of the Turkish Embassy. The Ankara government had revoked the citizenship of Abdürreşid İbrahim and maintained a distance from the Tatar community in Tokyo.[13] The guest of honor was Prince Hussein, because of Fascist Italy's close connections to Yemen. The Japanese admired their Italian allies, who had managed to secure a foothold closer to Mecca than the British or the Americans would have liked with their continued support for Prince Hussein's father, Imam

Prince Hussein of Yemen arriving at Tokyo Station, May 1938.
(Greater Japan Muslim League database, Waseda
University Library Special Collections)

Yahya. En route to Tokyo, Prince Hussein also stopped for an official visit in Japanese-occupied Shanghai.[14]

The history of Yemen's relationship with Fascist Italy is little known and important for the development of Japanese interests in creating links to Muslims around the world. In the 1870s Yemen was incorporated as a province into the Ottoman Empire. The Ottomans introduced state centralization and modernization projects to the region, but these programs faced obstacles and resistance from locals. By the beginning of the twentieth century, the Ottoman hold over Yemen was waning, which created a power vacuum in the region. After World War I, a number of Salafi-supported movements attempted to bring order to strategically positioned Yemen. One of these people was Yahya Hamid al-Din, who quickly adopted the military apparatus put in place by the Ottomans and presented Yemen as an important "element in the greater trans-regional project of Islamic unity and anti-imperial activism that was characteristic of the interwar period."[15]

Throughout the 1920s, as Yemen sought a position of leadership in the region in opposition to the British presence in Aden, power brokers in the country aligned themselves with Fascist Italy. In 1926, Imam Yahya signed a friendship treaty with Italy that advocated for stronger bilateral trade between the two countries. This quickly translated into a massive military aid from Italy, accompanied by Italian military advisers. This relationship be-

Sino-Muslims beyond Occupied China

tween Italy and Yemen explains why Imam Yahya's third son, Prince Hussein, was the guest of honor at the opening of the Tokyo Mosque in 1938. It also explains why Prince Hussein apparently greeted the guests in both Arabic and Italian.[16] In 1937, Imam Yahya wrote a letter to Mussolini on the occasion of the renewal of the Italian-Yemeni Treaty. He praised Mussolini and wrote that the accord "reflected the devout and amicable relationship between the two Kingdoms." He also emphasized "the aims of friendly collaboration which the Italian government has shown toward our Kingdom as a fine example for Islamic countries and Muslim people" of how Europeans and Arabs could work together.[17] Just six months after the re-signing of the Italian-Yemeni friendship treaty, Prince Hussein traveled to Tokyo.[18]

Japanese policymakers were anxious to gain the patronage of important Muslim leaders in the Middle East and beyond. By making Prince Hussein the guest of honor at the opening of the Tokyo Mosque, they were not only making overtures to Muslims around the world but also creating stronger bonds with their Fascist allies. High-ranking officials were invited at Japan's expense to the opening of the Tokyo Mosque, and the Tatar émigrés were introduced to dignitaries to highlight Japan's "long-standing" support for Muslims persecuted by the Soviets. With the building of the Tokyo Mosque, the Japanese Empire was attempting to show that it was the protector of Islam and an Axis power that extended religious freedom to everyone.[19]

The five delegates from the Japanese-sponsored All China Muslim League who were chosen to attend the opening of the mosque left occupied Beijing on May 1, 1938.[20] When they arrived in Kobe six days later, they were greeted by a Sino-Muslim named Wang Ruilan and Japanese officials. Wang was a prominent cleric from Beijing and a relative of Wang Haoran. Upon arriving in Tokyo, around fifty Tatars and a number of Sino-Muslims working or studying in Japan came to greet the delegates. The following morning, their Japanese hosts arranged a tour of Tokyo for the men, including a visit to the Imperial Palace, the Meiji Shrine, and the Yasukuni Shrine.[21]

Also in attendance at the opening of the mosque was Puguang of the Manchu Qing Aisin-Gioro household. Puguang was the younger and lesser-known cousin of the last emperor of China, Puyi. Puguang was related to Puyi through his uncle Zaifeng. Zaifeng was Puyi's father and more commonly known as Prince Chun, who served as Puyi's regent from 1908 until his 1911 abdication (which ended the Qing Dynasty). Years later, Puyi was lured out of exile by Japanese promises to reinstate him as "emperor" of Manchukuo. Puyi's cousin Puguang had converted to Islam when he married a Sino-Muslim opera singer named Xue Yanqing (her stage name was

A group of Sino-Muslims and their Japanese
hosts visit the Meiji Shrine, late 1930s.
(Greater Japan Muslim League database, Waseda
University Library Special Collections)

Huang Yongni). Puyi's cousin was an asset to the Japanese, as one of Puyi's close relatives and as a member of the Manchu Aisin-Gioro household who was not only a supporter of Islam but a Muslim himself. Puguang's presence at the opening of the Tokyo Mosque surely helped Japanese imperialists to imagine that they were presenting themselves as the legitimate protectors of Islam in the region.[22]

The opening of the Tokyo Mosque was used as a propaganda tool on the home islands and throughout the world. There were even coordinated propaganda efforts aimed specifically at Japanese children on the home islands. The May 1938 edition of the children's magazine *Kodomo* ("Children") published a three-page spread about the Tokyo Islamic School and the Tatar children who attended it to coincide with the opening of the mosque. The article includes a number of images of the Tatar children playing. It explains to young readers that the children who attended the school had escaped religious persecution in Soviet Russia.[23] It also contains two images of students writing in what is described as Arabic (J. *Arabia go*) and Japanese on a blackboard.[24] However, upon closer inspection, the text on the board in the

Children at the Tokyo Islamic School, 1938.
("Tōkyō kaikyō gakkō no kodomotachi." *Kodomo* 17, no. 6 [May 1938]).

photo appears to be East Turki rather than Arabic. The accompanying text indicates that these studious youngsters learned Japanese, Turkish (J. *Toruko go*), and Arabic in school, perhaps a nod to some of the policies Kobayashi was attempting to institute in occupied China. Overall, the propaganda efforts and campaigns surrounding the opening of the Tokyo Mosque were well coordinated and organized.

At the inauguration of the mosque, the Sino-Muslim guests participated in a ceremony where they offered a bronze vase to one of the Japanese dignitaries. In the prayers that followed, the group apparently prayed for world peace and better cooperation among Muslims.[25] The group then had an audience with Prince Hussein of Yemen, and, according to the report from their trip, a number of Turks and Afghans were on hand to meet the group from North China. Over the next few days, the group participated in several meetings.[26] Upon returning to Beijing, individual members of the group wrote a number of articles detailing the events of their trip and urging Muslims from North China to abandon their skepticism about imperial Japanese intentions and to accept aid from the Japanese government.

No doubt the group enjoyed touring Japan for three weeks for free, visiting zoos, parks, and shrines, and meeting Muslim dignitaries and officials.

Tang and his companions from North China met, interacted, and ate with important Muslims from all over the world, establishing connections and learning about the struggles of their coreligionists beyond the borders of China. The connections made and fostered in Tokyo were instrumental in shaping the worldview of men like Tang Yichen. Tang Yichen even wrote that he wished to return to Tokyo one day to open a Beijing-style halal restaurant.[27] This provides a window into some of Tang's explicit and implicit justifications for collaborating, as he planned to benefit economically from his connections to the Japanese Empire. In expressing his desire to open a halal restaurant in Tokyo, he likely knew that a Beijing-style noodle house would prosper thanks to the large contingent of Northern Chinese, both Muslim and non-Muslim, then residing and studying in Japan, as well as the growing Muslim community in Tokyo who sought out halal dining options.

While in Tokyo, Tang was also approached by Japanese officials about embarking on a Japanese-sponsored hajj. Following his return to Beijing he started planning for his upcoming pilgrimage and recruited four others to join him. The second part of this chapter follows Tang on his Japanese-sponsored hajj through a close reading of the journal he published upon returning to occupied China. But first, we need to assess and examine the Chinese Nationalist responses to the opening of the Tokyo Mosque and the Japanese Empire's ongoing diplomatic outreach to Muslims around the world.

The Nationalists: On the Defensive Again?

The opening of the Tokyo Mosque did not go unremarked upon by the Nationalists. One government report even declared that the Japanese government had achieved a grand success by getting Muslims from all over the world to attend.[28] However, the same report also noted that although the Japanese had managed to assemble Muslims from far-flung corners of the earth, some of the attendees were skeptical about the Japanese government's intentions.[29] According to the Nationalists, the Japanese government was simply eager to send advisers and sell military hardware to Iran, Turkey, and Afghanistan in order to build up and train armies in Muslim countries.[30]

In tandem with these plans, the Nationalists observed that the Japanese government was increasing the number of scholarships it awarded to Muslim students to study in Tokyo. The report noted that the Japanese Empire had been successful in its pleas to Muslims to resist the Soviets and Western imperialism.[31] In conclusion, the report suggested that the Nationalists needed to combat these and other perceived Japanese successes, such as the grand opening of the Tokyo Mosque.[32] This could be done by increasing the presence of the Chinese Foreign Ministry in Muslim countries and training more Arabic speakers. The Nationalist government was urged to take a page from the Japanese policy and extend more scholarships for Muslims to study in China.[33]

The report also noted that although the Nationalists had a number of valuable agents who were traveling around Asia and the Middle East attacking Japanese propaganda, these efforts needed to be increased. One of these allies was Xinjiang-born Turkic Muslim Īsa Yūsuf Alptekin (C. *Aisha*). Between November 1933 and February 1934, he had been the head of the first Eastern Turkestan Republic in Kashgar. After the Japanese surrender, he would serve as the head of the Soviet-backed Second East Turkestan Republic. Īsa's prominence and political clout meant that he was regularly sent on foreign diplomatic missions at the behest of the Nationalists. In 1938–39, he and Sino-Muslim Ma Fuliang were deployed to spread anti-Japanese messages throughout the Middle East, India, and Southeast Asia.

As early as 1934, Īsa was warning Muslims in China about Japan's plans to "warm up" to Islam. According to Īsa, Japan had a "crazy dream" (C. *fengkuang de menghua*) to unite all the Muslims of the world under one mantle.[34] Because there were very few Muslims in Japan, he noted that the Japanese were "grooming" (C. *huanyang*) Muslims in Northwest China (C. *Xibei*). Īsa repeatedly warned the Nationalists that if they let the Japanese become more involved with Islam and Muslims, this could give the Japanese a considerable political advantage.[35] From early on, Īsa clearly understood the utility of Muslims from China for Japan's aspirational plans beyond the mainland and tried to articulate these advantages to the Nationalist government.

On a trip to Egypt in 1940, Īsa gave a speech to the World Muslim Assembly in Cairo. The speech was transcribed, translated, and published in a number of periodicals back in China. Īsa began by urging greater cooperation (C. *hezuo*) between Muslims around the world, and he reminded the audience that a substantial population of Muslims in China was fighting the Japanese Empire.[36] Īsa also claimed that all Muslims in China came from an Arabic blood lineage (C. *Zhongguo de huibao you alabo xuetong*).[37] He bolstered his message with promises of business opportunities with China after the war and ended his speech by imploring Muslims to support the Chinese Nationalists in their efforts to defeat the Japanese Empire.[38] Although this speech likely appeased his benefactors back in Chongqing, some of this rhetoric might not have resonated with an Egyptian audience. After all, the Chinese Nationalists were aligned with the Allies and secured massive lend-lease loans as well as military advisers and military personnel from the United States ahead of the bombing of Pearl Harbor in December 1941.[39] Īsa concluded by urging Muslims around the world to "step up" (C. *jiajin*) and contribute to the Chinese war efforts to resist Japanese imperialism in Asia.[40]

After his tour of Egypt, Īsa went on to Turkey, Persia, Syria, Arabia, Iraq, Iran, and Afghanistan, spreading the message of resistance against the Japanese.[41] While on a diplomatic mission to India, Īsa also drew on the deep historical connections between India and China to make an impression on dignitaries there. He presented the ongoing war in China as an anticolonial struggle and once again urged Muslims to come together to fight against oppression. While Indian Muslims may have been sympathetic to the plight of Muslims living in China, trying to convince them that "China's war was also India's war" (C. *Zhongguo de dazhang shi wei Yindu de*) was a strategy likely to be questioned by Indians, who were fighting for independence from the British. Īsa's case illuminates how Nationalist-supported Muslims used the war with Japan to broaden their diplomatic engagement with South Asia and the Middle East. Īsa makes another appearance later in this chapter as he diverted his tour from Istanbul to Mecca in order to intercept Tang Yichen and his companions on their Japanese-sponsored hajj.

Īsa was not the only Nationalist-supported Muslim traveling on diplomatic and goodwill missions and spreading anti-Japanese propaganda. In 1938, Ma Tianying led the Chinese Muslim Nanyang Mission (C. *Zhongguo Huijiao Nanyang fangwentuan*), which stopped in Hong Kong before heading to Malaya and Singapore.[42] The Nationalists also enlisted the services of well-known and respected Sino-Muslim Da Pusheng. Da was deeply concerned about the lack of knowledge about the Japanese occupation among Muslims beyond China. His concern came from learning about correspondence between Muslim students who had studied abroad and the friends they had left behind in the places where they had studied. As letters came in from afar expressing sympathy and support for the situation in China, it seemed to Da that the true extent of Japanese belligerence was not being fully communicated in the media to Muslims beyond China. To rectify this, Da Pusheng and Bai Chongxi commissioned the translation of a number of tracts about Japanese imperial aggression in China into Farsi, Turkish, Persian, and Arabic.[43]

In some cases, these efforts led to responses like Egyptian prime minister Mustafa Pasha's pledge to try to improve Sino-Arab relations and to boycott Japanese goods.[44] In fact, the presence of Japanese goods "flooding" the Egyptian markets was a regular complaint from Nationalist-supported Muslim students studying in Egypt and North Africa, who reported on their experiences in short op-eds or articles published in Chinese-language journals.[45] It was true that the Japanese government was managing to insert itself into new markets in Central Asia, South Asia, the Middle East, and North Africa. In the next chapter, we will explore some of the ways it planned to use Sino-Muslims to hawk goods to Muslim consumers throughout North Africa and the Middle East.

Nationalist propaganda depicted World War II as a war against fascism. The Japanese government was "seducing" (C. *youhuo*) Muslims in China with scholarship opportunities and trips to Tokyo.[46] The Nationalists also claimed that the Japanese government was drawing Muslims "over to their side" (C. *lalong*) with a three-part plan: offering economic aid and incentives, extending outreach efforts to Muslims, and directing propaganda efforts at anti-British and anti-American Muslim leaders around the world.[47] According to Nationalist-supported Sino-Muslim Zhu Jianmin, the Japanese government deceived Muslims with their "crafty plots" (C. *guiji*), the most emblematic of which was the extravagant and well-attended program of ceremonies for the opening of the Tokyo Mosque.[48] For Zhu, the logic behind Japan's imperial aspirations was clear, and he contextualized the role that Sino-Muslims were imagined to play in fascist international politics: Sino-Muslims were supposed to foster "intimate connections" (C. *qinhe*) between the Japanese Empire and Muslims around the globe.[49] All of this was done under the guise of promoting religious freedom in the Japanese Empire, and Zhu claimed that none of it could have been achieved without the help of Muslims from China.[50]

Going Places with the Help of the Japanese: Sino-Muslims on the Move

After 1938, a growing number of Sino-Muslim students from occupied China went to Japan to study. One of these students was a young man named Bai Jinyu. During his time in Japan, Bai corresponded with Tang Yichen, who published some of their correspondence in the journal *Islam*.[51] Bai wrote to Tang about the well-integrated and growing community of Muslims from China in Tokyo, and about how he had been welcomed into the expanding network of Muslims from all over the colonized world. Bai was in Tokyo to learn Japanese, but he explained that his arrival was made much easier by the fact that a number of Muslims from North China already studying and working in the imperial capital helped him get acquainted with the city. Bai also indicated that Muslims from China traveled frequently back and forth between Tokyo and the mainland with news and goods.[52]

Bai's experience highlights two larger points regularly overlooked in the historiography of the war. First, there was a certain degree of freedom of movement for specific individuals living under Japanese occupation. There is a tendency to think of occupied North China as having an impermeable border, as a place where people who stayed after 1937 — either by choice or by force — were simply stuck. Although Bai was traveling to Japan under Japanese supervision, he came and went throughout East Asia and was in contact with many people who lived beyond the borders of the occupied territories. Second, Bai's account reveals an important and growing network of Muslims living and studying in Tokyo during the war. These men and women, who came from all over, exchanged ideas, helped each other out, and studied together, fostering a sense of community with Muslims they might not have had the chance to meet otherwise. Circumstances like the ones described by Bai and other young people caught the attention of the Nationalist government and increased its concern regarding the Japanese Empire's courting of Muslims.

A Beijinger named Ma Liangpu also studied Japanese in Tokyo in the years leading up to World War II. He was invited to accompany Tang Yichen as part of the Japanese-sponsored hajj, likely because of his Japanese-language skills. Ma played an important role translating articles about Islam from Japanese to Chinese and vice versa for his benefactors, articles that were published in Japanese-sponsored periodicals for Muslims throughout occupied China. The relationship for both parties was strategic but also forward-thinking and meant to foster long-term growth and an intimate relationship between Japanese and Muslim populations throughout East Asia.[53] For his part, Ma benefited from working for the Japanese by earning a decent salary and having the opportunity to study in Tokyo and learn another language, go on hajj for free, and broaden his horizons through interactions with other Muslims living and working in the imperial capital.[54]

The Japanese government sponsored a Sino-Muslim hajj delegation led by Tang Yichen. In some ways Tang is emblematic of people traveling during the war, and in other ways, because he published an account of his travels and his high level of visibility, he is anomalous. When Tang embarked on his Japanese-sponsored hajj he kept a careful diary, which he edited upon his return. It was first serialized in journals and then published as a book in 1943. Despite the familiarity of historians of Islam in both Japan and China with

Tang's hajj, no attention has been given to either the journal or the journey itself. In two separate works, Mao Yufeng mentions the Japanese-sponsored hajj trip in passing but pays no significant attention to Tang or his companions. Her argument that all Muslims were united in their vision for China throughout the war and that all Muslims in China actively supported the resistance against Japan would make it hard for her to include Tang's dissenting voice. She does acknowledge that the Japanese delegation was the reason that the Nationalists brought together students studying at Al-Azhar in 1938, but the stated purpose of her article is to focus on the "first and third *hajj* missions, both of which were initiated by Sino-Muslims and were supported by the Nationalist state under Chiang Kai-shek."[55] This sentiment is echoed by Cemil Aydin, who rightly characterizes the "chaotic political conditions of the era" but denies agency to Tang and his companions by presenting them as peons of the Japanese, and by dismissing propaganda efforts using hajj as general failures.[56] However, the efforts of Tang and his fellow pilgrims were less about proselytizing and spreading propaganda in Mecca and more about how the hajj was understood and received in Asia, where it was covered and reported on extensively in both pro-Allied and pro-Axis papers and journals.

Tang's journey reinforces the point that resistance to the Japanese on the mainland was anything but unified, and that the Sino-Muslim community remained deeply divided throughout the war. This particular hajj served as an ominous reminder to the Nationalists of the geopolitical situation in North China: more than half the Muslims who they claimed were part of the *Zhonghua minzu* were living under Japanese occupation, influenced to some degree by Japanese propaganda.[57] In the end, the Nationalist preoccupation with the Japanese-sponsored hajj gave the group the attention that imperial Japan had likely only dreamed the men would be able to achieve on their own.[58]

Japanese Motivations, Sino-Muslim Hajjis, and Nationalist Responses

Perhaps part of the reason that Tang's journal has not been examined until now is that it does not fit nicely into the bounded nationalist idea of what it meant to be a collaborator, nor does it laud the Japanese as protectors of Islam. Instead, Tang's journal offers a glimpse into the tensions and stresses of traveling on the eve of World War II and the everyday experiences of being a Chinese hajji. It also underscores the fraternity among Muslims from

China that often overrode political affiliation. Trying to decipher their "true" loyalties obscures the main point: Tang and his companions participated in an ongoing dialogue between the Nationalists and the Japanese Empire about the place and future of Sino-Muslims in East Asia.

In addition to facilitating connections with Muslims around the world, these exchanges were important for the ways the Japanese legitimized their imperial projects to themselves, their observers and critics, and their Axis allies. The Japanese Empire imagined that enabling travel for Muslims from China would help it gain the support of Muslims around the world. In order to do this, Muslims from the mainland needed to leave the occupied areas to meet, interact, converse, and share ideas with the many different people they encountered on their travels. Upon returning to China, they also shared their stories with their coreligionists to underscore that they had two common enemies: Western imperialism and Soviet Communism.

It is also important to keep in mind that both the Sino-Muslim hajjis and the Japanese Empire got what they wanted out of the pilgrimage. Tang and his companions got a free hajj. In his hajj journal, Tang reiterates that although the Japanese sponsored their pilgrimage, the men embarked on their religious journey because it was their fundamental duty as Muslims. Even for wealthy urban Muslims like Tang, however, the hajj was a long and arduous journey requiring a lifetime of saving. For their part, the Japanese established diplomatic relations with the Saudis almost immediately after Tang and his companions returned to China.[59] After the founding of the unified Kingdom of Saudi Arabia in 1932, the Japanese tried to establish diplomatic relations with the Saudi royal family.[60] However, Ibn Saud had little to do with the Japanese Empire until the late 1930s, when the pressing Japanese need for oil led to the first concerted outreach to the Saudi king. Before Tang and his companions left Saudi Arabia, they paid a visit to the palace for an audience with members of the Saudi royal family. There is no information in Tang's journal about how they managed to secure the audience, but this was surely not a usual affair. They offered the Saudi royalty gifts, including a jade vase brought on their journey in anticipation of the meeting.[61]

Almost immediately following the Japanese-sponsored hajj, the first-ever diplomatic mission of Japanese officials, led by career diplomat Masayuki Yokoyama, made its way to Mecca to try to secure an oil concession. The Saudis agreed to give the Japanese a small concession for drilling but "demanded a large up-front payment by the Japanese without allowing any geologists to survey the proposed concession area."[62] The negotiations for an oil concession ultimately failed because of British and U.S. intervention.[63] Unwilling to agree to the Saudi terms, the Japanese Empire shifted its search for oil and other commodities to the Dutch East Indies.

Although the Japanese government never secured oil rights, financing the Sino-Muslim hajjis was a relatively cheap and effective way for the Japanese Empire to establish diplomatic relations with Saudi Arabia. We should not separate Tang's Japan-sponsored hajj from the empire's attempts to secure an oil concession and establish economic connections in the Middle East. In the end, because the Japanese were the "friends and guardians of Moslems [sic] in China," the Saudis did offer them something they had been after for a number of years: a legation in Jeddah.[64] In the Japanese Empire, cultural policy, or cultural engagements, regularly preceded economic and diplomatic engagement in unfamiliar regions. The forethought given to these policies demonstrates the interconnectedness of cultural policies and economic policies in long-term Japanese imperial ambitions.

The Japanese government was acutely aware of anti-Western, anticolonial movements as well as anticommunist sentiments among Muslim populations throughout the world, and it armed the Sino-Muslim hajjis with the vocabulary to present the British, French, and Soviets as oppressors and the Japanese as liberators. Though the war and their known affiliation with the Japanese Empire complicated their journey, Tang and his companions' familiarity with the international geopolitical situation enabled them to offer harsh critiques of European and Soviet policies directed at Muslims. The members of the group were also active participants in the growing transnational networks of Muslims, and were aware of the connections between themselves and Muslims from South Asia, Southeast Asia, Arabia, and even Africa.[65] At the same time, these men also asserted a strong sense of local identity as "Beijingers" that sometimes trumped other ethnic or political affiliations and, in some cases, even religious sentiment.

Movement and motion are a large part of Tang's story. The modes of transportation his group used, the places they visited, and their relative comfort or discomfort riding on trains, ships, cars, wagons, and even camels gives readers a glimpse into the ebbs and flows of performing hajj in the first half of the twentieth century.[66] Yet this profound sense of movement is anchored in Tang's deep attachment to Beijing. He and his companions escaped occupation (albeit temporarily) by traversing borders, and the group never encountered a single Japanese person on their journey beyond the boundaries of occupied China. At the same time, their travel was restricted because of their known affiliation with the Japanese Empire, and they regularly encountered Italian soldiers on their journey, finding them just as terrifying as the Japanese officers they faced in their daily lives back in Beijing.

Although the Japanese government sponsored the group, the men seemed rather ambivalent about working with their occupiers. In Tang's journal, the group regularly defends their cooperation with the Japanese but never goes as far as lauding their sponsors as protectors of Islam.[67] One other thing that becomes abundantly clear in reading Tang's hajj journal is that the Nationalist surveillance apparatus went well beyond gathering students from Egypt to intercept the five hajjis. In fact, the Nationalists, who had a well-developed network of agents and diplomats stationed throughout Asia, deployed overseas Chinese agents in Hong Kong, Singapore, Bombay, Egypt, and Arabia to confront the group.[68] The fact that Tang and his companions encountered Nationalist agents at almost every port they called on indicates the Nationalists' deep concern about Japanese successes working with Muslims in North China.

Perfect Timing: Tang's Hajj and Larger Geopolitical Maneuverings

One of the tensions in historical writing is striking a balance between the stories of the quotidian in relation to how the lives of historical actors were — or were not — impacted by global forces. This dilemma forces historians to dedicate themselves to "finding the right ratios" between the voices of the people who pepper our narratives and extrapolating to make larger, global claims "in order to bring about their inevitable co-existence."[69] In this case, the intertwining of Tang's hajj and the ways he internalized and wrote about state-directed policies creates complex — and in some cases messy — narratives about Japan's imperial ambitions and the impact of those aspirations on the lives of Sino-Muslims.

The timing of Tang and his companions' journey was significant. The Anti-Comintern Pact had been signed by the Germans and the Japanese Empire in November 1936, joined by the Italians in November 1937. But since there was no formal declaration of war in Europe, the situation between the would-be Axis powers and the other European powers was tense, although not impossible, for the group to navigate. By early 1942, their trip would have been impossible since the Allies had defeated Italy and the Vichy regime in North and East Africa, and the British occupied the entire western coast of the Red Sea. At this specific moment in 1938, cooperation between the Italians and the Japanese enabled five Muslims from occupied Beijing to go on a Japanese-sponsored hajj pilgrimage to Mecca. Without visa sponsorship from the Italian consulate in Shanghai and passage on an Italian steamship, the pilgrims would have never made it from Japanese-occupied China to Italian-occupied Eritrea. From Eritrea, they boarded another Italian vessel that ferried them across the Red Sea to Jeddah. Supported in their religious journey by the Japanese Empire, in some ways these five men were pawns, deeply involved in the international diplomacy of the war; in other ways, the hajjis from North China navigated obstacles they faced using their own agency.

All of this is important for a number of reasons. First, it helps to broaden our understanding of what "wartime China" means. By examining the experiences of non-Han Chinese traveling around the world during the war, we get a better sense of how these people imagined themselves participating in the war, and how they mediated their relationship to both the Chinese state and the Japanese Empire. Second, it expands our spatial imagination of how Japanese policymakers, militarists, and non-Japanese people living under the empire viewed the untapped and vast potential of the Japanese imperial reach. In abstract terms, four days after bombing Pearl Harbor, the Japanese offered the Germans a plan to divide Africa and Eurasia among the Axis powers. The main purpose was to delimit "operational spheres," but the Germans were concerned that an arbitrary division down the seventieth meridian would lead to political skirmishes between the two powers. Yet, in practice, this arbitrary division of the world into Axis spheres never prohibited the Japanese imperial apparatus from imagining larger territorial acquisitions and expanding markets to the Middle East and beyond. Here, examining the travels of Sino-Muslims beyond what is traditionally imagined as the geographical extent of Greater East Asia reveals that the Japanese Empire thought of its imperial project as one much larger and further reaching than currently conceived.

Five Muslims from China on a Japanese-Sponsored Hajj

The Japanese sponsorship of five Muslims from Beijing to perform hajj on the brink of World War II provides a window into the ways Muslims living under the Japanese occupation positioned themselves vis-à-vis the Japanese Empire, the Chinese Nationalists, other world powers, and individual Muslims they encountered on their journey. The Japanese government relied on a number of prominent Muslims from Beijing to accomplish an imperial objective, and Tang Yichen played a large role facilitating interactions between the Muslim community living in occupied North China and the Japanese Empire. The four men who joined Tang were Zhang Ying, Su Ruixiang, Liu Derun, and Ma Liangpu. Zhang and Su were clerics from Beijing, and Liu and Ma were entrepreneurs. Ma is the Sino-Muslim mentioned earlier in this chapter who had studied in Tokyo and was fluent in Japanese.[70]

Tang's journal clearly states that he published the journal to set the record straight, to allow readers to come to their own conclusions about his group's "supposed" political motivations. According to Tang, the men were deeply conflicted about accepting Japanese sponsorship for their pilgrimage and painfully aware of the complications caused by being associated with the Japanese Empire.[71] Yet, at the time of their hajj, Tang was the head of the Japanese-sponsored All China Muslim League, which he had helped establish earlier the same year.[72] In his writing, his guarded ambivalence toward the Japanese Empire provides a much more complicated picture of Sino-Muslim receptiveness to state-directed policies. Tang was not simply a shill who parroted the Japanese party line, and he worked with his occupiers for his own benefit. In this regard, Japanese colonial authorities did not always have the final say when it came to implementing their imperial objectives through the use of nonstate actors.

In a number of publications, Nationalist-supported Muslims took direct aim at Tang and his entourage. In his travelogue *Journal of Travels to the West*, Ma Songting calls out Tang and his companions as traitors (C. *hanjian*). Pang Shiqian (1902–58), a student-delegate summoned by the Nationalists from Al-Azhar to intervene in Tang's hajj, included a section in his own hajj journal about the men.[73] In yet another dispatch from Egypt, Zhang Huaide explained that Ma Songting sent a telegram from China asking him to gather the students studying in Egypt to travel to Mecca to keep watch over Tang and his companions.[74] Zhang had heard that the Japanese government had paid the hajjis 15,000 yuan each to complete their journey.[75] The criticisms levied against Tang and his benefactors indicate that the Nationalists were concerned about the Japanese-sponsored hajjis. Some of this reproach may be fair since it was reported in numerous outlets that the Japanese "spies" complicated and obstructed the movements and plans of the Nationalist-supported hajj delegation.[76] But, given the proliferation of Nationalist-sponsored publications about Tang's hajj, it is clear that it was well-known among the Sino-Muslim community living in Free China that Muslims from occupied China were going on a hajj sponsored by the Japanese government.

It was in response to these critics that Tang decided to publish his own version of events.[77] Throughout his journal, Tang emphasizes that although his group and the Nationalist-sponsored Muslims sent from Al-Azhar to intercept them were originally suspicious of each other, they ended up spending a lot of time together, since many of them had known each other before the war.[78] Through his quotidian anecdotes of shared meals and tourism, Tang argues that shared identity as Sino-Muslims overrode political divisions between the Nationalist- and Japanese-backed hajj delegations. Delving into the day-to-day of their hajj sheds light on the ways the ordinariness of their everyday activities and concerns regularly undermined the political concerns of their backers.

In his journal, Tang used the word *Huabei*—or North China—to describe the region under Japanese occupation. This was likely intentional. Much less loaded than *Manchukuo*, the term was familiar to Chinese readers and also rather vague. Although Beijing was not in Manchukuo, it was still under Japanese occupation, and Tang's use of *Huabei* to name the region he and his companions hailed from also evokes a sense of a shared political geography with the boundaries of the area under Japanese occupation.[79] The choice of the word *Huabei* also highlights that Tang's account was not a real-time journal but a carefully crafted apologia. Intent on quashing what he called "rumors and lies," Tang repeats over and over that the men set out on a journey with no political ambitions and were simply performing hajj. The specific time and place his hajj occurred had an impact on both the social and cultural production of the piece that is reflected in the recording and the subsequent commentary on his journey.

British Colonial Control of the Hajj and Sino-Muslims

Even before leaving Beijing, Tang and his companions encountered seemingly insurmountable obstacles. Under normal circumstances, Muslims would have obtained the required paperwork for the hajj from the Chinese Department of Foreign Affairs (C. *Zhongguo zhengfu waijiaobu*) in Shanghai before traveling by ship to Singapore via Hong Kong. From Singapore, they would sail to Jeddah via Sri Lanka and Bombay, perhaps with a stop in Egypt. However, all of these ports were under British control. This posed a problem for the group, and Tang pointed out that since the Nationalist government had not returned from "exile," they would be unable to get the passport stamps needed to complete their journey in Shanghai.[80] Tang thus danced around a sensitive issue with oblique language: the Japanese army had occupied both Beijing and Shanghai and the Japanese government had forced the Nationalists to flee. This meant that there was no way the Nationalist government could provide them with the visas they needed to get to Mecca via British colonial ports.

Even with generous funding, Tang's hajj almost did not happen. A few months before their departure, the group began making repeated visits to the British consular office in Beijing. However the Japanese alliance with Fascist Italy and Nazi Germany made the British unwilling to help. They never refused Tang and his companions outright; instead, they gave them an impossible scenario: since the group would be disembarking in Egypt, the British officials claimed that the travelers would first need to visit the Egyptian Embassy in either Mumbai or Tokyo to get the proper visa stamps. But the group could not get to Mumbai without stamps from the British. Tang briefly contemplated a trip to Japan but decided the trip would be prohibitively expensive.[81] In the end, the men resolved to travel to Shanghai on a Japanese boat from Dalian to try to get the required visa stamps from the Italians. Getting their visas from the Italians determined their route, the ports of call where they would be allowed to disembark, the people they would meet, and the languages they would need.

Leaving Home: "We'll Miss the Beef Noodles"

The group met to set off on their long journey on December 19, 1938. Before heading to the train station, however, the men wanted one last taste of home. They went to a restaurant for a steaming bowl of Beijing-style beef noodles. The theme of missing Beijing and Beijing-style cuisine runs through Tang's entire journal, and the meals they ate were an important part of their journey.[82] Finding halal places to eat required great effort. The group was always happiest when they encountered other "Chinese" restaurants serving familiar dishes, like in Singapore, or at a small Uyghur-run restaurant in Jeddah that served dumplings.

During their journey from Beijing to Dalian, Tang remarked on the increased presence of Japanese soldiers and Japanese civilians in the cities where the train stopped. He said that the group was happy to have Ma Liangpu as part of their entourage because he spoke fluent Japanese. This was Tang's first mention of Ma's Japanese-language abilities and their first of many encounters with a foreign language. Ma's Japanese skills proved useful at the beginning and the end of their journey, as he was able to help the group buy train and boat tickets and interact with the Japanese officers they encountered throughout occupied China. On more than one occasion, Ma defused tense situations between Japanese officers on trains and the other hajjis who could not speak Japanese.[83] One can only imagine how many similar encounters escalated to violence as Japanese soldiers exerted their dominance over non-Japanese speaking Chinese civilians trying to go about their daily business in occupied China.

Once on the boat from Dalian to Shanghai, the group encountered a problem that they would face on their entire journey: the lack of halal food at sea. In the small teahouse onboard, the cook noticed that they were Muslim (presumably from their white caps) and told them there was little for them to eat on the ship. Tang and his companions subsisted on tea and bread. When the boat docked for a short time in Qingdao, they bought a fish that the chef agreed to fry separately for them. They garnished it with sesame oil (C. *xiangyou*) that they had brought with them from Beijing in anticipation of these types of situations. It is likely that most of the food on the ship would have been cooked in lard, so bringing their own cooking oils showed that the men were well-versed in the difficulties of maintaining a halal diet in a place where Muslims were a minority.

Shanghai: Strangers in Their Own Land

As the boat approached Shanghai, Tang delicately broached the issue of the "Shanghai Incident" (C. *Shanghai shibian*). Tang's vocabulary choice once again indicates his familiarity with the political euphemisms preferred by the Japanese Empire. "Incident" was an innocuous term used by the Japanese Empire to explain the high numbers of Chinese civilian and military casualties caused by intense fighting in the late summer and fall of 1937 that preceded the Japanese occupation of Shanghai that November.[84] Tang and his companions had never been to Shanghai. They found the burgeoning metropolis overwhelming. Their fears of being robbed and unfamiliarity with the city were amplified by the fact that everyone seemed to know that they were not locals (C. *buxiang bendi*) before they uttered a word in their thick northern accents.[85] Shanghai had a smaller Muslim population than Beijing, so Shanghainese were less familiar with Muslims and there were fewer halal places for them to eat. In order to follow a halal diet, the men bought a small grill and kettle and tried cooking for themselves in their hotel room. When Tang burned himself while making tea, he wondered, "If we can't even make tea for ourselves, how will we ever get to Mecca?"

While in Shanghai, the group tried their luck again at the British Consulate but were firmly rebuffed by the Gurkha guards. Dismayed, Tang wondered why the Japanese had not helped them secure travel documents, and then resolved again to visit the Italian consulate.[86] After two or three anxious days exhausting what they thought were all possible avenues to get to Mecca, they received a phone call at their hotel from a Shanghainese travel agent who had secured them visas and passage. The travel agent explained that they would travel on an Italian boat to Massawa in Eritrea with Italian passport stamps. The agent suggested that while docked in Hong Kong, Singapore, Colombo, and Mumbai, the men should stay on the boat to avoid British customs officials. Once in Eritrea, the hajjis would have to figure out for themselves how to get across the Red Sea to Jeddah.[87] Although it was risky, the group decided to take the chance. They spent a few frantic days buying provisions, including white cloth and sandals for *ihram*, the sacred state that all Muslims must enter before beginning a pilgrimage.[88]

Beyond Occupation

On January 3, 1939, the group departed Shanghai on an Italian steamship with around seventy Western passengers and thirty Chinese passengers. Tang and his companions often felt awkward on the Italian ship, adding a certain degree of anxiety to their journey. The Italian crew spoke only English and Italian, which posed a problem for the group. Although they spoke French, Arabic, Chinese, and Japanese between them, none of them spoke any Italian, and only a few words of English. Like most people who have traveled to a place where they do not speak the language, the group enjoyed a good laugh at the comedy of errors that ensued when they had to resort to frantic gestures to make waiters understand what they could and could not eat.[89] After this experience, Tang expressed deep regret for not bringing a Chinese-English dictionary, which, in addition to making it easier to communicate with ship staff, also would have enabled them to read the daily news cables.[90]

Three days after leaving Shanghai, the boat arrived in Hong Kong, where they chose not to disembark. Although they were not forbidden from leaving the boat, they were concerned that their paperwork might make it difficult to get back onboard.[91] Luckily, small junks with hawkers selling fruit, snacks, and other necessities approached the ship, allowing them to restock their perishable provisions. Two days later, the boat arrived in Singapore. They were once again anxious about disembarking, but two British customs agents explained that because Singapore was not their final destination, they

Sino-Muslims beyond Occupied China

could get off the ship without a problem. After spending the morning touring Singapore and complaining about the stifling humidity, Tang and his friends returned to the ship to find two Chinese men waiting for them. This was their first encounter with the elaborate Nationalist surveillance apparatus. The men apparently asked Tang, "Are you the five gentlemen from *Huabei*?" Tang replied that they were.[92] One of the men told them that they had received a cable from the Chongqing government that five Muslims were on a "mission" (C. *shiming*) to Mecca. The Nationalist affiliates told the would-be hajjis that they were there to try to stop the men from continuing their journey. Tang simply replied that it was the duty of all Muslims to go to Mecca and it would be truly unfortunate if the men detained them after they had come this far.

After a tense interaction, the agents demanded to see the group's travel documents and requested that they go with them to their office. At the office, they photographed the men and told them that their pictures would appear the next day in *Xingzhou Daily*, the Chinese-language Singapore newspaper. According to the agents, this would expose the travelers' identities and their intentions to spread propaganda for the Japanese Empire throughout Asia. These threats didn't intimidate Tang, since their ship would be well into the Indian Ocean by the time the evening edition of the newspaper came out the next day. In the end, the agents returned their travel documents, and the group left the office in search of a halal restaurant.[93] Luckily, their taxi driver was Muslim and he dropped them at a restaurant where everyone was wearing a "red Turkish hat," presumably a fez.[94] They were extremely happy to eat fried rice with lamb, fried bread, barbequed lamb (C. *kaoyangrou*), and spicy beef (C. *laniurou*). Although the food was probably not the Northern Chinese fare they were used to, it was halal, and Tang used the vocabulary at his disposal to describe the dishes.[95]

A few days after leaving Singapore, Tang spotted some islands in the distance. One of the stewards announced that they were arriving in Colombo (C. *Gelunbo*). When the boat steamed into port, Tang remarked that everything was very different and strange looking, and that the local customs and language were completely incomprehensible. This tension between their northern Chinese identity and their identification with the global *umma* becomes most evident when the group encountered Muslims with habits and customs different from their own, like in South Asia and East Africa. In Tang's writing, these differences are regularly mediated through racialist discourse, and the observations of difference between themselves and Muslims from South Asia, East Africa, and the Arabian Peninsula may say more about their "Chineseness" than about their adherence to a universal religion.[96] Coming from China, the men were aware of the influence of Buddhism on Chinese society over the millennia. But on numerous occasions, the cultural differences witnessed by Tang between South Asian Muslims and Chinese Muslims provides a glimpse into the ways Tang and his companions practiced and expressed their religious beliefs and the great difference they saw between their coreligionists and themselves. In Colombo, this difference is expressed most clearly in the group's disgust at the South Asian custom of eating with one's hands.[97] In these encounters, Tang reveals his own lack of cultural relativity and highlights the group's insensitivity to cultural practices different from their own. Throughout his journal, Tang questions the religiosity of people who ate in this unfamiliar way. Having never been anywhere beyond East Asia, instead of viewing the custom of not eating food with his hands as specifically East Asian, Tang assumes that the South Asians he sees eating with their hands are less civilized Muslims. This trope reinforces the deeply embedded racial hierarchies that were essential to the Japanese imperial project.

After the boat sailed from Colombo, another Nationalist operative confronted the men. He asked them about their "mission" and inquired how they felt about leaving *Huabei* when the situation there was so dire. Tang repeated that it was the responsibility of all Muslims to perform hajj. The Nationalist agent then told them he had read about their "mission" in a newspaper and received a cable about their journey from Singapore. He also told Tang and Ma that he worked for the Chinese Foreign Ministry (C. *Zhongguo waijiaobu buyuan*). After hearing this, Tang and Ma quietly excused themselves and the men went their separate ways. The agent disembarked in Mumbai.[98] The well-connected and informed network of agents positioned throughout the overseas-Chinese community in Southeast Asia and the Indian Ocean highlights the organizational aptitude of the Nationalists during the war, something they are not generally recognized for.

Soon after the boat entered the Gulf of Aden, the stewards informed the group that they would be reaching their final destination, Massawa (C. *Masadian gang*). Massawa is an important port city in Eritrea, which was then occupied by the Italians. The area was home to numerous Bedouin tribes who had been subjects of the Ottoman Empire since the sixteenth century. After the completion of the Suez Canal in 1869, the Egyptians, with the help of the British, had ousted the Ottomans from Massawa, briefly bringing the entire region along the eastern shore of the Red Sea under British control. By 1885, the burgeoning Italian Empire made a play for Massawa, which only mildly irritated the British, who were much more concerned with French expansion in North and East Africa than with what they considered to be half-baked Italian attempts at empire-building. However, in 1889, regional power brokers, led by the Ethiopians, entered into the Treaty of Uccialli with the Italians. The treaty ceded parts of Eritrea and Ethiopia to Italy in return for protection against the British. The treaty also allowed Italy to control the foreign affairs of their new East African holdings. Shortly after, the Ethiopians rebelled and expelled the oppressive Italians, leaving Italy with only the small piece of land now known as Eritrea.

In the years leading up to World War II, the Italians invested a lot of money in colonial infrastructure and development in Eritrea, which the Fascists referred to as *colonia primogenita* in comparison to their later acquisitions of Libya and Italian Somaliland. However, the Italians were not able to hold onto their colonial possessions, and by 1941 East Africa was firmly under British control.[99] Despite their short rule in Eritrea, from the descriptions provided by Tang, the Italian military and civilian presence made quite an impression on the region.

After disembarking in Massawa, the group was taken to a holding room in the customs office, since they spoke neither Italian nor what Tang calls the "Abyssinian language." After a few tense hours, Italian special police (C. *yiguo tejing*) escorted the group to their hotel and explained to them in French that they needed to stay in Massawa under medical quarantine. Once an Italian doctor gave them a clean bill of health, they would be able to book passage to Jeddah.[100]

Much like in Colombo, Tang assumes an air of superiority. His extensive commentary about the cultural differences between East African Muslims and Chinese Muslims is steeped in the racialist discourses of the early twentieth century. Tang thought it remarkable to be in a place where there were so many Muslims, but he also found it noteworthy that many of them were black Africans rather than the lighter-skinned Arabs or Egyptians he was expecting to see. At the same time, Tang and his companions also mentioned that they felt very at home in East Africa, knowing that they were among a large number of believers. Although it may seem incongruous, there was no apparent tension for Tang between his racial — and sometimes racist — observations about East Africa and his deep appreciation for being in a place where the majority of the population was Muslim.

The following morning after prayers and breakfast, the group found a car waiting to take them to the Italian hospital. Once cleared for travel, the group purchased tickets for Jeddah. However, when they woke up on

Wednesday morning and were getting ready to board the boat, Ma was visibly ill. Tang convinced Ma to hold himself together, and when people inquired about Ma's state, Tang told them that the extremely hot weather in East Africa was affecting him, which the customs officials seemed to believe.[101] Onboard, they met a cleric from Sudan. They chatted with him in Arabic, and he provided information about his home, which the group found fascinating. As they approached Jeddah, the group took out their new white cloth and leather sandals to prepare themselves for *ihram*. Once cleansed and dressed, Tang commented that it was strange to see everyone wearing white, the color of burial shrouds in China.[102] In some ways, this observation exemplifies just how "Chinese" the group was at a seminal moment on their hajj. It also highlights the variety of Islamic practices, which adapted over time to localities where they took root.

When the group passed through Saudi customs, the customs officer told Tang that the Saudis had been expecting them. The previous day, eighteen Chinese students had arrived from Egypt and alerted the customs officers about the five Sino-Muslims from *Huabei* traveling on the Japanese Empire's dime. Tang describes this event matter-of-factly, turning quickly to his excitement about finally being in Jeddah, the principal gateway to Mecca. However, this is another indication that their movements were being monitored and tracked.[103] Tang and his companions found lodgings and a local guide in Jeddah. After returning from a walk around town with their guide, they received a letter written in Arabic and signed by Ma Jian, Zong Hongqing, Wang Shiqing, and Ma Fuliang. Tang was elated at the possibility of seeing old friends and classmates from North China in Saudi Arabia.[104] He did not know that the men had been sent by the Nationalists to intercept the group and to attempt to dissuade them from their suspected pro-Japanese views.

The Hajj

The group started their morning with a prayer followed by a visit to the Zamzam Well and the Kaaba (C. *ke'erbai*). Finally in Mecca, the holiest site of Islam, Tang lamented that it was hard for them to get close to the Kaaba due to the crowds.[105] After completing seven circuits of the Kaaba, the group decided that they wanted to do it again. So they did! They were able to visit the Kaaba repeatedly during their time in Mecca, indicating that the hajj was not as rigidly prescribed as it is today. Of course, there were fewer pilgrims during the 1930s, but the fluidity and flexibility of their journey contrasts with the very structured contemporary hajj. After visiting the Kaaba, the group left for Mount Arafat (C. *Haxilei shan*) by car. When they stopped in Mina for watermelon and grapes, the shopkeeper mentioned that another group of Chinese pilgrims had been through earlier that day. Tang and his companions were hopeful that they would be reunited with their old friends sometime during their pilgrimage.[106] The fact that the Sino-Muslim pilgrims were highly visible to Arab shopkeepers and customs agents suggests that there were probably few other groups from China on the hajj that year, although some groups of Central Asian Muslims living in Xinjiang had come overland. Tang remarks on the bloodthirsty Arabian mosquitoes and the unhygienic toilets. He prayed that it would not rain because he was concerned that this might cause the latrines to overflow—a worry he returns to a number of times in his journal.[107] The men from Beijing did not feel that the Arabs had high standards of hygiene. This suggests the influence of social conditioning and the sanitation and public health campaigns run in China in the 1920s and 1930s. Perhaps Tang and his companions also emphasized the "backwardness" of Arabs with regards to sanitation and hygiene as evidence that Arabs were being held back by European imperialists.[108] Yet there was no acknowledgment by Tang that these hygiene campaigns had originated in the West and had sprung up in cities like Tianjin and Shanghai where Europeans had a large presence.

Old Friends, Together in Mecca: Meeting Up with the Nationalist-Sponsored Hajjis

After they finally met up with the Nationalist-sponsored Muslim group, Tang describes the emergence of an unlikely new friendship between himself and Ma Fuliang. The two men knew of each other but had not met before their encounter in the Saudi desert. However, after a brief conversation, Tang and Ma realized that they had many mutual acquaintances. Ma Fuliang was in Saudi Arabia waiting for Īsa, the prominent Uyghur who was called from his diplomatic work in Turkey to meet the Nationalist-supported hajj delegation. Like Īsa, Ma was sent abroad by the Nationalists on a diplomatic tour of the Middle East, India, and Southeast Asia during the war. This information was not included in Tang's journal, but it helps demonstrate just how precarious some of these supposed political affiliations were, and how tightly connected these men were to one another.

After spending some time together, Ma asked Tang whether just the five of them were on the hajj or if other people were in their party, perhaps implying that Japanese agents might be accompanying them. Tang denied that there were others and Ma told him a rumor he had heard that five *Huabei* Muslims had been involved in "an incident" in Singapore and had murdered a man in Mumbai. This rumor-mongering by the Nationalist operatives could indicate that they were expected to report on nefarious intentions of Tang's group, but that when they were unable to provide their superiors with factual information, they simply made things up. Regardless, Ma told Tang that after spending time with the men he was sure they were incapable of murder. In his journal, Tang seems happy to have won the trust of their new friends — that is, the Nationalist-sponsored group sent to spy on them. Yet, in his journal, this was likely a way of trying to establish a connection with the Nationalists by stressing his interactions with well-known Nationalist Muslims like Īsa and Ma Fuliang.

The men talked about the latest news and Ma relayed information about a large group of pilgrims from Xinjiang who were supposedly massacred by the Soviets on the Afghan border.[109] However, official British reports dispelled these claims as a wild rumor circulated among anti-British and anti-Soviet Muslims. British colonial officials were less than impressed that the "bogus representatives" sent from Al-Azhar by the Chinese Nationalists were stoking this rumor mill, which the pro-Japanese Muslims then repeated, shared, and published as fact upon their return to China.[110] Ma also explained that very few Turks were permitted to go on hajj that year because of the impending war. He told Tang that normally 30,000 or more Turks would perform hajj, but only a fraction of that number had been granted visas to travel through the Levant in 1938–39 since the British were dealing both with the flight of European Jews to the Holy Lands and the Arab Uprising. Unlike the rumor about the hajjis murdered by Soviet agents, it is true that in 1938–39 the British were denying transit visas through the Levant to the majority of Turks who applied. The British were concerned that an extra 30,000 to 40,000 people traveling through the region would be too much for them to monitor, so they simply told Turks to find another route to Mecca (which some did) or to try again another year. These informal networks of information were key to the ways Muslims got news about their coreligionists; true or not, these stories created a sense of community and camaraderie that, in this case, superseded political loyalties and allegiances.

The following day was Eid al-Adha, the tenth day of the twelfth lunar month (C. *layue*), which marks the beginning of the Festival of Sacrifice. One of the members of the group from Egypt told Tang that he was happy they could share this holy experience. Yet, in the next breath, he questioned

Tang's intentions, asking if the "mission" had any political affiliations. Annoyed by the continuing interrogation of his motives, Tang replied that he found these assumptions both unfair and tedious.[111] Tang's repeated denial of any political allegiance to the Japanese Empire prompted another member of the group to tell him that they had been sent from Egypt with the specific task of communicating frequently with the Chongqing government about Tang and his companions' movements.[112] Apparently shocked by this news, Tang did not know how to respond. Disillusioned, upset, and too tired to walk, the men hired camels to take them back to their hotel.

To celebrate Eid al-Adha, the group bought five sheep to be slaughtered. Tang invited Ma Fuliang and the Sino-Muslim students from Egypt to participate in the ceremony and share some of the mutton from the sacrifice. Over dinner, the conversation turned to tea. Although tea was slightly different everywhere they had been, everyone they encountered drank it. As they enjoyed a characteristically "Chinese" global commodity, political boundaries once again dissolved. Ma Fuliang was excited for the cookout because it had been around three years since he had eaten anything with "Beijing flavor" (C. *Beijing weidao*).[113] This statement is corroborated by one of the nationalist-supported commentaries. Zhang Huaide writes that the Japanese-sponsored hajjis brought their own soy sauce, spices, and oils to cook with, foresight appreciated by everyone who attended the feast.[114] Once again, local identity trumped all else, and Tang's group easily won over the Nationalist supporters with the flavors of their homeland.

Tang's seemingly incongruous views about Arabs and the Middle East need to be unpacked. On the one hand, Tang says that his group was sympathetic to the plight of Muslims living under the yoke of Western imperialism throughout the Middle East. In their many encounters with Arabs, Tang repeatedly notes that Arabs suffered tremendously at the hands of the British and the French. This quite obviously reflects the fascist, anti-imperialist message of the Japanese Empire. On the other hand, Tang expresses his discomfort about the physicality of Arab merchants in Jeddah's markets and bookstores. Tang is also shocked by the lack of theological texts available in the bookstores. These observations lead him to reflect on his time in Saudi Arabia. He expresses the need for an intellectual revival in the region, which he feels is indicated by the lack of theological texts and what he imagines to the uncivilized behavior of Arab merchants. His views also diverge from the experiences of other Sino-Muslim hajjis, such as Hu Songshan, who found himself discriminated against, not because he was Muslim but because he was Chinese.[115]

In the vocabulary of his benefactors, Tang explains that Arabs needed to throw off their colonial oppressors and reawaken, since they are the progenitors of the most glorious religion, followed by more than 300 million people worldwide.[116] This familiar rhetoric echoes the Japanese anti-imperialist discourse in East Asia in the late 1930s and early 1940s. Beyond that, however, he presents Arabs as a mirror for Sino-Muslims, whom he sees as distinct and separate from Arabs, and in many ways more civilized. This jockeying for cultural and civilizational superiority presents a complicated picture of how Tang understood himself in relation to the Muslims he and his group met on their journey.

Homeward Bound

As he prepared to leave Mecca, Tang confessed that he was happy he would never have to ride a camel again, which he complained was way more trouble than it was worth (C. *tai mafan le*).[117] Of course, Tang would have been familiar with camels, which were commonly seen in markets around Beijing, but he may not have ever ridden one until he arrived in Arabia.[118] Although banal, these quotidian details provide insights into Tang's character and into the variety of experiences the group had on their journey. While they waited for their boat in Jeddah, they visited the Chinese Guild Hall (C. *Zhongguo huiguan*) established a few years before by a Gansu Muslim, Ma Shaoyun. Tang explained that Ma had originally planned to build a Hezhou Guild Hall (C. *Hezhou huiguan*) in Jeddah but that not enough people from Hezhou went on hajj, so he named it the Chinese Guild Hall instead.[119] Tang's comments help contextualize the broad reach of native-place associations, not just for Han Chinese but also for Sino-Muslims traveling abroad in an era of increasing worldwide travel. In some ways, Sino-Muslims shared more in common with Han Chinese than they did with non-Chinese Muslims, at least in terms of the cultural fabric and social institutions common among overseas Chinese communities around the world.

Initially, the group had trouble getting passage back to Eritrea. Although plenty of boats moved through the Red Sea, they were full of Italian army officers traveling to East Africa or Jews and other groups fleeing Germany and Eastern Europe on whatever vessels would take them.[120] They finally departed the day before the Chinese Lunar New Year. The group celebrated by drinking coffee and barbequing a fish that they caught off the stern of the boat. With a few days to spare in Massawa, the men managed to track down all the ingredients needed to make dumplings (C. *bao jiaozi*) and celebrate the Lunar New Year. This small gesture of spending an evening cooking together further reminds us that although Tang and his companions were devout and pious Muslims, they were also active participants in distinctly East Asian rituals. The group spent the evening recreating a comforting and familiar atmosphere far from their homes and families.

The first thing the group did after arriving back in Shanghai was go to a halal restaurant. The restaurateurs were apparently shocked by how much food the men consumed, but Tang explained that it had been more than two months since they had eaten "real" Chinese food.[121] The following morning Ma went to buy the boat tickets to Qingdao while Tang and Su headed to the market near the Hongkou Bridge to get provisions for the trip. When they arrived at the Hongkou Bridge, they were stopped by a Japanese soldier who asked them in Chinese what they were doing there. Tang's explanation that they were buying provisions for their boat ride to Qingdao seemed to satisfy the soldier.[122] The tense encounters with the Japanese soldiers highlight that although the men had accepted Japanese money to fund their pilgrimage, this did not diminish the anxiety the Japanese military presence could inspire in them.[123] After almost three months of traveling, Tang and his companions arrived back in Beijing. The first thing they did after greeting their families was head to their favorite halal restaurant on Oxen Street for a steaming bowl of Beijing-style beef noodle soup.

Tang's Afterthoughts and Conclusions

The journey broadened Tang's knowledge and understanding of the variety of Islamic practices in South Asia, East Africa, and the Middle East. The increasingly frequent circulations of Muslims facilitated dialogue among Muslims and contributed to the creation of a larger, more integrated, and global understanding of what it meant to be a Muslim during the war.[124] Tang was never shy about questioning the motives or even the religiosity of the Arab, African, and South Asian Muslims he encountered based on what he deemed to be religiously inappropriate behavior. Yet, in the end, he completed one of the pillars of Islam surrounded by Muslims from all over the world, sharing this deeply religious experience with them. It is also important to remember that long after the end of the Japanese Empire, Tang and his friends were still hajjis in the eyes of their local community and the global *umma*.

In his concluding remarks, Tang offers readers insights into his group's journey. Once again, relying on the vocabulary of his occupiers, Tang blamed the British for the majority of the obstacles the group encountered during their hajj.[125] Tang used the initial British refusal of their hajj visas to launch a polemic critique of British policies toward Muslims throughout the British Empire. Tang said the British had quashed the dreams of Muslims all over the world by preventing them from completing hajj. Tang urged his readers to support groups who resisted the British, like the Balochis in Afghanistan. At the same time, Tang added a paternalistic twist to his argument about Baluchistan. For him, the Balochis were much worse off than Muslims from North China and therefore deserving of help in their fight against the British.[126] Tang positions himself somewhere between the Japanese and Afghans in the hierarchy of the Japanese imperial project, with the latter below him. Once again, Tang's own writings about Muslims reinforced the deeply embedded social order of the Japanese Empire and also included Muslims living *beyond* the empire in the imperial imagination.

Tang also reflected on the different ways people practiced Islam in the places they visited. Tang recognized that a religion as widespread as Islam was not static, unchanging, or monolithic. As Tang saw it, the elapsed time and the immense geographic space of the *dar-al-Islam* manifested in diverse expressions of the Islamic faith. In his journal, he dwells on these markers of difference, such as Indian and East African Muslims eating with their hands.[127] But Tang's objective was to get Muslims around the world to rise up against Western imperialists and the Soviet communists. In his view, the British and the Soviets were oppressing Muslims and denying them the right to fulfill their fundamental religious obligations, while the Japanese Empire was providing Muslims with the support that they needed.

Focusing on the specific moment when this journey was possible and the five Sino-Muslims who accepted Japanese funds to complete hajj reveals some of the ways minorities in wartime China acted as political intermediaries, influenced policy decisions, and made tactical political moves for both the Nationalists and the Japanese Empire. Looking at larger patterns of increased interactions between the Nationalists and the Allied powers, the Japanese Empire and their fascist allies, and Sino-Muslims provides an important global perspective. Yet Tang's journal also supplements this story of geopolitical wartime maneuvering and offers a bridge to the quotidian trials of performing hajj in the 1930s. The reality is that both the Nationalist- and the Japanese-sponsored hajj were overtly political, and all the men who participated were sponsored by their respective benefactors. That their strong and shared local identity regularly trumped any affiliation with the Chinese nation-state or the Japanese Empire is a testament to the malleability of political loyalties. We should never lose sight of the fact that in between the Axis and Allies political maneuverings for the hearts and minds of Muslims around the world were Muslims themselves.

What is also clear is that by the 1930s, the role that Sino-Muslims played in influencing domestic policy and international politics was disproportionate to their small numbers in the Chinese population.[128] Knowing how much was at stake in their dealings with Muslims, the Axis and the Allies were more likely to cater to them. The Japanese government financed Tang and his companions' hajj as a relatively cheap and easy way to gain supporters among Muslims around the world. Questioning whether or not the Japanese Empire's efforts were entirely successful misses the point: the Asian ally of the Nazis and the Italian Fascists was mobilizing Muslims from East Asia in ways similar to what their European counterparts were attempting in North Africa, the Balkans, and the Middle East. As Tang's hajj demonstrates, the war with Japan also precipitated more aggressive Nationalist recruitment and alignment campaigns among Muslim populations in China, as well as Nationalist leaders' increased recognition of the diplomatic potential of engaging Sino-Muslims to create ties with countries that were either predominantly Muslim or had sizable Muslim populations. Just how the Japanese Empire planned to use Sino-Muslims to foster linkages with Muslims around the world and to bolster its connections with the other Axis powers is the focus of this book's two remaining chapters.

4

DEPLOYING ISLAM

Sino-Muslims and Japan's Aspirational Empire

By 1942, U.S. observers in China noted that the Japanese government had exerted a "vast amount of propaganda energy" to recruit Sino-Muslims. These efforts were meant to "induce" Sino-Muslims, "as part of a larger Islamic world, to join in the cherished Japanese scheme of hegemony over Greater East Asia," and to support "separatist tendencies in the Muslim minority groups" throughout China's vast borderlands.[1] But these ambitious plans did not end at the edges of Greater East Asia.[2] This chapter places Japanese imperial objectives concerning Islam and Sino-Muslims living under occupation in the larger currents of fascist efforts to subvert capitalism, colonialism, and Soviet Communism during World War II. The chapter takes Japanese imperial aspirations to enter new, predominantly Muslim markets as a springboard for examining a number of specific cases where members of the Greater Japan Muslim League envisioned Sino-Muslims playing a key role in the convergences and interactions between Japan's Islamic policy on the mainland and its broader, long-term policies for the maintenance and expansion of empire. In these plans, Sino-Muslims were the linchpin in Japan's overtures to Muslims around the world, and they were always presented as a necessary component of Japan's attempts to undermine the Allies.

After Pearl Harbor, regions with large Muslim populations, such as the Philippines and Burma, and regions with majority Muslim populations, like the Dutch East Indies and British Malaya, came under Japanese control. However, the plans to use Sino-Muslims throughout Japan's expanding empire were in the works long before the occupation of Southeast Asia. In a secret report published in 1939, the Greater Japan Muslim League emphasized the important relationship between the economy, Muslims, and the

South Seas (J. *Nanyō*). The report highlighted *Nanyō* as a region about the same size as China with a large, untapped market of would-be Muslim consumers.[3] To gain access to these markets, the Greater Japan Muslim League suggested that the government promote the successful results of its development campaigns among Sino-Muslim populations living in Manchukuo.[4] Furthermore, assisting Muslims in their nationalist campaigns against the Dutch and the British throughout the region would lead Muslims to buy Japanese goods, ensuring that capital and resources would remain in the region.[5] Sino-Muslims were meant to serve as the empire's ambassadors to Muslims around the globe, starting in Southeast Asia. By shifting the focus to Muslims living throughout the Greater East Asia Co-Prosperity Sphere and to expanding markets throughout Asia, North Africa, and the Middle East, it becomes clear just how important Sino-Muslims were to Japan's aspirations for empire. In the end, of course, these plans failed, as resources were diverted to protecting the home islands and imperial Japan was eventually defeated. However, putting these plans into perspective provides insight into the seminal and significant role members of the Greater Japan Muslim League imagined Muslims would play in the maintenance of empire had Japan won the war.

Interactions between the Japanese Empire and Muslims throughout Asia were varied, characterized by both cooperation and conflict. In their adamant denial that they were themselves a colonial power, Japanese imperialists deployed strong anti-Western and anti-Soviet propaganda that appealed to anticolonial Muslim nationalist sentiments. In these tropes, the Japanese Empire and the "Islamic world" were presented as simultaneously experiencing a revival. Only through a deeper understanding of each other's cultures, customs, and beliefs could they join together and defeat their common enemies.[6] This plea for mutual cultural revival and understanding went hand in hand with Japan's search for new markets and its continued efforts to undermine capital flows emanating from the North Atlantic. Although historians tend to focus on "connections and convergences," paying attention to the "disruptions and displacements" of both capital and people provides new insights into wartime history.[7] From this perspective, the Axis economic bloc — and in this case, the Japanese Empire in particular — successfully challenged the global capitalist world order through the creation of new markets made available by wartime instability.[8]

Once again, these overtures did not go unnoticed by the Chinese Nationalists, who explicitly stated in policy reports that "Japan's Muslim policy" had started in Manchukuo and after 1941 was replicated and implemented in other parts of the empire. According to the Nationalists, the Japanese used a "carrot and stick" (C. *enwei bingyong*) approach to lure Muslims to their side. By the Nationalists' own accounts, these policies seemed to be working, as Muslims throughout Asia became increasingly active participants in Japan's "international Muslim conspiracy."[9] Nationalist-supported Sino-Muslim Yang Jingzhi even described the Japanese Imperial Army as "fomenting coups" (C. *yunniang zhengbian*) and "launching serious incidents" (C. *fadong feichang shijian*) in Muslim-majority and Muslim-minority places throughout Asia.[10] This claim might be a bit of a stretch, however, since the only successful precedent Yang could provide as evidence was the Japanese-facilitated coup in Thailand (where there is a small Muslim population along the border with present-day Malaysia).

Perhaps Yang's claims served more as a warning of what could happen if the Chinese Nationalists did not increase their diplomatic engagement with Muslims around the globe.[11] To drive his point home, Yang relayed some personal experiences from his travels through occupied China. He describes an incident where an older cleric was publicly shamed for speaking out against the Japanese occupation. The cleric taught at a Muslim school that came under Japanese control but was fired after making an anti-Japanese statement in public to Japanese officers and onlookers. He apparently said something to the effect that Muslims in China would never be convinced that the Japanese Empire supported Islam. According to Yang, the old man then presented the Japanese officers with an ultimatum: "If you want to kill me, just kill me, but I will not say that I agree with you or what you are doing."[12] For Yang, this was proof that some Muslims living under occupation were actively resisting the Japanese and were willing to die for what they believed in.

Yang went on to urge the Nationalists to consider the fate not only of Muslims in Free China but also of Muslims living under occupation throughout the Japanese Empire. His plea was meant to strengthen resistance against the Japanese occupation, and to increase the Chinese Nationalist backing of Muslims beyond China in their propaganda war against the Japanese Empire. In their campaign to subvert Western imperialism, the Nationalists noted that "Japan's Muslim policy" was directly tied to the establishment of economic opportunities for the Japanese Empire, and to finding ways to increase imports to and exports from predominantly Muslim regions.[13] Here, once again, it seems that the Nationalists' effort to engage with Muslims was a direct response to imperial Japan's efforts to undermine the Nationalists' allies.

Inserting Sino-Muslims into Visions for a Greater East Asia

Fascism offered an alternate path to "overcome the crisis of capitalism and resolve the problems of class conflict and authority in modern industrial society."[14] Through cooperation and a shared vision of a world free of Western domination, the technocrats of the Japanese Empire were able to exert influence on policy and its implementation in Manchukuo in ways that went beyond their capabilities on the home islands.[15] For Janis Mimura, the Greater East Asia Co-Prosperity Sphere was a "complex ideological matrix" that "fused" different strands of ideology which were both widely appealing and pragmatic in their management of empire.[16] In this respect, the well-coordinated policies involving the potential deployment of Sino-Muslims as intermediaries between the Japanese Empire and the far-flung Muslim-dominated regions of the world for economic gain are completely reasonable.

The amount of intellectual energy invested in understanding the people living in the Japanese Empire was immense and should not be reduced to simply "a problem of Japanese chauvinism or duplicity."[17] Whittling down Japanese imperial aspirations to pure conceit misses the crucial point that colonized peoples around the world aspired to create economies free from Western intervention.[18] This provides a catalyst for investigating how Japanese bureaucrats imagined the future of Asia refracted through Sino-Muslim intermediaries and then projected that future outward from Manchukuo to their plans and visions beyond Greater East Asia. As the war went on, the Greater Japan Muslim League helped Japanese officials articulate a clearer vision for the role they imagined Muslims living under occupation playing in Japan's visions for Asia.[19]

In fact, research published in Japanese often mentions that Muslims from China would be useful for creating a larger, more coherent, global religious policy.[20] In the third installment of the 1938 volume of the Japanese journal *Islam*, a short introductory article about Muslims in China is followed by a longer essay about South Asia's Muslims (J. *Ajia nanpō no kaikyōto*) and Southeast Asia's Muslims (J. *Nanyō kaikyōto*). The thread that ties these articles together is Sino-Muslims. Both articles begin by explaining the contentious relationship between Western powers (J. *rekkyō*) and Islam, but only after lauding Japanese efforts to help Muslim populations in China free themselves from the oppressive clutches of Chiang Kai-shek's Western-backed regime.[21] Drawing connections and parallels between the different experiences of Muslims around the world flattens specific and individualized experiences with colonial encounters, yet at the same time, it helped create a sense of commonality between Muslims who likely had vastly different lived experiences. Through the example of Sino-Muslims, Japanese policymakers were offering an aspirational and attainable model to Muslims around the world.

Muslims from China were also integral to the ways Japanese intellectuals projected their visions for a Greater East Asia. Articles about Islam published in Japan were sprinkled with statistics and offered evidence of just how important Muslims—and particularly Muslims in China—were to Japan's larger imperial aims.[22] By drawing attention to Pan-Islamism and Islamic movements in the post–World War I era, these narratives attempted to connect Sino-Muslims to global political trends of national self-determination and freedom from colonial oppression.[23] Although Japanese intellectuals wrote about Pan-Islamism, the Japanese imperial government never promoted a specifically "pan-Islamic" ideology. It did, however, "assume the existence of a global community of Muslims, joined by a common faith[, who were] inherently interested in the plight of their co-religionists many thousands of miles away."[24] On a more pragmatic level, members of the Greater Japan Muslim League had collected large quantities of data about Muslim communities throughout Southeast Asia. When the plans for the Greater East Asia Co-Prosperity Sphere were put into place, the Japanese government recognized the need to more closely align the goals of these researchers with its larger imperial aspirations.[25] The policies that had been implemented on the mainland and among the Muslim community in Manchukuo (J. *Manchukuo no kaikyōto*) were used to highlight the emancipatory powers of the Japanese Empire with regards to Muslims.[26] Here, Pan-Islamism and Pan-Asianism overlapped at a shared point: Sino-Muslims.

At the same time, it is important to remember that Islam and Muslims were never central to imperial Japan's policy initiatives and decision making. The position of Muslims in the periphery of policymaking and the lives of regular Japanese subjects is seen in descriptive articles published in popular Japanese monthlies, like *Japan and Japanese People*. Faraway places like the Philippines and the Dutch East Indies were presented to Japanese subjects on the home islands, and in many instances Islam was inserted as an afterthought or an add-on.[27] In the Philippines, where the majority of the population is Roman Catholic, Japanese policymakers relied on the Spanish-speaking Catholic elites to provide information about the Moro, a Muslim population who resisted conversion by the Spanish and lived in the southern islands, close to the Sultanate of Borneo. In one particular instance, a

Filipino author explained to Japanese readers on the home islands how the Moro had converted to Islam, but his discussion is framed by their ongoing resistance to Catholicism. This negative presentation of the Moro gave the Filipino author a segue into his argument that the Moro in particular would benefit from the goodwill of the Japanese Empire.[28] This outlook is perhaps emblematic of the overall attitudes of most Japanese bureaucrats and Japanese subjects toward Islam: Muslims were an afterthought, only important if they could be placed within the framework of Japan's larger imperial ambitions.

Yet this space on the margins of empire provides new insights into the operations and aspirations of the Japanese imperial project. What is clear is that even if Islam was not central in the minds of all the policymakers and Japanese subjects living on the home islands, a devoted group of Japanese imperialists and scholars were adamant about emphasizing their efforts to win the support of Muslims from North China to the rest of the world. These efforts were intended to create strong cultural and economic ties to regions with predominantly Muslim populations. How—and why—this was achieved is the focus of the rest of this chapter.

Going Both Ways: Japanese Muslims Abroad and Muslim Visitors to Japan

Both Pan-Islamism and Pan-Asianism are transnational ideologies, and beyond simply being reactions to Western imperialism and Soviet Communism, they gave disenfranchised peoples an aspirational ideal for a new world order. Wartime Tokyo was at the intersection of these two ideologies. Pan-alternatives were not purely an effect of the world order imposed by Western colonial powers; they were also a way for people to reconceptualize the interregional relationships between ethnicities and groups of people that long predated Western colonial incursions throughout Asia and the Middle East.[29] The "theoretical elasticity" of both Pan-Asianism and Pan-Islamism made them broadly appealing and inclusive enough for many of those trying to figure out their place in the world during the war.[30] In the bustling metropolis, Muslims from all over the world were provided with financial aid from the Japanese Empire, and they met to learn, discuss, and debate the common issues they were facing at home.[31] The Japanese government gave Sino-Muslims the freedom to operate between their local communities and global Islamic movements.[32] The war gave Muslims the opportunity to imagine a postcolonial world, and Muslims throughout Asia figured out how to bridge their own local concerns with the concerns of Muslims around the world.

The simple fact was that there were hundreds of millions of Muslims in *Nanyō*, and the Japanese government believed that governing Muslims required a distinct policy to ensure that they did not turn to the Soviet Union in their anti-imperial struggles. In certain places, the government acknowledged that they needed to take countermeasures against communist successes at winning over Muslims in *Nanyō*, and that there was a need for a direct and well-coordinated policy for Muslims who had fallen under the influence of the Comintern or who had developed communist sympathies.[33] In order to combat these sympathies, Japanese scholar Suzuki Tomihide suggested that the Japanese foster pan-Islamic sentiments and help connect Muslims throughout *Nanyō* to the larger community of believers. Suzuki imagined that this would enable Muslims in *Nanyō* to fully realize that they were oppressed by both the Soviets and the Western imperialists.[34] Only through the promotion of a sense of community among Muslims around the world would the Japanese Empire be able to develop countermeasures (J. *taisaku*) to help Muslims free themselves from these forces holding them back.[35]

Efforts to examine the strands of imperial policies directed at Islam unspooling from North China throughout the empire provides an opportunity to move past treating the Japanese imperial project as a set of discrete encounters between colonial officials and the army with individual states or specific colonies. Treating Japan's attitude and policies toward Muslims holistically rather than as parts of a fragmented whole helps to reterritorialize Japanese imperial space. When we place Muslims at the center of Japanese imperial visions for a Greater East Asia, we maintain that Japanese imperial space was bounded not by colonial borders but rather by commonalities such as an imagined shared history, a long record of diplomatic relations, trade, and, later, the notion of a common destiny.[36] When Muslims become the focus of grand visions for a Greater East Asia, it also becomes clear that the Middle East, North Africa, Central Asia, and South Asia were seminal to the projection of Japanese imperial space and the untapped potential for empire. As the Japanese imperial project looked for new markets in predominantly Muslim places, the Japanese backed up their plans with references to reform, religious inclusion, and freedom from Western domination, all essential parts of both Pan-Asian and Pan-Islamic discourses *and* approaches they had tested out in Sino-Muslim communities.

When Japanese Muslim Suzuki Takeshi published a memoir about his hajj, he used the platform as an attempt to clarify and amplify the few tenuous connections between the "Islamic world" and the handful of Muslim Japanese. In line with imperial orthodoxy, Suzuki argued that the fact Japanese Muslims were few in number was inconsequential given that everyone who lived within the Japanese Empire was an imperial subject (J. *kokumin*).[37] Suzuki presented the Japanese Empire as a bastion of religious freedom and expression, where Muslims were free to practice Islam as they pleased.[38] Beyond ideology and religious tolerance, the underlying importance of commercial links between the Middle East and Japan was not lost on Suzuki. As knowledge about Islam and Middle Eastern culture expanded throughout the Japanese Empire, Suzuki suggested in the introduction to his published hajj journal that manufacturers begin making commercial products specifically for Muslim markets. He explained the Islamic concepts of halal and haram, and helpfully informed his readers that alcohol and pork products should be avoided in all entrepreneurial engagements with Muslims. This cultural sensitivity and knowledge about their expanding consumer base was supposed to be useful for strategists who planned to export everything from tea to rubber to tapioca to Muslim consumers as the Japanese Empire looked for new markets for the natural and manufactured resources circulating in its imperial space. Suzuki's personal proposal was to sell water bottles printed with Japanese motifs (such as cherry blossoms and pagodas) to Muslim merchants for long journeys through arid deserts.[39] For Suzuki, the Japanese Empire had an opportunity to deepen its commercial ties with the Middle East by fostering cultural ones, and this meant that the Japanese needed to be supporters of Islam who were sensitive to the specific religious needs of Muslims.

Around the same time that Suzuki was on his hajj, prominent Muslims from around the world were invited to Japan and Manchukuo by Japanese military advisers to observe the treatment of Muslims living in the Japanese Empire. In 1938, one account of these visits was translated into Japanese from Arabic and published in a Japanese journal.[40] Yahia Abdul Mesa was born in the Hejaz (J. *Hijāzu*) and later studied in Italy. Mesa stayed in Japan for six months and attended the opening of the Tokyo Mosque. At first, Mesa found there to be little in common between Japan and the Middle East.[41] However, over time, he began to appreciate the similarities between Japanese and Middle Eastern Islamic cultural mores. Although he acknowledged that there were important differences between Muslims from the Middle East and Japanese people, he explained that he came to see Asian people (J. *tōyōjin*) as much more compassionate and tolerant than Western-ers.[42] After talking with Japanese people and traveling around Japan, Mesa felt that the Middle East had a lot to learn from the Japanese and considered the country a strong ally.[43]

At this point, Mesa's analysis and observations turned to Muslims in China. After a brief description of the tensions between China and Japan, he stated that he had no reason to believe that the Japanese Empire had any ill intent toward Muslims because of its continued support of Sino-Muslim populations on the mainland.[44] According to Mesa, Western powers sug-gested that the Japanese Empire harbored malice toward Muslims because the British and the Soviets had their own aspirations on the mainland. The Japanese Empire was adamant about building a New Asia (J. *shin Ajia kense-tsu*), and Sino-Muslims were an integral part of this vision.[45] In his writings, Mesa also used Sino-Muslims to express how Middle Easterners like himself were aware of Japanese outreach to Muslims. Using the language of his bene-factors, Mesa highlights just how integral Sino-Muslims were to the expan-sion and maintenance of imperial Japanese connections to Muslims around the world. Suzuki and Mesa are just two men who were part of these larger networks of globally minded individuals traveling around the world during the war. They understood their surroundings and spoke about the Japanese Empire and Muslims beyond East Asia as being both interconnected and dependent on each other.

Practical Applications, Part I: Sino-Muslims and the Formation of the Idea of the Greater East Asia Co-Prosperity Sphere

Although the Japanese occupation of Southeast Asia was uneven and did not last as long as the occupation of North China, it was not inconsequen-tial. Since the end of the war, scholars have debated how much the Japanese occupation influenced the minds and psyches of the people in the places they occupied.[46] After Pearl Harbor, as Japanese imperialists asserted more direct control over the region, they appealed to anticolonial nationals, many of them Muslim, who had been ostracized in the region's Dutch, French, and British colonial possessions.[47] When we focus on Japan's Islamic policies and place the occupation of Southeast Asia in the broader context of Japanese imperialism in the Pacific, it becomes clear that imperial Japan used and ex-trapolated lessons from North China in its governance of new regions with large or predominantly Muslim populations that came under its control after

Pearl Harbor. Japanese bureaucrats who had honed their skills on the mainland were deployed throughout Southeast Asia, where they adapted the lessons they had learned in China to different local contexts.[48]

By 1941, there was a pressing need to articulate a clearer policy with regards to Muslims, and when Japanese imperial officials visited places like Borneo and the Philippines they framed their experiences with Sino-Muslims as a model that could be adapted and used in these places.[49] For example, in Borneo, Japanese military officials observed that the majority of the population was Muslim, but according to officials who visited the small sultanate between Malaya and the Philippines, the country was less developed than many parts of North China. When the officials approached Muslim students in Borneo about the possibility of traveling to Tokyo to study, a number of them jumped at the opportunity. The Greater Japan Muslim League told Borneans that studying in Tokyo would give them the opportunity to meet and interact with other Muslims from places like Manchukuo, where Muslims had been under Japanese tutelage for several years. In turn, these Muslims could take what they learned from the Sino-Muslims and others living and studying in Tokyo, and help Borneo develop along the lines of Manchukuo.[50] Here, Sino-Muslims were presented as both an aspirational and attainable model for Muslims coming under Japanese control throughout the growing empire.

The occupied-Dutch East Indies also provided a place to implement policies that had been initiated in North China. Even though the Japanese occupation of the region now known as Indonesia was relatively short, it had a profound impact.[51] After the Netherlands surrendered to the Nazis in May 1940, the Germans informed Tokyo that they were "not interested in the problem of the Netherlands East Indies," which the Japanese took as carte blanche to coordinate an attack on the archipelago. Six months later, the cabinet of Prime Minister Prince Fumimaro Konoe approved a fifteen-point plan to stimulate economic and social development in the region. However, the Japanese Empire was exerting both political and economic pressure on the Dutch East Indies long before this.[52] Historian Satō Shigeru maintains that putting the Japanese occupation of the Dutch East Indies into a longer perspective rather than treating it as a disruptive interregnum offers more insights into the impact of the occupation on the economic, social, and political life of the archipelago's inhabitants.[53] Aiko Inomata Kurasawa also characterizes the Japanese policies in Java in particular as a "combination of control and mobilization," which had a profound and lasting impact on the region.[54]

Sino-Muslims and Japan's Aspirational Empire

Javanese youth at a botanical garden, 1937.
(Greater Japan Muslim League database, Waseda
University Library Special Collections)

After the Japanese military occupied Java and Sumatra beginning in March 1942, some of the first bureaucrats to arrive were experts trained in Islamic studies.[55] Japanese colonial officials also quickly recruited the handful of Japanese Muslims who were living on Java to help them with their operations.[56] After its experiences in North China, the Japanese government noted that "Islam appeared to be a powerful force which could be utilized for the realization of [Japan's] aims in Indonesia."[57] It was understood in Japanese policy and military circles that for the occupation to succeed with the few numbers of troops expected to be stationed on Java and Sumatra, the support of local Muslims, as well as of Muslim organizations and associations, would be essential.[58]

In the Dutch East Indies, the Japanese occupying forces implemented a number of policies specifically directed at Muslims. The introduction to the reprint of the 1943 secret Japanese military document *Survey on the Situation of Islam in Java* explains that although the Japanese policies toward Islam in Java had a lasting impact on the social and political fabric of Indonesia, they also involved a lot "of rather hasty information gathering and make-shift policy making."[59] The sixteen-chapter secret report covers topics ranging from the history of Islam in the archipelago to the ways Islam was practiced on Java, to surveys of Islamic organizations and schools. It also contains lists of hajjis and Javanese who had studied at Al-Azhar in Egypt, followed by a section about the relationship between Muslims from the archipelago and Muslims around the world.[60] In many ways, these documents mirrored the compilations of information about Muslims in North China and were intended to provide the occupying forces with necessary information about an unfamiliar population.

What is particularly noteworthy in this instance is the reliance on Dutch colonial data collection, and the wholesale reproduction of these data by Japanese imperial officials without any interrogation of the information or methods of collection.[61] For instance, Dutch statistics tell a particular story about the monitoring and maintenance of hajj by Dutch imperial officials over a sixty-year period. From 1879, when the Dutch started collecting data on hajjis, until the beginning of the twentieth century, the number of hajjis appears to have remained relatively stable. The numbers began to increase in the lead-up to World War I but, like in other parts of the world, they declined drastically after 1914. Numbers picked up gradually after World War I but were impacted again by the Great Depression. When war broke out in Europe, the Dutch stopped all pilgrimage from the colony.[62]

It is important to remember that these are official colonial statistics, and that others likely performed hajj on their own, circumventing the legal roadblocks imposed by the colonial state. The main point, however, is that these data tell an important story about global geopolitics and were produced in a specific context for use by the Dutch to maintain control over colonial subjects in colonial spaces. For all of their anti-Western, anti-imperial rhetoric, the Japanese government simply replicated and reproduced these data because they served the needs of Japan's own imperial project and helped to reinforce Japanese objectives regarding how to manage Muslim populations. In many ways, this reliance on Dutch data says more about the similarities between colonial monitoring apparatuses than about differences between the imperial enterprises of the Axis and the Allies.

Another tactic the occupying Japanese forces used in Java was the mobilization of Muslim leaders. Clerics were courted and entrusted with disseminating propaganda to their congregations, and held responsible for the actions of their worshippers.[63] This was a direct departure from Dutch policies, which had generally tried to avoid relying on indigenous religious elites.

With the help of local clerics and Muslim elites in the archipelago, the Japanese military deployed its plans to "grasp people's minds" (J. *minshin hāku*) and to "indoctrinate and tame" (J. *senbu kōsaku*) the locals through propaganda.[64] Because the majority of the population was illiterate, getting clerics to disseminate their messages was considered a successful propaganda tactic on Java and Sumatra.

The Japanese military also reached out to Indonesian nationalists who had been exiled or ostracized by the Dutch, and anti-Dutch sentiment among younger, nationalistic Muslims was "allowed to flourish" in the starkly anti-Western environment.[65] In the end, the Japanese government was partially responsible for ushering in a new generation of Muslim leadership by putting the future leaders of postcolonial Indonesia like Sukarno, Mohammad Hatta, and Dewantara into positions of prominence.[66] Sukarno and Hatta were skeptical of imperial Japan and outspoken critics of the Japanese invasion of Manchuria, but they quickly got swept up in the politics surrounding the decisive Japanese defeat of the Dutch.[67] Sukarno, the future president of postcolonial Indonesia, got his first real break during the Japanese occupation.[68] The Japanese government had been courting Hatta, who would become the first vice president of Indonesia under Sukarno, since the early 1930s. Hatta first visited Japan in 1933 as a guest of the Asia Association, although he never fully embraced Japan like other anticolonial leaders.[69] In 1935, he was exiled to a remote island in the archipelago for anti-Dutch agitation, but he was one of the first people rehabilitated after the Japanese arrived to "liberate" the islands. Like Sukarno, Hatta was given a position of prominence as adviser to the occupation government. Although Japanese bureaucrats likely knew about his anti-Japanese sentiments, his prominence made him indispensable to the occupation, and he was treated very well after his return from exile.[70]

At an event held in Batavia in April 1943 to celebrate the birthday of Emperor Hirohito, Sukarno was one of the invited guest speakers. To mark the occasion, Sukarno praised the Japanese as liberators and vowed to support the Japanese Empire in its efforts to defeat Western imperialism.[71] Later the same year, Sukarno and Hatta traveled to Japan to participate in the Greater East Asia Conference, and their efforts in resisting Dutch colonialism were rewarded by the emperor. While in Japan, Sukarno and Hatta also had an audience with General Hideki Tōjō, in which they implored him to expedite Indonesian independence, but the Indonesian delegation left dejected.[72] This younger generation of Muslims were useful to the Japanese for two reasons: unlike their elders, they had not been educated in Europe;

and they were ardent anticolonial nationalists.[73] Under the guidance of the Japanese, these anticolonial Muslim youth leaders "gained experience in administration, political organization and military affairs," which they carried over into the postwar era.[74]

As in their interactions with Sino-Muslim communities within the Japanese Empire, nationalist Muslims living throughout *Nanyō* were active agents with their own objectives and not simply passive victims of Japanese imperialism.[75] Men like Sukarno and Hatta capitalized on the occupation, and among the most well-known Southeast Asian collaborators "most were pragmatists and were simply concerned with their own survival and advancing whatever their nationalist causes were."[76] In China, collaborators were marked as traitors who had betrayed the vision for the nation, and like in France, they became easy scapegoats for the plethora of problems that plagued China after World War II. In other parts of Southeast Asia, however, collaborators fared much better than their Sino-Muslim brothers in co-prosperity, and men like Sukarno quickly recast themselves as liberators from Western imperialism in the early postwar years.[77]

It was the Japanese, not the Dutch or the British, who privileged mixing Islam and politics throughout Southeast Asia, and this had a lasting impact on the region.[78] By undermining the Dutch in order to privilege young Muslim Indonesian nationalists like Sukarno and Hatta, the Japanese helped create a new generation of power brokers in Southeast Asian politics that would outlast their short rule.[79] The occupation government worked hard to "present itself as one with Java's majority religion," and "Muslims in Batavia were treated to Japanese public pledges," promising religious freedom and espousing kinship with the Prophet.[80] Yet these promises were often seen as incongruous with what were perceived as fundamental mistakes in understanding the specificities of Islamic practices in the archipelago, and with the ongoing violence inflicted on locals by the Japanese military.[81] As Muslim leaders grappled with the deep contradictions of Japanese rule, they began to use their newfound voices to promote anticolonial Indonesian nationalist movements.[82] Like the Sino-Muslims who hedged their bets and supported the Japanese Empire, Muslim reformers in Indonesia made decisions based on what they thought was best for themselves and their future.[83] In working with the Japanese Empire, men like Sukarno and Hatta had their own purposes in mind, principally to give their anticolonial movements momentum.[84]

In Malaya, the Japanese military faced much more opposition to its rule. The occupation of Malaya highlights some of the variations of Japanese colonial rule throughout the empire with regards to the management of Muslims. During the four-year occupation, the local population was completely and brutally mobilized to support the Japanese wartime economy. Muslims had initially looked to imperial Japan as a potential liberating force from British imperialism, and, like in the Dutch East Indies, the Japanese Empire had started campaigns to disrupt the British presence on the peninsula in the late 1930s by funding of anti-British Malaya nationalists and the Malaya Muslim Youth League.[85] Other organizations were also founded with Japanese support, such as the Kesatuan Melayu Muda (League of Malay Youth), which was started by Malayan journalist Ibrahim bin Haji Yaacoob (1911–79).[86]

However, Malaya differed for a number of reasons. For one, the large overseas Chinese and South Asian communities proved a persistent challenge for the Japanese military. The Indians and Chinese who lived in Malaya were often more attached to burgeoning nationalist movements in their native places than to any sense of an indigenous, Malayan nationalism. Overseas Chinese connections to the Chinese Nationalists thus posed a direct threat to Japanese efforts to maintain order on the peninsula, and Nationalist operatives worked hard through native-place associations to undermine Japanese imperial ambitions in the region. Unfortunately, the overseas Chinese (C. *huaqiao*) community living in Malaya was swept up in the geopolitical maneuverings of the war. Chiang Kai-shek urged the large Chinese community in Malaya to resist the Japanese invaders. In response, the Japanese army launched annihilation campaigns specifically targeting ethnic Chinese. According to estimates, upward of 40,000 Chinese living in Malaya were massacred after being targeted by the Japanese as either Chinese Nationalist or Chinese Communist supporters.[87] These murderous pacification campaigns attest to the brutality of the war and the Japanese Empire's perception of overseas Chinese as a threat to its maintenance of order and stability throughout East Asia. The pacification campaigns directed at overseas Chinese also quashed any idea among Malayan nationalists that the Japanese Empire could be seen as a liberating force.

Overseas Chinese living in Malaya regularly sent dispatches to Chongqing to keep the Nationalist government informed about the slaughter of their communities by the Japanese army and the slash-and-burn tactics used in the aftermath of these massacres.[88] Overseas Sino-Muslims living in Malaya were not immune from Japanese army violence directed specifically at "Chinese" nationals. When the Nationalist-sponsored Muslim Mission (C. *Huijiao fangwentuan*) visited Singapore to raise support for the war effort, it reported back to Chongqing about the massacre (C. *can'an*) of a Sino-Muslim community living under occupation in Malaya and asked the Nationalists to send relief efforts.[89] This is another indication of the multiplicity of identities embodied in the Sino-Muslim experience. In this particular case, the Japanese Empire perceived overseas Sino-Muslims as more "Chinese" than "Muslim." Contrary to its ongoing efforts almost everywhere else in the empire, Japan never saw overseas Sino-Muslim communities in Malaya as potential allies, only as a direct threat.

Throughout the Japanese Empire, Muslims' wartime experiences and expectations were uneven and diverse. Yet there was still a coherent and clear understanding of the Japanese government's willingness and ability to instrumentalize Islam in the service of its long-term visions of empire. The Japanese Empire had to adapt to situations on the ground in the places that it occupied, but there is at least one area where policy implementation with regards to Muslims was consistent: the attempts to teach the Japanese language to Muslim students in Muslim schools and madrasahs throughout the Greater East Asia Co-Prosperity Sphere. In this regard, the Japanese government took a page from its North China playbook, incorporating many of the lessons it had learned there trying to teach Japanese to young Muslims.

Plans for Learning Japanese and Language Reforms in Muslim Schools throughout the Empire

As Japanese military officials and Japanese bureaucrats secured control over the occupied Dutch East Indies, they adapted policies tried out on the home islands and in other parts of their empire to their experiences in Java and Sumatra. This was particularly apparent in their youth training programs, the publication of Islamic journals in Indonesian, teacher-training programs, and Japanese-language courses in both public schools and madrasahs.[90] From the beginning of the occupation, the army "regarded the Islamic policy as an important link in the occupation policy, and conducted organized activities from the beginning of the occupation as the most important aspect of the cultural and educational policy."[91] Throughout Southeast Asia, the Japanese-language education of Sino-Muslims was presented to students and parents as a model that worked. Japanese imperialists drew parallels between the plights of Sino-Muslims oppressed by Chiang Kai-shek and Javanese Muslims, Moro, and Muslim Malayans under Dutch, U.S., and British rule, respectively.[92] The progress that Sino-Muslims made learning Japanese was presented as a tangible outcome of the Japanese Empire's desire to help

Muslims free themselves from Western imperialism and create a new Asia.[93] As the Japanese presence in *Nanyō* began to result in tangible changes in the political and cultural landscape, Japanese bureaucrats needed to figure out just where these people would fit into their imperial schemas.[94]

As in North China, the Japanese focused on educational reforms in Muslim schools throughout Southeast Asia. Some scholars contend that the emphasis on language and curriculum reform was the occupation's most lasting impact on the region. One of the reasons for this was that beyond the promotion of Japanese-language learning, Japanese officials also supported the standardization of indigenous languages like Burmese, Malay, Indonesian, and Tagalog to be taught alongside mandatory Japanese-language classes.[95] By standardizing indigenous languages and moving away from the Dutch or British educational models (and the teaching of Dutch and English, respectively), nationalist movements in the region were able to disassociate themselves from Western colonial powers using standardized languages with the help of the Japanese Empire.[96] In the Dutch East Indies, Japanese officials banned the teaching and use of Dutch in schools, and the Japanese language was made compulsory. All schools had to teach it along with Indonesian (J. *Indoneshia go*), and one other local language such as Javanese (J. *Jawa go*) at a ratio of 7:2:1 classes per week.[97] By banning Dutch, the elite that had been cultivated under the Dutch regime was ostracized, giving way to those who had been suppressed for their nonconformism and nationalism. As in North China, this also allowed the Japanese government to educate occupied people in their own particular vocabulary of opposition to imperialism and Soviet Communism.

The policy called "the national language is Japanese" (J. *kokugo to shite no Nihongo*), which had been implemented in Taiwan for over fifty years, Korea for almost thirty-five years, and in Manchukuo since its founding, was then exported to territories in Southeast Asia.[98] Owing in part to Japan's previous experience, curriculum reforms in Southeast Asia were implemented quickly and with purpose, and "comprised of standardized national schools for which tuition was free and with a uniform curriculum that laid a heavy stress on Japanese subjects and physical training."[99] These schools were popular, receiving more applications than they had openings since educational opportunities had been so limited by the Dutch and British.[100] Again, following the model used in other parts of the empire, the Japanese government began hosting Japanese-language contests in Jakarta. Of course, in Java, the majority of these students were Muslim. As with Sino-Muslims, outstanding students were sent to Tokyo for three years as part of a program for "special foreign students from the southern regions" (J. *nanpō tokubetsu ryūgakusei*).[101] And, similarly to the experience in Manchukuo, students at these schools put on pro-Japanese plays for their communities that relayed messages of anticolonial resistance to audiences in Indonesian.[102]

In Malaya, overseas Chinese who had not been killed by the Japanese army learned Chinese and Japanese in schools. However, by 1943, as the perceived threat of overseas Chinese communities supporting the resistance to Japanese rule in Southeast Asia intensified, Japanese officials banned Chinese-language learning altogether.[103] Other students learned Malay, Hindu, or Tamil and Japanese, depending on their heritage. For instance, an Indian National School was set up "under the auspices of the Indian Independence League" with the intent of promoting "Indian culture, national spirit, Hindustani music, handicraft, gardening and other subjects."[104] Like Javanese and Sumatrans, Malayans received "rigorous training" in the Japanese language and "Japanese spirit" (J. *Nihon seishin*).[105] All of these efforts were geared to creating a new East Asia where the subjects of the Japanese Empire could converse proficiently with one another in Japanese. These were ambitious and long-term plans deeply connected to Japanese efforts to undermine Western capitalism through the creation of a new economic bloc centered in Tokyo.[106]

Although these policies were started in Taiwan and Korea, the one difference that separates these places from occupied China and Southeast Asia was the presence of Muslim schools. As in North China, the occupying Japanese forces faced objections and resistance to these Japanese-language policies in "Islamic schools" (J. *isuramu no gakkō*) in the occupied-Dutch East Indies. In some schools, a policy of accommodation and compromise was adopted, and fewer Japanese-language classes were required.[107] These schools had a long tradition of rejecting any form of Dutch-language learning, and traditionally placed no emphasis on educating women. However, the education of Muslim women had been a priority for Japanese bureaucrats, and, in 1942, when twenty-three Indonesian Muslim students left the archipelago to study at universities in Japan, a handful of them were women.[108] Like the Sino-Muslim women in Manchukuo who were chosen to continue their studies in Japan, these women were also seen as valuable assets for the implementation of long-term language and policy goals.[109]

These types of cultural policies were integral to maintaining the guise of imperial legitimacy, and they often went hand in hand with more overt economic policies for resource extraction and exploitation of labor. Cultural policies directed at Muslims throughout East Asia and Southeast Asia hinged on their viability for creating economic profit. In the case of education and teaching Muslim youth to speak Japanese, members of the Greater Japan Muslim League were able to highlight tangible economic benefits from their experiences with Sino-Muslims, leading to the policies' implementation throughout the empire. At the same time, cultural and social policies for Muslims helped encourage Japan's visions for an Asian economic bloc free from Western dominance. From here, the Greater Japan Muslim League promoted and implemented plans to expand the imperial horizon beyond East Asia and Southeast Asia into places with predominantly Muslim populations. How they proposed to achieve these ambitious plans is the topic of the following section.

Practical Applications, Part II: Hoping to Form Commercial Networks beyond the Greater East Asia Co-Prosperity Sphere with the Help of Tea and Sino-Muslims

The following photograph shows Afghan men visiting Japan in 1941 on an "economic inspection tour" of the Japanese home islands while the world is embroiled in a devastating global war. The men look relaxed as they are served tea by Japanese geishas under a tent. The image, captured by a member of the Greater Japan Muslim League for press coverage of the tour, provides an illuminating glimpse into the experiences of Muslim guests invited to Japan during the war. On this particular tour, the Afghan delegates visited factories, arsenals, naval schools, and important Japanese cultural sites, like the Meiji Shrine and Ueno Park in Tokyo. However, as Muslims, the initial stop on their tour was different from those made by non-Muslim visitors to the home islands: they were first taken to the Tokyo Mosque, erected in 1938 as a goodwill gesture by the Japanese Empire to Muslims around the world.

The image also raises a number of important questions directly related to the larger aims of this book. For instance, why are these men drinking tea in this staged image? How did the Japanese leverage tea as a diplomatic tool during World War II? Why Afghans? And, perhaps most important, what role were Sino-Muslims intended to play in these economic and cultural outreach efforts? Gestures and ventures by Japanese imperialists toward groups like the men on the Afghan economic tour would have been much more difficult without an important global commodity like tea and Sino-Muslims to sell it. Attempting to create economic networks and trading global commodities with the help of Sino-Muslims was just one of the ways the Japanese Empire was planning to extend its imperial purview beyond what we

Afghan men visit Tokyo on an "economic inspection tour"
of the home islands, 1941.
(Greater Japan Muslim League database, Waseda
University Library Special Collections)

would typically consider to be the geographical confines of the Greater East Asia Co-Prosperity Sphere, into places such as Afghanistan, North Africa, and the Middle East.

The Axis economic bloc attempted to reorder the ways goods circulated during the war, shifting tastes, building consumer markets in largely Muslim regions, and simultaneously creating and destroying markets for tea and other commodities.[110] Afghans were not subjects of the Japanese Empire, but they were from a predominantly Muslim region strategically positioned between British India and Soviet Central Asia. Afghanistan was also one of the only countries to maintain neutrality throughout World War II. Tea was a commodity with growing and expanding markets, opened because of the war. The Japanese Empire became a "space of circulation" for people, goods, and services, yet these flows and exchanges were also deeply embedded in the global circulation of capital.[111] Products like tea from occupied regions in China, Taiwan, the Dutch East Indies, Malaya, and Burma, as well as high-quality green tea cultivated on the Japanese home islands, circulated not only within the empire but outside of it as well.

Tea provides a window into the Greater Japan Muslim League's vision of the imperial project as much farther reaching than how it is conceived now. By taking into account the ways the Japanese Empire sought new markets beyond the area traditionally considered to be the Greater East Asia Co-Prosperity Sphere, we get the sense that Japanese policymakers fixated on Sino-Muslims as they set their gaze on the Middle East, South Asia, and North Africa as places for economic expansion and domination. With tea and Sino-Muslims at the center, alternative narratives about the Japanese Empire's long-term goals percolate to the surface.[112]

Placing tea at the center of the discussion of Japan's wartime ambitions does a number of things. Tea highlights the Allies' insecurities about Japan's economic advance into new markets. European fears about Japanese entry into African and Maghreb tea markets might have been exaggerated, but they were not unfounded. Japanese exports to Africa increased exponentially in the years after the Great Depression, and they made enough of an impact for European colonial powers to express growing concern with "Japan's 'penetration' of Africa."[113] Throughout the 1930s, the British and South Africans placed increasingly strict embargos on Japanese imports to the African continent.[114] The economic insecurities of white South Africans in the post-Depression era were further fueled by racism and the perception that "multitudes of Japanese emigrants" who stopped in South Africa on their way to Brazil might decide to settle in South Africa.[115] In the tense years leading up to World War II, the racialized fears of white South Africans were amplified by Japan's potential to infiltrate markets the South Africans had once dominated.

When we shift our focus away from oil as the only commodity that drove Japanese imperial aggression and expansion into Southeast Asia, new stories emerge about the ways that the Japanese Empire sought to subvert the global capitalist system by creating a self-sufficient non-Western economic bloc. The Japanese were interested in commodities beyond oil and rubber in their growing empire in Southeast Asia. In 1942, Takahashi Sejima published *Sketching Indonesia*, which outlined the history of the archipelago and analyzed various exports from the islands in addition to oil and rubber, like tea.[116] Other notable products exported from the islands included Javanese coffee (J. *Jawa kōhī*), cinchona bark (J. *kina*), palm oil (J. *aburayashi*), and coal (J. *sekitan*).[117] Many of these commodities, like tea and cinchona bark (used to make the antimalarial medicine quinine), were already well integrated into global markets.

Tea ranked behind only oil, rubber, and tin in exports from the Dutch East Indies, accounting for around 20 percent of all tea sold in markets in London.[118] Japanese policymakers knew that tea exports from the Dutch East Indies dwarfed Japanese exports by an average of around 150 million pounds per year between 1927 and 1940, and that the commodity was central to the export economy in Java and Sumatra at the time of the occupation.[119] Although this statistic should not be used as a marker of the decision to invade and occupy the Dutch East Indies, it was something that the Greater Japan Muslim League and the tea producers on the home islands would have made clear to Japanese military advisers and policymakers as they embarked on their campaigns to defeat the Dutch and occupy their colonial holdings in Southeast Asia.[120]

The Greater Japan Muslim League's plans to sell tea to Muslims around the world with the help of Sino-Muslims was just one of the ways they attempted to disrupt global flows of capital dominated by the West. When we unravel some of the ways the well-traveled and highly educated members of the Greater Japan Muslim League explained Middle Eastern tea-drinking habits to both everyday Japanese readers and imperial policymakers, it becomes clear that beyond the marketization of this important global commodity, the Japanese also practiced tea diplomacy and intended to "deploy" Sino-Muslims as cultural ambassadors to promote good relations and trade with a commodity familiar to the majority of Muslims.[121] These outreach efforts were partly meant to increase tea exports from the Japanese Empire, and partly meant to grease the wheels of diplomacy with regions not generally considered when studying imperial Japanese foreign policy during the war.

In her book about tea and the British Empire, Erica Rappaport points out that tea provides one locus for examining the daily lives of subjects of empire from all different walks of life while simultaneously underscoring "how the British Empire exerted power over land, labor, tastes, and the daily habits of millions of people living in so many parts of the globe."[122] In a similar way, illuminating Japan's policies regarding tea provides new perspectives on the impact of wartime cultural, social, and economic policy decisions throughout the empire. The Greater Japan Muslim League understood that tea was a commodity that connected Muslims around the world. As we saw in chapter 3, Sino-Muslim Tang Yichen and his companions reflected on the universality of tea as a product shared and enjoyed by all the Muslims they encountered on their Japanese-sponsored hajj. Although the Muslims he met on his journey prepared tea differently depending on where they lived, he remarked that all Muslims could take pleasure in sharing a pot of tea with their coreligionists around the world.[123] For Tang, this global commodity broke down barriers of difference between his group and the other Muslims they encountered on their journey.

In this way, tea becomes a prism through which we can examine the overlapping interests of the Japanese Empire and its long-term plans for integrating Sino-Muslims into a non-Western economic bloc under the aegis of Japan's imperial project. Fostering friendly relationships with Muslims around the world was one of the mandates of the Greater Japan Muslim League, and it was through Sino-Muslims that the league wanted to begin promoting this cultural agenda of tea diplomacy. In this case, diplomatic engagements went hand in hand with trade relations, and the Greater Japan Muslim League readily acknowledged that the main aim of its extensive research about Islam and tea was to create potential markets for Japanese goods throughout the "Muslim world."[124] It was just one commodity, but the Greater Japan Muslim League claimed that Muslims around the world considered it a necessity (J. *hitsuyuhin*).[125] And unlike rubber or oil, there was deep cultural meaning for both Japanese and Sino-Muslims involved in the production, sale, and consumption of tea.

Japanese policymakers also appreciated tea as a commodity with a seemingly endless market potential and a capacity to disrupt British and Dutch economic networks. In their writing about tea, members of the Greater Japan Muslim League liked to point out that Japan was a small island country like Britain, and, like Britain, the Japanese home islands had few natural resources. The British had successfully colonized bigger places in order to extract resources that had created an "English economic bloc" (J. *igirisu no keizai burokku*). The Greater Japan Muslim League argued that in order to become self-sufficient (J. *jikyū jisoku*) Japan would need to rely on exports from its colonies—Manchukuo, North China (J. *hokushi*), and Central China (J. *chūshi*)—to places where Muslims lived. Members of the Greater Japan Muslim League expressed a great sense of urgency (J. *shōbi*) to connect with Muslim markets that had been neglected or overlooked in the past.[126] In this regard, the sale of tea to these new markets required not just an economic policy but a cultural one as well. Japan's imperial aspirations to sell tea with the help of Sino-Muslims make clear the broad reach of these policies developed to disrupt Western-driven circulations of global capital. This project of creating and maintaining the far-reaching connections between Muslims and the Japanese Empire should not be examined separately from Japan's expanding cultural and social outreach, nor from the efforts to make the people in its empire understandable to the subjects on the home islands. Japanese policymakers and diplomats needed to be well-versed in the cultural and social behaviors of these regions beyond their imperial purview. In turn, this provided an opportunity for members of the Greater Japan Muslim League to present information, data, and statistics they collected in digestible forms for career bureaucrats in ways that served the needs of the growing empire.

Before World War I, Japan bought little from the Middle East and North Africa and enjoyed enormous trade surpluses on the light industrial goods and cotton textiles that it exported to the region. However, given their country's increasing reliance on oil, Japanese imperial bureaucrats quickly realized that this favorable trade balance could shift. As connections and investments in the Middle East increased, Japanese bureaucrats were keen to understand their trading partners and find ways to expand these important relationships. As there was only a handful of Japanese Muslims at this time, the government used its ongoing association with Sino-Muslims to demonstrate that it was serious about respecting the different cultural and religious traditions of its new Middle Eastern trading partners.[127] These expanding commercial and industrial networks required middlemen, and in these plans for empire, Japanese bureaucrats envisioned that Sino-Muslims would help facilitate these commercial networks.[128] Sino-Muslims were offered as a case study to explain how tea consumption patterns in the daily lives of Muslims were different from Japanese tea consumption patterns. Around the same time that Tang embarked on his hajj, the Greater Japan Muslim League published a number of privately circulated dossiers for imperial officials along with a number of journal articles in well-read circulars about new markets in the Middle East and North Africa for tea grown in Manchukuo and Japan. Likely avid tea drinkers themselves, members of the Greater Japan Muslim League observed Muslim tea-drinking habits to report back to imperial officials on the viability of the region as a place for Japanese tea exports.

Like Sino-Muslims, tea is only a small part of the story of the Japanese imperial project. At the same time, an examination of tea does unveil Japanese aspirations to dominate a specific sector of the global economy. These "side stories" of empire provide a different take on what Japan wanted to accomplish during the war, as well as who and what was needed to bring their aspirations to fruition. The "dense webs of social meaning" surrounding the consumption, marketing, and sale of this global commodity to Muslims frame the deep entanglement of the Japanese Empire's economic policies with social and cultural policies.[129] This helps explain why the Japanese imperial project produced and reproduced images like the one of the Afghan men drinking tea to make Muslims legible to Japanese subjects at home. The aim of the Greater Japan Muslim League was to communicate to Japanese people that Muslims also appreciated tea and understood the importance of associated rituals and traditions, the difference of these rituals notwithstanding.

In other words, the efforts of the Greater Japan Muslim League were twofold: first, to expand into markets disrupted by the war where there were majority Muslim populations and, second, to continue the league's efforts to make Muslims legible to subjects of the expanding Japanese Empire. Through a close reading of newly mined documents produced between 1938 and 1941, the following section provides a fresh look at how scholars of Islam in Japan represented Muslims as both similar and different from Japanese subjects. In turn, these observations bring into question both the spatial and temporal boundaries of the Japanese Empire while examining Japanese constructions and perceptions of "others" beyond their East Asian colonial possessions.

The Cultural Component: Tea in China and Japan

Tea culture flourished among elites in China during the Tang Dynasty (618–907). In 780, Lu Yu compiled his now-famous *Classic of Tea*, which imbued tea drinking with Daoist and Buddhist philosophy, as well as Confucian etiquette, transforming it into a ceremonial art.[130] It was also around this time that tea is generally thought to have made its way to Japan via itinerant Buddhist monks.[131] Tea was such an important commodity for agrarian Chinese dynasties that it was brought under state control in the eleventh century, and all tea trade was controlled by the Tea and Horse Bureau (C. *Chamasi*). The bureau was responsible for producing, buying, selling, and offering as gifts bricks of tea from Yunnan and Sichuan to nomads in exchange for horses from the Mongolian steppes and the Tibetan plateau. From this tea and horse trade came the Chinese axiom "use tea to manage the barbarians" (C. *yichazhiyi*), as Han officials relied on nomads' dependence on tea to facilitate diplomatic engagements along the northern and western frontiers.

By the Southern Song Dynasty (1127–1279), tea had transformed from a luxury commodity consumed by elites into a daily staple in the lives of people across the socioeconomic spectrum. Revered for its taste and medicinal qualities, tea's preparation also required boiling water, which lowered transmission rates of waterborne illnesses.[132] During the Ming Dynasty (1368–1644), the Hongwu emperor decreed that brick tea would be replaced by leaf tea, reducing the time and labor used to grind tea and press it into bricks. This shift gave way to a new fashion of steeping and brewing leaves rather than mixing ground tea with hot water in a fashion similar to today's Japanese matcha. Although nomads continued to favor brick tea for its greater portability and longer shelf life, by the time the British and the Dutch arrived in southern China, settled agricultural workers and elites in the Chinese heartland were consuming steeped-leaf tea.

As in China, tea drinking in Japan became associated with aesthetics and philosophy, and the tea ceremony (J. *chanoyu*) "animated the material world and endowed it with spiritual, social, and political significance."[133] Between the Meiji Restoration and the Satsuma Rebellion in 1877, Japan's tea exports blossomed, with the majority of exports heading across the Pacific to the United States.[134] In the twentieth century, the aesthetics associated with Japanese tea culture were exported as Westerners became fascinated by orientalist visions of Japanese tea ceremonies. In 1906, Okakura Kakuzō (also known as Tenshin), a Japanese intellectual who spent many years in the United States, published the first edition of his well-read book about Japanese tea culture, *The Book of Tea*. The book is both a scathing critique of Western individualism and chauvinism and an introduction to the history of tea-drinking ceremonies in Japan.[135] For Okakura, all aspects of Japanese culture, including cuisine, art, and literature, were inseparable from the appreciation of tea and the ceremonies that accompanied drinking it.[136] Tea is also a central thread in discourses about China and Japan "losing out" to the West in the nineteenth century after the Qing defeat in the Opium Wars and Commodore Perry's subsequent arrival in Japan in 1853. The deep and long relationship between tea, ritual, and defeat at the hands of Westerners may help explain the care that Japanese wartime intellectuals dedicated to the subject. Or perhaps these bureaucrats simply valued the commodity's long history in East Asia and potential to disrupt global markets.

Taking Sides: Teatime and Aligning with the Axis

Until World War I, Japan was the largest exporter of tea to the United States. However, this statistic is somewhat misleading since most of the tea came from Formosa, the island now known as Taiwan, which Japan acquired as spoils of war from the Qing Empire in the aftermath of the First Sino-Japanese War (1894–95).[137] Much like the Indian tea sold on British markets, Formosan tea was an imperial commodity, grown and produced in Japan's first colonial acquisition beyond the archipelago, shipped to the United States via Kobe, and marketed as a Japanese product. It was not until the end of World War I that tea exports from India outpaced Japanese tea exports to U.S. markets. This partly had to do with the shifting tastes of U.S. consumers, who in the nineteenth century had preferred green tea but began to drink more black tea in the twentieth century.

The Great Depression was extremely disruptive to international tea markets. Tea prices plummeted in the late 1920s as demand decreased drastically. After the Great Depression, tea-producing empires were anxious to get prices and consumption back to pre-Depression levels. This necessitated limiting exports and expanding the consumer base for tea into new markets such as India or Africa, where tea was grown but generally not consumed. In order to continue to exert worldwide dominance over the tea trade, the British and the Dutch initiated the "international commodity control" of tea in 1933 through the creation of an allied bloc of tea producers, known as the International Tea Agreement (ITA).[138] The ITA was not solely an economic pact, and the arrangement was clearly dictated by the politics on the European continent, as Hitler and Mussolini tightened their control over Germany and Italy in the 1930s.[139]

Although the British and the Dutch tried to convince Japan to join the ITA, the Japanese declined the offer.[140] The Chinese government also was eager to get the price of tea back up to pre-Depression levels, so it agreed to export quotas imposed by the Dutch and British but never joined the ITA. In the interwar years, the provisions of the agreement meant that the British and the Dutch limited their tea trade to "intra-empire," circulating commodities produced in their respective empires within them. This "intra-empire" trade provided the space and freedom for entrepreneurs from the Japanese Empire to start tapping into new markets. Before the outbreak of World War II, Japanese officials went searching for new consumers in places such as North Africa, the Balkans, and Central Asia.[141] Of course, many of these regions were places that also had predominantly Muslim populations.

The Great Depression also had a negative impact on Japanese tea imports to the United States and Canada. This sent Japanese tea producers to the Middle East looking for new markets. In 1931, French consular officials at the Commerce Bureau in Casablanca sent inquiries to both the French consul in Yokohama and Shanghai about an envoy of Japanese tea merchants who were distributing free green tea around Morocco.[142] Apparently, a Japanese representative of the Central Tea Association of Japan arrived in Morocco to circulate tea among "les indigènes," and the French consul expressed concern because the tea pleased the palates of locals, who had previously been uninterested in Japanese green tea.[143] The man in question was Mr. Torī, one of the directors of the Central Tea Association of Japan. On the trip, he traveled with his entourage to Oudjda, Fez, Meknes, Rabat, Casablanca, and Marrakesh before leaving for Tunisia and Algeria.[144] According to the French consular officer who compiled the report about Mr. Torī's visit, Japanese entrepreneurs had expended large sums of money trying to reinvigorate tea markets in the United States and Canada, without much success. After these failures, they decided to turn to new markets in North Africa. The French were concerned about Japanese tea imports because of their own "intra-empire" trade, as they had started importing tea from Indochina to Morocco in the early 1920s. Until 1930, however, most of the green tea consumed in Morocco was imported from China, including the famous "gunpowder tea," which is rolled into pellets and easy to steep with mint, as was the custom in Morocco. In the end, the efforts by Mr. Torī and his associates yielded little to no increases in tea sales for the Japanese, as the markets and margins were still too small and too insular. However, by 1939, the French Commerce office in Morocco expressed growing concern about the repercussions of Japanese military operations on the production and exportation of green tea from Indochina to France's North African colonies.[145]

The ITA "ceased to have practical significance" after the Japanese occupation of the Dutch East Indies in early 1942, but the British continued to control the circulation of tea for the Allies throughout the war.[146] Throughout the conflict, tea remained an important concern for the Allies and the Axis. In 1942, the loss of Burma to the Japanese was not only a striking military blow for the British and their Chinese allies, but it was also felt throughout the British tea industry. At the time, Britain relied heavily on tea exports from Darjeeling to supply soldiers on the front lines and civilians back home.[147] The loss of Burma was so concerning to the Allies that "the Director of Tea at the Ministry of Food and the Combined Food Board in Washington became the sole purchaser of tea for the Allies and certain neutral countries," and children's tea rations were cut back because of the growing fear that the British would also lose the tea fields in Darjeeling to the advancing Japanese army.[148] During World War II, decisions about tea and tea fields were perhaps not central to wartime decision making for both the Axis and the Allied powers, but they were not entirely peripheral: in addition to being a global commodity, tea's availability impacted the morale of troops and civilians alike.

Japanese Tea Policy: Commodities, Labor, Empire, and Muslims

One of the striking things about Japanese tea policy was its ambition. Japanese writing about tea during the war also reveals the extent to which the Japanese were aware of and concerned with the intersections between race, class, and ethnicity, and the division of labor throughout their empire. In these writings, Japanese policymakers acknowledged the importance of Sino-Muslims as longtime intermediaries and middlemen in the tea trade and the potential value of these traders as Japan looked to expand markets in predominantly Muslim places. Sino-Muslims living under occupation also provided the lens through which scholars of the Greater Japan Muslim League filtered the daily tea-drinking habits of Muslims. They explained things like the Islamic custom of dipping a small piece of bread in a cup of tea with a dash of sugar after morning prayers. The "rituals and rites" associated with tea played an important yet different role in Japanese, Chinese,

Young women from the Mongolian-Muslim Inspection
tour participate in a tea ceremony in Kyoto.
(Greater Japan Muslim League database, Waseda
University Library Special Collections)

and Islamic cultures, but in all cases the consumption of tea replicated and reinforced social order within the empire and Muslim communities.[149]

Unlike other commodities, tea had emancipatory capabilities. Tea was presented as a "powerful force" (J. *iryoku*) capable of inciting revolution for freedom against the oppressive British Empire. In this view, taxes on tea (J. *chazei*) imposed by the British had fueled demands in thirteen American colonies for freedom from the Crown.[150] In this way, tea could guide politics and free people from imperialism.[151] These emancipatory possibilities were then refracted back on the potential for the Japanese Empire to create a non-Western economic bloc, as evidenced by the last section heading in a report published about tea by the Greater Japan Muslim League: "Islamic Countries and Our Economic Bloc" (J. *Kaikyō shokoku to waga keizai burokku*).[152]

These emancipatory possibilities were also meant to help people throughout Asia free themselves from colonial oppression, and Japanese writers wrote frequently about the economy in *Nanyō* and the relationship to Japanese tea.[153] In *New Asia*, a widely read Japanese circular, prominent tea scholar Hosoya Kiyoshi briefed readers on Dutch imperialism in Asia

Sino-Muslims and Japan's Aspirational Empire

and its impact on the tea economy. He noted that tea had been traded and consumed throughout the South Seas for hundreds of years, and when the Dutch colonized Java, they quickly established large tea plantations outside Batavia.[154] In the 1820s, the Dutch commissioned Japanese tea merchants and growers from the home islands to accompany them to Batavia to help set up plantations there. For Hosoya, this meant that the Japanese had a hand in the growth and production of the tea industry in *Nanyō* and were therefore entitled to a cut of the profits. In Hosoya's telling, the Dutch exploited the Javanese and Sumatrans the same way as they had the Japanese tea merchants. Although his comparison may be overblown, Hosoya's point is clear: Asia was for the Asians, and everyone living in the region had been exploited or used by Western powers at some point.[155]

Traditionally important tea-producing regions of Japan, like Shizuoka Prefecture, also enlisted the services of the Greater Japan Muslim League to write about the potential for new markets for Japanese tea in the Middle East, North Africa, and other places with large Muslim populations.[156] In one case, Matsumoro Takayoshi, the major-general of the army on the mainland as well as the military overseer of the Greater Japan Muslim League, contributed a piece to the *Tea Journal*, a monthly published by the Shizuoka Tea Producers Association. After lauding tea from Shizuoka, Matsumoro informed his readers that he had spent a great deal of his youth in China, Mongolia, and Turkestan. Having established his credentials, Matsumoro told readers that the Greater Japan Muslim League was working hard to improve the lives of Sino-Muslims on the mainland (J. *tairiku*).[157]

Matsumoro explained that the relationship between Sino-Muslims and tea was deep and symbolic: Sino-Muslims drank tea after all five of their daily prayers, imbuing it with religious meaning. Beyond this, Matsumoro maintained that since Muslims had arrived in China, tea had been central to both the daily religious lives and economic well-being of Sino-Muslims, as many worked as middlemen in the tea trade between the tea-producing regions of Yunnan and Guangzhou and the tea-buying regions of Central Asia and Persia.[158] Matsumoro reiterated the importance of Sino-Muslims as traders between the Mongolian, Siberian, and Tibetan nomads, and urged his Japanese readers to understand their potential in the expansion of the Japanese tea industry as Shizuoka began increasing exports to the Middle East and other regions with majority Muslim populations.

In terms of supplying Japanese tea to Muslim markets, the Greater Japan Muslim League made an ethnoreligious argument about the value of Sino-Muslims in distribution chains. But when it came to consumption, the argument shifted to the framework of class. Some tea was a luxury commodity and other tea was swill, made for the masses. For the Greater Japan Muslim League, there were some Muslims who were sophisticated and cosmopolitan enough to be able to appreciate the high-end green tea grown on the home islands, whereas regular middle- and lower-class Muslims would be satisfied to drink the lower-quality tea grown and produced throughout the empire.[159] In some ways, this vision for tea exports replicated the deeply entrenched hierarchies of empire, with the Japanese at the top, and the people living throughout their empire below them, aspiring to be as civilized as the Japanese.[160]

In his 1941 book *Patriotic Used Tea Leaves*, Hosoya Kiyoshi goes to great pains to explain the historical relationship between the British Commonwealth and tea, the United States and tea, and nomads and tea.[161] However, the chapters dealing specifically with Muslims and the Asian tea economy are most useful and relevant here. After taking a few pages to explain the world's Muslim populations to readers, Hosoya compares the religious significance of tea for Muslims on religious pilgrimages to tea's symbolism for Tibetan lamas (J. *rama*) making pilgrimages to the Tashilhunpo Temple, the seat of the Panchen Lama in Shigatse.[162] This analogy would likely have resonated with Japanese readers, who were much more familiar with Buddhist practices than with Islamic ones. It also helped establish the religious significance of tea as a universal beverage consumed around the world by Buddhists and Muslims alike.

Hosoya also fixates on the supposed health benefits of drinking tea and tea's potential for improving the health of both Muslims and Japanese people. According to Hosoya, the drying process involved in making green tea allows it to retain more vitamin C than fermented black tea. Since taking fruit on long overland and seagoing voyages might not be possible, Hosoya suggests that tea could help solve the Navy's scurvy problem.[163] The Russo-Japanese War illustrates the benefits of tea in relation to military prowess. During the war, a high proportion of the Russian Navy suffered from scurvy on the long trip from the Black Sea and had to fight the Japanese in poor health.[164] Although Hosoya does not go as far as to attribute the Japanese victory to the Russians' not drinking green tea, he does imply that tea should be a central component in maintaining the health of the Japanese military. He extends this argument to Japan's imperialist and expansionist policies.

For Hosoya, tea policy (J. *cha seisaku*) was important for the empire because it had a number of different impacts on the nation beyond the economy alone. As Japan's empire expanded into *Nanyō* and Inner Asia, it could be useful to help those less well-nourished than the Japanese themselves by introducing them to Japanese green tea, boosting their daily intake of vitamin C.[165] Here, the perceived benevolence of the Japanese imperial project was tied to a commodity that could increase military might and help improve the health of Japan's subjects from Java to Mongolia. Hosoya's point was that Japanese green tea was a way to bring continuity, stability, and health to the vast and growing Japanese Empire. Taking this argument a step further, Matsumoro wrote elsewhere that because tea was a commodity consumed around the world, it required a "global policy" (J. *sekai seisaku*).[166] Matsumoro's plan was to disrupt current markets and displace Europeans as the top tea providers while extending Japanese tea sales into new markets. Muslims around the world were central to this global drive to sell more tea from the home islands and the colonies.

In this scenario, oppressed colonial peoples and Muslims living under the yoke of European imperialism *needed* the Japanese to provide them with tea. Since Sino-Muslims demonstrated that tea also served a religious function, they could be used as free advertising in places where tea drinking was not the norm to help expand markets and develop new Muslim consumers.[167] To illustrate this point, Matsumoro explained that although India produced the majority of the world's tea, almost no Indians drank it. More to the point, he informed his readers that there were over 85 million Muslims in India who were woefully oppressed by the British: they were all waiting to be freed from the clutches of imperialism by a cup of Japanese tea.[168]

Sino-Muslims were instrumental to this particular Japanese vision for two reasons: first, they could be used as examples to highlight the benefits of consuming tea to Muslims who might not already be consumers; second, and perhaps more important, they were exemplary models of how economic support from the Japanese government could help Muslims develop without reliance on the West.[169] Through development of the economy and increased access to education, Japanese policymakers imagined that Sino-Muslims would reciprocate and create stronger commercial ties with places where Japan could export goods.[170] This global tea policy was also meant to convey the benevolence of the Japanese government toward Muslims around the world. The Greater Japan Muslim League wanted to highlight that tea produced in China was incentivized by Japanese economic investment that helped propel the development of Sino-Muslim communities.[171] Matsumoro even suggested that through cooperation with Sino-Muslims, the Greater Japan Muslim League might see large increases in the exports of tea from China, and he recommended that the Japanese government offer loans to Sino-Muslim communities willing to either grow or produce tea for export. In turn, this would contribute to the economic development of Sino-Muslim communities and the overall economic success of the Japanese Empire.[172] In other words, the promotion of cultural exchanges and the fostering of friendly diplomatic relations went hand in hand with the development of commercial and economic networks that would promote Muslim countries as a place where Japanese goods could be sold, creating a non-Western economic bloc well beyond the boundaries of the Japanese Empire.

Tea and the World of Islam

As tea exports from Japan increased following the Great Depression, markets in many Muslim countries also expanded.[173] While tea markets in Britain, her dominions, and the United States were saturated, the real potential for growth was in emerging markets, which happened to be in predominantly Muslim regions of the world. In 1939, a year after the establishment of the Greater Japan Muslim League, the group published a thirty-five-page dossier about Japanese tea exports to new and emerging markets in Muslim regions around the world.[174] From the outset, the export of tea was framed within the context of the ongoing "Holy War" and the potential for future markets after Japan emerged victorious. Like the war against imperialism in Asia, the tea business was presented by the Greater Japan Muslim League as a "sacred enterprise" (J. *chagyō ga seigyō to shite*) that had been ruined and exploited by capitalism, the British Empire, and British corporations, particularly Lipton.[175] Without a hint of irony, Lipton was presented as an evil imperialist company that took advantage of rural Indian tea plantation workers, but it was also heralded as a model for how the Japanese Empire could sell tea in global markets. Coupled with low tariffs and a "laissez-faire economic policy" (J. *hōnin shugi*), tea could be exported from China to the new, predominantly Muslim markets. The Greater Japan Muslim League's plan for domination of tea markets throughout the "Muslim world" would be possible with cheap labor from China, and with Sino-Muslims to work as middlemen selling tea to Muslim consumers.[176] New wartime markets provided an opportunity for certain sectors of the Japanese economy, and while militarists were busy preparing for Pearl Harbor, smaller sectors of the economy, like the tea producers' guild and the Greater Japan Muslim League, saw a space in the market and prepared to act.

The Greater Japan Muslim League also noted a connection between European colonial powers and the type of tea consumed across North Africa and the Middle East. Colonial subjects living under British rule in Egypt preferred black tea, highlighting the extent of "intra-empire" trade and the influence of British cultural habits over people living under their imperial purview, whereas in other parts of North Africa, the ratios of black to green tea varied.[177] Beyond North Africa, the Greater Japan Muslim League commented, British customs had influenced tea consumption in Persia and Afghanistan, and the league noted that many Persians drank black tea in the winter and green tea during the summer. Other Muslims like the Sarts, Kyrgyz, Turks, and Tatars in the Soviet Union also drank green tea, unlike the Russians, who favored black tea.[178] This was seen as an opportunity to export both high-quality green tea from the Japanese home islands and lower-quality black tea from China to different North African and Central Asian countries depending on the drinking habits of their inhabitants.

The information about the tea-drinking preferences of Muslims around the world also provides a segue into a criticism of Soviet colonial policies in Xinjiang. The Greater Japan Muslim League inferred that the Soviets had influenced the tea-drinking habits of Muslims living in the region. This mention of Uyghur Muslims in Xinjiang and their tea-consumption patterns was likely an opportunity to underscore the oppression of Muslims in China's western borderlands under Soviet control rather than a concerted effort to sell Japanese tea to Uyghurs. The league pointed out that Xinjiang was an ethnically and religiously diverse region with many overlapping customs and cultures, but that the majority of Uyghurs consumed black tea, which was different from all the other Muslim groups in the region.[179] It seems unlikely that there was ever a Soviet plot to get Uyghurs to drink black tea, and the difference in tea-drinking habits was likely attributable to the different lifestyles of the predominantly nomadic Muslim groups, like the Kyrgyz, and the sedentary, oasis-dwelling Uyghurs. The availability of tea in remote western regions during the war could also have been a factor in Uyghur tea-drinking habits. However, the Greater Japan Muslim League was clearly trying to make a point about the influence that colonial powers had over the customs and habits of the daily lives of Muslims around the world, particularly those living under Soviet and British rule.

Tea production and distribution was also seen as a way to increase the economic output of both China and Japan during the war, and as a way for Sino-Muslims to free themselves from the Chinese Nationalists. To emphasize the emancipatory possibilities of a thriving tea industry and the potential of this renewed industry to help Muslims around the world, the Greater Japan Muslim League drew inspiration from the American Revolution and the Boston Tea Party as a historical allegory.[180] In this instance, this example is cited to highlight—or perhaps even overemphasize—the importance of tea as a commodity in world political and economic history.[181] The suggestions for implementation of this global tea policy were straightforward: export more high-quality green tea from Japan and more black tea from China. The league also suggested a more coordinated tea policy for the empire. Part of this meant mounting propaganda campaigns about Japanese tea to inform markets in Muslim countries, where the potential for growth was the highest.

The linchpin in all these plans was the cooperation of Sino-Muslims. With their supposed business acumen and religious connections to the Middle East, Sino-Muslims were meant to facilitate and maintain these trading networks with Muslim merchants around the world.[182] The Greater Japan Muslim League used a Chinese idiomatic phrase to explain that this comprehensive policy would "kill two birds with one stone" (C. *yiju-liande*), as the revenue increase from expanding tea markets could help the Japanese Empire and increase the standard of living among Muslims in China. In the end, the league noted that if the global tea policy was successful, it could be replicated with other commodities, such as manufactured goods from Japan, silk, tobacco, and wool, thus creating a network of small shops beyond the empire that stocked and sold Japanese-produced goods to Muslims with the help of Sino-Muslim intermediaries.[183] For the Greater Japan Muslim League, the Muslims who lived in Manchukuo and the surrounding border areas were the perfect salespeople to take Japanese green tea—and potentially all kinds of commodities produced in the empire—to Muslims around the globe.[184]

Conclusions

Erica Rappaport's work about tea and the British Empire is useful for framing the conclusions about the significance of tea and Sino-Muslims to the Japanese imperial project. While Rappaport illustrates how tea and "global capitalism has produced both ideologies of internationalism and multiple articulations of nationalism and racism" in the British Empire, the same could be said for the Japanese imperial project and the circulation of commodities within the Japanese Empire and beyond it.[185] By presenting itself as a benevolent liberator from colonial oppression, the Japanese Empire disrupted and intervened in the circulation of an important global commodity.

However, in order to accomplish this, it needed a global war to create a massive disruption in the circulation of currency and commodities.

Exploring the history of tea "outside" of the Japanese Empire "allows us to see the empire as a set of relationships between producers and consumers, as a taste and as a habit, as an everyday encounter." It also enables us to highlight that "imperial culture did not always take an obvious measurable, detectable form and that it can be felt far beyond formal imperial boundaries."[186] Here the informal boundaries of empire are brought into question. Japan's Islamic policies and its global tea policies might not have been central to the war effort, but foregrounding them begins to reconfigure the spatial boundaries of the Japanese Empire and provides opportunities to deepen understandings of the pluralities of Japanese imperial power and Japanese imperial space. The Japanese Empire meant something different to Muslims than it did to Japanese subjects living in Tokyo, and the ways individuals arranged the empire in their minds and projected it through maps, vocabulary, travel, contact with other people, and the consumption of commodities begins to tell a more variegated story about the Japanese imperial project.[187]

In the post–World War II era of decolonization and communist victories throughout Asia, tea began to take on a new meaning, transitioning from an imperial commodity to a national one. Throughout the postwar years, new nations, such as the prosocialist government in Ceylon, nationalized tea fields throughout Asia.[188] At the same time, the bureaucrats and technocrats of the now-defunct Japanese Empire drew on their wartime connections to reach out to the networks they had created and cultivated during the war. After the San Francisco Treaty was ratified in 1952, Japan's oil imports rose dramatically, and between 1952 and 1970 around 80 percent of oil used in Japan came from the Middle East. It is sometimes assumed that the Japanese government and the oil-producing nations in the Middle East had no extensive relationships during the war. However, it was the networks that the Japanese Empire worked so hard to create and maintain starting in the interwar period through to the end of World War II that allowed the Japanese government to quickly and efficiently reinsert itself into the region following the end of the U.S. occupation.[189]

At the end of her book, Rappaport calls on scholars beyond the British Empire to examine the global circulations of tea as a way to complicate her narrative because, as she rightfully acknowledges, "there is not just one empire of tea but several interconnected domains from which power emanated from different centers."[190] The case presented here provides insights into disruptions in the wartime economy that complement her work by inserting the Japanese Empire into the story of tea. The Japanese Empire hoped to capitalize on the chaos wrought in Europe by the Nazis to enter new and lucrative markets with the help of Sino-Muslims. The next chapter explores how these inter-Axis connections created new histories, new opportunities, and new spaces during the war beyond the Greater East Asia Co-Prosperity Sphere, all with Sino-Muslims at the forefront of the agenda.

5

FASCIST ENTANGLEMENTS

Islamic Spaces and Overlapping Interests

"Go West!"

"Japan's Near East Conspiracy,"
Chinese Ministry of Foreign Affairs, 1940

"Defeat the bear using Fascism!"

Matsubara Hiroshi, Minzoku-ron, *1937*

Read together, the quotations above and the map below frame the central argument of this chapter. They bring together various threads of Japanese imperial policy during the war. "Go West!" and "Defeat the bear using Fascism!" encapsulate the plans to defeat the Allies. The map of the distribution of Muslims throughout Asia and Africa illustrates that in order to achieve these ambitious plans, the Japanese Empire needed to continue its appeals to Muslims over two continents. The Japanese Empire had grand plans involving Muslims, and in order to implement them, it looked to the Italian Fascists and the Nazis to validate, justify, and legitimate its own policies. As the Japanese Empire trudged west, the Nazis forged east, and they met roughly in the middle: Afghanistan.

This chapter travels to the fringes of fascist empires to get a sense of the spaces and places the Japanese Empire imagined it would go, and the ways policymakers believed it would get there. These aspirational aims for em-

Map of the distribution of Muslims produced by the
Greater Japan Muslim League, 1939.
(Dai Nihon Kaikyō Kyōkai, *Kaikyō ken hayawakari*, 1939)

pire would never have been possible without the help and support of Sino-Muslims. Displacing Tokyo, the nexus of the Japanese Empire, to Muslim spaces beyond the edges of empire frames the global ambitions of the Japanese imperial project. Examining these spaces provides a glimpse into the coordinated—and sometimes not so coordinated—efforts by the Japanese Empire and the other Axis powers to bring Muslims from around the world together in order to defeat their common enemies.

The chapter takes imperial Japan's policies toward Sino-Muslims and places them in larger currents of the global war as a way of evaluating imperial Japan's approaches and overtures to Muslims around the world. Doing this highlights the rhetorical and ideological similarities linking the three Axis powers' geopolitical concerns about Western imperialism and Soviet Communism from the perspective of their respective engagement with Muslims under their purview. Taking what it had learned from its engagement with Sino-Muslims, the Japanese Empire compared its efforts to the Italian campaigns in North and East Africa, and to Germany's forays into Muslim regions in the Balkans and the Middle East during both world wars. The chapter ends with a focus on an Islamic space generally considered to be beyond the sphere of Nazi and Japanese influence during the war: Afghanistan. The focus on Afghanistan reveals how both the Nazis and the Japanese

Islamic Spaces and Overlapping Interests

imperialists framed their connections to the region through the use of origin myths and historical narratives. The Nazis linked their past to a distant and mythologized Aryan race, and the Japanese Empire connected itself to a pre-Islamic Buddhist past. Both powers understood the political importance of the region as an Islamic space sandwiched between Soviet Russia and British India, but in order to exert influence in present-day Afghanistan, they needed to draw on pre-Islamic connections to an imagined Afghan past.

However, in order to get to Afghanistan, the story needs to start in occupied China. After that, the chapter makes two short detours: first to Detroit, Michigan, home of the Nation of Islam, where Japanese agents worked to foster anti-American sentiment among African American Muslim populations in the years leading up to Pearl Harbor; then to North Africa, where imperial Japan observed, assessed, and reported on Fascist Italy's colonial policies and treatment of Muslims in the Mediterranean. These detours help frame the global reach of Japan's imperial ambitions regarding Muslims during the war and reveal the ways Japan hoped Muslims would help it achieve its plans for victory over the Western powers and the Soviets.

On a practical day-to-day level, Japanese officials stationed in Kabul understood the value of having Afghans on their side in the war against the Allies. Through connections made with individual Afghans, Japanese officials envisioned the region as a space where Axis interests could converge. Afghanistan was also an important place for the Japanese Empire to gather intelligence about the movement of Muslims throughout Asia. The Japanese envoy posted in Kabul reported back to Tokyo with news of the whereabouts of Muslims from China and India, and also acted as a go-between for negotiating peace talks and relaying messages from Muslims who had been exiled from British India, displaced from Xinjiang, or were transiting through the region.[1]

Japanese bureaucrats working in Kabul also communicated to Tokyo that they could easily lure Afghans over to "Japan's side" (J. *Nihon gawa*) with relatively inexpensive strategies, such as opening Japanese-sponsored schools, or offering support to parties that opposed the British and Soviets.[2] In order to do this, they maintained that the government should cooperate with the Germans and the Italians to persuade Muslims in Afghanistan to back the "Axis side" (J. *nichidokui-gawa*). These bureaucrats imagined that if their efforts were successful, they could use Afghans to help the Axis powers lure the Turks and the Saudis into the war on their side.[3]

When we examine Japan's wartime expansion through the lens of Islam and Muslims, a number of things become clear. First, the Chinese Nationalists and their allies were deeply concerned about imperial Japan's plans to "go West" and connect with Muslims beyond East Asia. Second, although many of the predominantly Muslim places lay beyond the Greater East Asia Co-Prosperity Sphere, this did not preclude members of the Greater Japan Muslim League and other Japanese bureaucrats from envisioning them as areas for potential Japanese imperial expansion, or as places where imperial Japan should exert influence. At the same time, Japanese imperialists were always anxious about the spread of Soviet Communism into regions under their control, an apprehension shared by the Axis powers at the other end of the Eurasian continent.

Scrutinizing the Japanese Empire's foreign relations with Afghanistan provides just as many insights into its imperial aspirations abroad as it does about how Japanese bureaucrats conceived of their imperial projects at home. Historian Louise Young points out that academics often overlook an important "truism" in Japanese history, namely that "foreign affairs and domestic affairs occupy a single frame."[4] In other words, there is a pressing need for historians of imperial Japan to explore how *all* facets of Japanese foreign affairs impacted the home islands during the war and vice versa. This type of history writing is meant to "shrink the boundary between national, transnational, and international history" in a way that emphasizes that none of these categories are disparate or discrete forms of historical writing.[5] By centering Islam and Sino-Muslims in the discussion of Japan's wartime ambitions, it becomes clear that places like Afghanistan and Detroit were never peripheral to some Japanese bureaucrats and policymakers during the war. Rather, they were interconnected and integral components in the war against Soviet Communism and Western imperialism. Although these far-off places are not part of the standard narrative about World War II in the Pacific, including them offers new insights into the management of the Japanese Empire both at home and abroad.

In order to grasp the full scope of the Japanese imperial project, historians of East Asia need to "suspend the judgement of hindsight, and . . . look at the wartime empire on its own terms."[6] This can only be done through a holistic approach that seriously considers the aims and aspirations of the Japanese imperial project with regards to the Muslims Japan envisioned participating in it.[7] Only by taking a broad approach to Japan's wartime handling of diverse peoples in different situations can we start to assess both the failures and successes of Japan's policy across a broader temporal and geographic spectrum. As historians begin to seriously consider the projects of global fascist imperialisms, new perspectives on the Axis and the interactions among the Germans, the Italians, and the Japanese begin to surface.[8] Engaging with fascist projects on their terms provides a better understanding of the commonalities between the Axis powers and their ongoing appeals to Muslims around the world as viable alternatives to hegemony based on either an idealized white liberal democratic order or Soviet Communism.[9]

At the same time, the Japanese Empire's connections to the Axis powers in Europe often complicated or damaged diplomatic relationships it had worked hard to cultivate, and political maneuverings in Europe regularly overshadowed Japanese policies geared to appeasing Muslims. For example, the Japanese Empire opened an embassy in Istanbul in March 1925, about six months after the Japanese government ratified the Treaty of Lausanne, the international accord that recognized the newly formed Turkish Republic. By 1926, imperial Japan had opened a consulate in Alexandria, followed by a legation in Cairo a few years later. Diplomatic relations with the Egyptians paved the way for legations and consulates in Tehran, Beirut, and Baghdad.[10] However, after Germany and Japan signed the Anti-Comintern Pact in 1936, Turkish-Japanese and Egyptian-Japanese relations cooled as a result of the growing tensions between the British and the Germans.

Likewise, in 1938, the United States had started extracting oil from recently discovered oil fields in Saudi Arabia and was increasingly concerned with security and stability in the region. The same year, Sheikh Hafiz Wahhabi attended the opening of the Tokyo Mosque. While in Tokyo, the sheikh reportedly told Japanese officials that the Saudis were prepared to do business with Japan—which likely dismayed their British and U.S. allies.[11] After the sheikh's visit, the Japanese government sponsored Tang Yichen and four other Sino-Muslims to go on hajj, during which they had an audience with members of the Saudi royal family. As we saw in chapter 3, in April 1939, after the hajjis returned to Beijing, the Japanese Empire sent a number of representatives, including the envoy to Egypt, Masayuki Yokoyama, to Riyadh and Jeddah to negotiate for an oil concession. An agreement was never reached.

By September 1939, Europe was at war and the situation in the Middle East had changed dramatically. Less than a year later, the war spread to North Africa and the Middle East, leading to the closure of the Suez Canal to Japanese shipments. Japanese consulates and legations in Beirut, Baghdad, Tehran, and Alexandria were shut down at the behest of the Allies.[12] These types of maneuverings between the Axis powers and the Allies made lasting impressions on people living throughout Asia and the Middle East. The involvement of Sino-Muslims like Tang Yichen as facilitators for the Japanese diplomatic engagements with Muslims gives us as sense of their utility to the larger geostrategic aims of the Japanese Empire.

Through the framework of global fascism, Muslims are centered in the discussion about the ways the Axis and the Allies vied for power. The Nazis, the Japanese Empire, and the Italian Fascists often had competing and conflicting agendas with regards to Muslims under and outside of their respective control.[13] By assessing the ways Japanese bureaucrats observed and monitored interactions with Muslims by Fascist Italy and Nazi Germany, and through an interrogation of their respective geopolitical concerns in Afghanistan, it is clear that in what might be called the "suburbs" of empire, the Axis powers regularly shared intelligence, mimicked each other's policies, and even coordinated policy regarding Muslim populations. At the same time, their outlook and approaches varied as the ideological frameworks and methods for appealing to minorities by the Japanese Empire, the Italian Fascists, and the Nazis meant that the ways they talked about and engaged with Muslim populations differed vastly. The ways local Muslim populations mediated their relationships with the Axis powers provide further insights into Japanese imperialists' strategies to curry favor with Muslims.

Japanese Overtures and Chinese Nationalist Responses

The Chinese Nationalists worried about imperial Japan's appeals to Muslims not only in occupied China but also around the world. In addition to reporting on the situation in occupied China, the Chinese Nationalist Foreign Ministry's internally circulating document "Japan's Near East Conspiracy" (1940) provided insights into the ways the Japanese imperial apparatus was attempting to win the hearts and minds of Muslims around the globe.[14] According to the report, the Japanese were secretly making connections with Muslims in the Near East and Far East, "lying low" (C. *yinfu*) and operating behind the scenes. The report also claimed that the Japanese army incentivized support from Muslim populations by promoting infrastructure and development projects. For instance, the Chinese Nationalists reported that in Baluchistan (C. *Biluzhi*), the Japanese government promised to help the Balochis defeat the British and offered to sponsor development programs. "Japan's Near East Conspiracy" concluded that this overextending arm of the Japanese imperial government meddled with Muslims beyond the borders of occupied China, and was a threat that needed to be taken seriously.[15] As the Nationalists presented the scenario, the problem was that not all Muslims understood such efforts as part of the Japanese Empire's plot to win over Muslims around the world, and they feared that economic incentives could easily convince Muslims to work with Japanese imperialists. Any Muslim with "ambition" (C. *yexin*), the Nationalists reasoned, might be lured into working with the Japanese for the right price.[16] This meant that it was the duty of the Chinese Nationalists to warn all Muslims—even those outside China—of Japan's evil plans and intentions.[17]

According to the Nationalists, these efforts were all part of the Japanese Empire's "international Muslim conspiracy" (C. *guoji Huijiao yinmou*), which was coordinated with the Italians and the Nazis to lure Muslims over to the Axis side.[18] The Chinese Nationalists even claimed that the Italians and Japanese had signed a top-secret pact to conspire with Muslims all over the world to stop the spread of communism.[19] Moreover, in their overtures to Muslim power brokers in the Middle East, the Nationalists maintained that Japanese imperialists used their connections to the Axis to establish a rapport with Muslims, and that they were quick to send lavish gifts to dignitaries. To demonstrate this point, the Nationalists noted that when King Farouk (c. *Faluke*) of Egypt married Princess Farial in November 1938, the Japanese government sent a large and expensive sword (C. *baojian*) to the newlyweds engraved with suns and crescent moons to symbolize the symbiotic and lasting relationship between imperial Japan and Muslims.[20]

The Nationalist government also recognized that in a relatively short time, Japanese politicians had managed to expand their diplomatic relationships with a number of predominantly Muslim countries. According to Nationalist sources, there were even increasing fears in some diplomatic circles that the Persians would reject the British in favor of the Japanese Empire, which was supposedly supplying them with arms and training officers at the Japanese Naval Academy.[21] The Afghans were also said to be expanding their diplomatic and economic ties with the Japanese Empire in order to upgrade their industrial capacity and train their army.[22] The Chinese Nationalists took note of the interactions and stepped up their own diplomatic engagement with these places.

Xinjiang and the Oppression of Muslims in Central Asia under Soviet Rule

The oppression of Muslims living in Soviet Central Asia was a real concern for many educated Muslims. It was also a useful propaganda tool for the Axis powers. Japanese policymakers were aware of anti-Soviet nationalist movements and presented a number of explanations for the Soviet suppression of Muslims in Central Asia. According to the Greater Japan Muslim League, Vladimir Lenin and Joseph Stalin had made promises to Muslims when they had first adopted a policy of "conciliation and appeasement."[23] However, Sovietization policies and land reform campaigns led many Muslims to flee to Persia and Afghanistan. Land reform campaigns were particularly difficult on nomads, and forced settlements had led the Kazakhs and other communities of nomads to mount armed rebellions (J. *busō hanran*) against the Soviets.[24]

As with Sino-Muslims, Japanese imperialists framed themselves as saviors who could help liberate Central Asian Muslims from the Soviets. To reinforce this point, the Greater Japan Muslim League reminded readers of the endemic problems with alcoholism in the steppe. It was the Russians who had brought vodka to the region, and although Islam prohibits drinking, many Central Asians suffered from alcoholism. The Greater Japan Muslim League also reported that Russians had made feeble attempts at industrialization in Central Asia. However, the people who benefited from industry were not local Muslims but Russian migrants. These examples of exploitative and hazardous policies were used to legitimize the Japanese Empire's own potential involvement in the region.[25] Such problems predated the establishment of the Soviet Union, but the conflation of Soviet Russia with pre-Soviet Russia may have been an effort to reinforce the notion that Central Asian Muslims had long been under attack from the Russian metropole. Or perhaps by pointing to problems that had started under the tsars and continued unabated into the Soviet era, the Greater Japan Muslim League sought to demonstrate the Soviets' inability to improve lives of Central Asian Muslims.

However, at the same time, the Japanese bureaucrats' lengthy and scathing critique of the treatment of Muslim minorities inadvertently reinforced the nationality categories imposed by the Soviets in Central Asia. In a report detailing the situation among Muslims in the Soviet Union, the Greater Japan Muslim League simply adopted the Soviet nationality designations for groups such as the Kazakhs, Kyrgyz, Uzbeks, and Turkmen. Each group receives separate treatment, which begins by rehearsing the essentialized characteristics of these respective Muslim nationalities as categorized by the Soviets. For example, according to the Greater Japan Muslim League, as settled peoples, Uzbeks were more civilized and cultured than the nomadic Central Asian Muslims, whereas Turkmen were said to be a fierce warrior people (J. *hyōkan torukumen-zoku*).[26] As in the Japanese Empire's replication of Dutch colonial data regarding the hajj, this suggests more similarities than differences between the imperial powers' attempts at state-making in the early twentieth century. This story continues later in this chapter, where the overlapping interests of the Axis and Allies created power vacuums and new spaces for Japanese imperial expansion with regards to regions with predominately Muslim populations. But first, a quick stop in Detroit will highlight the Japanese Empire's truly global ambitions to be seen as emancipators of Muslim communities around the world and as a viable alternative to the governments that enabled the post–World War I world order.

Detroit: Japanese Interest in African American Muslims and the Nation of Islam

In 1942, a Japanese agent known as Takahashi Satokata was arrested in the United States. Takahashi was a suspected member of the Black Dragon Society, and shortly before his arrest he supposedly pronounced to African Americans that imperial Japan would be their savior: "Leave the sinking ship of Western civilization. It has reached its end: the Pacific. Beyond lies your friend: Japan, the lifeboat of racial love, made radiant by the star of the East, the Rising Sun."[27] In its ongoing efforts to undermine Western imperial powers, the Japanese government covertly sponsored a number of individuals like Takahashi to infiltrate groups and associations for disenfranchised or underrepresented people, and to spread pro-Japanese propaganda in the United States during the 1930s. In the years leading up to the bombing of Pearl Harbor, Japanese agents did manage to exert influence on a number of African American Muslim groups in the United States. Once again, these "side stories" of empire fall between the cracks of the larger narratives concerning religion, race, and war in the Pacific theater. Including them illuminates how imperial Japan's attempts to win over Muslims did not stop at the edges of the Greater East Asia Co-Prosperity Sphere but were, in fact, truly global ambitions.

African Americans were initially quite supportive of the Japanese Empire, especially after its defeat of the Russians in 1905.[28] For many, the victory undermined theories of white racial superiority deeply embedded in U.S. politics and social life.[29] The Japanese Empire provided African Americans with a model where a "reordering of racial hegemony" was possible, and Pan-Africanist scholars and activists like W. E. B. Du Bois and Marcus Garvey were instrumental in projecting to African Americans the idea that the Japanese Empire was on their side.[30] Historian Shana Redmond claims that the actual impact of the Japanese Empire's agents on the African American community is "difficult, if not impossible, to quantify" but that until Pearl Harbor many prominent African American intellectuals "had only positive impressions of the Japanese and their achievements." This admiration was gained through both real and "imaginary" expressions of Japanese imperial power in the political, technological, and cultural realms.[31]

As with other disenfranchised groups—such as Sino-Muslims—the Japanese government invited African Americans to visit the home islands and their colonies. In one highly publicized visit a few years before the establishment of Manchukuo, well-known civil rights activist and African American writer James Weldon Johnson traveled to Yokohama to attend the Institute of Pacific Relations conference in Kyoto.[32] Other African American activists, like W. E. B. Du Bois, traveled to Japan and returned to the United States with nothing but praise for the Japanese government.[33] In 1936, Du Bois toured the world, and during that trip spent a week in Manchukuo after visiting Shanghai.[34] In Shanghai, Du Bois was disgusted by the accoutrements of imperialism that made the city both famous and infamous. He was also shocked by the exploitation of Chinese workers and servants by Europeans and Americans, which reminded him of slavery in the United States.[35] After Shanghai, Du Bois was invited to visit Manchukuo by the Japanese government, and his highly curated tour impressed him. After spending a few days in Manchukuo, Du Bois dubbed the Japanese efforts in the region a "perfectly epitomized . . . vision of a new anti-racist community."[36] Reflecting on his time in the quasi-sovereign state whose legitimacy was rejected by the majority of the international community, Du Bois noted that "there is, however, no apparent discrimination between motherland and colony in this respect. Nowhere else in the world, to my knowledge, is this true. And why? Because Japanese and Manchukuoans are so nearly related in race that there is nor can be no race prejudice."[37]

Historians with the blessing of hindsight might now say that Du Bois gulped the Japanese Kool-Aid. Although his writings about Manchukuo at the time of his visit are shockingly uncritical, Du Bois was "infatuated" with the optics of the Japanese Empire.[38] Yet, unlike his visit to chaotic and hedonistic Shanghai, Du Bois's tour of Manchukuo was a highly orchestrated affair. Du Bois also had his own agenda, and his writings about Manchukuo should be refracted through what he was hoping to achieve for African Americans in the United States. As he actively supported the Japanese Empire, Du Bois also "developed harsh critiques of American racism against ethnic minorities."[39] Du Bois worked through this conundrum by claiming that Chiang's Nationalist government was a puppet of the white imperialists, thus reducing Japan's invasion of Manchuria to a profound failure of the Wilsonian moment in the post–World War I era.[40]

This perspective helps place the history of African Americans in the Pacific milieu, and Du Bois's support for imperial Japan and the policies it was executing in Manchukuo "illuminates the ironic side of racial liberation" while exposing the deep contradictions in imperial Japan's ongoing efforts to win over colonized and disenfranchised people around the world.[41] Like Du Bois, many other African Americans turned a blind eye to Japanese aggression throughout Asia until the bombing of Pearl Harbor. Ideas that a victory for the Axis would mean a victory over white imperialists were circulated in the United States, and echoed the contemporary understanding of race as a zero-sum game between whites and everyone else.[42] In the aftermath of World War II, "these Afro-Asian political alliances were revived and continued to link African Americans to the 'darker nations' in collective response to the hegemony of the West."[43]

Deeply entangled with African American admiration for imperial Japan were concerted efforts by agents working in the service of empire to infiltrate Muslim African American groups.[44] The Nation of Islam, founded in Detroit in 1930, is an African American political and religious movement based on the teachings of Islam. Its support for the Japanese Empire mixed with the "unfolding messianic nationalist sentiment" brought about by the Great Depression's economic destruction wrought on African American communities that had moved north to cities like Detroit and Chicago after the U.S. Civil War. In the months before Pearl Harbor, a number of Japanese agents were arrested by the Federal Bureau of Investigation (FBI) on suspicion of working to infiltrate the Nation of Islam and other similar groups in the United States.[45] All connections between Japanese agents and the Nation of Islam were severed after Pearl Harbor, and raids in September 1942 on three splinter groups of the organization led to the arrest of the majority of the African American Muslims who held known pro-Japanese views.[46]

In total, eighty-five people were arrested, many on charges of draft-dodging. In the U.S. media, the sympathies of African American Muslims toward the Japanese Empire were downplayed, and the well-publicized "arrests of a handful of black dissidents on sedition charges during World War II seemed much more geared towards the intimidation" of African Americans by law enforcement than any real concern about an underground Japanese–African American plot to destroy the United States from within.[47] Yet this should not be interpreted as evidence that Japanese agents had no impact on members of the Nation of Islam, nor does it exclude the possibility that the Japanese Empire was making concerted efforts to connect with African American Muslims. In fact, one of the better-known splinter groups of the Nation of Islam, Development of Our Own, was heavily influenced by Japanese propaganda.[48] Development of Our Own was established in 1933 in Detroit but had branches throughout the Midwest, with around 10,000 members across fourteen chapters. Some members pledged allegiance to Emperor Hirohito, and the organization developed a Confucian- and Buddhist-inspired code of conduct, which was introduced to them by the elusive Japanese agent Takahashi Satokata. Takahashi claimed to have connections to the Black Dragon Society, but his links to the Japanese imperial government remain dubious. What is clear is that he was active in the African American Muslim community, urging support of the Japanese Empire around the Midwest throughout the 1930s.[49]

These actions were not coordinated through the Greater Japan Muslim League, yet the organization was aware of the power of disenfranchised and marginalized peoples to foment dissent. In the end, although Japanese propaganda aimed at U.S. Muslims may have only appealed to a marginalized few, it raised enough concern to inspire an FBI investigation that led to the arrest and incarceration of a relatively large number of U.S. citizens after the outbreak of the Pacific War. The attempts to infiltrate Muslim organizations and religious groups in the United States were part of the Japanese Empire's efforts to undermine Western imperialism. To do this, Japan needed to both connect to and distance itself from the rhetoric and policies of its Axis partners. For African American Muslims, the Japanese Empire was a much more credible champion than the Nazis or the Italians.[50] The Japanese Empire faced a dilemma: although it wanted to be similar to its Nazi and Italian Fascist allies, its approaches toward ethnic and religious minorities in China and the United States often differentiated it from its European partners. The differences in the Axis powers' approaches were grounded in their respective conceptualizations of race and racial hierarchy, which were deeply embedded in the ideological underpinnings of their imperial projects. How the Japanese Empire attempted to balance these tensions surrounding Muslims and Islamic spaces is the focus of the rest of this chapter.

The Berlin-Rome-Tokyo Axis and Sino-Muslims

The Japanese Empire needed ways to connect itself rhetorically and ideologically to the Italian Fascists and the Nazis, and this was not always easy for policymakers to do. Through the creation of origin stories and the retelling of Muslim pasts, the Greater Japan Muslim League projected deep historical connections to Sino-Muslims on the mainland in ways similar to what the Nazis and the Italians were doing among Mediterranean Muslim populations. For their part, Sino-Muslim travelers relayed their experiences meeting diasporic communities of Muslims living in Rome or Berlin to readers back home, offering a mirror for the experiences of Muslims living and studying in Tokyo. Accounts of such connections, intended to foster Pan-Islamism through a sense of shared experience for all Muslims living under the Axis umbrella, were also meant to showcase the Muslim networks facilitated by Axis cooperation as evidence of Japanese, Italian Fascist, and Nazi support for Islam.[51] The deep histories created by the Axis powers were the cultural justifications for more practical and immediate actions that would have been impossible without them.

Japanese policymakers learned from German and Italian mistakes and successes with Muslim populations throughout North Africa, the Balkans, and the Middle East from before World War I up until the end of World War II.[52] In a number of instances, Japanese policies closely mirrored both German and Italian models for dealing with Muslims, although Japanese policymakers were always quick to point out the differences.[53] Before Pearl Harbor, the Greater Japan Muslim League was keenly aware that in areas under Japan's control, Muslims made up a minority of the population, unlike in North Africa and the Middle East, or in parts of the Balkans, where Muslims were the sizable majority. This presented a different set of challenges for imperial Japan. The Greater Japan Muslim League also wrote about the Nazis' and the Italian Fascists' experiences with Muslims to defend Japan's own approaches to managing Muslims.[54] Central to these efforts was a secret document written in 1938 that outlined both the German and the Italian approaches for handling Muslims under their control. Although it also provides information about the Germans, the document is simply titled "Italy's Muslim Policy" (J. *Itaria no Kaikyō seisaku*).[55] It outlined both the historical and contemporary relationship between the Italian Empire and its North African colonies, and drew on German experiences in World War I with the Ottoman Empire, as well as on Nazi Germany's forays into the Balkans and the Middle East as powerful case studies for the Japanese Empire's handling of Muslims living under its control.

Part I: The Italians—Policies Worth Emulating?

There is general consensus among historians that Fascist Italy's ventures into North Africa were an abject failure, and that the Italian pacification campaigns against North Africans were violent and brutal.[56] Latecomers (like the Germans) to the scramble for Africa, the Italians managed to secure a foothold in East Africa by the 1880s. They were rebuffed by the French in their attempts to encroach on what is now Tunisia but managed to establish a colony in Libya, which they were forced to give up after World War I. After Mussolini's march on Rome, one of his first objectives was to "reconquer" parts of North Africa that had been under Italian control. Between 1922 and 1931, the Italians launched a "bloody colonial war," killing around one-tenth of the local populations in the region.[57] By the outbreak of World War II, over 40,000 Italian colonists were settled on land stolen from Berbers and Arabs trying to eke out a living in the North African desert.[58]

In many regards, the model colonist envisioned by Mussolini was the diametric opposite of the dregs of society sent to North Africa. Although there were Italian laws intended to protect the rights of locals, Italian settlers regularly broke them with impunity, and the colonists were notorious for their violence against local populations. "This contradiction . . . lay at the heart of the Fascist imperial project" in Africa.[59] The oppression was so brutal that when the Allies defeated the Italians in the African campaigns during World War II, many locals happily sided with the British in order to kill Italian colonists in retribution. After years of oppression, murders, and rapes at the hands of Italian colonists, North Africans initially saw the British as liberators.[60]

So why, then, did members of the Greater Japan Muslim League praise Mussolini and his advisers for what they considered to be successful policies handling Muslims in the region? The truths regarding Italian rule in North Africa did not stop the Japanese Empire from admiring and presenting Mussolini's policies there as great accomplishments. Through parallels and comparisons, "Italy's Muslim Policy" outlined the relationship between Italy and Muslims in North and East Africa, and at the same time confirmed to military advisers that the Japanese Empire faced similar predicaments as the Nazis and the Italian Fascists.[61]

The Greater Japan Muslim League compared the situation in Japan to that in Italy, where there were also very few Muslims living in the first years of the twentieth century. It also noted Italy's late arrival to colonialism in Africa. Comparing Japan's situation to Italy's, the league deemed both of these factors to be advantageous for the Italians.[62] The report singled out Libya as the place where Italian policies and strategies were the most successful.[63] According to the Greater Japan Muslim League, before World War I, the Ottomans had assisted the Libyans in their fight against Italian imperialism. At that time, the Italians had not understood that governing Muslims would be different from governing Italians. This lack of understanding and respect for local customs and culture, along with the overwhelming number of colonists sent to Libya in the first decade of the twentieth century, had led to armed resistance against Italian rule. However, after World War I, the Italians had learned from their mistakes and started developing heavy industry in Libya. According to the Greater Japan Muslim League, Italy also shifted its policies to promote goodwill and cultural understanding (J. *yūkō-teki bunka seisaku*) between Italians and local Muslims.[64] As part of the larger plan to promote development and cultural understanding, the report indicated that the Italians funded the building of mosques, schools, hospitals, bridges, and roads.

For the bureaucrats who authored the secret document, these were tangible markers of the Italian presence in Libya. The Italians changed the colony's physical landscape by developing industry and providing jobs for locals. This resulted in a higher standard of living among certain segments of the population. The report stated that in a few years the Italians had managed to transform their reputation in Libya and were seen much more positively.[65] The "successes" of the fascist ally in Libya allowed Japanese bureaucrats to offer implicit justification for their own investment in Sino-Muslims.

Mussolini himself offered another justificatory parallel by visiting Tripoli to declare himself the protector of Islam (J. *Kaikyō no hogo-sha*).[66] At the time, Mussolini was promising a beneficial relationship between Fascism and Islam to Muslims throughout the region. In its propaganda in North Africa, the Greater Japan Muslim League noted that the Italians pointed to the French and the British as the real enemies of Muslims, and that the Italian government funded and armed anti-British and anti-French colonial movements throughout the region.[67] "Italy's Muslim Policy" also noted that the Italians invited Muslim students to Rome from India, China, and Afghanistan to participate in the Asian Student Congress (J. *Ajia gakusei kaigi*) in 1933. At the congress, Mussolini addressed the 500 students in attendance with a rousing speech about the Italian Fascists' plans to help Muslims free themselves from colonialism. Furthermore, the secret report noted that the Italians were exporting their vision of Fascist youth culture to their North African colonies, where they had established a number of Green Shirt organizations (J. *midori shatsu tō*). The Greater Japan Muslim League claimed that many young Muslims happily signed up, since being a part of the organization could give them the opportunity to study in Rome.[68] Taken together, these policies were tactics for recruiting young and impressionable Muslims that Japanese imperialists were already replicating in Asia. The authors of "Italy's Muslim Policy" believed that Japan could learn from the Italians, but they also cautioned policymakers and militarists to proceed with caution when adopting Italian models throughout Asia.

The Greater Japan Muslim League considered the Italians to be successful in inciting anti-British violence among Muslim populations in North Africa and the Middle East, as demonstrated by Italian support for the Arab Revolts. The league also admired the Arabic-language radio stations that the Italians used to broadcast in North Africa, and the league also produced radio broadcasts directed at Muslim populations living throughout Asia during the war.[69] Through radio propaganda and their continued support of Muslims in the Levant, the organization claimed, the Italians had won the approval of certain segments of the Muslim populations in India, Syria, Iraq, and Egypt.

In addition, the report stated that the Italians were supplying arms to the Aga Khan (J. *Aga Kan*) to fight the British in India.[70] Japanese observers described this policy as one that could work with Muslim populations in East Asia. By arming Muslim communities that were oppressed by the British, Japan could demonstrate its support for Muslim-backed nationalist movements in places like Malaya and Afghanistan. "Italy's Muslim Policy" concluded that unlike the British, who were intent on dominating Muslims for the purpose of extracting as much oil as possible from the Middle East, the Italians were trying to cooperate with Muslims for their mutual benefit. It was from this "cooperative model" that Japanese analysts thought they could learn the most. By following the Italians' lead, the report concluded, the Japanese Empire could make similar inroads with the Muslim populations that had recently come under its direct control.

For their part, Italian scholars were also interested in Japanese involvement with Muslims in China and published regularly about Sino-Muslims in widely circulated journals like *Oriente Moderno*. The stories highlight the transnational movement and connections that these Muslim elites maintained and cultivated with the support of the Axis powers throughout the global war, and *Oriente Moderno* covered a wide variety of topics concerning Muslims moving around the world with Axis backing. One article mentioned that five Muslim students had traveled from Manchukuo to enroll at Al-Azhar with support from the Japanese. The students in question were not Sino-Muslims but refugees who had fled the Bolsheviks and were being sponsored by an organization that attempted to "reunite Turkish Muslims who were refugees from Russian territory."[71] *Oriente Moderno* used this story to highlight the ways the Japanese Empire supported anti-Soviet Muslims.[72]

In December 1937, a news story appeared about representatives from Arab nations who had recently returned from attending the "Young Asia Congress" in Tokyo. The congress reportedly brought together over 200 youths from India, Siam, Inner Mongolia, Arab nations, North China, and Manchukuo. At the meeting, students discussed a number of pressing issues, including ways they could help oppose European and U.S. interference in the Sino-Japanese conflict, and how Asian countries could pressure the British to stop supplying arms to the Nationalists via Hong Kong. They also discussed the possibility of other Asian nations joining the Anti-Comintern Pact.[73] These efforts directed at students in the fight against communism and imperialism were always presented as the most successful way for the Axis powers to demonstrate their continued support for one another.

Italian readers also learned, from an Axis perspective, about the history of Islam in China and where the Japanese Empire fit into this narrative. In 1938, *Oriente Moderno* ran translations of a number of lectures delivered in Cairo by Nationalist-supported Sino-Muslim Ma Jian. The lecture series was meant to introduce Egyptians to the particularities of Islam in China.[74] Drawing on earlier works written in Europe, the Italian translator editorialized Ma's speech to make Chinese Islamic traditions appear backward and associated with cult-like ancestor worship. This presentation of Muslims from China as being less pious and less "Islamic" than other Muslims gave the Italian translator the chance to plug the redemptive qualities of the Japanese Empire.[75] Although Muslims in China participated in the "Confucian Cult," he explained that they were not quite as "backward" as they had once been. For this they could thank their increased interactions with "great Islamic nations," which were facilitated by their engagement with the Japanese Empire, whose "well-known Islamic policy . . . might offer them new reasons to detach themselves still more from their countrymen of different faiths."[76] For Italian readers, *Oriente Moderno* helped to broaden the idea of the varieties and variances of Islamic practices around the world while also acknowledging Japanese imperial aspirations involving Sino-Muslims.

Part II: The Germans—Go East!

Japan's admiration and support of its European allies' policies toward Muslims extended to German policies from before World War I. In the years leading up to World War I, Kaiser Wilhelm II was deeply involved in the Ottoman Empire. His undertakings there proved a powerful case study for Japanese imperialists, who hoped to learn from some of the kaiser's over-ambitious political blunders in the region. Although the Greater Japan Muslim League admired his bold moves, it also used them as a warning for Japanese strategists and militarists, whose grand visions for a Greater Asia would similarly require them to appeal to large numbers of Muslims without overstepping their own political and religious limitations. Kaiser Wilhelm's maneuverings in the Ottoman Empire highlighted how he fashioned himself as a benevolent protector of the Ottomans while antagonizing colonial powers throughout the region. The kaiser's vision of weltpolitik included a plan to unite East and West through Constantinople with the Berlin to Baghdad railroad.[77] His plans ensured German access to the Arabian Gulf without reliance on the Suez Canal and provided a direct, German-controlled route to India.[78] Wilhelm's foreign policy plan *Drang nach Osten* ("push eastward") consisted of a continental drive into Ottoman territory. It also had an important cultural component. In the plan, he emphasized that Germans should learn about Islam, and in return they would spread German culture to Muslims.

After visiting the Ottoman Sultan Abdul Hamid in the Sublime Porte, Kaiser Wilhelm declared the German people the eternal friends of the Ottomans. Allying himself with the sultan meant that Wilhelm was "meddling in the affairs of other powers with Muslim subjects—not least French North Africa, Russian Central Asia, and the British Empire, which alone contained some 100 million Muslims spread out over British India, Egypt, and the Gulf States."[79] On this same trip, he continued to travel throughout the region and came away with an orientalist appreciation for Islam. At one point, Wilhelm reportedly declared that he was interested in converting to Islam. Although this declaration was likely a political gesture, it prompted references to "Hajji Wilhelm" in Arabic newspapers around the region.[80]

Historians tend to agree that in their efforts to mobilize Muslims, the gravest mistake that the Germans made during World War I was to underestimate the political backlash from sponsoring an Ottoman call for jihad. In retrospect, the jihad is considered a massive political miscalculation, but at the time it alarmed the British, the French, and the Russians, who decided to keep troops in the Middle East that could have been diverted to the European Front.[81] On November 11, 1914, the Ottoman sheikh al-Islam Ürgüplü Hayri issued five fatwas with German backing. Three days later, in an elaborate ceremony at the Fatih Mosque in Constantinople, Sultan Mehmed V declared it "the duty of Muslims everywhere on earth to wage war on [Entente] infidels."[82] However, there were serious theological problems with the fatwas.[83] They were distinguished by "the open-ended selection of targets — including Entente civilians, along with armies — and the pointed exemptions for German and Austro-Hungarian nationals, for which there was no precedent."[84] Mehmed V's declaration was also considered by many Muslims to be a symbolic last-ditch effort by the sultan to retain power despite his lack of legitimacy in the eyes of his subjects.[85] In essence, the observers from the Greater Japan Muslim League came to similar conclusions as a number of prominent historians of modern Germany: they felt that Wilhelm's efforts were perceived by the Entente powers and by Muslims as overreach into territory that did not concern him.

During the interwar period, German interest in Islam was predominantly scholarly. However, as in Japan, this changed suddenly with the outbreak of World War II in Europe. In 1938, Hitler had *Mein Kampf* translated into Arabic, and it was distributed in Arabic-speaking regions. As in Japan, it was also during this time that the interests of German intellectuals interested in Islam became more closely aligned with the Nazi Party. Japanese policymakers wrote about German policies in order to legitimize their own imperial aspirations and create closer ties with the Axis powers in the 1930s.[86] If the authors of "Italy's Muslim Policy" understood the drawbacks of the kaiser's plans to call for a jihad against the Entente powers in World War I, they also felt they could learn from and apply the concepts of *Drang nach Osten* (J. *Dorangu naha osuten*) in Asia.[87] In the eyes of the Greater Japan Muslim League, *Drang nach Osten* was coined to justify German expansion into Slavic lands in the nineteenth century, but the term had been appropriated by Hitler in the 1930s as a major tenet of Nazism, which involved the Germanization of Slavic and other non-German peoples.[88] Later, Hitler relied on these same ideas to create his *Islampolitik*, and, according to Japanese observers, these expansionist Nazi campaigns during World War II were simply *Drang nach Osten* repackaged for the war.[89] In the same section, the report also remarked on an alleged German plan to send a secret envoy (J. *misshi*) to get the Afghans to declare a jihad (J. *Kaikyō senső*) on the Allies.[90]

One Sino-Muslim observer writing in Japanese-occupied China remarked that the Nazis had the most successful Islamic policy among the "old European powers" (C. *Ouzhou lieqiang*).[91] Unlike the British, the Germans paid attention to the needs and demands of Muslims rather than blindly trying to "win over governments" (C. *lalong zhengfu*) with financial incentives.[92] Moreover, the Nazis had planned to bring an end to "Jewish capitalism" (C. *youtai ziben zhuyi*), which, according to the Sino-Muslim commentator, appealed to Muslims throughout the world.[93] These ideas not only parroted Nazi racialized ideologies but also reveal how some Sino-Muslims might have been supportive of Nazi policies toward Jews in this particular historical moment.

In Nazi racial categorizations, Arabs were considered Semites. Perhaps not surprisingly then, the rhetoric of "anti-Jewish" rather than "anti-Semite" appeared much more frequently in Nazi propaganda directed at Muslims living in British- and French-occupied regions of the Middle East.[94] The Greater Japan Muslim League acknowledged that one of the Nazis' biggest problems in appealing widely to Arabs and other nonwhites was their overt anti-Semitic racism. This particular brand of Nazi racism was presented as an opportunity: because the Japanese were not white and had no previous colonial encounters with other nonwhite peoples, they could more easily attract non-Western people to their own imperial ideology, which was not overtly anti-Semitic. They also had no long-standing grievances with any peoples in the Middle East or North Africa. In reality, of course, Japanese militarists and bureaucrats also had their own racial hierarchies of empire and were often explicitly racist in the formulation of their policies. Japan itself was also not immune to anti-Semitism, and the virulent hatred of Jews (of whom there were almost none in Japan) was tactically used by ultranationalist ideologues and the Japanese Imperial Army to attack Japanese Communists and other groups based on racialized tropes throughout the war.[95] In this case, however, the differences between how the Japanese Empire ordered people and how the Nazis constructed racial hierarchies was presented as a point of entry for the Japanese imperial project into places with large numbers of Muslims beyond East Asia.

German and Japanese outreach to Muslims did overlap in one very surprising place. Japanese observers commented on the favorable treatment of Sino-Muslim communities in the German-occupied Qingdao region prior to the Japanese takeover after World War I. One commenter noted that the Japanese needed to thank the Germans for their generous treatment of Muslims in Shandong.[96] Although tenuous, this connection of the German presence in Qingdao to the Japanese occupation with regards specifically to Sino-Muslim communities served an important purpose. Although the Japanese Empire's reception of the Shandong peninsula as part of the spoils of war after World War I goes unmentioned, the suggestion of a connection between the ways the Germans and the Japanese treated Muslims living in the same place reinforced the Axis relationship. Japanese policymakers concocted some abstruse connections to their own involvement with Sino-Muslims with invented German policy successes in Asia.

Stories that connected the Japanese Empire to the Germans and the Italians by comparing their treatment of Muslims living under the Axis purview did a number of things. First, they allowed the Japanese Empire to express a sense of camaraderie linking the Axis powers and a shared policy concern. Second, such narratives allowed the Japanese Empire to continue to vilify the Western imperialists and the Soviets and claim that the Axis powers treated Muslims better than the Allies did. As the Nazis pressed east with *Islampolitik*, the Japanese Empire pushed west, and their respective imperial interests and concern about Islam inevitably began to converge in places we might not expect, like Afghanistan.

Geographies of Empire and the Spaces in Between: Go East! Go West! We'll Meet in . . . Afghanistan!

This section takes us to a place generally not considered when examining the wartime objectives of either the Nazis or the Japanese Empire: Afghanistan. By placing Muslims and Muslim spaces in the context of the Japanese Empire's anti-Western, anti-Soviet agitation throughout World War II, peripheries are centered, new actors emerge, and new stories about Japan's wartime ambitions unfold. Here, Afghanistan becomes the locus of wartime geopolitical maneuverings in Asia between the Axis and the Allies, and between the competing imperial aspirations of the Nazis and the Japanese Empire. As one of the only nations to maintain neutrality during the war, Afghanistan provides a space for thinking about how the Axis and Allies vied for power in a region generally not taken into consideration when discussing the history of World War II. Although the British exerted a fair amount of influence over Afghan politics in this period, Afghans themselves remained opposed to joining the war effort, and they maintained a pro-Axis neutrality throughout the war. The focus on Afghanistan therefore provides the opportunity to complicate the idea of neutrality, and to highlight that neutrality during wartime is never really value-free. In Afghanistan, the Axis powers interacted in a place predominantly populated by Muslims, yet this story is almost entirely absent from the historiography of the Japanese Empire and Nazi Germany.

Bringing the peripheries of World War II into focus affords new perspectives on the management of the Japanese Empire and Nazi Germany, on their imperial ambitions, and on their respective outlooks regarding Muslim populations. By decentering the European and Pacific theaters, a focus on Afghanistan offers fresh insights into this truly global war from the vantage point of the Muslim populations who inhabited spaces often imagined as marginal to Berlin and Tokyo. However, as historian Robert Crews has aptly pointed out, Afghans "never imagined themselves as peripheral to the rest of the world," during World War II or at any other time in their long history.[97] In fact, in the years leading up to the war, Afghans were "imperial cosmopolitans" who traveled to Rome, Berlin, and Tokyo to study. In this regard, elite Afghans facilitated connections between the Axis powers in a way that gave them agency vis-à-vis both the Nazis and Japanese imperialists.

The focus on Afghanistan and the Axis does a number of things. Taking both the Nazis' and imperial Japan's efforts to understand the Afghan past seriously and within the geopolitical context of the war provides new insights into the ways ideological discussions surrounding, "antiquarianism, Aryanism, liberalism . . . socialism," and Buddhism informed Japanese, German, and Afghan historical discourses.[98] There is also a growing body of historiography in English concerning Afghanistan and its past. However, despite the important and deep connections between Japan and Afghanistan throughout the 1930s and 1940s, the Japanese are mostly absent from these histories, with the exception of a few Japanese actors regularly dismissed as spies.[99] By taking Japanese ambitions in the region seriously, we begin to see how the policies that started in North China among Sino-Muslims catalyzed Japanese imperial outreach into these aspirational spaces of empire.

Placing Afghanistan within the larger context of geopolitical maneuverings in Inner Asia also decenters China as the focus of Japan's policies directed specifically at Muslims throughout the region. By framing the discussion around the ways Tokyo was often much more concerned with Russian (and later Soviet) and British incursions into the region than with those of the Chinese Nationalists, new possibilities for Japanese interest in the region are unveiled.[100] For example, early on, Japanese policymakers in the late nineteenth century watched "negotiations regarding the Russian return of Ili to the Qing closely," as a way to gauge how the Qing would handle diplomatic negotiations concerning the Ryukyus and Formosa.[101] Then, after the Russo-Japanese War, Japan stepped up its intelligence gathering about Rus-

Islamic Spaces and Overlapping Interests

sia throughout Inner Asia to figure out ways to "trigger political disturbances in China," but "with the ultimate goal of fomenting broader opposition to the Russian presence in Central Asia."[102]

Afghanistan also provides an illuminating case study for examining the overlapping, often conflicting imperial objectives of the Germans and the Japanese with regards to Muslim populations. Through an exploration of the ways both the Japanese and the Germans created and manipulated connections to an Afghan past — connections later internalized by Afghans — we get a different sense of how race and religion played into the imperial outlook of the Nazis and the Japanese Empire beyond what we would generally consider to be their spheres of influence. This engagement with the Axis "peripheries" provides an interesting juxtaposition for examining Nazi and Japanese imperial plans in a highly strategic geopolitical location with a deep history.

By drawing on symbols from the past in their overtures to the Afghans, Japanese policymakers regularly "played up the common trait of respect for the warrior tradition and for the male-dominated patriarchal family systems," which supposedly differentiated them from Westerners.[103] They drew on deep, imagined connections to a pre-Islamic Buddhist past between Japan and Afghanistan that was often embodied in the commonalities between some essentialized version of Afghan tribalism and Japanese *bushidō* culture. The Nazis relied on symbols from the past too and, in the case of Afghanistan, managed to tie the historical destiny of the German people to a mythologized Aryan race from a distant Afghan past. These stories "served as modern myths binding the collective together," and connected people from Afghanistan to either the Nazis or imperial Japan in ways that would have been impossible without them.[104] It was through these imagined historical connections that the Nazis and Japanese imperialists presented themselves as allies to the Afghans. However, in reality their relationship was utterly modern: both the Germans' and the Japanese Empire's diplomatic engagements with Afghanistan only began at the turn of the twentieth century.

As for the Afghans, they had been dealing with the Russians and the British for almost seventy years before Japanese and German explorers and archaeologists began casing the region for artifacts to fill museums and mantelpieces back home. In the 1830s, while the British Empire was securing its hold over India and making inroads into Qing Central Asian markets, it became increasingly interested in the area north of India as a bulwark against Russian imperial expansion. By the end of the 1830s, the British attacked what is now Afghanistan, but they were defeated three years later. This would come to be known as the First Anglo-Afghan War. After their initial victory over the British, the people living in the arid Hindu Kush came into increased contact with the world beyond their immediate periphery, commencing what Nile Green calls a "product of dialogical exchange" between Afghans and the modern world.[105]

The British continued to exert influence in the region, and in 1878, the Second Anglo-Afghan War broke out. The Russians, who were increasingly concerned with British interference in regional affairs, refused to offer support to Afghans, and although the war was "not quite as disastrous as the first," it was counted as a "debacle" in London even though the British were victorious and Afghanistan was made into a British protectorate.[106] By the end of the nineteenth century, there were a number of competing local political power brokers in Afghanistan. Some wanted independence from the British, while others were happy to maintain the status quo. In 1880, as British troops withdrew from the region at the end of the Second Anglo-Afghan War, one of these local power brokers, Abd al-Rahman, "seized power" in Afghanistan.[107] Abd al-Rahman took this opportunity as the big power players—the Russians and the British—were more concerned with one another than with local politics. He managed to maintain a precarious hold on power by ostracizing families who did not support him and sending many elite Afghans into exile. After his death in 1901, families who had been banished during his rule started to return to Afghanistan.[108] While exiled in the Ottoman Empire or British India, these exiles got a glimpse into the fin-de-siècle Ottoman reforms and the political administration of the British raj. These experiences had a deep impact on the exiles, and many returned home poised to reform Afghanistan and return it to its former position as an independent and vital player in Asian politics.

After Japan's victory over Russia in 1905, political reformers throughout Asia were eager to send military personnel to Japan for instruction, and Afghanistan was no exception. In 1907, General Ayub Khan, a veteran of the Second Anglo-Afghan War, visited the Tokyo Naval Academy and stayed in Japan for about three months. Throughout the first two decades of the twentieth century, the Afghan affinity toward imperial Japan continued to grow, and after World War I the Afghan government attempted to establish diplomatic relations with Tokyo. However, the British put political pressure on the Japanese government to deny the Afghan request to open a legation in Tokyo, and the Japanese acquiesced. It was not until the 1930s that Afghanistan and the Japanese Empire would formally establish diplomatic relations.

As Afghanistan began its reengagement with the wider world, the wider world also became interested in Afghanistan. Japanese explorers were among the first non-Europeans to make expeditions to the region, close on the heels of European orientalist adventurers and archaeologists like Sven Hedin. Between 1902 and 1914, Japanese Buddhists, led by Tachibana Zui-chō of the Nishi Honganji branch of the Jōdo Shinshū sect, were sponsored by the eccentric Japanese count Ōtani Kōzui to undertake three exploratory expeditions to Chinese Turkestan, Pakistan, and Northern India. Although these particular expeditions did not make their way to Afghanistan, the purpose of these types of trips was to uncover the pre-Islamic Buddhist connections between Japan and the region, as well as to extract Buddhist art, scriptures, and artifacts for museums and private collections on the home islands.[109]

In the years following the Meiji Restoration, Japanese Buddhism was "in a state of crisis as a result of imperial efforts to establish Shintō as a state religion."[110] During this time, wealthy Japanese patrons sponsored religious reform campaigns, some of which involved sending monks to overseas Buddhist communities to "reconnect" with their roots. Ōtani was one of these men. He had a vision of a pan-Asian Buddhist past that he wanted to recover in the face of what he perceived as the Japanese state's assault on Buddhism.[111] Ōtani's objectives and motives were different than later imperial objectives, but the rhetoric of deep historical connections dating back to the transmission of Buddhism to Japan via China was drawn upon regularly to justify Japanese imperial expansion into the region thirty years later.[112]

There was a lot of speculation surrounding Ōtani's intentions and Tachibana's wanderings around the Taklimakan Desert, over the Karakorum Pass, and through Pakistan to meet up with his benefactor in Bombay. These suspicions came from Western powers, owing in part to the tense political climate in British India, and in part to the ongoing friction between the Russians and the Japanese Empire in the aftermath of the Russo-Japanese War. Remarking on the possibility of Tachibana's nefarious intentions, U.S. professor Chester Fuson wrote, "Into this far interior of Asia, the Japanese also have penetrated. Two Japanese, ostensibly archaeological explorers but suspected by the other foreigners of being secret service men," were in the area on "private business, which may have been to keep informed as to Russian power in Central Asia."[113] These claims might have some credibility, as shortly after the earliest Ōtani mission, the first foreign mission from Afghanistan was sent to imperial Japan. Yet the Japanese were not exceptional in this regard: Western explorers were also providing intelligence to European governments and attempting to undermine each other's power in the region.

At the other end of the Eurasian continent, the Germans were also developing an interest in Afghanistan and the region surrounding it. The first official German mission to Afghanistan took place during World War I. On a trip back from Central Asia to Sweden, famed traveler and geographer Sven Hedin stopped in Berlin for a meeting with Kaiser Wilhelm. Hedin told the kaiser that the "Afghans were burning with desire" to free themselves from the British.[114] This pleased Wilhelm, and in order to get a better sense of where the Afghan people stood on British rule, he arranged for a delegation to leave promptly. On the journey, Werner-Otto von Hentig and Oskar Niedermayer were joined by an Indian guide named Mahendra Pratap and by Mohammed Barakatullah, the "second-ranking member of the Indian Revolutionary Committee in Berlin." Barakatullah had spent six years in New York promoting anti-British revolutionary causes before making his way to Tokyo. In Tokyo, he taught Hindi at the Tokyo University of Foreign Studies before moving to Germany.[115]

The journey took the group overland via Constantinople and down through Iraq. En route, von Hentig noted that "this was the route previously taken . . . by Alexander the Great, the Apostle Paul and Friedrich Barbarossa."[116] By connecting their own journey to the Ancient Greeks, a companion of Jesus Christ, and one of the most revered Holy Roman emperors, von Hentig was not only claiming to be in illustrious company but also asserting that he and his companions were fulfilling a historical destiny. When they finally arrived in Afghanistan, the Germans requested an audience with Habibullah, the pro-British emir, and the two parties drafted a friendship treaty that included provisions for diplomatic exchanges between Afghanistan and Germany, accompanied by an infusion of German military aid to Afghanistan. It seems that the Germans and the Afghans were both fully aware that the friendship treaty was a formality, as both parties knew that the British would never allow the Germans to send weapons and military advisers to Afghanistan.

Publicly, the emir stated that he supported the treaty; however, this was likely to indicate his support for maintaining the status quo in the German-backed Ottoman Empire rather than an indication of any real desire to engage in diplomatic relations with the Germans. The delegation returned to Germany and relayed their experiences to the kaiser. The men claimed that in their negotiations with the Afghans they had faced "daily frustrations with delicate and moving targets" that led to "precarious arrangements, implausible alliances, and marriages of convenience."[117] However, the situation on the ground in Afghanistan changed quickly, and in the months that followed their return to Berlin, Habibullah was murdered. The identity of his assassin was never discovered. One of his brothers, Amanullah, came to power. Amanullah was more amenable to a relationship with the Germans, leading to the opening of a German school in Kabul and the implementation of reforms that had been suggested by the German delegation in the friendship treaty.

After the end of the Third Anglo-Afghan War in August 1919, Amanullah Khan declared independence from the British and began "pursuing a third power strategy" to ensure that Afghans were supported in their ongoing efforts to thwart British and Russian influences.[118] Around this time, the first delegation of Afghani diplomats traveled to Berlin. However, it was not until 1932 that Dr. Fritz Grobba went to Afghanistan for a diplomatic visit on behalf of the Nazi Party. Grobba had been the German consul in Kabul in the 1920s after Germany and Afghanistan established diplomatic relations in 1923. He worked for some years in the Middle East branch of the Weimar government's Foreign Ministry and was appointed German ambassador to Iraq in the fall of 1932. Grobba worked closely with the government in Kabul and was instrumental in the establishment of stronger ties between Germany and Afghanistan.[119]

The Italians also engaged in bilateral relations with the Afghans in the years after World War I. In fact, Italy was the first nation to recognize the sovereignty of Afghanistan, leading to cordial relations between the two nations. In 1921, after the two countries signed a friendship treaty, the Afghans opened a legation in Rome. When Amahullah Khan was deposed in 1919, he fled to Rome on an Italian army plane and remained in Italy during his exile. The Italians also sent a number of engineers to help with Afghan development projects, and in exchange a number of Afghan students were sent to study in Italy throughout the 1920s and early 1930s.[120]

It was not until 1931 that the Japanese and Afghan governments established official diplomatic relations. By 1933, the Afghans had opened a legation in Tokyo, and the following spring they broke ground on a new building in the imperial capital. A few months later, the Japanese government opened a legation in Kabul. In the history of Japanese-Afghan relations, 1934 marks the true beginning of bilateral diplomatic relations between the two states. One Afghan commentator wrote that in 1934, "the wishes of the Afghans and the Japanese came true," as reciprocal legations would make diplomatic and trade negotiations between the two countries much easier.[121] By 1935, there was an exchange of teachers and other professionals, and the Afghan government put out a notice in Japan advertising a number of high-ranking jobs that could be filled by Japanese professionals, such as engineers and lawyers. In return, the Japanese government invited Afghan students to study in Tokyo, and the first group of Afghan students sponsored by the International Students Association (J. *Kokusai gakuyū-kai*) arrived in February 1936.[122]

These efforts were also part of a growing desire by both the Japanese and Afghan governments to increase trade between the two countries. U.S. observers noted that by 1939, cheap Japanese manufactured goods such as low-quality silk and chinaware had "ousted all Russian and Indian goods" of a similar kind in the markets of Kabul and Kandahar.[123] Silk and livestock made up the majority of Japanese exports to the region. In return, the Afghans exported lamb and sheep, as well as sheepskins, dried fruit, and raw cotton to Japan. Consumption of green tea in Afghanistan skyrocketed after Japanese producers began exporting it there in 1931. In 1933, the Shizuoka Prefecture Tea Producers Association (J. *Shizuoka ken cha-gyō kumiai*) reported that just 2,500 pounds of Japanese green tea was exported to Afghanistan, but by 1939 that number had risen to just over 2 million pounds.[124] By 1937, Japan was Afghanistan's largest trading partner, followed by Britain, America, Germany, Burma, Java, and China. However, only one year later, Germany had superseded Britain and the United States to become Afghanistan's second most important trading partner.[125] Nazi preparations for war meant that they needed suppliers who were not aligned with the British or the Soviets, and Afghanistan also proved to be an untapped market for both of the Axis powers.

After official diplomatic and trade relations between Afghanistan and the Japanese Empire were established, Afghan students began traveling to Tokyo on scholarships from the Japanese government. By 1936, there was a Japanese-Afghanistan Club in Tokyo whose stated objectives were to "improve the friendship between the two nations, publish bulletins several times a year, and hold welcome and farewell parties for officials of both nations as well as tea parties for exchange students from Afghanistan."[126] Most of the scholarship students were enrolled at Kyoto Imperial University and Tokyo Imperial University, where they studied practical majors such as economics, agricultural sciences, politics, and industrial spinning (both wool and silk). With support from the Japanese government, these students were to return to Afghanistan and use what they had learned to facilitate development and trade between the two countries. By contrast, the European exchange students studied more esoteric subjects like East Asian cultures, Buddhism, and

Japanese art.[127] By 1941, Afghan students continued to make up a large proportion of the scholarship students in Japan from places beyond East Asia, with six students being awarded full scholarships that year. Learning skills such as industrial weaving prepared the Afghan students to return home to "serve the plan to develop the Greater East Asia Co-Prosperity Sphere" and help expand it into regions not under Japanese occupation or control.[128] Although Afghanistan was never a part of the Greater East Asia Co-Prosperity Sphere, there seem to have been plans in place to include the people who lived in the region. Such educational endeavors were a relatively inexpensive way to promote Japanese imperial objectives in a place not part of the Japanese Empire.

The U.S. Office of Strategic Services (oss) collected intelligence on a number of returned Afghan students who had studied in Tokyo during the war. The oss surmised that the Japanese Empire reaped many benefits from supporting educational exchanges beyond the economic advantages for the Japanese imperial project. According to a classified report, the Japanese government was successfully cultivating anti-Soviet, anti-British, anticommunist, and anti–Hindu Congress Party sentiment among the students for a small price.[129] In fact, the oss claimed that Japan's efforts to win the hearts and minds of Muslims had been "gratifying" in this regard, and their objectives in Afghanistan were met by "the Japanese Legation at Kabul and by returning Afghan businessmen and students who had been entertained and indoctrinated in Japan."[130]

In 1941, the perceived success of the Japanese Empire's efforts in Afghanistan was bolstered when the first special Afghan mission was sent to Tokyo. The Tokyo newspaper *Nichi Nichi* reported that "this is but a part of the program of the Afghanistan ruler to free his country from Occidental dominance under the guidance of Japan as the leader of all Asiatic nations." Once again, this could be dismissed as wartime propaganda, but even as late as 1943, the oss took the Japanese threat in Afghanistan seriously. For U.S. observers, the Japanese Empire had found "ready followers among the fiercely nationalistic and religious Afghans."[131] The perception that the Japanese were effective in their overtures to Afghans underscores that Japanese efforts to undermine Western imperialism and Soviet Communism with the help of Muslims from around the world remained a deep concern for the Allies throughout the war.

This concern was echoed in a State Department debriefing of Afghan students Abdullah Khan, Ghulam Naqshband Khan, and Abdul Hakim Khan, who had returned to Kabul overland in April 1943 via Siberia and

Tashkent after studying in Japan. According to the report provided by State Department officials, "These students, with three others, had been sent to Japan by the Afghan government in 1936 as a result of an offer by the Japanese government to have all their expenses paid by the Cultural Relations Section of the Japanese Foreign Office."[132] The students all came from elite Afghan families, and although some of them returned professing support for Japan, others were more skeptical of imperial Japanese intentions. In the report, one of the students claimed, "When the Japanese radio announced the loss of a cruiser off Guadalcanal, the people became so despondent that it was necessary immediately to issue 'news' of the sinking of three American cruisers."[133] Given that the United States actually lost six cruisers off Guadalcanal and the Japanese lost three, the students were either misinformed or mistaken. However, their statement does indicate that they were conscious of the geopolitical situation in the Pacific and how it impacted their own position vis-à-vis their imperial hosts.

According to the State Department, the Japanese were also stoking anti-Soviet agitation in Afghanistan by aiding the large numbers of nomads who lived between Soviet Central Asia and Afghanistan. The State Department reported that nomads had developed a "deep hostility to all restrictions" imposed by the Soviets on their lifestyles, and Japanese officials attempted to tap into this animosity from their bases in Kabul and Kandahar.[134] From the perspective of those living in the Soviet peripheries, the Japanese Empire was aiding them in their ongoing efforts to thwart Soviet encroachment and resist regulations that restricted their movement.

Afghan history in the twentieth century is marred by "political upheavals, *coup d'état*, foreign invasion, civil war and frequent shifts of political power."[135] Yet during World War II, despite being enveloped by the Allies on all sides after the Soviets joined the war in 1941, Afghanistan somehow managed to maintain neutrality. After Operation Barbarossa, and under increasing pressure from the British and the Soviets, many Axis nationals were expelled from Afghanistan. The Germans and the Italians left a small staff to manage affairs, but the Soviets could not compel the Afghans to demand that the Japanese bureaucrats also be expelled because of the neutrality pact between the Soviets and the Japanese government.

However, connections to an Afghan past went beyond trade and geopolitical maneuverings for both the Nazis and the Japanese Empire. Both powers grounded their relationships with Afghanistan in a series of fabricated historical myths, which were used to bolster the political and economic connections between Afghans and Germans, or Afghans and Japanese subjects in the context of the ongoing war. The myths and stories were based on an essentialized and racialized past and were meant to provide the justification for both the Nazis' and Japanese Empire's interests in the region. The cultural justifications for these relationships on the fringes of empire facilitated trade and economic development there.

Afghanistan: Islam, Aryans, Buddhism—or Just Geopolitics?

In many ways, the Japanese government's interest in Afghanistan was always closely aligned with its interests in China and with its Islamic policy, and Afghanistan was essential to the Japanese Empire's anti-Soviet and anti-Nationalist agitation in Xinjiang.[136] The Chinese Nationalists reported that Japanese imperialists presented themselves as advocates for Islam (C. *tichang Huijiao*) by using their work among Sino-Muslim communities as a model, and packaged their propaganda intended for Central and South Asian Muslims in veiled promises of religious freedom and developmental aid.[137] Soviet attacks and ventures over the Pamir Mountains "aroused undistinguished sympathy in Afghanistan" for Muslims living in and around Xinjiang, and during the war the Japanese government was suspected of funneling money and arms to anti-Soviet fighters throughout the region from its bases in Kabul and Kandahar. U.S. observers noted that the Japanese Empire maintained a "keen interest" in Xinjiang, which meant that it was keeping "in close touch with Moslem [*sic*] refugees from that area[,] some of whom arrived in Kabul" from throughout the region.[138] Through debriefings and intelligence gathered from refugees and informants in Kabul, the Japanese government extended its reach into predominantly Muslim regions that it hoped one day to bring under its direct control.

At the same time, both the Japanese Empire and the Nazis had only started official diplomatic relations with Afghanistan a few years before the outbreak of World War II. In an effort to bolster their legitimacy among Afghans, both the Nazis and the Japanese Empire tried very hard to project connections to the region into a distant, imagined past. In this regard, the Afghan past became an ideological space where the political and economic goals of Japanese imperialists and the Nazis overlapped, converged, and conflicted.

Japanese connections to an Islamic past were always tenuous, but that never stopped Japanese imperialists from asserting interactions with Afghans for over a millennium.[139] Unlike in China, where they had connected themselves to Sino-Muslims through Ming Dynasty Muslim literati, there were no ways for scholars of Islam in Japan to make up connections to Muslims in Afghanistan before the early twentieth century. This meant that Japanese scholars opted for other avenues, establishing links through pre-Islamic Buddhist ties and ideas about circulations of goods and peoples on the early modern Silk Road (J. *shiruku rōdo*). For instance, in writings about Afghanistan published in Japan, Japanese scholars explained that lapis lazuli, which on the Eurasian continent is primarily mined in Afghanistan, had been highly prized in Japan as one of the "seven treasures" (J. *shichihō*) for hundreds of years, according to archaeological evidence in tombs on the home islands.[140]

Japanese academics also claimed closeness to Afghans through their mutual appreciation for moral valor associated with Shinto *bushidō* rituals, which were presented as the counterpart for Afghan patriarchal honor codes.[141] In this instance, the myth of the valiant and martial Aryan was a mirror for samurai warriors. As the Ōtani missions had done earlier in the twentieth century, Japanese scholars of Buddhism also tried to reinvigorate ideas about historical connections to Central Asian Buddhists. In the 1930s, as Afghans began to reclaim their own Buddhist past through a reconnection with Persian historiography, Japanese intellectuals latched onto these discourses in order to highlight connections between the two places.[142]

Some scholars even searched for parallels in the political development of the Meiji state and the Afghan state in the late nineteenth century. In this argument, both countries had undergone massive reform programs—the Meiji Restoration in Japan and the reforms of Amir Sher Ali in Afghanistan—around the same time. During this period, both places had modernized their armies, abolished the feudal system and tax-farming, and set up proper postal services, all of which had set the two nations on a parallel historical path toward friendship, development, and trade in the twentieth century.[143] In one final comparison, Afghanistan and Japan were described as places that respected religious freedom. Japanese academics explained that although Islam was the state religion in Afghanistan, people openly practiced Zoroastrianism, Buddhism, and Judaism. The ecumenical spirit of the Afghans was framed by Japanese intellectuals as a way to stress the inclusive policies of religious freedom throughout the Japanese Empire. These similarities were meant to underlie the presumed fact that Afghans and Japanese subjects were simply destined to have a deep respect for one another.

Throughout the 1930s, as the Japanese Empire's interests in Afghanistan deepened, the published material available about the distant region also in-

Islamic Spaces and Overlapping Interests

creased. Scholars like Murata Shōzō published works with titles such as *Afghanistan's Foreign Relations after the Great War* in order to bring the history of Afghanistan to a broader audience on the home islands.[144] Murata's survey begins with an examination of Afghan foreign relations with the Russian Empire and the British Empire to provide context for bilateral relations with individual nation-states after World War I. He explains that following the Congress of Berlin in 1878, the Russians had turned their attention from the Balkans and Ottoman lands and had begun to press further into Central Asia, which had alarmed the British raj. For Murata, the Russians were simply trying to ensure that trade routes through "Chinese-occupied Turkestan" (J. *Shina-ryō Torukisutan*) were secured.[145] Murata also clarified for his readers that in their attempts to control Afghanistan, the British had drawn an arbitrary 2,430 km border between what is now Pakistan and Afghanistan in the wake of the Afghan defeat in the Second Anglo-Afghan War. This political demarcation, known as the Durand Line, was established in 1896 to delineate Russian and British spheres of influence in the region. Because Afghanistan was sandwiched between these two imperial powers, Murata felt that Afghans were constantly searching for allies who would help them build a modern army and develop infrastructure, and for markets to which they could export raw materials they produced, such as wool and opium.[146] He framed this as an opportunity for the Japanese Empire to exert more influence in what Murata described as a volatile and complicated region.

Sino-Muslims living under Japanese occupation also wrote about the indignities suffered by Afghans, especially the Balochis, at the hands of the British. In his hajj journal, Tang Yichen wrote that he believed that Muslim regions with a strong British colonial presence were the most volatile because the British had a long history of intervening in the religious affairs of others. Tang also expressed hope that Muslims around the world would react violently to British rule and argued that his readers should support groups who resisted the British, such as the Balochis in Afghanistan. For Tang, the ongoing insurgency in Baluchistan provided a clear example of a group of Muslims who were successfully opposing the British and were much worse off than Muslims from North China, and therefore deserving of support from the Japanese Empire.[147]

These writings were meant to introduce readers to the history of Afghanistan while simultaneously justifying Japanese imperial interest in the region. They also reinforced social and spatial hierarchies deeply embedded in the Japanese imperial project. By offering the Balochis as a group of Muslims worthy of their support, Tang was implicitly arguing that he and his friends had already been served by the benevolence of the Japanese Empire, and now it was time for other Muslims, especially those who lived on the fringes of the Japanese Empire and were woefully oppressed by the British or the Soviets, to experience the same transformative powers.

Like the Japanese Empire, the Nazis searched for ways to connect themselves to Afghan pasts. Similarly, origin myths played an important role in the production and validation of Nazi ideology. Fascist regimes are not alone in their desire to politicize history, but during World War II, the Axis powers expended enormous amounts of intellectual energy fabricating connections and building an environment to accentuate these imagined links.[148] In his work on the ways the Nazis drew on Greek and Roman antiquity to legitimize power, historian Johann Chaputot clearly displays how "history was rewritten in order to annex Greeks and Romans to the Nordic race" in an effort to demonstrate how "ideology partially overlaps with genealogy." In turn, these intersections between the past and the present were meant to "clarify the affinities that existed between Nazism and history, between the race and the traces of its past, between the definition of German identity and the search for its origins."[149] In other words, through the rewriting of their own history, the Nazis convinced themselves that German ancestry was connected to classical antiquity in a direct and linear way.[150]

In Afghanistan, the Nazis joined their own past to the myth of the Aryan race, which was both a modern and a Western invention.[151] The story is complex but helps contextualize the lengths to which the Nazis went in order to legitimate themselves and their own pasts. The word *Aryan* is a neologism, indicating a place, Ariya, described by Herodotus. Ariya was removed from its meaning in the nineteenth century when it was appropriated to define an essentialized people who inhabited the place described by Herodotus. In the nineteenth century, Aryan came to be understood as a racial designation of a pure and true classical race. Reza Zia-Ebrahimi explains that this, "confusion between Ariya and Aryan is a particularly acute case of anachronism," and "one that has distorted ancient sources beyond recognition and exploited them to confer credibility to the Aryan myth."[152] Nazi origin myths also drew heavily from writings by Tacitus, who referred to a people known as the "Germanos indigenas." Tacitus explained that these "Germanos indigenas" had originally descended from Nordics, had strong features, and exhibited qualities of moral prowess. Once again, these stories were removed from their context to provide "the foundation myth of German autochthony."[153] In order to connect the Aryan myth of a pure race to the German peoples, these nearly 2,000-year-old observations made by Herodotus

Islamic Spaces and Overlapping Interests

and Tacitus were appropriated and entwined with eighteenth-century theories about Indo-European languages.[154]

In the eighteenth century, linguists developed a theory of common ancestry between Greek, Latin, Sanskrit, and Persian, now known as the "Indo-European" theory. In this schematic linguistic tree, "Semitic" languages like Hebrew and Arabic were labeled as separate and distinct from "Indo-European" languages. In essence, by creating distinct categories of languages, European linguists were able to link languages to newly emerging ideas about race and racial superiority. The consequence of racializing linguistics was that the two categories were conflated in a highly romanticized and teleological way, which drew false parallels between the people whom the Nazis imagined to be the Aryans and the Germans.[155] These myths were then connected to the historical legacy of the Aryans, who in Nazi ideology were the progenitors of all the great civilizations.

In fact, it was the invention of an "Aryan" race that gave Hitler and Nazis the flexibility to include racial affinity with the "great civilizations" like the Egyptians and the Chinese. In Hitler's worldview, these peoples, like the Germans, had also originally descended from Aryans, but had diluted their civilizational aptitude and racial purity over time through intermarriage with lesser races, thus leading to a period of decline since antiquity.[156] Through the "annexation of a culturally prestigious past" that was both fabricated and racialized, the Nazis claimed superiority over others, and connected themselves to distant peoples in ways that made geopolitics easier to maneuver and ideas of racial superiority seem plausible to some.[157] In 1936 these theories were put into practice, and the racial affinity between the Nazis and the "Aryans" was clearly drawn when Persians and others, such as Egyptian Christians, were exempted from the Nuremburg Laws.[158]

It was the Nazis who instilled Afghans with the idea that their region was part of the homeland of the "Aryans." In Afghanistan, this racialist myth took on a life of its own and continued to exist long after the German defeat and the discrediting of Nazi racial ideology in Europe. Through schools in Afghanistan, which had originally been established under the conditions of the German-Afghan friendship treaty, the Nazis devoted significant propaganda efforts and energy to promoting these historical anachronisms and myths, which in turn, helped "publicize racist nationalism that was similar to the nationalist ideology of the Nazi Party in Germany."[159] As the war went on, these ideas were internalized by Afghans, who began to believe that the myth of the Aryan race could serve a particular purpose at a particular historical moment. To this end, Nile Green maintains that in Afghanistan, "the writings of Orientalists" and other Europeans were "co-opted for nationalist purposes," and that this "notion of Aryana acquired its own distinct trajectory in Afghanistan and would later proliferate into the names of hotels, restaurants and the national airline, Ariana, founded in 1955."[160]

In Afghanistan, on the margins of fascist imperial projects, the Japanese Empire and the Nazis had to work extra hard to connect themselves to the people who lived in these strategically important areas. In both cases, the myths about how Afghanistan fit into Japanese and Nazi imperial schemas far beyond their respective empires served to validate their legitimacy at home. Through the creation of deep historical connections to Afghanistan, both powers simultaneously reinforced claims to the region, albeit in different ways. Through these deep histories that connected Japan and Germany to Afghanistan in a way that made sense to those back in the metropole, both powers promoted and constructed trade and economic relationships with Muslims in the present, wartime moment.

Conclusions

The Japanese Empire was well-tuned to the anticolonial struggles of different communities of Muslim people around the world, from the Nation of Islam in Detroit all the way to the Balochis' ongoing insurgence against the British based in Afghanistan. As "have-not" countries, the Japanese, the Italians, and the Germans provided an alternative model to Soviet Communism and the perceived hollowness of the Western democratic liberal order that was appealing to Muslims who were seeking alternative paths to independence. Both Sino-Muslims and the Japanese Empire understood full well that like in China, World War I had had massive repercussions (C. *fanxiang*) on Muslims throughout the colonized world. The false promises and empty rhetoric of Woodrow Wilson's "internationalism" and "self-determination" provided fuel and ideas for many of the indigenous anti-imperial movements among Muslim communities around the world.[161]

Drawing on many of the precedents it had established in North China with Sino-Muslim populations, the Japanese Empire extended its reach into places beyond its direct control. Japanese imperialists were able to legitimize their overtures to Muslims around the world by featuring the experiences of Sino-Muslims. They created and maintained connections with their Axis partners through engagement with Muslims who were adamantly anticolonial and anti-Soviet. This foray to the edges of both the Japanese and the Nazi spheres of influence during World War II has sought to entice others to

Islamic Spaces and Overlapping Interests

look more closely at places and peoples not generally considered part of the narratives of World War II and to move beyond the Greater East Asia Co-Prosperity Sphere to tell new stories about the Japanese Empire. Locating the history of wartime Japan at the margins opens up the possibility of exploring the various articulations of what Japanese imperial space meant for subjects — and potential subjects — of the Japanese Empire. Hopefully, this observation will open new avenues for scholarship into the maintenance and operation of fascist empires in the twentieth century.

CONCLUSION

Sino-Muslims, Fascist Legacies, and the Cold War in East Asia

In 1944, an analyst at the Office of Strategic Services remarked on the subject of Sino-Muslims that "even if the Japanese lose the war and have to withdraw from the Chinese mainland, they may be able to leave behind a disaffected, pro-Japanese minority group that they can continue to control."[1] These concerns never materialized. The OSS analyst's observation is a striking reminder that the Chinese Nationalists and their wartime allies were so concerned with imperial Japan's overtures to Muslims that they wondered if Sino-Muslims would remain loyal to the Japanese Empire even in the face of defeat. Yet, imperial Japan's influence in Muslim communities throughout North China and around the world ended abruptly in August 1945. However, many of the Japanese wartime policies aimed at Muslims and the virulent anti-Western and anti-Soviet propaganda that accompanied these outreach efforts were resurrected, repackaged, and redeployed by the Chinese Communists after their takeover of the mainland *and* by the Nationalists-in-exile on Taiwan in the early years of the Cold War.

After Japan's surrender, the Nationalists finally had the opportunity to draw the borders of China where they had wanted them to be for almost forty years.[2] But a civil war between the Chinese Communists and the Nationalists began almost immediately, and the Nationalists continued to experience "unexpected and overwhelming" problems attempting to bring the borderlands and its inhabitants under their control.[3] It was not until its victory over the Nationalists that the Communist Party was able to begin the process of consolidating borders and imposing state-directed classifications on the people who lived in these borderlands in a violent and systematic way.[4]

Overlooking the Japanese Empire's policies aimed at an important group that is now part of the People's Republic of China only serves to reinforce the Chinese Communist Party's own story about how these non-Han communities were incorporated into the party's vision of the nation-state. Since the Communist victory over the Nationalists, the Communist Party has attempted to project an infallible vision of what it means to be a citizen of the People's Republic of China. But this vision inhibits the possibility that collaborating with the Japanese Empire appealed to many Muslims during the war and discounts the ways diverse groups of Sino-Muslims envisioned their place in the world at that particular moment. Only by including the Japanese Empire's objectives and long-term goals with regards to Muslim populations can we begin to unpack the far-reaching implications of Japanese imperialism in East Asia. At the same time, in order to understand the complexities of the post–World War II geopolitical landscape in the region, it is imperative to include the wartime voices of minority actors.

In the immediate postwar era, Pan-Asianism was relegated to the ideological dustbin of history because of its uncomfortably close association with Japanese militarism. However, the obvious echoes of the anti-imperialist and anti-Soviet messages propounded by the Japanese Empire to Muslims reverberated in the new rallying calls for Afro-Asian solidarity. In other words, the idea of what "Asia" meant throughout the 1950s and 1960s was once again reenvisioned and repackaged to reflect the particular postwar, postcolonial moment, but its new fashioners drew heavily from the imperial formation and vocabulary of the Japanese Empire.[5]

At the First Afro-Asian Conference held in Bandung in 1955, anticolonial agitators such as Indonesian president Sukarno, Chinese foreign minister Zhou Enlai, U Nu of Burma, Egyptian president Gamal Abdel Nasser, and Indian prime minister Jawaharlal Nehru triumphantly proclaimed a new era of Afro-Asian solidarity. In the discussions at Bandung, "professions of global solidarity against colonialism, proclamations of the . . . new force of neutralism, and demands for economic development," crystalized around the idea of a nonaligned movement.[6] At the time, the fact that many of these men had been given their first real "break" by consorting with the Japanese imperial project was downplayed in the name of postcolonial solidarity.[7]

Yet many of the men in attendance at Bandung had been groomed by the

Japanese Empire and had been provided with the vocabulary they needed to move ahead with their post–World War II decolonization battles through their engagement with imperial Japan.[8] Just as Japanese political theorists and politicians from the late nineteenth century through to the end of the Pacific War defined their "national spirit" in opposition to the West, the idea of an "Asia for the Asians" was seriously discussed at Bandung.[9] With this in mind, it is quite obvious that the "genealogy of nonalignment, anticolonialism, and global distributive justices in the 1950s" is located in the global Axis imperial rhetoric of opposition to colonialism, Westernism, and Soviet Communism of the 1930s and 1940s.[10]

By uncovering imperial Japan's efforts to attract the loyalty of Sino-Muslims, this book has revealed continuities between the Japanese wartime imperial project and the post–World War II order that followed it in Asia. Ethan Mark's work on Indonesia under Japanese occupation reinforces my own conclusions, and in this case, it is worth quoting him at length:

> In public discourse across the former empire, the militant racial and cultural exceptionalism and anti-Westernism emphasised during the war years now gave way to a universalist modernism and internationalism that rejected racism, fascism in all its forms, whether Japanese or Western. Yet in many postwar and postcolonial national contexts, Asianism as transnational ideology—defined, that is, as a worldview with a lengthy historical lineage not limited to or originating out of Japanese experience alone but rather out of a shared political, social, and cultural problematic—proved of more lasting durability.[11]

Salvaging the strands of Japanese imperial policies with regards to Islam and Muslims presents the opportunity to acknowledge the consistency and continuities surrounding "Asianism" as a political ideology and of "Asia" as a geopolitical space across the World War II/Cold War divide. After the war, everything having to do with Japanese imperialism was cast as malevolent, and some of the realities of the Japanese occupation on the mainland were purged from Communist Party–driven historical narratives. Here, the atrocities committed against civilians during the war are rightfully commemorated and memorialized. But the successes, such as the efforts the Japanese made to connect Muslims around the world, are neglected.

After all, the Japanese Empire was actively attempting to create a non-Western economic bloc that would subvert Western imperialism and global capitalism by diverting resources to the region or keeping them in Asia with the help of disenfranchised minorities living across the continent. For the most part, historians are still reluctant to admit that remnants of fascist pasts reverberate through the geopolitical landscape of East Asia. Historian Maggie Clinton reminds us that this is in part because of the "particular perversity" associated with "assessing a fascist movement in terms of its success."[12] This point is essential for reassessing the impact of Japanese imperialism on the formation of ethnoreligious identities within the modern Chinese nation-state.

In his examination of the budding relationship between the Chinese Communist government and Egypt during the Suez Canal crisis in 1956, Kyle Haddad-Fonda argues that "the actual impact of imperialism — whether American, British, or Japanese — on the psyche of the Chinese people" underscores the fact that "the CCP was consistently able to utilize imperialist rhetoric as a way of appealing to its citizens."[13] Understanding the antecedents of these postwar relationships requires that we "distinguish between imperialism as a historical reality and the idea of imperialism as manifested in the collective memory."[14] In this instance, this discrepancy between the "historical reality" and the "collective memory" of Japanese imperialism is particularly salient because it offers the chance to create a distinction between the assessment of the actual long-term impacts of wartime imperialism on those who are excluded from state-driven narratives.

Recasting the Japanese imperial project within the larger framework of global Axis imperialisms also helps to center the Japanese Empire in postcolonial experience in Asia. Surely the Bandung Moment was "born of the challenges of grappling with the legacies of European imperialism," coupled with an "unprecedented number of peoples across the world actively reimagining, changing, and prefiguring the rules of the global order."[15] But what about the legacies of Japanese imperialism and Japan's Axis partners on the Global South? Should we also not look for the antecedents of the anti-Western, developmentalist discourses situated in this particular moment in Japanese imperial propaganda and efforts geared to winning the hearts and minds of Muslims around the world during World War II?

Including Sino-Muslim Voices in the Telling of China's Wartime History

The first half of this book highlighted the variety of Sino-Muslim voices as a way of restoring agency to minority actors coming to terms with their place in a changing world. Their experiences serve as a counterweight to dominant narratives that have strived to impose a tidy story of complete and collective resistance to Japanese imperialism and the occupation. Yet, even within the Sino-Muslim community that supported the Chinese Nationalists, there was a spectrum of ideas about what it meant to be modern, Muslim, or a modern Sino-Muslim. In order to push back against state-driven narratives that emphasize a top-down approach to the incorporation of non-Han communities into nation-building projects, historians must recover these marginalized voices and facilitate understanding of how these people imagined themselves participating—or not—in nation-building initiatives.

In the years immediately following the Japanese surrender, Sino-Muslims continued to voice concerns about their place in the emerging visions for the state. In fact, even before the war ended, Sino-Muslims who had supported the Nationalist government began to call in the promises made to them in return for their support resisting the Japanese during the war. After Italy was defeated and Joseph Goebbels, Hitler's "right-hand man" (C. youbi), committed suicide on May 1, 1945, a Nationalist-supported Sino-Muslim named Ke Xing wrote an op-ed predicting that the war would be over in a few months.[16] In the piece, he posited a number of rhetorical questions to his readers: "What would peace look like? Who would China's 'new allies' [C. mengguo] be? Where would Sino-Muslims fit into this new postwar nation-state?"[17] Ke Xing then asked his readers to look outward and suggested that ushering in a new era required an increased focus on improving relations with Muslim countries and developing schools and Arabic-language training programs.[18]

Shortly after the partition of India and Pakistan in 1947, Muslims in China regularly invoked Pakistan as a positive example of Muslim self-governance in an attempt to get the Nationalists to implement policy changes that would improve their own situation. With deep respect and admiration, Sino-Muslims wrote about the "peaceful and successful" transfer of power from the British military to the new leadership in Islamabad and expressed their faith in the promise for a new future.[19] The idea of a country created specifically for Muslims was intriguing, and in that specific historical moment Pakistan offered a glimpse of what could be for Sino-Muslims living in the new postwar, postcolonial era.

In these writings, some Sino-Muslims also suggested creating a governmental agency for Muslim (C. Hui) and Tibetan development in the aftermath of the war. Others suggested sending more Muslim students abroad on scholarships to study in predominantly Muslim places, particularly Egypt and Indonesia. Beyond this, Sino-Muslim elites continued to urge the

Nationalist government to send delegations abroad to reengage with newly formed Muslim governments in places like Indonesia and Pakistan, and to reinforce existing diplomatic relationships with places like Egypt.[20] Here, certain groups of Sino-Muslims continued to articulate their own ideas about how they should interact with the state and with Muslims beyond the borders of China after the war with Japan was over.[21]

When the People's Republic was founded in October 1949, the Chinese Communists started the process of defining and bounding minority communities as distinct "nationalities" (C. *minzu*). But none of this was new. For almost half a century, the Japanese and the Nationalists had been jockeying with a diverse group of Sino-Muslims trying to come to a suitable arrangement for defining their place (or places) in either imperial or national schemas. In the People's Republic, state-sponsored authorities investigated claims to "nationhood"; among the more than 400 groups who applied, fifty-five were granted minority status.[22] The new state adhered to the Stalinist criteria for delineating official identification as a state-sanctioned ethnic minority (C. *shaoshu minzu*). In order to get this recognition, groups had to prove that they possessed a common language, locality, economy, and culture. However, these criteria are amorphous and should never be understood as objective. Communities also used them to their own ends.

Like its political predecessors, the new Communist state was never able to simply impose categories on the people it governed.[23] In the early 1950s, prominent Sino-Muslim and Marxist historian Bai Shouyi maintained that Islam should be referred to as *Yisilan jiao* rather than *Huijiao* because the *Hui* were a distinct group of Muslims who were adherents of the universal religion of Islam. By identifying "Huiness" as separate from Islam, Bai was attempting to legitimize the group's claims to a separate ethnic classification.[24] The point here is that as with the Japanese and the Nationalists before them, Sino-Muslims living in the People's Republic engaged with state-proscribed categories and suited them to their needs as best they could. These categories were never simply imposed, nor were they static.[25]

In foreign policy, the new Communist regime "downplayed its Marxist ideology and focused instead on its commitment to thwarting imperialism around the globe."[26] As Communist China looked outward to assert itself on the international scene, the co-optation and support of its Muslim population was one way to achieve this.[27] Another way was through engagement with new, postcolonial Muslim nation-states. For example, throughout the Suez Canal Crisis in 1956, the Chinese Communist Party provided consistent, if not outspoken, backing to Nasser's government in Egypt.[28] When the Suez Crisis culminated in the invasion of Egypt by the United Kingdom, France, and Israel, the Chinese Communist Party contributed 20 million Swiss francs to subsidize the Egyptian war effort. This symbolic gesture should be understood as part of the anti-imperialist struggle for nonaligned sovereignty and solidarity in the postwar era, as well as a way for the Chinese Communists to distance themselves from the Soviets in the aftermath of the Korean War.[29]

During the Suez Crisis, Mao Zedong, like both his Nationalist and Japanese predecessors, paid disproportionate attention to Chinese Muslims and rallied them behind the cause.[30] At home, Chinese citizens were "temporarily consumed" with the Suez Canal crisis, and "both the media and the government placed particular emphasis on Chinese Muslims, who were accorded a special role in the demonstrations by virtue of their religious link to the Egyptian people." In this case, the media attention paid to Muslims during the crisis "must be seen as a political statement on the part of the PRC government, which had long endeavored to include Muslims — as well as other minority religious and ethnic groups — within its definition of the Chinese nation."[31] By piggybacking on policies that had worked for both the Chinese Nationalists and the Japanese Empire during the war with regards to managing Muslim populations, the new Communist government rebranded these policies to suit its own specific postwar needs.

At the same time, the Nationalist government-in-exile on Taiwan and longtime Nationalist-supporting Sino-Muslims like Bai Chongxi amped up their efforts to undermine the Chinese Communists through diplomatic engagement with newly formed postcolonial states.[32] Part of the Republic of China's efforts involved offering strong support to anti-imperial nationalists in their ongoing fight against communism.[33] Chiang Kai-shek made Bai Chongxi the head of the Chinese Muslim Association based in Taipei, and through this organization Bai continued his engagement with Muslim dignitaries as he had done throughout the war. The Republic of China also allocated funds to build the Taipei Grand Mosque, and in 1958 Muslim dignitaries who supported anticommunist movements were invited from throughout Southeast Asia, South Asia, and the Middle East to attend the opening. In the 1950s, deploying Sino-Muslims like Bai Chongxi on diplomatic missions to spread anticommunist propaganda was a tried and true method honed during World War II and should be understood as part of the Nationalist plans to retake the mainland from the Chinese Communists by undermining their own outreach to Muslims. These efforts to instrumentalize Islam in East Asia quite obviously mirror the ways the Japanese Empire attempted to gain the favor of Muslims throughout the war.

Epilogue: History Lessons

It is now undeniable that the current party-state in China has launched a violent and repressive campaign against the Uyghurs who live in western China. Since 2016, the state has arrested and interned somewhere in the range of 1 million Uyghurs and placed them in "reeducation" facilities.[34] Uyghur families are separated, and children are sent to orphanages in coastal regions to be adopted by Han families. Mosques are closed indefinitely. Uyghur women are forced to marry Han Chinese men. Muslims are forced to eat pork and renounce their faith, and law-abiding expatriate Uyghurs are extradited back to China without due process.[35]

The justification provided by the state for these actions is that the Uyghurs pose a threat to domestic stability and are easily radicalized by Islamic terrorists. The rhetoric of the post–September 11 War on Terror gave the Chinese government the vocabulary it needed to institute increasingly hardline policies in Xinjiang starting in 2009 after interethnic riots between Han Chinese and Uyghurs broke out in the provincial capital of Urumqi. The reality is that the threat of terrorism from Uyghurs is largely exaggerated by the Chinese state apparatus, and beyond a few individuals, claims of links between Uyghurs and terrorist groups such as ISIS or Al-Qaeda are hard to substantiate. For Xinjiang observers, domestic attacks by Uyghurs are directed at oppressive state policies that are aimed at breaking the Uyghurs rather than any sort of coordinated Islamist threat.[36]

The ongoing campaigns against the Uyghurs also have unmistakable reverberations in Sino-Muslim communities, and Islamophobia is rampant in the People's Republic of China.[37] Recently there have been campaigns to "de-Arabize" Islam by removing all Arabic signage on Muslim storefronts in Chinese cities or forcing Muslim parents to give their children Han Chinese names.[38] In other words, there are active campaigns to Sinicize Islam and Muslims through much more repressive and aggressive policies than have been used by the Communists, the Nationalists, or the Japanese in the past 100 years.

As the current party-state exerts itself economically and militarily in the Indian Ocean, Southeast Asia, and Africa through Belt and Road Initiatives, the state also attempts to "appropriate its own ethnic Muslim heritage to meet the changing global order by making use of the Hui Muslims to forge a closer alliance with the Muslim world."[39] The deep contradiction here is that countries with large or majority Muslim populations exchange economic incentives from the party-state in return for their silence and complicity in the Communist Party's ongoing repression of Muslims within the borders of the Chinese state. These inconsistencies are especially glaring in places with established overseas Sino-Muslim communities, like Indonesia and Malaysia.[40]

The Sino-Muslim community in Indonesia makes up less than 6 percent of the total population of ethnic and overseas Chinese living in Indonesia. Given that ethnic Chinese and overseas Chinese make up just over 1 percent of the population, this means that Sino-Muslims living there are a minute fragment of the entire population of the archipelago.[41] However small, there is a renewed interest by the Chinese government to reconnect China's Islamic past to Indonesia in the post-Suharto present. This desire has resulted in the "proliferation of Chinese-Style Mosques" including the Masjid Cheng Hoo (C. *Zheng He Qingzhensi*), which pays homage to the Ming-era Muslim admiral Zheng He, who commanded expeditionary fleets through Southeast Asia and the Indian Ocean.[42]

Similarly, during the 1980s and 1990s, Muslim students from the poorer northwestern regions of China chose cheaper, Muslim-majority locations for studying abroad such as Malaysia, Egypt, Saudi Arabia, and Turkey. In the early 1980s, the first Muslim students from China in more than thirty years traveled to Egypt to study at Al-Azhar, where students reestablished connections that had been made in the late nineteenth and early twentieth century. The communities of Sino-Muslims in places like Malaysia, Saudi Arabia, and Egypt are important for business and development in the interior of China, but they have also allowed the Communist apparatus to present itself as protector of the interests of their Muslim citizens abroad while suppressing them at home.

As the world begins to pay more attention to the plight of the Uyghurs, a coordinated response from predominantly Muslim countries along with increasingly punitive restrictions on global corporations that use materials such as cotton and tomato paste produced in factories that use Uyghur forced labor might be the only way to elicit any kind of reaction from the party-state. Embargos and sanctions could start to impact economic growth in coastal regions of the Chinese mainland, and a coordinated political response from Muslim states where the party-state has invested a lot of money in infrastructure and technology programs might also put pressure on the regime. In China, as technology and the police state become more closely entwined and state-driven efforts to eliminate the Uyghurs accelerate, we should be reminded that while some religious groups participated in projects that increased their political worth to the Axis powers during World War II, others were simply exterminated.

Glossary

NAMES

Japanese Names to *rōmaji*

天川信雄	Amakawa Nobuo	大川周明	Ōkawa Shūmei
新井白石	Arai Hakuseki	大谷光瑞	Ōtani Kōzui
林銑十郎	Hayashi Senjūrō	坂本健一	Sakamoto Ken'ichi
福田規矩男	Fukuda Kikuo	桜井匡	Sakurai Masashi
川村狂堂	Kawamura Kyōdō	鈴木剛	Suzuki Takeshi
細谷清	Hosoya Kiyoshi	橘瑞超	Tachibana Zuichō
小林元	Kobayashi Hajime	高垣信三	Tagataki Shinzō
近衞文麿	Konoe Fumimaro	田島大輔	Tajima Daisuke
松田寿男	Matsuda Hisao	店田廣文	Tanada Hirofumi
松室孝良	Matsumuro Takayoshi	田中逸平	Tanaka Ippei
松岡洋右	Matsuoka Yōsuke	都甲文雄	Togō Fumio
村田昌三	Murata Shōzō	若林半	Wakabayashi Han
岡倉 覚三	Okakura Kakuzō	山岡光太郎	Yamaoka Kotaro

Chinese Names to Pinyin

艾沙	Aisha (Īsa Yūsuf Alptekin)	馬鴻逵	Ma Hongkui
白崇禧	Bai Chongxi	馬堅	Ma Jian
白今愚	Bai Jinyu	馬家昇	Ma Jiasheng
白淑芳	Bai Shufang	馬良璞	Ma Liangpu
達浦生	Da Pusheng	馬少雲	Ma Shaoyun
丁淑媛	Ding Shuyuan	馬松亭	Ma Songting
丁在欽	Ding Zaiqin	馬肇彭	Ma Zhaopeng
哈德成	Ha Decheng	龐士謙	Pang Shiqian
李福順	Li Fushun	薛文波	Xue Wenbo
李宗慶	Li Zongqing	沙蕾	Sha Lei
劉德潤	Liu Derun	尚止戈	Shang Zhige
劉錦標	Liu Jinbiao	蘇瑞祥	Su Ruixiang
馬步芳	Ma Bufang	唐父子	Tang Fuzi
馬步青	Ma Buqing	唐易塵	Tang Yichen
馬福良	Ma Fuliang	唐雨田	Tang Yutian

Chinese Names to Pinyin, continued

王岱興	Wang Daiyu	張懷德	Zhang Huaide
王浩然	Wang Haoran	張王某	Zhang Wangmou
王連鈺	Wang Lianyu	張英	Zhang Ying
王瑞蘭	Wang Ruilan	趙雲陞	Zhao Yunsheng
王士清	Wang Shiqing	朱建民	Zhu Jianmin
雪艷琴	Xue Yanqin	宗鴻青	Zong Hongqing
楊敬之	Yang Jingzhi		

WORDS AND PHRASES

Characters	Pinyin	*rōmaji*	Translation
アガ・カン		Aga Kan	Aga Khan
アジア南方の回教徒		Ajia nanpō no kaikyōto	South Asian Muslims
アーリアン人種		ārian jinshu	Aryans
イギリスの経済ブロック		igirisu no keizai burokku	English economic bloc
イスラム文化協會		Isuramu Bunka Kyōkai	Islamic Culture Society
キナ		kina	cinchona bark
タタル問題		tataru mondai	the Tatar problem
タタル語		tatarugo	Tatar language
ドラング・ナハ・オステン		dorangu naha osuten	Drang nach Osten
ハム人種		hamu jinshu	Ham race
ヒジャーズ		Hijāzu	the Hejaz
ファシスト黨旗		fashisuto tōki	Nazi swastika flag
ムガル帝国		Mugaru Teikoku	Mughal Empire
ラマ教		ramakyō	Tibetan lama; Tibetan Buddhism
レネサンス		renesansu	renaissance

Characters	Pinyin	*rōmaji*	Translation
阿訇	ahong		imam; ahung
阿雅蘇非亞	aya sufeiya		Hagia Sofia
哀	ai		lament
愛國愛教	aiguo aijiao		love the nation, love Islam
愛國茶殼		aikoku chagara	patriotic tea leaves
愛教愛國	aijiao aiguo		love Islam, love the nation
八達嶺	badaling		section of the Great Wall North of Beijing
八一三	bayisan		Occupation of Shanghai
白酒	baijiu		Chinese liquor
白人		hakujin	white people
白石	baishi		white jade
包饺子	bao jiaozi		make dumplings
薄荷茶		hakkacha	green tea with mint
寶劍	baojian		sword
北京味道	Beijing weidao		Beijing flavor
俾路支	Biluzhi		Baluchistan
必需品		hitsujuhin	daily necessity
邊疆教育	bianjiang jiaoyu		school on the border; borderland schools
辮发/辮子	bianfa/bianzi		queue
不懂阿拉伯語	budong alaboyu		did not understand Arabic

Characters	Pinyin	*rōmaji*	Translation
不像本地	buxiang bendi		do not look/act/ sound like locals
不振	buzhen		lack of vitality
部落民		Burakumin	Burakumin
惨案	can'an		massacre
策進救國與教工作	cejin jiuguo yu jiao gongzuo		policies that would work to save both their country and religion
茶の湯		chanoyu	tea ceremony
茶馬司	Chamasi		Tea and Horse Bureau
茶政策		cha seisaku	tea policy
吃苦	chiku		to eat bitterness
赤鬼		akaoni	red devil, communist
大アジア主義		dai Ajia shugi	Greater East Asianism
大東亞解放戰	dadongya jiefang zhan		Greater East Asia Liberation War
大陸	dalu	tairiku	mainland China
大陸主義		tairiku shugi	expand on land
大日本回教協會		Dai Nihon Kaikyō Kyōkai	Greater Japan Muslim League
大同	datong	daidō	great harmony
大亞細亞協會		Dai Ajia Kyōkai	Great East Asia Association
等閑		naozari	overlooked (in the past)
低能	dineng		feeble-minded
敵後	dihou	teki-go	behind enemy lines

Characters	Pinyin	*rōmaji*	Translation
东亚	Dongya	Tōa	East Asia
東洋人	dongyang ren	tōyō jin	East Asian
篤信	duxin		devout believer; faithful
対策		taisaku	countermeasures
恩威並用	enwei bingyong		carrot and stick (idiomatic phrase)
法魯克	Faluke		King Farouk
反響	fanxiang		massive repercussions
放任主義		hōnin shugi	laissez-faire economics
非回教徒		hi kaikyōto	non-Muslim
風行一時	fengxing yishi		in fashion
瘋狂的夢話	fengkuang de menghua		crazy dream
哥倫坡	Gelunbo		Colombo
格迪目	gedimu		Qadim
公民教徒	gongmin jiaotu		religious citizens
古羅馬所以的政策	gu Luoma suoyi de zhengce		Ancient Roman policies
廣安門	Guang'anmen		Guang'an Gate (Beijing)
詭計	guiji		crafty plots
国民	guomin	kokumin	the people; citizens
國際回教陰謀	guoji Huijiao yinmou		international Islam conspiracy
國際學友會		Kokusai gakuyū-Kai	International Students' Association

Glossary

Characters	Pinyin	*rōmaji*	Translation
國民政府外交部	Guominzhengfu Wajiao Bu		National Government Ministry of Foreign Affairs
國語運動	Guoyu Yundong		National Language movement
哈里發	halifa		caliph
哈皙勒山	Haxile Shan		Mount Arafat
還都	huandu		a government to return to a capital after exile
海洋主義		kaiyō shugi	expand in the sea
漢奸	hanjian		traitor
漢克塔布	Han Ketabu		Han Kitab
合衆国		Gasshūkoku	United States
合作	hezuo		cooperation
和樂	hele		happy and harmonious
黑龍會		kokuryūkai	Black Dragon Society
紅土耳其帽子	hong tu'erqi maozi		fez
後進		kōshin	backward
華僑回教徒		kakyō Kaikyōto	overseas Chinese Muslims
懷柔政策	huairou zhengce		policy of conciliation and appeasement
豢養	huanyang		to groom
回華僑	hui huaqiao		overseas Chinese Muslims
回回色		kaikai-shoku	more Islamic (more religious)
回教ノ保護者		Kaikyō no hogo-sha	protector of Islam

Characters	Pinyin	*rōmaji*	Translation
回教班		Kaikyō Han	Islam Division
回教弟兄會	Huijiao Dixionghui		Muslim Brotherhood
回教訪問團	Huijiao Fangwentuan		Muslim Mission
回教聖戰		Kaikyō seisen	jihad
回教世界	Huijiao shijie	Kaikyō sekai	Islamic world/Muslim world
回教問題		Kaikyō mondai	Islamic problem
回教政策		Kaikyō seisaku	Islamic policy/Muslim policy
回教之友	Huijiao zhiyou		friends of Islam
回教諸国と我が経済ブロック		Kaikyō shokoku to waga keizai burokku	Muslim countries and our economic bloc
回教專号	Huijiao zhuanhao		special Islam issue (of a periodical)
回民一家	huimin yijia		Muslim family; Muslims as a collective
加爾格達各大學	Jiaergedage Daxue		Calcutta University
加緊	jiajin		stepping up
勁敵	jingdi		formidable opponents
禁忌	jinji		taboo
浄土真宗		Jōdo shinshū	Jōdo Shinshū sect
静岡県茶業組合		Shizuoka Ken Cha-gyō Kumiai	Shizuoka Prefecture Tea Producers Association
救國救教	jiuguo jiujiao		save the country, save Islam
攫取	juequ		to seize

Characters	Pinyin	*rōmaji*	Translation
開羅	Kailuo		Cairo
烤羊肉串	kao yangrouchuan		barbecue lamb kebabs
克爾拜	ke'erbai		Kaaba
拉攏	la long		draw over to your side
拉攏政府	lalong zhengfu		win over governments
辣牛肉	la niurou		spicy beef
臘月	layue		twelfth month of the lunar year
列強		rekkyō	Western powers
綠シャツ黨		midori shatsu tō	Green Shirts
瑪撒淀港	Masadian gang		Massawa Port
賣國	maiguo		sell out your country; traitor
賣國與賣教	maiguo yu maijiao		sell out the country and sell out Islam
美術工藝		bijutsu kōgei	handicrafts; fine handmade crafts
盟國	mengguo		Allies
迷信	mixin	meishin	superstition; superstitious belief
密使		misshi	secret envoy/secret agent
民心把握		minshin ha'aku	grasp people's minds
莫臥兒	mowo'er		Mughal [Empire]
南方特別留学生		nanpō tokubetsu ryūgakusei	special foreign students from the southern areas
南洋		Nanyō	South Seas

Characters	Pinyin	*rōmaji*	Translation
南洋の回教徒		Nanyō kaikyōto	Southeast Asian Muslims
牛街	Niu Jie	Gyū Gai	Oxen Street, Muslim neighborhood in Beijing
歐洲列強	Ouzhou lieqiang		old European powers
叛亂	panluan	hanran	armed rebellion
剽悍トルクメン族		hyōkan Torukumen-zoku	fierce warrior Turkmen
貧愚	pinyu		stupid; foolish
七寶		shichihō	seven treasures
焦眉		shobi	great urgency
親和	qinhe		intimate connections
親善關係		shinzen kankei	goodwill relationship; friendly relationship
全面抗戰	quanmian kangzhan		everyone resisted the Japanese
日本側		Nihon gawa	on the Japanese side
日本回教協會		Nihon Kaikyō kyōkai	Japanese Islamic Association
日本精神		Nihon seishin	Japanese spirit
日独伊側		Nichidokui-gawa	Axis-side
日蘇關係	ri-su guanxi		Japanese-Soviet Relations
日支事件		nisshi jiken	"China Incident"
桑税		kuwazei	taxes on tea
僧兵		sōhei	warrior monk; priest soldier
上海事變	Shanghai shibian		"Shanghai Incident"

Characters	Pinyin	*rōmaji*	Translation
深い理解		fukai rikai	deep understanding
神		kami	god
石炭		sekitan	coal
石油		sekiyu	oil
使命	shiming		mission
世界政策		sekai seisaku	global policy
鬆湖會戰	Songhu huizhan		alternate term for Battle of Suzhou Creek
蘇丹	Sudan		Sudan
提倡回教	tichang Huijiao		to promote Islam
天橋清真寺	Tianqiao qingzhensi		Tianqiao Mosque
威力		iryoku	powerful force
文化	wenhua		culture, civilization
文化政策		bunka seisaku	cultural policy
五族共和	wuzu gonghe		Five Races, One Union
西本願寺		Nishi Honganji	Nishi Honganji branch of Buddhism
西道堂	xidaotang		Sect of Islam in China
香油	xiangyou		sesame oil
向西亞進出	xiang xiya jinchu		Go West!
新アジア建設		shin Ajia kensetsu	to build a New Asia
新京伊斯蘭協會	Xinjing Yisilan Xiehui		Xinjing Muslim Association

Characters	Pinyin	*rōmaji*	Translation
宣撫工作		senbu kōsaku	indoctrinate and tame; pacification
巡禮	xunli		pilgrimage; the hajj
亞剌比亞經典	yalabiya jingdian		Arabic classics
亞細亞學生會議	Yaxiya Xuesheng Huiyi	Ajia Gakusei Kaigi	Asian Student Congress
野心	yexin		wild ambition
一舉兩得	yijuliangde		kill two birds with one stone (idiomatic phrase)
伊赫瓦尼	yihewani		*Ikhwan*
伊斯蘭主義	Yısılan zhuyi		Islamism
伊太利ノ回教政策		Itaria no Kaikyō seisaku	Italy's Muslim/ Islamic Policy
以茶治夷	yichazhiyi		use tea to control the barbarians
義國特警	yiguo tejing		Italian special police
隱伏	yinfu		lying low
印度尼西亞回教運動	Yindunixiya Huijiao Yundong		Indonesian Muslim Movement
永久和平	yongjiu heping		perpetual peace
優秀	youxiu		outstanding; splendid
油椰子		aburayashi	palm oil
猶太資本主義	youtai ziben zhuyi		"Jewish capitalism"
友好的文化政策		yūkō-teki bunka seisaku	goodwill/friendly cultural policy between Italians and local Muslims
誘惑	youhuo		seducing
醞釀政變	yunniang zhengbian		fomenting coups

Characters	Pinyin	*rōmaji*	Translation
在海外	zai haiwai		being/living abroad
佔住	zhanzhu		occupation
支那領トルキスタン		Shina-ryō Torukisutan	"Chinese-occupied Turkestan"
支那人		Shinajin	Chinese person
支那人化	Zhinarenhua	Shinajinka	Sinification
中国会馆	Zhongguo huiguan		Chinese guild hall
中國的回胞有阿拉伯血統	Zhongguo de huibao you alabo xuetong		Muslims from China had Arabic blood lineage
中國的教胞們	Zhongguo de jiaobaomen		Chinese fellow-Muslims
中國回教總聯合會	Zhongguo Huijiao Zonglianhehui		All China Muslim League
中華民族	Zhonghua minzu		Chinese nation
忠實	zhongshi		loyal and faithful
軸心國協力的政策	zhouxinguo xieli de zhengce		Axis powers were united in a common effort to coordinate policy
自給自足		jikyū jisoku	self-sufficient
自治	zizhi		autonomy
自主	zizhu		self-determination
宗教自由	zongjiao ziyou		religious freedom
坐在籬笆上	zuozai liba shang		sitting on a bamboo fence

Notes

INTRODUCTION

1. "Japan's Near East Conspiracy." In referring to the Chinese Nationalist Party on the mainland and in Taiwan, English-speaking news media and dictionaries often use the Wade-Giles romanization, "Kuomintang." As I indicate in "A Note on Romanization," this book uses the pinyin system, or "Guomindang."

2. "Japan's Near East Conspiracy."

3. Lipman, *Familiar Strangers*, xii–xxxvi; Thum, "The Uyghurs in Modern China," 2.

4. "Tong huimin xiaoxue."

5. Green, "Anti-colonial Japanophilia," 2.

6. Reese, *Imperial Muslims*, 1.

7. There are a number of scholars who have written about this topic in Japanese. See Yamazaki (née Unno), "Nihon no Kaikyō kōsaku" (2012); Shimada, "Shōwa senzenki" (2015); Tuoheti, *Nihon ni okeru* (2019).

8. Brown, "The Konoe Cabinet," 169.

9. King and Poulton, introduction, 3.

10. Morris-Suzuki, "Introduction," 8–9.

11. Morris-Suzuki, 9.

12. Morris-Suzuki, 9.

13. Reese, *Imperial Muslims*, 9; also see Motadel, "The Global Authoritarian Moment."

14. Erikson and Samila, "Social Networks," 151–53.

15. Erikson and Samila, "Social Networks," 151–52; Cooke and Lawrence, introduction, 1–28.

16. Erikson and Samila, "Social Networks," 154.

17. Tilly, "Retrieving European Lives," 31.

18. Wetherell, "Historical Social Network Analysis," 126.

19. Cooke and Lawrence, foreword, xii, see also 2.

20. Duara, "Asia Redux," 963.

21. Ambaras, *Japan's Imperial Underworlds*, 1–28; Duara, "Asia Redux," 963.

22. See Matsumoto, "Sino-Muslims' Identity"; Matsumoto, "Rationalizing Patriotism"; Mao, "A Muslim Vision."

23. Lary, introduction, 1–10; Schoppa, *In a Sea of Bitterness*, 1–8.

24. Woo, "Chinese Collaboration," 235.

25. Barrett, "Introduction," 4.

26. Taylor, *Disappearing Acts*, 13.

27. Chatani, *Nation-Empire*, 2–4.

28. Rezrazi, "Pan-Asianism."

29. Lary, introduction, 4.

30. See Duara, "The Discourse of Civilization."

31. Esenbel, introduction, 3.

32. Lei, "The Chinese Islamic," 138–42.

33. Ethan Mark comes to a similar conclusion in his examination of the Japanese occupation of Java. Mark, *Japan's Occupation*, 293–303.

34. "Chinese Islamic Association."

35. "Chinese Islamic Association."

36. Brook, "Toward Independence," 317–37; Jeans, "Third-Party Collaborators," 114–32.

37. "Chinese Islamic Association."

38. Yang, *Riben zhi Huijiao zhengce*.

39. See Brophy, *Uyghur Nation*; Atwill, *Islamic Shangri-La*; Mullaney, *Coming to Terms with the Nation*; and Weiner; *The Chinese Revolution*.

40. See Leibold, *Reconfiguring Chinese Nationalism*; and Lin, *Modern China's Ethnic Frontiers*.

41. Brophy, *Uyghur Nation*, 5–6.

42. Brophy, 9.

43. Brophy, *Uyghur Nation*, 18, 274; Halevi, "Is China a House of Islam?"

44. See Elliott, *The Manchu Way*; Millward, *Beyond the Pass*; and Rawski, *The Last Emperors*.

45. Mitter, *The Manchurian Myth*, 14–15; Cieciura, "Ethnicity or Religion?"

46. Cieciura, "Ethnicity or Religion?"

47. Elliott, "*Hushuo*."

48. Elliott.

49. Millward, *Beyond the Pass*, 1–19.

50. Gladney, "Clashed Civilizations?," 122.

51. Cieciura, "Ethnicity or Religion?"

52. I must thank one of the blind reviewers for bringing this point to my attention.

53. Gladney, "Clashed Civilizations?," 122.

54. Lin, *Tibet and Nationalist China's Frontier*, 10.

55. Halevi, "Is China a House of Islam?," 64.

56. Chen, "Chinese Heirs to Muhammad," introduction.

57. Chen, chap. 5.

58. Lin, *Tibet and Nationalist China's Frontier*, 22–26; Lipman, "Ethnicity and Politics," 285–316.

59. Aydin, "Japan's Pan-Asianism," 1–4.

60. Having recognized Manchukuo as a sovereign state in 1934 as part of its negotiations with Japan concerning the invasion of Ethiopia, in 1937 Fascist Italy joined the pact as well.

61. Aydin, "Japan's Pan-Asianism," 1–4.

62. Galambos and Kōichi, "Japanese Exploration"; Galambos, "Japanese 'Spies'"; Noda, "Japanese Spies."

63. Aydin, "Overcoming Eurocentrism?," 137.

64. Hotta, *Pan-Asianism*, 184, 226; Szpilman, "Between Pan-Asianism and Nationalism."

65. Saaler and Szpilman, "Introduction," 1–2.

66. Saaler, "Pan-Asianism," 9.

67. Saaler, 7.

68. Mark, *Japan's Occupation*, 3.

69. See Motadel, *Islam and Nazi Germany's War*; Kirby, "The Internationalization of China."

70. Aydin, "Overcoming Eurocentrism?," 138.

71. Aydin, "Japan's Pan-Asianism," 5.

72. Aydin, 5.

73. Nishimura, "Northeast China in Chongqing Politics," 174.

74. Nishimura, 176.

75. "Nihon to Kaikyō Ajia," 28.

76. Taketani, "The Cartography," 81.

77. Taketani, 81.

78. Taketani, 82.

79. Taketani, 83.

80. Mitter, "Classifying Citizens," 251.

81. "Japanese Infiltration among Muslims in China."

82. Lin, *Tibet and Nationalist China's Frontier*, 39.

83. Lin, xi, see also 45.

84. Lin, 13.

85. Lin, 15.

86. Lin, 45.

87. Carter, *Creating a Chinese Harbin*, 6–7.

88. Mitter, "Evil Empire?," 146.

89. Mitter, 147.

90. Mitter, 163.

91. Please see the "Brief Note on Sources" for more on my archival work. Also see Ambaras, *Japan's Imperial Underworlds*, 1–28.

92. Wu, "The Silent Half Speaks," 208.

93. Wu, 208.

94. Cieciura, "Ethnicity or Religion?"

95. Gladney, "Clashed Civilizations?," 120–21.

96. Cieciura, "Ethnicity or Religion?"

97. Brook, *Collaboration*, 88.

98. I consulted numerous works in thinking about this project. A few of these are Hoffmann, "Collaborationism," 375–95; Bertrand, *Collaborationism in France*; Diamond, *Women and the Second World War in France*; Kaplan, *The Collaborator*; and Rousso, *Le syndrome de Vichy*.

99. Brook, *Collaboration*, 88.

100. Barrett, "Introduction," 4.

101. Brook, *Collaboration*, 1–31.

102. See Kuhn, *Origins of the Modern Chinese State*; and Duara, *Rescuing History from the Nation*.

103. A notable exception among Chinese colleagues is the work of Pan Min. See Pan, *Jiangsu riwei*. In 2000, Jiang Wen also directed and starred in a dark comedy called *Guize laile!* (*Devils on the Doorstep*). Although it was banned on the mainland, it is a

good indication that certain segments of the population are thinking critically about the Japanese occupation.

104. Wakeman, "*Hanjian*," 298–99.

105. Brook, *Collaboration*, 88.

106. Mitter, "Contention and Redemption," 44–45.

107. See Kobayashi, "Nihongo to kaimin jidō"; and "Dai Ajia sensō to Kaikyō."

108. Lipman, *Familiar Strangers*, xxxiv.

109. Mitter, "Historiographical Review," 529.

110. See Brook, *Collaboration*; Lincoln, *Urbanizing China in War and Peace*; Pan, *Jiangsu riwei*.

111. Carroll, *Edge of Empires*, 130, see also 180.

112. Carroll, 12.

113. Moon, *Populist Collaborators*, 3–5.

114. Moon, 5.

115. Palmer, *Fighting for the Enemy*, 4–17.

116. Palmer, *Fighting for the Enemy*, 17, see also 24; Mimura, *Planning for Empire*, 190.

117. Palmer, *Fighting for the Enemy*, 12.

118. Schoppa, *In a Sea of Bitterness* 261.

119. Schoppa, 6.

120. Schoppa, 1–8, 188–213.

121. Schoppa, 7.

122. Wien, *Arab Nationalism*, 3–4.

123. Wien, 6.

124. See Aydin, *The Idea of the Muslim World*; Manger, *Muslim Diversity*.

125. See Aydin, *The Idea of the Muslim World*.

126. Khalid, "A Secular Islam," 576.

127. Halevi, "Is China a House of Islam?," 37.

128. See Martin, *Affirmative Action Empire*.

129. Moon, *Populist Collaborators*, 286.

130. Perdue, "Empire and Nation."

131. McDonald, *Placing Empire*, xv.

132. McDonald, xv.

133. Ambaras, *Japan's Imperial Underworlds*, 3.

134. McDonald, *Placing Empire*, 25–49.

135. Chatani, *Nation-Empire*, 1–24.

136. See Young, *Japan's Total Empire*, v.

137. Cemil Aydin expresses an opposing view in his article "Overcoming Eurocentrism?" He writes that "the Islamic world was not in direct relation to the national identity construction in Japan, and thus interest in Islam did not involve the nation-building dimensions that Stefan Tanaka emphasized [in *Japan's Orient*]" (140).

138. Hanscom and Washburn, "Introduction," 5.

139. Kushner, "Introduction," 1.

140. See Gladney, "Clashed Civilizations?," 123–25; Snow, *Red Star over China*; and Salisbury, *The Long March*.

141. Pianciola and Sartori, "*Waqf* in Turkestan," 475–98.

142. Lindbeck, "Communism, Islam and Nationalism in China," 475.

143. Gladney, "Clashed Civilizations?," 124.

144. See Weiner, *The Chinese Revolution.*

145. Hammond, "Managing Muslims."

CHAPTER 1

1. Ando, "Japan's 'Hui-Muslim' Campaigns," 22, see also 28–29.

2. "Japan Courting Islamic People."

3. "Kaisoku," 6.

4. "Kaisoku," 7.

5. "Kaisoku," 7–9.

6. Matsumisha, "Nihon Kaikyō kyokai," 1–10.

7. Matsumisha, 2.

8. Matsumisha, 3–4.

9. Matsumisha, 5.

10. Matsumisha, 9.

11. Matsumisha, 10.

12. Mimura, *Planning for Empire*, 1–3.

13. Mimura, 109.

14. Mimura, 139.

15. Mimura, 4.

16. "Japanese Infiltration among Muslims in China."

17. "Japanese Infiltration among Muslims in China."

18. Hoover, "Chinese Muslims Are Tough," 720.

19. See Millward, *Beyond the Pass*; and Perdue, *China Marches West.*

20. See Atwill, *The Chinese Sultanate*; Hodong, *Holy War in China*; and Lipman, *Familiar Strangers*, chap. 4.

21. Petersen, *Interpreting Islam in China*, 1–25.

22. Halevi, "Is China a House of Islam?," 43–44.

23. See Erie, *China and Islam*; Thum, *The Sacred Routes*; and Aubin, "Islam on the Wings of Nationalism," 252.

24. Halevi, "Is China a House of Islam?," 35–37.

25. See Atwill, *The Chinese Sultanate*; and Hodong, *Holy War in China.*

26. Lipman, *Familiar Strangers*, 167–68.

27. Lipman, 169.

28. Lipman, 169.

29. Lipman, 170–71.

30. Lipman, 175.

31. Lipman, 176–77.

32. Tuttle, *Tibetan Buddhists*, 3.

33. Lipman, *Familiar Strangers*, 200. An imam is generally known in Chinese as an *ahong*. The term is derived from the Persian word *akhund*. For purposes of clarity, henceforth an "ahong" will be referred to as a cleric.

34. Josephson, *The Invention of Religion*, 1–3.

35. Josephson, 7–10.

36. Josephson, 10, see also 3–4.

37. Rocklin, *The Regulation of Religion*, 4–5, 12.

38. Bodde, "Chinese Muslims in Occupied Areas," 330; Aydin, "Japan's Pan-Asianism."

39. Ando, "Japan's 'Hui-Muslim' Campaigns," 26.

40. Krämer, "Pan-Asianism's Religious Undercurrents," 621. Also see Sugita, *Nihonjin no chūtō hakken.*

41. Esenbel, introduction, 6–7.

42. Esenbel, 6.

43. Krämer, "Pan-Asianism's Religious Undercurrents," 621. Mita's translation of the Quran is sometimes considered the first "true" translation because it was rendered from the original Arabic by a Muslim. It was published in 1972.

44. Krämer, "Pan-Asianism's Religious Undercurrents," 619–21.

45. Krämer, 621.

46. Krämer, 622, see also 627–31.

47. "Umar Mita."

48. See Krämer, "Pan-Asianism's Religious Undercurrents," 619–21; Esenbel, *Japan, Turkey and the World of Islam,* 201–02.

49. See Allen, "Waiting for Tōjō"; and Evanzz, "The FBI and the Nation of Islam."

50. Misawa, "Shintoism and Islam," 122.

51. Ando, "Japan's 'Hui-Muslim' Campaigns," 23.

52. Misawa, "Shintoism and Islam," 122.

53. Azade-Ayse Rorlich uses the term *Volga Tatars* in her book of the same title.

54. See Yamazaki (née Unno), "Abdürreşid İbrahim's Journey to China"; Brandenburg, "The Multiple Publics of a Transnational Activist"; and Komatsu, "Abdurreshid Ibrahim."

55. Krämer, "Pan-Asianism's Religious Undercurrents," 622–23.

56. See Duara, *Culture, Power, and the State.*

57. Esenbel, *Japan, Turkey and the World of Islam,* 201–2.

58. Maxey, *The "Greatest Problem,"* 1–2.

59. Maxey, 3–4.

60. Maxey, 244.

61. Maxey, 235–36.

62. Maxey, 56, see also 90.

63. Maxey, 56, see also 90.

64. Cieciura, "Ethnicity or Religion?"

65. Yamazaki (née Unno), "Cutting Off the Queue."

66. Yamazaki (née Unno).

67. Wong, "Thirty Years of Chinese-Arabic Cultural Relationship," 16.

68. Wong, 16.

69. Matsumoto, "Rationalizing Patriotism," 139.

70. Sha, "Aiguo yu aijiao," 99.

71. Sha, 99.

72. "Zhanhou huibao."

73. Wang, "Zuijin de kangzhan xingshi," 7.

74. Sha, "Aiguo yu aijiao," 99.

75. Ma, "Xibei huimin." Ma regularly cited the verse about the rise and fall of nations that did not follow the will of Allah (Quran 13.2 8:18). These verses describe the destruction that Allah wrought on the tribes (nations) that did not obey his command.

76. Ma, 25.

77. Na, "Bali de Huijiao."

78. Na.

79. Ding, "Bei feizhou."

80. Ding.

81. Ma, "Huijiao minzhong," 22.

82. Zhao, "Sanshinian."

83. Ma, "Huijiao minzhong," 24.

84. Ma, 27.

85. Tanada, "Senchūki Nihon," 96–97.

86. Duara, "The Discourse of Civilization," 111.

87. Duara, 111.

88. Duara, 111.

89. Suzuki, "An Aspect of Middle Eastern and Islamic Studies," 196.

90. Tanada, "Islamic Research Institutes," 92.

91. The organization was dissolved three months after the end of the Pacific War during the U.S. occupation of Japan. It was then reconstituted as the Nihon Isuramu Kyōkai. In the early 1960s, the contents of the Greater Japan Muslim League's extensive library were donated to Waseda University, which now houses the largest collection of works on Islam in Japan.

92. Levent, "Turanism in Japan," 310.

93. Levent, "Turanism in Japan," 311. For more on this, also see Aydin, *The Politics of Anti-Westernism in Asia*, 176–77.

94. Tanada, "Islamic Research Institutes," 92.

95. Tanada, "Senchūki Nihon," 119–20.

96. DuBois, "Japanese Print Media," 232–33.

97. Yamazaki, "Nicchū sensō-ki no chūgoku," 2. Xinjing was quite literally the "new capital" of Manchukuo between 1932 and 1945. After the war, it reverted to its previous name, Changchun, and is the current capital of Jilin province.

98. Ando, "Japan's 'Hui-Muslim' Campaigns," 31.

99. Sakurai, *Daitōa Kaikyō hattatsu-shi*, 167.

100. "Hokushi Kaikyō minzoku kyōkai setsuritsuan."

101. Schoppa, *In a Sea of Bitterness*, 13.

102. Yang, *Riben zhi Huijiao zhengce*, 13.

103. Yang, 13. Zhang was educated in Japan before leaving for New York to pursue graduate studies at Columbia University. He often helped the Japanese government recruit students to study in Japan.

104. Ando, "Japan's 'Hui-Muslim' Campaigns," 29–30.

105. Juzi, "Riben chuanli Huijiao," 50–52.

106. Shimbo, "Nihon senryōka," 232–62.

107. There are numerous examples of reports that document the economic specialization of Muslims in North China, among them Nīda, "Pekin no kaikyōto shōkō hito."

108. See Nīda, "Pekin no kaikyōto shōkō hito," 253; Shimbo, "Nihon senryōka," 242–43.

109. Nīda, "Pekin no kaikyōto shōkō hito," 253.

110. Moon, *Populist Collaborators*, 8–10.

111. Krämer, "Pan-Asianism's Religious Undercurrents," 619.

112. Hotta, *Pan-Asianism*, 1–18.

113. Duara, "The Discourse of Civilization," 111.

114. DuBois, "Japanese Print Media," 224.

115. "Nihon to Kaikyō Ajia," 28.
116. Tuttle, *Tibetan Buddhists*, 68.
117. Tuttle, 83.
118. Tuttle, 6.
119. Tuttle, 68.
120. Duara, "The Discourse of Civilization," 102.
121. Tuttle, *Tibetan Buddhists*, 4.
122. Saaler and Szpilman, "Introduction," 20.
123. "Sun Yatsen on the Role of Chinese Muslims."
124. Saaler and Szpilman, "Introduction," 28.
125. Saaler and Szpilman, 28.
126. Krämer, "Pan-Asianism's Religious Undercurrents," 628; Ando, "Japan's 'Hui-Muslim' Campaigns," 25.
127. Aydin, "Overcoming Eurocentrism?," 152.
128. Aydin, 152.
129. Misawa, "Shintoism and Islam," 130–32.
130. Misawa, 134–35.
131. Ando, "Japan's 'Hui-Muslim' Campaigns," 24.
132. Dufourmont, "Tanaka Ippei," 87.
133. Tanaka, *Isuramu to dai Ajia shugi*.
134. Misawa, "Shintoism and Islam," 119.
135. Krämer, "Pan-Asianism's Religious Undercurrents," 624.
136. Misawa, "Shintoism and Islam," 124. He translated Liu's biography of the Prophet into Japanese. Dufourmont, "Tanaka Ippei," 89.
137. Dufourmont, "Tanaka Ippei," 91.
138. Liu Jielian, *Tianfang zhisheng shi lu nian pian*. Translated by Tanaka Ippei (*Tenpo shisei jitsuroku*, 1941).
139. Tanaka, *Tenpo shisei jitsuroku*, 11–12.
140. Tanaka, 427.
141. Dufourmont, "Tanaka Ippei," 91.
142. Suzuki, *Nihon kaikyōto*, 15.
143. Suzuki, 15.
144. Suzuki, 16.
145. Amakawa, *Daitōasensō to sekai*, 184–86.
146. See Motadel, *Islam and Nazi Germany's War*; Chapoutot, *Greeks, Romans, and Germans*.
147. Chen, "Chinese Heirs to Muhammad," 4–10.
148. *Nihon to kaikyōto*, chap. 9.
149. *Nihon to kaikyōto*, chap. 9.
150. Juzi, "Riben chuanli Huijiao," 50–52. It is perhaps an overstatement to claim that the *Han Kitab* was "widely read" in Tokugawa Japan.
151. Togō, *Manshū shūkyō no gaikan*, 15–16.
152. Togō, 16.
153. Togō, 18.
154. Togō, 20.
155. Mei, "Zhuiyi jiwang," 23.
156. Mei, 24–25.

157. Mei, 24–25.

158. Mei, 24–25.

159. Bayliss, *On the Margins of Empire*, 1–22.

160. Moon, *Populist Collaborators*, 1–21.

161. Moon, *Populist Collaborators*, 287; Bayliss, *On the Margins of Empire*, 11.

162. Bayliss, *On the Margins of Empire*, 14.

163. Bayliss, 47.

164. Duus, *The Abacus and the Sword*, 413–24.

165. Bayliss, *On the Margins of Empire*, 83.

166. Nīda, "Pekin no kaikyōto," 241–65.

167. *Tatāru mondai.*

168. Bayliss, *On the Margins of Empire*, 51.

169. Bayliss, 390.

170. Sakurai, *Daitōa Kaikyō*, 162–64.

171. "Tōa ni okeru."

172. "Tōa ni okeru."

173. "Huijiao de libaitang," 12–14.

174. "Huijiao de libaitang," 13.

175. Shimizu, "The Japanese Trade Contact," 29.

176. Zhu, "Riben yu Yisilanjiao," 135.

177. DuBois, "Japanese Print Media," 217.

178. DuBois, "The Transformation of Religion," 1–4.

CHAPTER 2

1. Wang, "Zuijin de kangzhan xingshi," 7.

2. Bai Chongxi, speech delivered at the first National Convention of the Chinese Muslims' National Salvation Association, published in *The Bulletin of the Chinese Muslims' National Salvation Association* 1, no. 1 (October 1939).

3. Yang, *Riben zhi Huijiao zhengce*, 34.

4. Cooke and Lawrence, introduction, 17.

5. "Nihon to Kaikyō Ajia," 28.

6. "Nihon to Kaikyō Ajia," 28.

7. Green, "Anti-colonial Japanophilia," 13–15.

8. "Nihon to Kaikyō Ajia," 28. Also see Mitter, "Classifying Citizens," 248, see also 251.

9. For example, Satō, "Indonesia ni okeru I"; and Rezrazi, "Pan-Asianism."

10. Schoppa, *In a Sea of Bitterness*, 1–8.

11. Clinton, *Revolutionary Nativism*, 13–17.

12. Carroll, *Edge of Empires*, 184. Also see Rana Mitter's work on Manchukuo for more on this.

13. Mitter, "Classifying Citizens," 248–51.

14. Benite, "Nine Years in Egypt," 1–21.

15. Files relating to the Chinese Islamic Association in Malaya.

16. "Japanese Infiltration among Muslims in China."

17. Zhu, "Riben yu Yisilanjiao," 132.

18. "Japanese Infiltration among Muslims in China."

19. "Japanese Infiltration among Muslims in China."

20. "Japanese Infiltration among Muslims in China."

21. "Japanese Infiltration among Muslims in China."

22. See "Shina kaikyōto no shin dōkō"; "Ma Hongkui to Shina no kai kyōto."

23. Bai, "Zhongguo Huijiao."

24. Bai, 2.

25. Mitter, "Classifying Citizens," 254.

26. Yang, *Riben zhi Huijiao zhengce*, 19.

27. Yang, 52.

28. Yang, 18.

29. Yang, 26–28. In this case, the Japanese army bought upward of 90 percent of the wool coming through large trading entrepôts in border towns like Zhangjiakou.

30. Yang, 28.

31. Yang, 29–31.

32. Yang, 27.

33. Yang, 21.

34. Schoppa, *In a Sea of Bitterness*, 164–87.

35. Yang, *Riben zhi Huijiao zhengce*, 21.

36. Zhu, "Riben yu Yisilanjiao," 132.

37. Zhu, 133.

38. Zhu, 135.

39. Xue, "Huijiao shijie," 34.

40. Xue, 35.

41. Xue, 36.

42. See Goodman, *Native Place*.

43. Mao, "A Muslim Vision," 375.

44. Mao, "Muslim Educational Reform," 143, see also 149.

45. Lincicome, *Imperial Subjects*, xvii.

46. Lincicome, xxvi.

47. Lincicome, xxii–xxvi.

48. Gladney, "Making Muslims," 55–56.

49. Sino-Muslim students were not the only ones traveling to imperial Japan for educational opportunities. For instance, in 1906 around 12,000 Chinese students went there, including eight Mongolians. For more about this, see Yokota, "1906-Nen ni okeru Mongorujin-gakusei"; and Yokota, "Naimoko-'Harqin,'" 104. Also in 1943, the Japanese occupation authorities selected twenty-seven students from the Philippines to travel to Tokyo based on their presumed capacity to return to Manila and help the occupation government. While in Tokyo, they learned Japanese and attended the Police Academy. A number of the students were billeted with Japanese Catholics. See Goodman, *An Experiment in Wartime Intercultural Relations*.

50. Hoover, "Chinese Muslims Are Tough," 721.

51. *Indians in Japan*, 54.

52. Wiest, "Catholic Elementary and Secondary Schools," 102.

53. "Pekin kaikyōto saikin."

54. Shimbo, "Nihon senryōka," 244–45.

55. Brook, *Collaboration*, 245.

56. Yang, *Riben zhi Huijiao zhengce*, 25.

57. Mitter, *The Manchurian Myth*, 122.

58. Cong, *Teachers' Schools*, 9.

59. Harrell, *Sowing the Seeds of Change*, 48.

60. Harrell, 40.

61. See Culp, *Articulating Citizenship*; Li, *Student Nationalism*; Cong, *Teachers' Schools*.

62. Michael, "Notes and Comments," 471–86.

63. Li, *Student Nationalism*, 81.

64. Michael, "Notes and Comments," 481.

65. Culp, *Articulating Citizenship*, 28.

66. Li, *Student Nationalism*, 144.

67. Cong, *Teachers' Schools*, 128, see also 204 and 285.

68. Madrasahs are private institutions supported by the Muslim community (*waqf* in Arabic) and financed by wealthy patrons. The pedagogical style in madrasahs during this period focused on rote memorization of the Quran, hadiths, and other theological texts. Schools lacked a cohesive central authority, so individual clerics taught based on their own knowledge. For more, see the work of Elisabeth Allès, especially "Muslim Religious Education in China."

69. Cong, *Teachers' Schools*, 3–17.

70. Allès, "Muslim Religious Education in China," 4.

71. Thøgersen, *A County of Culture*, 15.

72. Hayhoe, *Education and Modernization*, 242.

73. Wiest, "Catholic Elementary and Secondary Schools," 99.

74. Cong, *Teachers' Schools*, 72–73.

75. Thøgersen, *A County of Culture*, 3.

76. Cong, *Teachers' Schools*, 72, 78.

77. Gladney, "Making Muslims," 61.

78. Culp, *Articulating Citizenship*, 32; Cong, *Teachers' Schools*, 159–201.

79. "Kangzhan jianguo."

80. "Kangzhan jianguo."

81. "Kangzhan jianguo."

82. "Kangzhan jianguo."

83. Carnoy, *Education as Cultural Imperialism*, 8–16.

84. Thøgersen, *A County of Culture*, 8, 125; Treat, "Choosing to Collaborate," 89.

85. Thøgersen, *A County of Culture*, 240.

86. Zhao, "Lun Zhongguo Huijiao."

87. "Kangzhan jianguo."

88. "Kangzhan jianguo."

89. "Huijiao jiaoyu zhi gaige."

90. Ding, "Zenyang lai."

91. Ding.

92. "Huijiao jiaoyu zhi gaige."

93. "Shengjiao yu Guoxue,"

94. "Shengjiao yu Guoxue."

95. "Shengjiao yu Guoxue."

96. Mao, "Muslim Educational Reform," 143–70.

97. "Guanyu jinhou de Huijiao jiaoyu wenti."

98. "Guanyu jinhou de Huijiao jiaoyu wenti."

99. Culp, *Articulating Citizenship*, 64.

100. "Huijiao jiaoyu zhi gaige," 57–58.
101. Carnoy, *Education as Cultural Imperialism*, 1–5.
102. Kobayashi, "Nihongo to kaimin jidō," 37–39.
103. Kojima, "The Making of Ainu Citizenship."
104. Kobayashi, "Nihongo to kaimin jidō," 37.
105. Kojima, "The Making of Ainu Citizenship," 108.
106. Sakuma, "Shina kaikyōto no kyōiku josei."
107. "Pekin kaikyōto saikin."
108. "Pekin kaikyōto saikin."
109. "Pekin kaikyōto saikin."
110. Yang, *Riben zhi Huijiao zhengce*, 18.
111. "Pekin kaikyōto saikin."
112. "Guoren jiyi riwen."
113. "Juezhan xia jiang nei jiaoyu quan."
114. Mitter, "Evil Empire?," 156.
115. Koyama, "Domestic Roles," 85.
116. "Huimin shehui zhi liyi."
117. "Zenme jiao nide haizi."
118. Carnoy, *Education as Cultural Imperialism*, 19.
119. "Huimin xuexiao wei."
120. "Huimin xuexiao wei."
121. "Tong huimin xiaoxue."
122. "Hui Qingxuexiao xinsheng."
123. "Datong Huimin."
124. "Datong Huimin."
125. "Chengli riyu."
126. "Rihui nüsheng."
127. "Rihui nüsheng."
128. "Pekin kaikyōto saikin."
129. "Pekin kaikyōto saikin."
130. Sakuma, "Shina kaikyōto no kyōiku josei."
131. Sakuma.
132. Sakuma.
133. Sakuma.
134. Sakuma.
135. "Huiqing xuexiao."
136. "Datong Huimin."
137. Kobayashi, "Nihongo to kaimin jidō," 49.
138. Kobayashi, "49.
139. "Nihon to Kaikyō Ajia"; "Dai Ajia sensō to kaikyōken."
140. Kobayashi, "Nihongo to kaimin jidō," 36.
141. Kobayashi, 38.
142. Kobayashi, 39.
143. Kobayashi, 49.
144. Kobayashi, 39–40.
145. Kobayashi, 42.
146. Kobayashi, 42.

147. Kobayashi, 42–43.

148. Kobayashi, 52.

149. Kobayashi, 52. In personal correspondence with Rian Thum and James Ryan, they both referred to the language that the students were learning as "East Turki."

150. Yamada-sei, "Tōkyō Kaikyō gakkō."

151. Yamada-sei, 58.

152. Kobayashi, "Nihongo to kaimin jidō," 49.

153. Kobayashi, 50.

154. Kobayashi, 51.

155. Kobayashi, 54.

156. Kobayashi, 54.

157. Kushner, "Introduction," 1.

CHAPTER 3

1. See McDonald, *Placing Empire*; Ambaras, *Japan's Imperial Underworlds*; Yellen, *The Greater East Asia Co-Prosperity Sphere*; and Chatani, *Nation-Empire*.

2. McDonald, *Placing Empire*, xv.

3. Ambaras, *Japan's Imperial Underworlds*, 3.

4. McDonald, *Placing Empire*, 11.

5. McDonald, 13.

6. McDonald, 41.

7. "Guanyu Dongjing Qingzhensi."

8. Tang, *Maijia xunli ji*, 415.

9. Yamazaki (née Unno), "Abdürreşid İbrahim's Journey to China"; Komastu, "Abdürreşid Ibrahim."

10. Yamazaki (née Unno), "Nicchū sensōki," 2.

11. Yamazaki (née Unno), 2.

12. Yamazaki (née Unno), 2.

13. Personal correspondence with Selçuk Esenbel, December 28, 2018.

14. "Son of King of Yemen."

15. Willis, *Unmaking North and South*, 148.

16. See Willis, *Unmaking North and South*; Dresch, *A History of Modern Yemen*; and Al-Rasheed and Vitalis, *Counter-narratives*.

17. "Lettrera dell'Imam."

18. "Gircolare della Missione musulmana."

19. "Huijiao de libaitang," 12–14.

20. Ma, "Zhongguo Huijiao."

21. Ma.

22. Bodde, "Japan and the Muslims of China." For more in Japanese, also see Yamazaki (née Unno), "Nichū sensōki," 1–20.

23. "Tōkyō Kaikyō gakkō" (*Kodomo*).

24. "Tōkyō Kaikyō gakkō" (*Kodomo*).

25. See Ma, "Zhongguo Huijiao"; and Bai, "Bai Jinyu anda Riben."

26. Ma, "Zhongguo Huijiao."

27. Yamazaki (née Unno), "Nicchū sensōki," 9.

28. "Japan's Near East Conspiracy," part 4.

29. "Japan's Near East Conspiracy," part 4.

30. "Japan's Near East Conspiracy," part 5.

31. "Japan's Near East Conspiracy," part 6.

32. "Japan's Near East Conspiracy," part 7.

33. "Japan's Near East Conspiracy," part 7.

34. Aisha, "Quan Riben jiaru Huijiao," 39.

35. Aisha, 41.

36. Aisha, "Zhongguo Huijiao," 4–7.

37. Aisha, 4.

38. Aisha, 6.

39. Ma, "Jinhou woguo waijiao," 13–15.

40. Sun, "Kangzhan yilai Huijiao," 3–9; "Huijiao yu er ci ou zhan."

41. Wang, "Kangzhanzhong," 68–69.

42. Wang, 66–69.

43. Wang, 66.

44. Wang, 67.

45. Tianfeng, "Zhongguo guomin," 5.

46. Sha, "Riben diguo," 27.

47. Sha, 28.

48. Zhu, "Riben yu Yisilanjiao," 132.

49. Zhu, 132–33.

50. Zhu, 134.

51. Bai, "Bai Jinyu anda Riben."

52. Bai.

53. Ma, "Huijiao Dongxiang Riben," 11.

54. Cooke and Lawrence, introduction, 27.

55. Mao, "A Muslim Vision," 375.

56. Aydin, *The Idea of the Muslim World*, 166–67.

57. Tang, *Maijia xunli ji*, 415.

58. Zhang, "Zhongguo Huijiao," 36.

59. Shimizu, "The Japanese Trade Contact with the Middle East," 27–53.

60. Penn, "The Vicissitudes of Japan-Saudi Relations," 280.

61. "Military Intelligence Division Regional File Relating to China, 1922–1944."

62. Penn, "The Vicissitudes of Japan-Saudi Relations," 280.

63. Penn, 280.

64. Rush, *Records of the Hajj*, 343–48.

65. Reese, *Imperial Muslims*, 2.

66. Coleman and Eade, *Reframing Pilgrimage*, 2.

67. Yang, *Riben zhi Huijiao zhengce*, 61–62.

68. See Kirby, "The Internationalization of China."

69. Stegewerns, "The Dilemma of Nationalism," 5.

70. Tang, *Maijia xunli ji*, 407.

71. Tang, 407.

72. Yamazaki (née Unno), "Nicchū sensōki," 417.

73. See Pang, *Aiji jiu nian*.

74. Zhang, "Zhongguo Huijiao," 27–40.

75. Zhang, 33–38.

76. Lei, "The Chinese Islamic," 145–52.

77. Yamazaki (née Unno), "Nicchū sensōki," 7.

78. Yamazaki (née Unno), 10.

79. Tang, *Maijia xunli ji*, 412.

80. The term *huandu* literally means for a government to return to a capital city after exile. Tang, 408.

81. Tang, 415.

82. Cooke and Lawrence, introduction, 27.

83. Tang, *Maijia xunli ji*, 416.

84. In Chinese historiography, the occupation of Shanghai by the Japanese is sometimes referred to as the Battle of Songhu. *Songhu* is an alternate name for Suzhou Creek.

85. Tang, *Maijia xunli ji*, 420.

86. Tang, 420–21.

87. Tang, 422.

88. Tang, 423–24.

89. Tang, 427.

90. Tang, 428.

91. Tang, 428.

92. Tang, 428.

93. Tang, 429.

94. Tang, 429.

95. Tang, 430.

96. Fogel, *Articulating the Sinosphere*, 1–6.

97. Tang, *Maijia xunli ji*, 433.

98. Tang, 434.

99. See Trevaskis, *Eritrea*.

100. Tang, *Maijia xunli ji*, 437.

101. Tang, 439–40.

102. Tang, 441.

103. Tang, 442.

104. Tang, 443.

105. Tang, 445.

106. Tang, 445.

107. Tang, 445.

108. See Rogaski, *Hygienic Modernity*.

109. Tang, *Maijia xunli ji*, 447.

110. Rush, *Records of the Hajj*, 281, see also 347.

111. Tang, *Maijia xunli ji*, 406–76, esp. 447.

112. "Huijiao chaojin tuan gongzuo giakuang," 139.

113. Tang, *Maijia xunli ji*, 35.

114. Zhang, "Zhongguo Huijiao," 36.

115. Lipman, *Familiar Strangers*, 209–10.

116. Tang, *Maijia xunli ji*, 406–76, esp. 457.

117. Tang, 460.

118. See Lao She's novel *Rickshaw Boy* (C. *luotuo xiangzi*) for more on this.

119. Tang, *Maijia xunli ji*, 460.

120. Tang, 462.

121. Tang, 470.

122. Tang, 471.

123. Tang, 472.

124. Coleman and Eade, *Reframing Pilgrimage,* 8.

125. See Motadel, *Islam and Nazi Germany's War.*

126. Tang, *Maijia xunli ji,* 475.

127. Tang, 475.

128. Gladney, "Sino–Middle Eastern Perspective."

CHAPTER 4

1. Hoover, "Chinese Muslims Are Tough," 722.

2. Wen, "From Manchuria to Egypt," 176, see also 194.

3. Dai Nihon Kaikyō Kyōkai, *Ware ga Nanyō bōeki to kaikyōto,* 1–12.

4. Dai Nihon Kaikyō Kyōkai, 22–24.

5. Dai Nihon Kaikyō Kyōkai, 28.

6. *Nihon to kaikyōto,* 19.

7. Ravinder Frost and Schumacher, "Wartime Globalization," 1924.

8. Ravinder Frost and Schumacher, 1925.

9. Yang, *Riben zhi Huijiao zhengce,* 33.

10. Yang, 40.

11. Yang, 42–43.

12. Yang, 48.

13. Yang, 36.

14. Mimura, *Planning for Empire,* 4.

15. Mimura, 39, see also 69.

16. Mimura, 186.

17. Mimura, 186.

18. Mimura, 194.

19. Sakurai, "Manchukuo no Kaikyō."

20. Sakuma, "Shina no kaikyōto," 19–21.

21. "Ajia nanpō no kaikyōto"; "Nanyō kaikyōto."

22. Suda, *Tairiku seisaku,* 4.

23. Suda, 6–8.

24. Haddad-Fonda, "The Domestic Significance," 55–56.

25. Suzuki, "Nanpō Kaikyō," 35–41.

26. Suda, *Tairiku seisaku,* 6–8.

27. Rodriguez, "Fuirippin Kaikyō," 19–21; Sakei, *Manmū no minzoku.*

28. Rodriguez, "Fuirippin Kaikyō," 20.

29. Duara, "The Discourse of Civilization," 100.

30. Hotta, *Pan-Asianism,* 229.

31. Suda, *Tairiku seisaku,* 6.

32. Conrad and Duara, *Viewing Regionalisms,* 12–36.

33. Suzuki, "Nanpō Kaikyō," 35.

34. Suzuki, 39–41.

35. Suzuki, 41.

36. Saaler and Szpilman, "Introduction," 1–2.

37. Suzuki, *Nihon kaikyōto*, 16.

38. Suzuki, 16.

39. Suzuki, 17–18.

40. "Kaikyōto no Nihonjin mi."

41. "Kaikyōto no Nihonjin mi," 98.

42. "Kaikyōto no Nihonjin mi," 98.

43. "Kaikyōto no Nihonjin mi," 99.

44. "Kaikyōto no Nihonjin mi," 99.

45. "Kaikyōto no Nihonjin mi," 102.

46. Elsbree, *Japan's Role*, 41.

47. Elsbree, *Japan's Role*, 4; Mark, *Japan's Occupation*, 25–51, see also 66–67.

48. Mark, *Japan's Occupation*, 66.

49. Ōwada, "Kaikyō seisaku," 35–36.

50. Ōwada, 37.

51. Kurasawa, "Mobilization and Control," 26.

52. Aziz, *Japan's Colonialism and Indonesia*, 110–16.

53. Satō, "Indonesia, 1939–1942," 225–26. Michael Laffan's book *The Makings of Indonesian Islam* ends in 1942 with the Japanese occupation of the islands.

54. Kurasawa, "Mobilization and Control," chap. 1.

55. Benda, "The Beginnings," 553–54.

56. Aziz, *Japan's Colonialism*, 201.

57. Aziz, 210.

58. Kurasawa, "Mobilization and Control," chap. 1.

59. *Zen Jawa Kaikyō Jōkyō*, 24–25; quotation from Mark, *Japan's Occupation*, 58.

60. *Zen Jawa Kaikyō Jōkyō*, 25–26.

61. See Laffan, *The Makings of Indonesian Islam*.

62. *Zen Jawa Kaikyō Jōkyō*, 27.

63. Kurasawa, "Mobilization and Control," chap. 4; Mark, *Japan's Occupation*, 91.

64. Kurasawa, "Mobilization and Control," 318.

65. Kurasawa, "Mobilization and Control," 385–86; Mark, *Japan's Occupation*, 6.

66. Kurasawa, "Mobilization and Control," 475.

67. Mark, *Japan's Occupation*, 41–42, see also 188–89.

68. See Slamet, *Japanese Machinations*.

69. Aydin, "Japan's Pan-Asianism," 18; Mark, *Japan's Occupation*, 40–41.

70. Mark, *Japan's Occupation*, 94.

71. Slamet, *Japanese Machinations*, 9, see also 15.

72. Elsbree, *Japan's Role*, 49.

73. Benda, "The Japanese Interregnum," 78.

74. Silverstein, "The Importance of the Japanese Occupation," 3.

75. Laffan, *The Makings of Indonesian Islam*, 189, see also 231.

76. McCoy, introduction, 7.

77. Lebra, *Japanese-Trained Armies*, 17.

78. Reid, "Indonesia," 26–27; Mark, *Japan's Occupation*, 106.

79. Anderson, "Japan," 23–25.

80. Mark, *Japan's Occupation*, 107.

81. Mark, 108–10.

82. Kobayashi, "Kyai and Japanese Military."

83. Mark, *Japan's Occupation*, 28–29.

84. Aydin, "Japan's Pan-Asianism," 21.

85. Akashi, "The Japanese Occupation of Malaya," 78.

86. Saaler and Szpilman, "Introduction," 24–25.

87. Kheng, "The Social Impact," 95.

88. Files relating to Protecting Malaya's Overseas Chinese.

89. Files relating to the Chinese Islamic Association in Malaya.

90. Kurasawa, "Mobilization and Control," 10–13.

91. *Indoneshia ni okeru Nihon gunsei no kenkyu*, 227.

92. Harada, "Toā Kyōeiken."

93. Harada.

94. Mark, *Japan's Occupation*, 129.

95. Benda, "The Japanese Interregnum," 65–70.

96. Satō, "Indonesia ni okeru I," 111–24; Satō, "Indonesia ni okeru II," 152–66; Satō, "Indonesia ni okeru III," 143–50.

97. Satō, "Indonesia ni okeru II," 162.

98. Satō, "Indonesia ni okeru I," 122.

99. Elsbree, *Japan's Role*, 130.

100. Mark, *Japan's Occupation*, 141.

101. Akashi, "The Japanese Occupation of Malaya," 68.

102. Mark, *Japan's Occupation*, 143.

103. Kheng, "The Social Impact," 107.

104. *Indians in Japan*, 42.

105. Akashi, "The Japanese Occupation of Malaya," 65; *Indians in Japan*, 41.

106. Kheng, "The Social Impact," 107, 110.

107. Satō, "Indonesia ni okeru II," 158.

108. Satō, 159.

109. Satō, 159–61.

110. Hopper, "The Globalization of Dried Fruit," 178.

111. McDonald, *Placing Empire*, 84.

112. Satō, "Indonesia, 1939–1942," 229–31.

113. Bradshaw and Ransdell, "Japan, Britain," 1–21.

114. Bradshaw and Ransdell, 1.

115. Bradshaw and Ransdell, 6.

116. Takahashi, *Indoneshia Tenbyō*, 80–81.

117. Takahashi, 82–87.

118. Hosoya, "Nanyō shingyō," 24.

119. de Jong, "Japan Pushing Her Program," 238.

120. Wickizer, *Tea under International Regulation*, 181.

121. Sigley, "Tea and China's Rise."

122. Rappaport, *A Thirst for Empire*, 7.

123. Tang, *Maijia xunli ji*, 447.

124. "Dai Nihon Kaikyō kyōkai."

125. Dai Nihon Kaikyō Kyōkai, *Kaikyōken hayawakari*, 79–80.

126. Dai Nihon Kaikyō Kyōkai, 81.

127. Suzuki, *Nihon kaikyōto*, 14–15.

128. Juzi, "Riben chuanli Huijiao," 52.

129. Um, *Shipped but Not Sold*, 2.

130. Hinsch, *The Rise of Tea Culture*, 1–12.

131. Hinsch, 89.

132. Rappaport, *A Thirst for Empire*, 29–30.

133. Rappaport, 31.

134. Hellyer, "1874: Tea and Japan's New Trading Regime," 186–87.

135. Okakura, *The Book of Tea*, 1–2.

136. Okakura, 2–3.

137. Wickizer, *Tea under International Regulation*, 5, see also 9.

138. Rappaport, *A Thirst for Empire*, 266.

139. Rappaport, 266.

140. Wickizer, *Tea under International Regulation*, 72.

141. Wickizer, 33.

142. Archives du Maroc, Rabat.

143. Archives du Maroc, Rabat.

144. Archives du Maroc, Rabat.

145. Archives du Maroc, Rabat.

146. Wickizer, *Tea under International Regulation*, 137–48.

147. Rappaport, *A Thirst for Empire*, 307–8.

148. Rappaport, 307, 309.

149. Um, *Shipped but Not Sold*, 15.

150. Dai Nihon Kaikyō Kyōkai, *Kaikyōken hayawakari*, 76.

151. Dai Nihon Kaikyō Kyōkai, 77.

152. Dai Nihon Kaikyō Kyōkai, 1–4.

153. Hosoya, "Nanyō shingyō."

154. Hosoya, 22.

155. Hosoya, 28.

156. Matsumoro, "Nihon cha," 6–9.

157. Matsumoro, 6.

158. Matsumoro, 7.

159. Dai Nihon Kaikyō Kyokai, *Nihon cha no sekai-teki*, 1.

160. Dai Nihon Kaikyō Kyokai, 1.

161. Hosoya, *Ai kuni chagara*, 67.

162. Hosoya, 67.

163. Hosoya, 71.

164. Hosoya, 75.

165. Hosoya, 76.

166. Matsumoro, "Nihon cha," 8–9.

167. Matsumoro, 8–9.

168. Matsumoro, 10.

169. "Dai Nihon Kaikyō kyōkai."

170. Hosoya, *Ai kuni chagara*, 71.

171. "Dai Nihon Kaikyō kyōkai."

172. Matsumoro, "Nihon cha," 11.

173. Wickizer, *Tea under International Regulation*, 182.

174. Dai Nihon Kaikyō Kyokai, *Nihon cha no sekai-teki*, 1.

175. Dai Nihon Kaikyō Kyokai, 14.

176. Dai Nihon Kaikyō Kyokai, 17.

177. Dai Nihon Kaikyō Kyokai, 7.

178. Dai Nihon Kaikyō Kyokai, 8.

179. Dai Nihon Kaikyō Kyokai, 10.

180. Dai Nihon Kaikyō Kyokai, 2.

181. Dai Nihon Kaikyō Kyokai, 1.

182. Dai Nihon Kaikyō Kyokai, 27–28.

183. Dai Nihon Kaikyō Kyokai, 28.

184. Dai Nihon Kaikyō Kyokai, 29.

185. Rappaport, *A Thirst for Empire*, 340.

186. Rappaport, 407.

187. Kushner, "Introduction," 1–2.

188. Rappaport, *A Thirst for Empire*, 340.

189. Shimizu, "The Japanese Trade Contact with the Middle East," 29.

190. Rappaport, *A Thirst for Empire*, 407–8.

CHAPTER 5

1. "Mohammedism [*sic*]."

2. "Mohammedism [*sic*]."

3. "Mohammedism [*sic*]."

4. Young, "Early-Twentieth-Century Japan."

5. Young, 1118.

6. Young, 1125.

7. Young, 1124.

8. Saravia, *Fascist Pigs*, 3–4.

9. Shin, "'Deimperialization' in Early Postwar Japan," 33.

10. Shimizu, "The Japanese Trade Contact," 30; Levent, "Images of Japan," 124–25.

11. Shimizu, "The Japanese Trade Contact," 42–43.

12. Shimizu, 44–45.

13. See Motadel, *Islam and Nazi Germany's War*.

14. "Japan's Near East Conspiracy," sections 1–5.

15. "Japan's Near East Conspiracy," section 1.

16. "Japan's Near East Conspiracy," section 2.

17. "Japan's Near East Conspiracy," section 3.

18. Yang, *Riben zhi Huijiao zhengce*, 34.

19. Yang, 34.

20. Yang, 37.

21. Zhu, "Riben yu Yisilanjiao," 134.

22. Zhu, 134.

23. Dai Nihon Kaikyō Kyōkai, *Kunao suru no ren*, 5.

24. Dai Nihon Kaikyō Kyōkai, 8–9.

25. Dai Nihon Kaikyō Kyōkai, 13–14.

26. Dai Nihon Kaikyō Kyōkai, 16–18.

27. "Takahashi's Blacks," 27.

28. Redmond, *Social Movements*, 98.

29. Dower, *War without Mercy*, 175.

30. Kearney, *African American Views of the Japanese*, xxv.

31. Redmond, *Social Movements*, 82. Redmond is drawing heavily from Reginald Kearney's *African American Views of the Japanese*. John Dower's *War without Mercy* also underscores Japanese efforts to "influence black opinion in the United States," throughout the 1930s (174). Although Dower claims that their efforts were "largely ineffective," Japanese agents did manage to link up with a number of black Muslim communities in Detroit, Chicago, and St. Louis (175).

32. Taketani, "The Cartography," 79; Kearney, *African American Views of the Japanese*, 84.

33. Taketani, "The Cartography," 81.

34. Allen, "When Japan," 28.

35. Lee, "The Paradox," 521.

36. Lee, 522.

37. W. E. B. Du Bois, quoted in Lee, 523.

38. Kearney, *African American Views of the Japanese*, 88.

39. Lee, "The Paradox," 513.

40. Taketani, "The Cartography," 96.

41. Taketani, 80.

42. Allen, "Waiting for Tōjō," 43.

43. Redmond, *Social Movements*, 82.

44. Dower, *War without Mercy*, 347–48.

45. Evanzz, "The FBI and the Nation of Islam," 164.

46. Dower, *War without Mercy*, 175.

47. Allen, "Waiting for Tōjō," 52.

48. Allen, "When Japan," 31.

49. Allen, 32.

50. Redmond, *Social Movements*, 83.

51. Yang, "Wo zai ouzhou," 8.

52. "Italy's Muslim Policy," 15.

53. "Italy's Muslim Policy," 15.

54. Hammond, "Managing Muslims."

55. "Italy's Muslim Policy," 14.

56. Bernhard, "Behind the Battle Lines," 425–27.

57. Bernhard, 425–27.

58. Barrera, "Mussolini's Colonial Race Laws," 431.

59. Barrera, 436.

60. Bernhard, "Behind the Battle Lines," 428–29.

61. "Italy's Muslim Policy," 14.

62. "Italy's Muslim Policy," 14.

63. "Italy's Muslim Policy," 16.

64. "Italy's Muslim Policy," 16.

65. "Italy's Muslim Policy," 16.

66. "Italy's Muslim Policy," 16.

67. "Italy's Muslim Policy," 16.

68. "Italy's Muslim Policy," 27.

69. "Italy's Muslim Policy," 21–22; Shimada, "Senchū-ki Nihon no."

70. "Italy's Muslim Policy," 23–24.

71. "Cinque studenti musilimani."

72. "Ritorno di due 'ulama' di al-Azhar."

73. "Rappresentati di paesi arabi."

74. "La prima traduzione arabe."

75. "La prima traduzione arabe."

76. "La prima traduzione arabe."

77. McMeekin, *The Berlin-Baghdad Express*, 1–2.

78. McMeekin, 3.

79. McMeekin, 14.

80. McMeekin, 14.

81. Motadel, *Islam and Nazi Germany's War*, 25.

82. McMeekin, *The Berlin-Baghdad Express*, 124.

83. Motadel, *Islam and Nazi Germany's War*, 24.

84. McMeekin, *The Berlin-Baghdad Express*, 124.

85. Motadel, *Islam and Nazi Germany's War*, 27.

86. "Italy's Muslim Policy," 14.

87. "Italy's Muslim Policy," 16.

88. "Italy's Muslim Policy," 15.

89. Motadel, *Islam and Nazi Germany's War*, 16.

90. Murata, *Afuganisutan ni okeru*, 142.

91. Tian, "Yingde de Huijiao zhengce," 133.

92. Tian, 133.

93. Tian, 133.

94. Green, "Introduction," 15–17.

95. See Goodman, "Anti-Semitism in Japan."

96. "Guanyu Dongjing Qingzhensi."

97. Crews, *Afghan Modern*, 1–10.

98. Green, "Introduction," 49.

99. Noda, "Japanese Spies," 21–29.

100. Noda, 21.

101. Noda, 22.

102. Noda, 26.

103. "Infiltration Attempts among Muslims in Russia's Borderlands."

104. Saravia, *Fascist Pigs*, 5.

105. Green, "Introduction," 8.

106. Morrison, "Beyond the 'Great Game,'" 690.

107. Morrison, 691.

108. Green, "Introduction," 9.

109. Galambos and Kōichi, "Japanese Exploration."

110. Galambos and Kōichi, 115.

111. Galambos, "Japanese 'Spies,'" 34; Mark, *Japan's Occupation*, 66–67.

112. Galambos, "Japanese 'Spies'"; Yamato, "Kaikyō seisaku."

113. "Diary of Chester G. Fuson's Ten-Month Magnetic Survey Trip across Asia," quoted in Galambos, "Japanese 'Spies,'" 49.

114. Hughes, "The German Mission," 447.

115. Hughes, 458–59.

116. Hughes, 460.

117. Hughes, 471.

118. Green, "The Afghan Discovery of Buddha," 49.

119. Murata, *Afuganisutan ni okeru*, 142.

120. Murata, 149.

121. Murata, 149.

122. Murata, 149.

123. "General Records of the State Department, 1940–1944."

124. Murata, *Afuganisutan ni okeru*, 155–56.

125. Murata, 158.

126. "The International Student Institute."

127. "The International Student Institute."

128. "Japanese Infiltration among Muslims throughout the World."

129. "Japanese Infiltration among Muslims throughout the World."

130. "Japanese Infiltration among Muslims throughout the World."

131. "Japanese Infiltration among Muslims throughout the World."

132. "Infiltration Attempts among Muslims in Russia's Borderlands."

133. "Infiltration Attempts among Muslims in Russia's Borderlands."

134. "Infiltration Attempts among Muslims in Russia's Borderlands."

135. Green, "Introduction," 186.

136. "General Records of the State Department, 1940–1944."

137. Juzi, "Riben chuanli Huijiao," 50–53.

138. "General Records of the State Department, 1940–1944."

139. Juzi, "Riben chuanli Huijiao," 51.

140. Amin, *Afghan-Japan Relations*, 4–5.

141. Amin, 5.

142. Green, "The Afghan Discovery of Buddha," 47–70.

143. Amin, *Afghan-Japan Relations*, 10.

144. Murata, *Afuganisutan ni okeru*, section iv. Also see Tanabe, *Afuganisutan-zen*.

145. Murata, *Afuganisutan ni okeru*, 23.

146. Murata, 120–21.

147. Tang, *Maijia xunli ji*, 475.

148. Chapoutot, *Greeks, Romans, and Germans*, 2.

149. Chapoutot, 3, see also 6.

150. Chapoutot, 3, see also 6.

151. Zia-Ebrahimi, "Self-Orientalization," 446.

152. Zia-Ebrahimi, 448–49.

153. Chapoutot, *Greeks, Romans, and Germans*, 18.

154. Chapoutot, 20.

155. Zia-Ebrahimi, "Self-Orientalization," 448–49.

156. Chapoutot, *Greeks, Romans, and Germans*, 30–32.

157. Chapoutot, 394.

158. Zia-Ebrahimi, "Self-Orientalization," 460.

159. Nawid, "Writing National History," 193.

160. Green, "The Afghan Discovery of Buddha," 55; Green, "Introduction," 36.

161. Manela, "Imagining Woodrow Wilson in Asia."

CONCLUSION

1. "Japanese Infiltration among Muslims throughout the World."

2. Lary, introduction, 6.

3. Lin, *Tibet and Nationalist China's Frontier*, 159.

4. See Weiner, *The Chinese Revolution*.

5. Mark, "'Asia's' Transwar Lineage," 466.

6. Burke, "'Real Problems to Discuss,'" 53.

7. Shahabuddin, "Nationalism, Imperialism, and Bandung," 106.

8. Shahabuddin, 95–96.

9. Burke, "'Real Problems to Discuss," 84.

10. Chen, "Bandung, China," 180.

11. Mark, "'Asia's' Transwar Lineage," 466.

12. Clinton, *Revolutionary Nativism*, 193.

13. Haddad-Fonda, "Long Live Egypt and China," 3–4.

14. Haddad-Fonda, 3–4.

15. Eslava, Fakhri, and Neshiah, "The Spirit of Bandung," 3–4.

16. Ke, "Zhanhou Huijiao wenti."

17. Ke.

18. Ke.

19. Jing, "Huijiao xin yuguo."

20. Tewa, "Shijie huimin yundong."

21. Khalid, "A Secular Islam," 576.

22. Gladney, "Clashed Civilizations?," 208.

23. Gladney, 209.

24. Gladney, 122.

25. Lindbeck, "Communism, Islam and Nationalism in China," 473–76.

26. Haddad-Fonda, "The Domestic Significance," 46.

27. Haddad-Fonda, 46.

28. Haddad-Fonda, "Long Live Egypt and China," 4.

29. Haddad-Fonda, 3–4.

30. Haddad-Fonda, "The Domestic Significance," 21.

31. Haddad-Fonda, 46.

32. "Telegram to Pakistan from Bai Chongxi."

33. See Jacobs, "Exile Island."

34. Buckley and Ramsey, "'Absolutely No Mercy.'"

35. There are now ample sources from well-respected media outlets reporting on these events.

36. See Roberts, *The War on the Uyghurs*.

37. For diverse opinions on this, see "ChinaFile Conversations: Islamophobia in China." http://www.chinafile.com/conversation/islamophobia-china.

38. Wu, "Sign of the Times."

39. Ho, "Mobilizing the Muslim Minority," 106.

40. See Ngeow and Ma, "More Islamic."

41. Zhuang, *Chinese Muslims in Indonesia*, 11–12. There were a number of prominent Sino-Muslims in Sukarno's administration, such as Lie Kait Teng (C. 李傑定) and hajji Tan Kim Liong (C. 陳金龍), who was minister of health from 1953 to 1955.

42. Zhuang, *Chinese Muslims in Indonesia*, 18; Hew, "Cosmopolitan Islam," 175–96.

Works Cited

Aisha. "Quan Riben jiaru Huijiao." *Tianshan* 1, no. 2 (1934): 39.

—————. "Zhongguo Huijiao yu kangzhan." *Huijiao Luntan Banyuekan* 3, no. 11 (1940): 4–7.

"Ajia nanpō no kaikyōto ni tsuite." *Isuramu* 3 (April 1938): 3–10.

Akashi Yoji. "The Japanese Occupation of Malaya: Interruption or Transformation." In *Southeast Asia under Japanese Occupation*, edited by Alfred McCoy, 65–91. New Haven, CT: Yale University Press, 1980.

Al-Rasheed, Madawi, and Robert Vitalis, eds. *Counter-narratives: History, Contemporary Society, and Politics in Saudi Arabia and Yemen*. New York: Palgrave MacMillan, 2004.

Allen, Ernest, Jr. "Waiting for Tōjō: The Pro-Japan Vigil of Black Missourians, 1932–1942." *Gateway Heritage* (Fall 1995): 38–55.

—————. "When Japan Was 'Champion of the Darker Races': Satokata Takahashi and the Flowering of Black Messianic Nationalism." *Black Scholar* 24, no. 1 (1994): 28.

Allès, Elisabeth. "Muslim Religious Education in China." *China Perspectives* 45 (January–February 2003): 569–85.

Amakawa Nobuo. *Daitōasensō to sekai*. Tokyo: Sekai Seiji Kenkyūkai, 1941.

Ambaras, David R. *Japan's Imperial Underworlds: Intimate Encounters at the Borders of Empire*. Cambridge: Cambridge University Press, 2018.

Amin, Haron. *Afghan-Japan Relations: Lands under the Rising Sun*. Tokyo: Embassy of the Islamic Republic of Afghanistan, 2007.

Ando Junichiro. "Japan's 'Hui-Muslim' Campaigns (回民工作) in China from the 1910's to 1945." *Japan Association for Middle East Studies* 18, no. 2 (2003): 21–38.

Atwill, David. *The Chinese Sultanate: Islam, Ethnicity, and the Panthay Rebellion in Southwest China, 1856–1873*. Stanford, CA: Stanford University Press, 2005.

—————. *Islamic-Shangri-La: Inter-Asian Relations and Lhasa's Muslim Communities, 1600–1960*. Berkeley: University of California Press, 2018.

Aubin, Françoise. "Islam on the Wings of Nationalism: The Case of Muslim Intellectuals in Republican China." In *Intellectuals in the Modern Islamic World: Transmission, Transformation, and Communication*, edited by Stéphane A. Dudoignon, Komatsu Hisao, and Kosugi Yasushi, 241–72. New York: Routledge, 2006.

Aydin, Cemil. *The Idea of the Muslim World: A Global Intellectual History*. Cambridge, MA: Harvard University Press, 2017.

—————. "Japan's Pan-Asianism and the Legitimacy of Imperial Order, 1931–1945." *Asia-Pacific Journal* 6, no. 3 (March 3, 2008): 1–33.

———. "Overcoming Eurocentrism? Japan's Islamic Studies during the Era of the Greater East Asia War (1937–45)." In *The Islamic Middle East and Japan: Perceptions, Aspirations, and the Birth of Intra-Asian Modernity*, edited by Renée Worringer, 137–63. Princeton, NJ: Markus Wiener, 2007.

———. *The Politics of Anti-Westernism in Asia*. New York: Columbia University Press, 2007.

Aziz, M. A. *Japan's Colonialism and Indonesia*. The Hague: Martinus Nighoff, 1955.

Bai Chongxi. "Zhongguo Huijiao yu shijie Huijiao." *Qingzhen Duobao* 8 (1942): 2–4.

Bai Jinyu. "Bai Jinyu anda Riben." *Huijiao* 1, no. 6 (1938): 41–42.

Barrera, Guilia. "Mussolini's Colonial Race Laws and State-Settler Relations in Africa Orientiale Italiana (1935–1941)." *Journal of Modern Italian Studies* 8, no. 3 (2003): 425–43.

Barrett, David. "Introduction: Occupied China and the Limits of Accommodation." In *Chinese Collaboration with Japan, 1932–1945: The Limits of Accommodation*, edited by David P. Barrett and Larry N. Shyu, 1–17. Stanford, CA: Stanford University Press, 2001.

Bayliss, Jeffery Paul. *On the Margins of Empire: Buraku and Korean Identity in Prewar and Wartime Japan*. Cambridge, MA: Harvard University Press, 2013.

Benda, Harry. "The Beginnings of the Japanese Occupation of Java." *Far Eastern Review* 15, no. 4 (August 1956): 541–60.

———. "The Japanese Interregnum in Southeast Asia." In *Imperial Japan and Asia: A Reassessment*, edited by Grant Goodman, 65–79. New York: Occasional Papers of the East Asian Institute, 1967.

Benite, Zvi Ben-Dor. " 'Nine Years in Egypt': Al-Azhar University and the Arabization of Chinese Islam." *HAGAR: Studies in Culture, Polity and Identities* 8, no. 1 (Summer 2008): 1–21.

Bernhard, Patrick. "Behind the Battle Lines: Italian Atrocities and the Persecution of Arabs, Berbers, and Jews in North Africa during World War II." *Holocaust and Genocide Studies* 26, no. 3 (Winter 2012): 425–66.

Bertrand, Gordon M. *Collaborationism in France during the Second World War*. Ithaca, NY: Cornell University Press, 1980.

Bodde, Derk. "Chinese Muslims in Occupied Areas." *Far Eastern Review* 15, no. 21 (October 23, 1946): 330–33.

———. "Japan and the Muslims of China." *Far Eastern Survey* 15, no 20 (1946): 311–13.

Bradshaw, Richard, and Jim Ransdell. "Japan, Britain and the Yellow Peril in Africa in the 1930s." *Asia Pacific Journal* 9, no. 44, issue 2 (October 2011): 1–44.

Brandenburg, Ulrich. "The Multiple Publics of a Transnational Activist: Abdürreşid İbrahim, Pan-Asianism, and the Creation of Islam in Japan." *Die Welt des Islams* 58 (2018): 143–72.

Brook, Timothy. *Collaboration: Japanese Agents and Local Elites in Wartime China*. Cambridge: Cambridge University Press, 2005.

———. "Toward Independence: Christianity in China under Japanese Occupation, 1937–1945." In *Christianity and China: From the Eighteenth Century to the Present*, edited by Daniel H. Bays, 317–37. Stanford, CA: Stanford University Press, 1996.

Brophy, David John. *Uyghur Nation: Reform and Revolution on the Russia-China Frontier*. Cambridge, MA: Harvard University Press, 2016.

Brown, Roger H. "The Konoe Cabinet's 'Declaration of a New Order in East Asia.'" In

Pan-Asianism: A Documentary History, vol. 2, *1920–Present*, edited by Sven Saaler and Christopher Szpilman, 167–74. New York: Rowman & Littlefield, 2011.

Buckley, Chris, and Austin Ramsey. "'Absolutely No Mercy': Leaked Files Expose How China Organized Mass Detention of Muslims." *New York Times*, November 16, 2019. https://www.nytimes.com/interactive/2019/11/16/world/asia/china-xinjiang-documents.html.

Burke, Roland. "'Real Problems to Discuss': The Congress for Cultural Freedom's Asian and African Expeditions, 1951–1959." *Journal of World History* 27, no. 1 (March 2016): 53–85.

Carnoy, Martin. *Education as Cultural Imperialism*. New York: Addison-Wesley Longman, 1974.

Carroll, John D. *Edge of Empires: Chinese Elites and British Colonials in Hong Kong*. Cambridge, MA: Harvard University Press, 2005.

Carter, James H. *Creating a Chinese Harbin: Nationalism in an International City, 1916–1932*. Ithaca, NY: Cornell University Press, 2005.

Chapoutot, Johann. *Greeks, Romans, and Germans: How the Nazis Usurped Europe's Classical Past*. Oakland: University of California Press, 2016.

Chatani, Sayaka. *Nation-Empire: Ideology and Rural Youth Mobilization in Japan and Its Colonies*. New York: Columbia University Press, 2018.

Chen, Jessica Lilu. "Chinese Heirs to Muhammad: Writing Islamic History in Early Modern China." PhD diss., Stanford University, 2016.

Chen Yifeng. "Bandung, China, and the Making of a World Order in East Asia." In *Bandung, Global History, and International Law*, edited by Luis Eslava, Michael Fakhri, and Vasuki Neshiah, 177–93. Cambridge: Cambridge University Press, 2017.

"Chengli riyu jiazheng Jiangxi hui." *Mengjiang Xinbao*, August 27, 1938.

"Chinese Islamic Association." Military Intelligence Division Regional File relating to China, 1922–1954, 2610.50/2 British National Archives, Kew, England.

Cieciura, Wlodzimierz. "Ethnicity or Religion? Republican-Era Chinese Debates on Islam and Muslims." In *Sino-Muslim Intellectual Evolution from the 17th to the 21st Century*, edited by Jonathan Lipman, 107–46. Edinburgh, Scotland: University of Edinburgh, 2017.

"Cinque studenti musilimani della Manciuria iscritti all'Università religiosa di al-Azhar." *Oriente Moderno* 17, no. 3 (March 1937): 131.

Clinton, Maggie. *Revolutionary Nativism: Fascism and Culture in China, 1925–1937*. Durham, NC: Duke University Press, 2017.

Coleman, Simon, and John Eade. *Reframing Pilgrimage: Cultures in Motion*. New York: Routledge, 2004.

Cong Xiaoping. *Teachers' Schools and the Making of the Modern Chinese Nation-State, 1897–1937*. Vancouver: University of British Columbia Press, 2007.

Conrad, Sebastian, and Prasenjit Duara. *Viewing Regionalisms from East Asia*. Washington, DC: American Historical Association, 2013.

Cooke, Miriam, and Bruce B. Lawrence. Introduction to *Muslim Networks: From Hajj to Hip-Hop*, edited by Miriam Cooke and Bruce B. Lawrence, xi–xii; 1–28. Chapel Hill: University of North Carolina Press, 2005.

Crews, Robert. *Afghan Modern: The History of a Global Nation*. Cambridge, MA: Harvard University Press, 2015.

Culp, Robert. *Articulating Citizenship: Civic Education and Student Politics in Southeastern China, 1912–1940*. Cambridge, MA: Harvard University Press, 2007.

"Dai Ajia sensō to kaikyōken." *Kaikyōken* 6, no. 1 (1942): 2–7.

Dai Nihon Kaikyō Kyōkai. *Kaikyōken hayawakari*. Tokyo: Dai Nihon Kaikyō Kyōkai, 1939, 1–90.

———. *Kunao suru no ren Kaikyō min*. Tokyo: Dai Nihon Kaikyō Kyō Kai, 1939, 5.

———. *Nihon cha no sekai-teki senshutsu to kaikyōto*, 1–38. Tokyo: Dai Nihon Kaikyō Kyokai, 1939.

———. *Ware ga Nanyō bōeki to kaikyōto*. Tokyo: Dai Nihon Kaikyō Kyōkai, February 1939.

"Dai Nihon Kaikyō kyōkai to wa donna Kotoka." *Jigyō Kore Nihon* 18, no. 4 (April 1939): 69–74.

"Datong Huimin Qingnian xunlian." *Mengjiang Xinbao*, March xx, 1937.

de Jong, Ellen van Zyll. "Japan Pushing Her Program for Netherlands India." *FES* 9, no. 20 (October 9, 1940): 237–39.

Diamond, Hanna. *Women and the Second World War in France, 1939–1948: Choices and Constraints*. Harlow, UK: Longman, 1999.

Ding Xingwu. "Bei feizhou de falanxi diguo tunisi ren de aiguo sixiang." *Yisilan Xuesheng Zazhi* 1, no. 4 (1943): 17–19.

Ding Zaiqin. "Zenyang lai jianshe zhongguo huimin jiaoyu." *Chengshi Yuekan* 3 (1941): 99–100.

Dower, John. *War without Mercy: Race and Power in the Pacific War*. New York: Pantheon, 1987.

Dresch, Paul. *A History of Modern Yemen*. Cambridge: Cambridge University Press, 2000.

Duara, Prasenjit. "Asia Redux: Conceptualizing a Region for Our Times." *Journal of Asian Studies* 69, no. 4 (November 2010): 963–83.

———. *Culture, Power, and the State: Rural North China, 1940–1942*. Stanford, CA: Stanford University Press, 1988.

———. "The Discourse of Civilization and Pan-Asianism." *Journal of World History* 12, no. 1 (Spring 2001): 99–130.

———. *Rescuing History from the Nation: Questioning Narratives of Modern China*. Chicago: University of Chicago Press, 1995.

DuBois, Thomas. "Japanese Print Media and Manchurian Cultural Community: Religion in the Pages of the *Shengjing Times*, 1906–1944." In *Casting Faiths Imperialism and the Transformation of Religion in East and Southeast Asia*, edited by Thomas DuBois, 217–38. New York: Palgrave Macmillan, 2009.

———. "The Transformation of Religion in East and Southeast Asia: Paradigmatic Change in Regional Perspective." In *Casting Faiths: Imperialism and the Transformation of Religion in East and Southeast Asia*, edited by Thomas DuBois, 1–4. New York: Palgrave Macmillan, 2009.

Dufourmont, Eddy. "Tanaka Ippei: 'Islam and Pan-Asianism,' 1924." In *Pan-Asianism: A Documentary History, 1920–Present*, vol. 2, edited by Sven Saaler and Christopher W. A. Szpilman, 87–92. Lanham, MD: Rowman & Littlefield, 2017.

Duus, Peter. *The Abacus and the Sword: The Japanese Penetration of Korea, 1895–1910*. Berkeley: University of California Press, 1995.

Elliott, Mark. "*Hushuo*: The Northern Other and the Naming of the Han Chinese." In *Critical Han Studies: The History, Representation, and Identity of China's Majority*, edited by Tom Mullaney, James Leibold, Stéphane Gros, and Eric Vanden Bussche, 173–90. Berkeley: University of California Press, 2012.

———. *The Manchu Way: The Eight Banners and Ethnic Identity in Late Imperial China.* Stanford, CA: Stanford University Press, 2001.

Elsbree, Willard. *Japan's Role in Southeast Asian Nationalist Movements, 1940–1945.* Cambridge, MA: Harvard University Press, 1953.

Erie, Matthew. *China and Islam: The Prophet, the Party, and Law.* Cambridge: Cambridge University Press, 2016.

Erikson, Emily, and Smapsa Samila. "Social Networks and Port Traffic in Early Modern Overseas Trade." *Social Science History* 39 (Summer 2015): 151–73.

Esenbel, Selçuk. Introduction to *Japan on the Silk Road: Encounters and Perspectives of Politics and Culture in Eurasia,* edited by Selçuk Esenbel, 1–18. Leiden, the Netherlands: Brill, 2017.

———. *Japan, Turkey and the World of Islam.* Leiden, the Netherlands: Brill, 2011.

Eslava, Luis, Michael Fakhri, and Vasuki Neshiah. "The Spirit of Bandung." In *Bandung, Global History, and International Law,* edited by Luis Eslava, Michael Fakhri, and Vasuki Neshiah, 1–12. Cambridge: Cambridge University Press, 2016.

Evanzz, Karl. "The FBI and the Nation of Islam." In *The FBI and Religion: Faith and National Security before and after 9/11,* edited by Sylvester A. Johnson and Steven Weitzman, 155–76. Berkeley: University of California Press, 2017.

Files relating to Protecting Malaya's Overseas Chinese. Academia Historica, *Waijiaobu* (C. *Malaya—huaqiao*) 020-010706-0014.

Files relating to the Chinese Islamic Association in Malaya. Academia Historica, *Waijiaobu* (C. *Malaya—huaqiao*) 020-010706-0014.

Fogel, Joshua. *Articulating the Sinosphere: Sino-Japanese Relations in Space and Time.* Cambridge: Cambridge University Press, 2009.

Galambos, Imre. "Japanese 'Spies' along the Silk Road: British Suspicions Regarding the Second Ōtani Expedition (1908–1909)." *Japanese Religions* 35, nos. 1 and 2 (2012): 33–61.

Galambos, Imre, and Kitsudō Kōichi. "Japanese Exploration of Central Asia: The Ōtani Expeditions and Their British Connections." *Bulletin of the School of Oriental and African Studies* 75, no. 1 (February 2012): 113–34.

"General Records of the State Department, 1940–1944." *State Department Files: Japan in China* 1940-1944 894.20290H/S, H/2 Section 111 NARA RG 56.

"Gircolare della Missione musulmana cinese di fratellanza sull'inaugurazione della moschea di Tokio." *Oriente Moderno* 18, no. 6 (June 1938): 279.

Gladney, Dru. "Clashed Civilizations? Muslim and Chinese Identities in the PRC." In *Making Majorities: Constituting the Nation in Japan, Korea, China, Malaysia, Fiji, Turkey, and the United States,* edited by Dru Gladney, 106–31. Stanford, CA: Stanford University Press, 1998.

———. "Making Muslims in China: Education, Islamicization and Representation." In *China's National Minority Culture, Schooling, and Development,* edited by Gerard A. Postiglione, 55–94. New York: Falmer, 1999.

———. "Sino–Middle Eastern Perspective and Relations since the Gulf War: Views from Below." *International Journal of Middle East Studies* 26, no. 4 (November 1994): 677–91.

Goodman, Bryna. *Native Place, City, and Nation: Regional Networks and Identities in Shanghai, 1853–1937.* Berkeley: University of California Press, 1995.

Goodman, David. "Anti-Semitism in Japan: Its History and Current Implications." In *The Construction of Racial Identities in China and Japan*, edited by Frank Dikotter, 177–98. Honolulu: University of Hawai'i Press, 1997.

Goodman, Grant K. *An Experiment in Wartime Intercultural Relations: Philippine Students in Japan, 1943–1945*, 1–27. Ithaca, NY: Cornell University Southeast Asia Program (Data Paper no. 46), 1962.

Green, Nile. "The Afghan Discovery of Buddha: Civilizational History and the Nationalizing of Afghan Antiquity." *International Journal of Middle East Studies* 49 (2017): 47–70.

———. "Anti-colonial Japanophilia and the Constraints of an Islamic Japanology: Information and Affect in the Indian Encounter with Japan." *South Asian History and Culture* 4, no. 3 (2013): 1–23.

———. "Introduction: A History of Afghan Historiography." In *Afghan History through Afghan Eyes*, edited by Nile Green, 1–49. New York: Oxford University Press, 2015.

"Guanyu Dongjing Qingzhensi luocheng yu li zhi suo wen." *Yiguang* 97 (1938): 11–13.

"Guanyu jinhou de Huijiao jiaoyu wenti." *Yisilan Xuesheng Zashi* 1, no. 4 (1933): 35–40.

"Guoren jiyi riwen." *Datong Wenhua* 252, no. 257 (1932): 2–3.

Haddad-Fonda, Kyle. "The Domestic Significance of China's Policy toward Egypt, 1955–1957." *Chinese Historical Review* 21, no. 1 (May 2014): 45–64.

———. "Long Live Egypt: The Suez Crisis, Chinese Muslims, and the Construction of Chinese Nationalism." Unpublished paper, George Washington University, 2013 (cited with permission of author).

Halevi, Leor. "Is China a House of Islam? Chinese Questions, Arabic Answers, and the Translation of Salafism from Cairo to Canton, 1930–1932." *Die Welt des Islams* 59 (2019): 33–69.

Hammond, Kelly Anne. "Managing Muslims: Imperial Japan, Islamic Policy, and Axis Connections during WWII." *Journal of Global History* 12, no. 2 (July 2017): 251–73.

Hanscom, Christopher P., and Dennis Washburn, "Introduction: Representations of Race in East Asian Empires." In *The Affect of Difference: Representations of Race in East Asian Empire*, edited by Christopher P. Hanscom and Dennis Washburn, 1–18. Honolulu: University of Hawai'i Press, 2016.

Harada Kōzō. "Toā Kyōeiken to kaikyōto." *Zoku* 18, no. 11 (November 1941): 34–35.

Harrell, Paula. *Sowing the Seeds of Change: Chinese Students, Japanese Teachers, 1895–1905*. Stanford, CA: Stanford University Press, 1992.

Hayhoe, Ruth, ed. *Education and Modernization: The Chinese Experience*. New York: Oxford University Press, 1992.

Hellyer, Robert. "1874: Tea and Japan's New Trading Regime." In *Asia Inside Out*, edited by Eric Tagliacozzo, Helen F. Sui, and Peter Perdue, 186–206. Cambridge, MA: Harvard University Press, 2015.

Hew Wai-Weng. "Cosmopolitan Islam and Inclusive Chineseness: Chinese-Style Mosques in Indonesia." In *Religious Pluralism, State and Society in Asia*, edited by Chiara Formichi, 175–95. New York: Routledge, 2014.

Hinsch, Bret. *The Rise of Tea Culture in China: The Invention of the Individual*. Lanham, MD: Rowman & Littlefield, 2016.

Ho Yip-Wai. "Mobilizing the Muslim Minority for China's Development: Hui Muslims, Ethnic Relations and Sino-Arab Connections." *Journal of Comparative Asian Development* 12, no. 1 (2013): 84–112.

Hodong, Kim. *Holy War in China: The Muslim Rebellion and State in Chinese Central Asia, 1864–1877*. Stanford, CA: Stanford University Press, 2004.

Hoffmann, Stanley. "Collaborationism in France during World War II." *Journal of Modern History* 4 (September 1968): 375–95.

"Hokushi Kaikyō minzoku kyōkai setsuritsuan." Diplomatic Archives of the Japanese Ministry of Foreign Affairs. I-2-1-1-2/5 Secret Military Document, 1939.

Hoover, Lyman. "Chinese Muslims Are Tough." *Asia* 38, no. 12 (December 1938): 719–22.

Hopper, Matthew S. "The Globalization of Dried Fruit: Transformations in the Eastern Arabian Economy, 1860s–1920s." In *Global Muslims in the Age of Steam and Print*, edited by J. Gelvin and Nile Green, 158–84. Berkeley: University of California Press, 2014.

Hosoya Kiyoshi. *Ai kuni chagara*. Tokyo: Mengjiang Shaban, 1941.

———. "Nanyō shingyō to Nihon cha." *Shin Ajia* 10 (1940): 21–31.

Hotta Eri. *Pan-Asianism and Japan's War, 1931–1945*. New York: Palgrave Macmillan, 2007.

Hughes, Thomas L. "The German Mission to Afghanistan, 1915–1916." *German Studies Review* 25, no. 3 (October 2002): 447–96.

"Hui Qingxuexiao xinsheng." *Mengjiang Xinbao*, March 18, 1937.

""Huijiao chaojin tuan gongzuo giakuang." *Zhongguo Huimin jiuguo xiehui tongbao* 35 (1939): 139.

"Huijiao de libaitang." *Huijiao* 1, no. 2 (1938): 12–14.

"Huijiao jiaoyu zhi gaige." *Huiguang* 2, no. 2 (1935): 56–58.

"Huijiao yu er ci ou zhan." *Zhongguo Huijiao Jiuguo Hui Huibao* 1, no. 11 (1939): 10–12.

"Huimin shehui zhi liyi." *Mengjiang Xinbao*, February 12, 1938.

"Huimin xuexiao wei jingtong qi jian jinri ju xing riyu huaju ge sheng jiazhang jun xing canjia." *Mengjiang Xinbao*, November 10, 1937.

"Huiqing xuexiao xinsheng." *Mengjiang Xinbao*, March 18, 1937.

Indians in Japan and Occupied Areas: Their Support of Indian Independence; Biographies. U.S. Department of State, Office of Intelligence Records. Honolulu: Office of Strategic Services, October 20, 1944.

Indoneshia ni okeru Nihon gunsei no kenkyu. Tokyo: Okuma Memorial Social Science Research Institute, 1959.

"Infiltration Attempts among Muslims in Russia's Borderlands." Record of the Office of Strategic Services, R&A 890.1S (August 25, 1944). National Archives Research Administration, College Park, MD. RG 226 190-3-4-3 890.2.

"The International Student Institute." Japanese Ministry of Foreign Affairs. Microfilm reel: S318 9.1.10.0–8.

"Italy's Muslim Policy" (J. "Itaria no Kaikyō seisaku"). Diplomatic Archives of the Ministry of Foreign Affairs of Japan: "Muslim Relations": I-2-1-0-1/2 (1938).

Jacobs, Justin M. "Exile Island: Xinjiang Refugees and the 'One China' Policy in Nationalist Taiwan, 1949–1979." *Journal of Cold War Studies* 18, no. 1 (Winter 2016): 188–218.

"Japan Courting Islamic People: Contact with the Mohammedans under Close Attention." *Shanghai Times*, January 31, 1938.

"Japanese Infiltration among Muslims in China." Record of the Office of Strategic Services, R&A 890.1S (August 25, 1944). National Archives Research Administration, College Park, MD. RG 226 190-3-4-3 890.0.

"Japanese Infiltration among Muslims throughout the World." Record of the Office of Strategic Services, R&A 890.1S (August 25, 1944). National Archives Research Administration, College Park, MD. RG 226 190-3-4-3 890.1.

"Japan's Near East Conspiracy." GMD Foreign Ministry, Japan's Wartime Diplomatic Activities Folio 4, 41–78/Part 4/02–010102–0124, June 19, 1940.

Jeans, Roger B. "Third-Party Collaborators in Wartime China: The Case of the Chinese National Socialist Party." In *China in the Anti-Japanese War, 1937–1945: Politics, Culture and Society*, edited by David Barrett and Larry Shyu, 114–32. New York: Peter Lang, 2001.

Jing Feng. "Huijiao xin yuguo: Baxisedan." *Huimin qingnian* 4 (1947): 10–11.

Josephson, Jason Ananda. *The Invention of Religion in Japan.* Chicago: University of Chicago Press, 2012.

"Juezhan xia jiang nei jiaoyu quan." *Mengjiang Xinbao*, August 2, 1938.

Juzi. "Riben chuanli Huijiao xiehui zancheng." *Huiguang* 1, no. 1 (1924): 50–52.

"Kaikyōto no Nihonjin mi." *Kaikyō Ken* 2, no. 2 (1938): 98–103.

"Kaisoku." *Dai Nihon Kaikyō Kyokai*, April 1, 1939.

"Kangzhan jianguo yu fazhan huimin jiaoyu." *Chengshi Yuekan* 5, no. 12 (1938): 7.

Kaplan, Alice Yaeger. *The Collaborator: The Trial & Execution of Robert Brasillach.* Chicago: University of Chicago Press, 2000.

Ke Xing. "Zhanhou Huijiao wenti." *Zhongguo Huijiao Xiehui Bao* 6 (1944): 1–12.

Kearney, Reginald. *African American Views of the Japanese: Solidarity or Sedition?* Albany: State University of New York Press, 1998.

Khalid, Adeeb. "A Secular Islam: Nation, State, and Religion in Uzbekistan." *International Journal of Middle Eastern Studies* 35, no. 4 (November 2003): 573–98.

Kheng, Cheah Boon. "The Social Impact of the Japanese Occupation of Malaya, 1942–1945." In *Southeast Asia under Japanese Occupation*, edited by Alfred McCoy, 85–120. New Haven, CT: Yale University Southeast Asia Monograph Series, no. 22, 1980.

King, Richard, and Cody Poulton. Introduction to *Sino-Japanese Transculturation: From the Late Nineteenth Century to the End of the Pacific War*, edited by Richard King and Cody Poulton, 1–18. Lanham, MD: Lexington, 2012.

Kirby, William. "The Internationalization of China: Foreign Relations at Home and Abroad in the Republican Era." *China Quarterly* 150 (June 1997): 433–58.

Kobayashi Hajime. "Nihongo to kaimin jidō." *Kaikyōken* 57 (1940) 222–31.

Kobayashi Yasuko. "Kyai and Japanese Military." *Studia Islamika* 4, no. 3 (1997): 70–98.

Kojima Kyōko. "The Making of Ainu Citizenship from the Viewpoint of Gender and Ethnicity." In *Gender, Nation and State in Modern Japan*, edited by Andrea Germer, Vera Mackie, and Ulrike Wöhr, 101–19. New York: Routledge, 2014.

Komatsu Hisao. "Addurreshid Ibrahim and Japanese Approaches to Central Asia." In *Japan on the Silk Road: Encounters and Perspectives of Politics and Culture in Eurasia*, edited by Selçuk Esenbel, 145–54. Leiden, the Netherlands: Brill, 2018.

Koyama Shizuko. "Domestic Roles and the Incorporation of Women into the Nation-State: The Emergence and Development of the 'Good Wife, Wise Mother' Ideology." In *Gender, Nation and State in Modern Japan*, edited by Andrea Germer, Vera Mackie, and Ulrike Wöhr, 85–101. New York: Taylor and Francis, 2014.

Krämer, Hans Martin. "Pan-Asianism's Religious Undercurrents: The Reception of Islam and Translation of the Qur'ān in Twentieth-Century Japan." *Journal of Asian Studies* 73, no. 3 (August 2014): 619–40.

Kuhn, Philip. *Origins of the Modern Chinese State*. Stanford, CA: Stanford University Press, 2002.

Kurasawa Aiko Inomata. "Mobilization and Control: A Study of Social Change in Rural Java, 1942–1945." PhD diss., Cornell University, 1988.

Kushner, Barak. "Introduction: The Unevenness of the End of Empire." In *The Dismantling of Japan's Empire in East Asia: Deimperialization, Postwar Legitimation and Imperial Afterlife*, edited by Barak Kushner and Sherzod Muminov, 1–18. New York: Routledge, 2017.

Laffan, Michael. *The Makings of Indonesian Islam: Orientalism and the Narration of a Sufi Past*. Princeton, NJ: Princeton University Press, 2011.

Lary, Diana. Introduction to *Negotiating China's Destiny in WWII*, edited by Hans van der Ven, Diana Lary, and Stephen R. Mackinnon, 1–12. Stanford, CA: Stanford University Press, 2015.

Lebra, Joyce C. *Japanese-Trained Armies in Southeast Asia*. Hong Kong: Heinemann Education, 1977.

Lee, Seok-Won. "The Paradox of Racial Liberation: W. E. B. Du Bois and Pan-Asianism in Wartime Japan, 1931–1945." *Inter-Asia Cultural Studies* 16, no. 4 (2015): 513–34.

Leibold, James. *Reconfiguring Chinese Nationalism: How the Qing Frontier and Its Indigenes Became Chinese*. New York, NY: Palgrave Macmillian US, 2007.

Lei Wan. "The Chinese Islamic 'Goodwill Mission to the Middle East' during the Anti-Japanese War." *Divan* 15, no. 29 (2010): 133–70.

"Lettrera dell'Imam Yahya a Mussolini." *Oriente Moderno* 17, no. 11 (November 1937): 570.

Levent, Sinan. "Images of Japan Created by the Inter-war Turkish Press: The Role of *Cumhuriyet*, Turkish Daily Newspaper (1933–1939)." *Annals of the Japanese Association for Middle East Studies* 26, no. 2 (2010): 122–46.

———. "Turanism in Japan from Perspective of the Pan-Asiatic Journal, *Dai Ajia Shugi*." *Journal of the Graduate School of Asia-Pacific Studies* 20, no. 1 (2011): 307–25.

Li, Lincoln. *Student Nationalism in China, 1924–1949*. Albany: State University of New York Press, 1994.

Lin Hsiao-ting. *Tibet and Nationalist China's Frontier: Intrigues and Ethnopolitics, 1928–1949*. Vancouver: University of British Columbia Press, 2006.

Lin Hsiao-ting. *Modern China's Ethnic Frontiers: A Journey to the West*. New York, NY: Palgrave, 2010.

Lincicome, Mark. *Imperial Subjects as Global Citizens: Nationalism, Internationalism, and Education in Japan*. Lanham, MD: Lexington, 2009.

Lincoln, Toby. *Urbanizing China in War and Peace: The Case of Wuxi County*. Honolulu: University of Hawai'i Press, 2015.

Lindbeck, John M. H. "Communism, Islam and Nationalism in China." *Review of Politics* 12, no. 4 (October 1950): 473–88.

Lipman, Jonathan. "Ethnicity and Politics in Republican China: The Ma Family Warlords of Gansu." *Modern China* 10, no. 3 (July 1984): 285–316.

———. *Familiar Strangers: A History of Muslims in Northwest China*. Seattle: University of Washington Press, 1998.

Ma Hongkui. "Xibei huimin wenti zhi jiepou." *Qingzhen Doubao* 1 (1940): 23–25.

"Ma Hongkui to Shina no kai kyōto." *Kaikyōken* 6, no. 6 (June 1942): 377–88.

Ma Liangpu. "Huijiao Dongxiang Riben Huijiao xiehui shengri zhi yiyi" (translated from the Japanese). *Huijiao* 1, no. 6 (1938): 11.

―――. "Zhongguo Huijiao zong lianhe hui daibiao tuan canjia dongjing qingzhensi luocheng yu li ji." *Huijiao* 1, no. 3 (1938): 33–40.

Ma Wenfu. "Jinhou woguo waijiao zhengce de yantao." *Huijiao luntan banyuekan* 3, no. 5 (1940): 13–15.

Ma Zhaopeng, "Huijiao minzhong kangri wuli de xingqi." *Huimin Yanlun* 1, no. 1 (1939): 22.

Manela, Erez. "Imagining Woodrow Wilson in Asia: Dreams of East-West Hegemony and the Revolt against Empire in 1919." *American Historical Review* 111, no. 15 (December 2006): 1327–51.

Manger, Leif, ed. *Muslim Diversity: Local Islam in Global Contexts.* New York: Routledge, 2014.

Mao Yufeng. "Muslim Educational Reform in 20th-Century China: The Case of the Chengda Teachers Academy." *Extrême-Orient / Extrême Occiedent* 33 (2011): 143–70.

―――. "A Muslim Vision for the Chinese Nation: Chinese Pilgrimage Missions to Mecca during WWII." *Journal of Asian Studies* 70, no. 2 (May 2011): 373–95.

Mark, Ethan. "'Asia's' Transwar Lineage: Nationalism, Marxism, and 'Greater Asia' in an Indonesian Inflection." *Journal of Asian Studies* 65, no. 3 (August 2006): 463–91.

―――. *Japan's Occupation of Java in the Second World War: A Transnational History.* London: Bloomsbury Academic, 2018.

Martin, Terry. *Affirmative Action Empire: Nations and Nationalism in the Soviet Union, 1923–1939.* Ithaca, NY: Cornell University Press, 2001.

Matsumisha Hajime. "Nihon Kaikyō kyokai ni tsute no mondō." 1–11. Tokyo: Dai Nihon Kaikyō Kyokai, 1939.

Matsumoro Takayoshi. "Nihon cha no sekai shinshutsu-saku to kaikyōto mondai." *Cha gyōkai* 34, no. 2 (1939): 6–11.

Matsumoto Masumi. "Rationalizing Patriotism among Muslim Chinese: The Impact of the Middle East on the *Yuehua* Journal." In *Intellectuals in the Modern Islamic World: Transmission, Transformation, and Communication,* edited by Stéphane A. Dudoignon, Komatsu Hisao, and Kosugi Yasushi, 117–42. New York: Routledge, 2006.

―――. "Sino-Muslims' Identity and Thought during the Anti-Japanese War: Impact of the Middle East on Islamic Revival and Reform in China." *Annals of Japan Association for Middle East Studies* 18, no. 2 (2003): 39–54.

Maxey, Trent E. *The "Greatest Problem": Religion and State Formation in Meiji Japan.* Cambridge, MA: Harvard University Press, 2014.

McCoy, Alfred. Introduction to *Southeast Asia under Japanese Occupation,* edited by Alfred McCoy, 1–14. New Haven, CT: Yale University Press, 1980.

McDonald, Kate. *Placing Empire: Travel and the Social Imagination in Imperial Japan.* Berkeley: University of California Press, 2017.

McMeekin, Sean. *The Berlin-Baghdad Express: The Ottoman Empire and Germany's Bid for World Power.* Cambridge, MA: Harvard University Press, 2010.

Mei Cun. "Zhuiyi jiwang si ji jianglai: Rihuihan hezuo—zhenyi xinyide." *Huijiao* 1, no. 8 (1939): 23–26.

Michael, Franz. "Notes and Comments: Japan—Protector of Islam!" *Pacific Affairs* (September 1942): 471–86.

"Military Intelligence Division Regional File Relating to China, 1922–1944." 2610.50:

Microfilms RG 165 M 1513, Roll #9, National Archives Research Administration, College Park, MD. Record of the Office of Strategic Services.

Millward, James. *Beyond the Pass: Economy, Ethnicity, and Empire in Qing Central Asia, 1759–1864*. Stanford, CA: Stanford University Press, 1998.

Mimura, Janis. *Planning for Empire: Reform Bureaucrats and the Japanese Wartime State*. Ithaca, NY: Cornell University Press, 2011.

Misawa Nobuo. "Shintoism and Islam in Interwar Japan: How Did the Japanese Come to Believe in Islam?" *Orient* 46 (2011): 119–40.

Mitter, Rana. "Classifying Citizens in Nationalist China during World War II." *Modern Asian Studies* 45, no. 2 (March 2011): 243–75.

———. "Contention and Redemption: Ideologies of National Salvation in Republican China." *Totalitarian Movements and Political Religions* 3, no. 3 (September 2010): 44–74.

———. "Evil Empire? Competing Constructions of Japanese Imperialism in Manchuria, 1928–1937." In *Imperial Japan and National Identities in Asia, 1895–1945*, edited by Li Narangoa and Robert Cribb, 146–68. New York: Routledge Curzon, 2003.

———. "Historiographical Review: Modernity, Internationalization, and War in the History of Modern China." *Historical Journal* 48, no. 2 (January 2005): 523–43.

———. *The Manchurian Myth: Nationalism, Resistance and Collaboration in Modern China*. Berkeley: University of California Press, 2000.

"Mohammedism [*sic*]." Japanese Ministry of Foreign Affairs, Microfilm reel: S331 9.2.1.0–8.

Moon, Yumi. *Populist Collaborators: The Ilchinhoe and the Japanese Colonization of Korea, 1896–1910*. Ithaca, NY: Cornell University Press, 2013.

Morris-Suzuki, Tessa. "Introduction: Confronting the Ghosts of War in East Asia." In *East Asia beyond the History Wars: Confronting the Ghosts of Violence*, edited by Tessa Morris-Suzuki, Morris Low, Leonid Petrov, and Timothy Y. Tsu, 1–23. New York: Routledge, 2013.

Morrison, Alexander. "Beyond the 'Great Game': The Russian Origins of the Second Anglo-Afghan War." *Modern Asian Studies* 51, no. 3 (2017): 686–735.

Motadel, David. "The Global Authoritarian Moment and the Revolt against Empire." *American Historical Review* 124, no. 3 (June 2019): 843–77.

———. *Islam and Nazi Germany's War*. Cambridge, MA: Belknap Press of Harvard University, 2014.

Mullaney, Tom. *Coming to Terms with the Nation: Ethnic Classification in Modern China*. Berkeley: University of California Press, 2010.

Murata Shōzō. *Afuganisutan ni okeru taisen go no kokusai kankei*. Tokyo: Tōa Kenkyūshō, 1940.

Na Zhong. "Bali de Huijiao." *Yuehua* 7/8, no. 6 (March 1935): 27–28.

"Nanyō kaikyōto no seiji deki dōkō." *Isuramu* 3 (April 1938): 10–14.

Nawid, Senzil. "Writing National History: Afghan Historiography in the Twentieth Century." In *Afghan History through Afghan Eyes*, edited by Nile Green, 179–200. New York: Oxford University Press, 2015.

Ngeow, Chow Bing, and Ma Hailong. "More Islamic, No Less Chinese: Explorations into Overseas Chinese Muslim Identities in Malaysia." *Ethnic and Racial Studies* 39, no. 12 (2016): 2108–28.

Nīda Noboru. "Pekin no kaikyōto shōkō hito to sono nakama-teki shogen." *Kaikyōken* 8, no. 6. (1944): 241–65.

"Nihon to Kaikyō Ajia." *Dai Ajia Shugi* 6, no. 62 (1941).

Nihon to kaikyōto no kankei. Tokyo: Sanseido, 1943.

Nishimura Shigeo. "Northeast China in Chongqing Politics: The Influence of 'Recover the Northeast' on Domestic and International Politics." In *Negotiating China's Destiny in WWII*, edited by Han van de Ven, Diana Lary, and Stephen R. Mackinnon, 174–89. Stanford, CA: Stanford University Press, 2015.

Noda Jin. "Japanese Spies in Inner Asia during the Early Twentieth Century." *Silk Road* 16 (2018): 21–29.

Okakura Kakuzō. *The Book of Tea: A Japanese Harmony of Art, Culture, and the Simple Life.* 2nd ed. Sydney: Angus & Robertson, 1935.

Ōwada Masato. "Kaikyō seisaku yori mitaru tōa shin chitsujo kensetsu." *Aikuni Gakusei* 16 (August 1940): 35–36.

Palmer, Brandon. *Fighting for the Enemy: Koreans in Japan's War, 1937–1945.* Seattle: University of Washington Press, 2018.

Pan Min. *Jiangsu riwei jiceng zhengquan yanjiu.* Shanghai: Shanghai Renmin Chubanshe, 2006.

Pang Shiqian. *Aiji jiu nian.* Beijing: Beijing Yuehua Wenhua Fuwu Chuban, 1951.

Penn, Michael. "The Vicissitudes of Japan-Saudi Relations." In *East by Mid-east: Studies in Cultural and Strategic Connectivities*, edited by Anchi Hoh and Brandon Wheeler, 279–93. New York: Equinox, 2012.

Perdue, Peter C. "Empire and Nation in Comparative Perspective: Frontier Administration in Eighteenth Century China, India and the Ottoman Empire." In *Shared Histories of Modernity; China, India and the Ottoman Empire*, edited by Huri Islamoglu and Peter C. Perdue, 21–45. London: Routledge, 2009.

———. *China Marches West: The Qing Conquest of Central Eurasia.* Cambridge, MA: Belknap Press of Harvard University Press, 2007.

Petersen, Kristian. *Interpreting Islam in China: Pilgrimage, Scripture, and Language in the Han Kitab.* New York: Oxford University Press, 2017.

Pianciola, Niccolò, and Paolo Sartori. "*Waqf* in Turkestan: The Colonial Legacy and the Fate of an Islamic Institution in Early Soviet Central Asia, 1917–1924." *Central Asian Survey* 25, no. 4 (2007): 475–98.

"La prima traduzione arabe del *Lun yu* (Dialoghi) di Confucio." *Oriente Moderno* 18, no. 4 (April 1938): 184–85.

Rappaport, Erica. *A Thirst for Empire: How Tea Shaped the Modern World.* Princeton, NJ: Princeton University Press, 2017.

"Rappresentati di paesi arabi al Congresso 'Gionvane Asia' di Tokyo." *Oriente Moderno* 17, no. 12 (December 1937): 597.

Ravinder Frost, Mark, and Daniel Schumacher. "Wartime Globalization in Asia, 1937–1945, Conflicted Connections, and Convergences." *Modern Asian Studies* 51, no. 6 (2017): 1922–35.

Rawski, Evelyn S. *The Last Emperors: A Social History of Qing Imperial Institutions.* Berkeley: University of California Press, 1998.

Redmond, Shana L. *Social Movements and the Sound of Solidarity in the African Diaspora.* New York: New York University Press, 2014.

Reese, Scott S. *Imperial Muslims: Islam, Community and Authority in the Indian Ocean, 1839–1937*. Edinburgh, Scotland: University of Edinburgh Press, 2019.

Reid, Anthony. "Indonesia." In *Southeast Asia under Japanese Occupation*, edited by Alfred McCoy, 16–32. New Haven, CT: Yale University Press, 1980.

Rezrazi, El-Mustafa. "Pan-Asianism and the Japanese Islam: Hanato Uho — From Espionage to Pan-Islamist Activity." *Annals of Japan Association for Middle East Studies* 12 (1987): 89–112.

"Rihui nüsheng chuji lianhuan." *Mengjiang Xinbao*, March 4, 1937.

"Ritorno di due 'ulama' di al-Azhar dalla Cina." *Oriente Moderno* 17, no. 10 (October 1937): 506.

Roberts, Sean. *The War on the Uyghurs*. Princeton, NJ: Princeton University Press, 2020.

Rocklin, Alexander. *The Regulation of Religion and the Making of Hinduism in Colonial Trinidad*. Chapel Hill: University of North Carolina Press, 2019.

Rodriguez, Abe. "Fuirippin Kaikyō no chidō fūshū." *Nihon to Nihonjin* 6, no. 432 (June 1944): 19–21.

Rogaski, Ruth. *Hygienic Modernity: Meanings of Health and Disease in Treaty-Port China*. Berkeley: University of California Press, 2004.

Rorlich, Azade-Ayse. *The Volga Tatars: A Profile of National Resilience*. Stanford, CA: Hoover Institution Press, 1986.

Rousso, Henry. *Le syndrome de Vichy de 1944 à nos jours*. Paris: Seuil, 1987.

Rush, A. de L., ed. *Records of the Hajj: The Pilgrimage to Mecca*, vol. 5. Cambridge: Cambridge University Press, Archive Editions, 1993.

Saaler, Sven. "Pan-Asianism in Modern Japanese History: Overcoming the Nation, Creating a Region, Forging an Empire." In *Pan-Asianism in Modern Japanese History: Colonialism, Regionalism and Borders*, edited by Sven Saaler and J. Victor Koschmann, 1–19. New York: Routledge, 2007.

Saaler, Sven, and Christopher W. A. Szpilman. "Introduction: The Emergence of Pan-Asianism as an Ideal of Asian Identity and Solidarity, 1850–2008." In *Pan-Asianism: A Documentary History*, 1:1–42. Lanham, MD: Rowman & Littlefield, 2011.

Sakei Torakichi. *Manmū no minzoku*. Tokyo: Tōa Nihon Shā, 1943.

Sakuma Jirō. "Shina kaikyōto no kyōiku josei." *Isuramu* 4 (July 1938): 19–25.

Sakurai Masashi. *Daitōa Kaikyō hattatsu-shi*. Tokyo: Sanseidō, 1943.

Salisbury, Harrison. *The Long March: The Untold Story*. New York: Harper Collins, 1985.

Saravia, Tiago. *Fascist Pigs: Technoscientific Organisms and the History of Fascism*. Cambridge, MA: MIT Press, 2016.

Satō Masanori. "Indoneshia ni okeru gunsei no gengo seisaku I." *Taiheiyō Gakki Shi* 6 (April 1980): 111–24.

———. "Indoneshia ni okeru gunsei no gengo seisaku II." *Taiheiyō Gakki Shi* 7 (July 1980): 152–66.

———. "Indoneshia ni okeru gunsei no gengo seisaku III." *Taiheiyō Gakki Shi* 8 (October 1980): 143–50.

Satō Shigeru. "Indonesia, 1939–1942: Prelude to the Japanese Occupation." *Journal of Southeast Asian Studies* 37, no. 2 (June 2006): 225–48.

Schoppa, Keith R. *In a Sea of Bitterness: Refugees during the Sino-Japanese War*. Cambridge, MA: Harvard University Press, 2011.

Sha Lei. "Aiguo yu aijiao." *Huijiao Datong* 6 (1938): 99.

———. "Riben diguo zhuyi zhe gei Huijiao minzu de youhuo." *Huijiao Dazhong* 2 (1938): 27.

Shahabuddin, Mohammad. "Nationalism, Imperialism, and Bandung." In *Bandung, Global History, and International Law: Critical Pasts and Pending Futures*, edited by Louis Eslava, 95–107. Cambridge: Cambridge University Press, 2017.

"Shengjiao yu Guoxue." *Yiselan Xuesheng Zazhi* 1, no. 3 (1933): 14–16.

Shimada Daisuke. "Senchū-ki Nihon no nishiajia-muke senden rajio hōsō to dai Nihon Kaikyō kyōkai." *Media-Shi Kenkyū: Media History* 25 (May 2009): 92–111.

———. "Shōwa senzenki ni okeru Kaikyō seisaku ni kansuru kōsatsu: Dai Nippon Kaikyō kyokai o cyūshin ni." *Isshinkyō Sekai* 6 (2015): 644–86.

Shimbo Atsuko. "Nihon senryōka no pekin ni okeru kaimin kyōiku." In *Kyokaiku ni okeru kaiminzoku teki sōkoku*, edited by Watanabe Sōsuke and Takenaka Kenichi, 232–62. Tokyo: Tōhō Shoten, 2000.

Shimizu Hiroshi. "The Japanese Trade Contact with the Middle East: Lessons from the Pre-oil Period." In *Japan and the Contemporary Middle East*, edited by Sugihara Kaoru and J. A. Allen, 27–53. London: Routledge, 1993.

Shin Kawashima. " 'Deimperialization' in Early Postwar Japan." In *The Dismantling of Japan's Empire in East Asia: Deimperialization, Postwar Legitimation and Imperial Afterlife*, edited by Barak Kushner and Sherzod Muminov, 30–47. New York: Routledge, 2017.

"Shina kaikyōto no shin dōkō." *Tōa* 11, no. 4 (April 1938): 20–30.

"Tea and China's Rise: Tea, Nationalism and Culture in the 21st Century." *International Communications and Chinese Culture* 2, no. 3 (December 2015): 319–41.

Silverstein, Josef. "The Importance of the Japanese Occupation of Southeast Asia to the Political Scientist." In *Southeast Asia in WWII: Four Essays*, edited by Josef Silverstein, 1–11. New Haven, CT: Yale University Press, 1966.

Slamet, M. *Japanese Machinations, IV: A Japanese "Dalang" in Java*. Batavia: n.p., 1946.

Snow, Edgar. *Red Star over China*. New York: Grove, 1938.

"Son of King of Yemen is in Shanghai." *Shanghai Times*, May 3, 1938.

Stegewerns, Dick. "The Dilemma of Nationalism and Internationalism in Modern Japan: National Interest, Asian Brotherhood, International Cooperation or World Citizenship?" In *Nationalism and Internationalism in Imperial Japan: Autonomy, Asian Brotherhood, or World Citizenship*, edited by Dick Stegewerns, 3–16. London: Routledge, 2003.

Suda Masatsugu. *Tairiku seisaku to Kaikyō mondai*. Tokyo: Yani Yapon Mofubirī, October 1937.

Sugita Hideaki. *Nihonjin no chūtō hakken*. Tokyo: Tokyo University Press, 1995.

Sun Shengwu. "Kangzhan yilai Huijiao tongbao de guomin waijiao." *Huijiao luntan banyuekan* 2, no. 12 (1939): 3–9.

"Sun Yatsen on the Role of Chinese Muslims in China and the World." Document translated by Max Oidtmann and used with permission.

Suzuki Akira. "An Aspect of Middle Eastern and Islamic Studies in Wartime Japan: A Case of Hajime Kobayashi (1904–1963)." *Annals of the Japanese Association for Middle East Studies* 23, no. 2 (2007): 195–214.

Suzuki Takeshi. *Nihon kaikyōto no Mekka junrei-ki*. Tokyo: Greater Japan Printing, 1938.

Suzuki Tomohide. "Nanpō Kaikyō no kenkyū to Kaikyō taisaku." *Kokusai Bunka* 24 (March 1942): 35–41.

Szpilman, Christopher W. A. "Between Pan-Asianism and Nationalism: Mitsukawa

Kametaro and His Campaign to Reform Japan and Liberate Asia." In *Pan-Asianism in Modern Japanese History: Colonialism, Regionalism, and Borders*, edited by Sveen Saaler and Victor Koschmann, 85–100. New York: Routledge: 2007.

Takahashi Sejima. *Indoneshia Tenbyō*. Tokyo: Aikoku Shinbun Shuppansha, 1942.

"Takahashi's Blacks." *Time*, October 5, 1942.

Taketani, Etsuko. "The Cartography of the Black Pacific: James Weldon Johnson's *Along This Way*." *American Quarterly* 59, no. 1 (March 2007): 79–106.

Tanabe Yasunosuke. *Afuganisutan-zen*. Tokyo: Tōa Dōbunkai Chōsa Hensanbu, 1930.

Tanada Hirofumi. "Senchūki Nihon ni okeru Kaikyō kenkyū." *Shakaigaku Nenshi* 47, no. 3 (2006): 117–36.

———. "Islamic Research Institutes in Wartime Japan: Introductory Investigation of the 'Deposited Materials by the *Dai-Nippon Kaikyō Kyokai* (Great Japan Muslim League).'" *Annals of the Japanese Association of Middle East Studies* 28, no. 2 (2012): 85–106.

Tanaka Ippei. *Isuramu to dai Ajia shugi*. Tokyo, 1924.

———. *Tenpo shisei jitsuroku*. Tokyo: Dai Nihon Kaikyō Kyōkai Shippanbu, 1941.

Tanaka, Stefan. *Japan's Orient: Rendering Pasts into History*. Berkeley: University of California Press, 1993.

Tang Yichen. *Maijia xunli ji*. Beijing: Zhenzong Baoshe Kanben, 1945.

Tatāru mondai. Japanese Ministry of Foreign Affairs, Muslim Relations Section (1:2:1:0:1—1 DSCF 0107–0143): 1939.

Taylor, Diana. *Disappearing Acts: Specters of Gender and Nationalism in Argentina's "Dirty War*." Durham, NC: Duke University Press, 1997.

"Telegram to Pakistan from Bai Chongxi." International Religious Affairs, 020–029903–0003 (June 14, 1951). Academia Historica, Chinese Nationalist Foreign Ministry Archives.

Tewa Dua. "Shijie huimin yundong yu zhongguo Huijiao yundong." *Huixie* 4, no. 1–4 (1947): 1–2.

Thøgersen, Stig. *A County of Culture: Twentieth-Century China Seen from the Village Schools of Zouping, Shandong*. Ann Arbor: University of Michigan Press, 2002.

Thum, Rian. *The Sacred Routes of Uyghur History*. Cambridge, MA: Harvard University Press, 2014.

Thum, Rian. "The Uyghurs in Modern China." In *Oxford Research Encyclopedia of Asian History*, edited by David Ludden (online only). New York: Oxford University Press, 2016.

Tian Xing. "Yingde de Huijiao zhengce." *Xin Dongfang* 4, no. 2 (August 1941): 133.

Tianfeng Puwu. "Zhongguo guomin waijiao zai Aiji." *Zhongguo Huijiao Jiuguo Huihuibao* 11/12 (1941): 5.

Tilly, Charles. "Retrieving European Lives." In *Reliving the Past: The Worlds of Social History*, edited by Olivier Zunz, 11–52. Chapel Hill: University of North Carolina Press, 1985.

"Tōa ni okeru Kaikyō seiryoku." *Dai Ajia Shugi* 6, no. 61 (1940): 23–27.

Togō Fumio. *Manshū shūkyō no gaikan*. Tokyo: Nichiman Bukkyō Kyōkai Honbu, 1936.

"Tōkyō Kaikyō gakkō no kodomotachi." *Kodomo* 17, no. 6 (May 1938).

"Tong huimin xiaoxue riyu fabiao hui." *Mengjiang Xinbao*. March 18, 1937.

Treat, John Whittier. "Choosing to Collaborate: Yi Kwang-su and the Moral Subject in Colonial Korea." *Journal of Asian Studies* 71, no. 1 (February 2012): 81–102.

Trevaskis, G. K. N. *Eritrea—A Colony in Transition: 1941–1954*. London: Oxford University Press, 1960.

Tuoheti, Alimu. *Nihon ni okeru isurāmu kenkyū-shi: Chūgoku-hen*. Tokyo: Shumpusha, 2019.

Tuttle, Gray. *Tibetan Buddhists in the Making of Modern China*. New York: Columbia University Press, 2005.

Um, Nancy. *Shipped but Not Sold: Material Culture and the Social Protocols of Trade during Yemen's Age of Coffee*. Honolulu: University of Hawai'i Press, 2017.

"Umar Mita: First Muslim Translator of the Qur'an to Japanese." *Islam in Japan Media Program*. islaminjapanmedia.org/umar-meta.

Wakeman, Frederic, Jr. "*Hanjian* (Traitor)! Collaboration and Retribution in Wartime Shanghai." In *Becoming Chinese: Passages to Modernity and Beyond*, edited by Wen-hsin Yeh, 298–341. Berkeley: University of California Press, 2000.

Wang Hao. "Kangzhanzhong de zhongguo huimin waijiao." *Xin Mumin* 2 (1943): 66–70.

Wang Shiming. "Zuijin de kangzhan xingshi." *Zhongguo Huijiao Jiuguo Huihui Kan* 2, no. 2 (1940): 7.

Weiner, Benno. *The Chinese Revolution on the Tibetan Frontier*. Ithaca, NY: Cornell University Press, 2020.

Wen Shuang. "From Manchuria to Egypt: Soybean's Global Migration and Transformation in the 20th Century." *Asian Journal of Middle Eastern and Islamic Studies* 13, no. 2 (April 2019): 176–94.

Wetherell, Charles. "Historical Social Network Analysis." *International Review of Social History* 43 (1998): 125–44.

Wickizer, Vernon Dale. *Tea under International Regulation*. Stanford, CA: Food Research Institute at Stanford University Press, 1944.

Wien, Peter. *Arab Nationalism: The Politics of History and Culture in the Modern Middle East*. New York: Routledge, 2017.

Wiest, Jean-Paul. "Catholic Elementary and Secondary Schools and China's Drive toward a Modern Educational System (1850–1950)." *Extrême-Orient / Extrême-Occident* 33 (2011): 91–113.

Willis, John M. *Unmaking North and South: Cartographies of the Yemeni Past*. New York: Columbia University Press, 2012.

Wong, J. Y., ed. "Thirty Years of Chinese-Arabic Cultural Relationship." In *Sun Yatsen: His International Ideas and International Connections*, edited by J. Y. Wong, 15–38. Sydney: Wild Peony, 1987.

Woo, Orodic Y. K. "Chinese Collaboration with Japan: Localizing the Study of the War." In *Chinese Collaboration with Japan, 1932–1945: The Limits of Accommodation*, edited by David P. Barrett and Larry N. Shyu, 226–36. Stanford, CA: Stanford University Press: 2001.

Wu Huizhong. "Sign of the Times: China's Capital Orders Arabic, Muslim Symbols Taken Down." *Reuters*, July 30, 2019. https://www.reuters.com/article/us-china-religion -islam/sign-of-the-times-chinas-capital-orders-arabic-muslim-symbols-taken-down -idUSKCN1UQ0JF.

Wu, Shellen. "The Silent Half Speaks." *Journal of Chinese History* 2 (2018): 203–10.

Xue Wenbo. "Huijiao shijie de mogui huodong." *Huijiao Jiuguo Huihuibao* 1, no. 8 (1939): 34.

Yamada-sei. "Tōkyō Kaikyō gakkō man tōnen shukagakai kiji." *Nihon Oyo Nihonjin* 349 (June 1, 1937): 58–62.

Yamato Masadomi, "Kaikyō seisaku yori mitaru tōa shin chitsushō sensatsu." *Aikoku Gakusei* 16 (August 1940): 35–39.

Yamazaki (née Unno) Noriko. "Abdürreşid İbrahim's Journey to China: Muslim Communities in the Late Qing as Seen by a Russian-Tatar Intellectual." *Central Asian Review* 33, no. 3 (2014): 405–20.

———. "Cutting Off the Queue for Faith, Preserving the Queue for Face: Chinese Muslims' Queue-Cutting Movements in North China during the Xinhai Revolution Period." *Asian Studies* 6, no. 22 (January 2018): 11–31.

———. "Nicchū sensōki no chūgoku musurimu shakai ni okeru 'shin'nichiha' musurimu ni kansuru ichikōsatsu: Chūgoku Kaikyō sō rengō-kai no Tang Yichen o chūshin ni." *Monthly Journal of Chinese Affairs / Zhongguo Yanjiu Yuebao* 65, no. 9 (2011): 1–20.

———. "Nihon no Kaikyō kōsaku [Japan's Islamic Campaigns]." In *60 Chapters for Learning about Muslims in China/Chūgoku no musurimu wo shiru tame no*, edited by the Society for Chinese Studies, 268–72. Tokyo: Akashi Shoten, 2012.

Yang Jingzhi. *Riben zhi Huijiao zhengce*. Chongqing: Yisilan Wenhua Xuehui, 1943.

Yang Zigang. "Wo zai ouzhou zuyjian dao de yisilan xiongdi." *Zhongguo Huijiao Jiuguo Yuekan* 7, nos. 8–12 (1944): 1–8.

Yellen, Jeremy A. *The Greater East Asia Co-Prosperity Sphere*. New York: Columbia University Press, 2019.

Yokota Motoko. "1906-Nen ni okeru Mongorujin-gakusei no Nihon ryūgaku." *East West South North* 15 (2009): 155–72.

———. "Naimoko-'Harqin' hata gakudō seito no Nihon tome gaku." *Ajia Minzoku Zōkei Gakkaish* 5 (2006): 91–108.

Young, Louise. "Early-Twentieth-Century Japan in a Global Context: Japan's New International History." *American Historical Review* 119, no. 4 (October 2014): 1117–28.

———. *Japan's Total Empire: Manchuria and the Culture of Wartime Imperialism*. Berkeley: University of California Press, 1999.

Zen Jawa Kaikyō Jōkyō Chōsasho. Jakarta: Headquarters of the Osama Group, Sixteenth Army, 1943.

"Zenme jiao nide haizi." *Mengjiang Xinbao*. February 2, 1938.

Zhang Huaide. "Zhongguo Huijiao chaojin riji." *Huimin Yanlun* 1, no. 11 (1939): 36.

"Zhanhou huibao yingyou de nuli." *Qingzhen Duobao* 18 (1945): 2–3.

Zhao Tangqi. "Lun Zhongguo Huijiao zhi guomin jiaoyu." *Xing Hui Pian*, 1908: 64–72.

Zhao Zhenwu. "Sanshinian lai zhi zhongguo Huijiao wenhuagaikuang." *Yugong* 5, no. 11 (August 1936): 15.

Zhu Jianmin. "Riben yu Yisilanjiao." *Huijiao Datong* 8/9 (1938): 132–35.

Zhuang Wubin. *Chinese Muslims in Indonesia*. New York: Select, 2008.

Zia-Ebrahimi, Reza. "Self-Orientalization and Dislocation: The Uses and Abuses of the 'Aryan' Discourse in Iran." *Iranian Studies* 44, no. 4 (July 2011): 445–75.

Index

data collection, Japanese policy of, 14, 33, 35–36, 50–54, 64; Black Dragon Society, 44; Dutch East Indies, 156; Greater Japan Muslim League, 149, 156, 168; religious associations, 51

data collection, Nationalist reconnaissance missions, 75–79

data collection, U.S. Office of Strategic Services, 211

Ding Zaiqin: educational reforms, 91

diplomatic relations, 29–30, 66–67, 151, 178, 187–88, 189; *Ertuğrul* shipwreck, impact of, 45–46; İsa Yūsuf Alptekin, 119–20; Japan/Afghanistan relations, 205, 206, 209–10, 213; Japan/Saudi relations, 124–25; Japanese support of *hajj*, 121–29; Japanese withdrawal from League of Nations, 14; Sino-Muslims, use of, 1–2, 4, 23–24, 26, 37, 43, 46, 73, 93, 109, 110, 143, 227–28; tea, tea drinking, and the tea trade, 163, 166–68; Tokyo Mosque, 113–14

divided China, 11–14, 16–17, 123

division and isolation of Sino-Muslim communities, 42, 72, 91–92, 101

Drang nach Osten policy, 200–202

Du Bois, W. E. B., 191–93

Dutch East Indies, 109, 154–56; anticolonial sentiment, 157–58; data collection, Japanese policy of, 156; exploitation of nationalism by Japanese, 157, 223; language reforms, 160–62; mobilization of Muslim leaders, 156–57. *See also* Indonesia

educational reforms to influence Sino-Muslims (Japanese reforms), 80–83, 105–6; Ainu language, 93; curriculum changes in Muslim schools, 28–29; education of women, 94–95, 97–98; family participation, 96–97; importance of, 84–85; incentive scholarships, 82–83, 85, 100–101, 121; Japanese language, 83–84, 96, 97; methods and motivations, 98–100, 101–5; propaganda and promotion, 95, 97; resistance, 88–89, 93–98, 102–5; Southeast Asia, 160–63

educational reforms to influence Sino-Muslims (Nationalist reforms), 85–87, 106; curriculum changes in Muslim schools, 28–29; language reforms, 80–81; resistance, 88–89; Three People's Principles, 87. *See also* madrassas; schools

Eritrea, 127, 132, 134–35, 140

ethnographic data: Japanese expansionism, use to justify, 33–34, 54, 64

ethnonationalism, 5, 6, 8–9

ethnopolitics, 8; Qing empire, 10–11

ethnoreligious identity, 10, 38–39, 105, 175–76, 224

expansionism, 29; "advance on land", 42; Axis partners, 29–30, 200–202; *Drang nach Osten* policy, 200–202; East Asia, 29; ethnographic data, use to justify expansionism, 33–34, 54, 64; Fascist Italy, 196–99; international trade, 29; Nazi Germany, 200–202; religious associations and, 51, 67; Russian imperial expansion, 205

fascism and Japan's fascist aspirations, 15–16, 148, 183–84; Berlin-Rome-Tokyo Axis, 194–218; Japan's interest in Fascist Italy, 184. *See also* Afghanistan; Fascist Italy; Nazi Germany

Fascist Italy, 12–13, 109; African occupations, 134–36; Eritrea, 134–35; expansionist ambitions, 196–99; *Italy's Muslim Policy*, 29, 196–98; Japanese admiration for, 194–95, 196–99; Mussolini as "protector of Islam," 197–98; Yemen, relationship with, 114–15

France: French colonialism, 44, 49, 139, 153, 197, 200–201; Muslim Brotherhood, 49; Suez crisis, 226–27; tea trade, concerns about Japanese control of, 172–73; World War II collaboration, 18, 158

"Free" China, 26, 48, 69, 73, 78, 85, 92, 128, 147

frontier issues, 8–9, 17, 170

Garvey, Marcus, 191–92

global Muslim networks, 3–4, 23–24, 25–27,

Konoe Fumimaro, 154
Korean peninsula, 21, 32–33, 34–35;
    Japanese educational reforms, 93, 161–62;
    Japanese treatment of minorities, 63–65;
    March First Movement, 64
Kwantung Army, 12

language and identity, 89–92
language reforms: assimilation policies,
    90–91; centrality of, 89–92; Chinese
    language learning, 91–92; Dutch East
    Indies, 160–62; educational reforms
    (Japanese reforms), 83–84, 96, 97, 105–7,
    160–63; educational reforms (Nationalist
    reforms), 80–81, 106; educational
    reforms generally, 28–29, 80–84, 90;
    Japanese language learning, 92, 93–98;
    Korea, 162; Malaya, 162; New Culture
    Movement, 87; North China, 161, 162;
    occupied China, 93–98; Southeast Asia,
    160–63; Taiwan, 161, 162
League of Nations, 12, 14
legitimacy of Japanese support for Islam,
    42–43, 72, 148–49

Ma Bufang, 74–75
Ma Buqing, 74–75
Ma clans, 12, 39
madrasahs, 80, 85–87, 106, 160
Ma Fuliang, 119, 136, 137–38, 139
Ma Fuxiang, 39–40
Ma Hongbin, 40
Ma Hongkui, 40, 48, 74–75
Ma Jian, 136, 199
Malaya, 109, 145, 154, 158–60, 198, 229;
    language reforms, 161, 162; relationship
    between Muslims and *Guomindang*, 159–
    60; resistance, 158–59; tea trade, 165
Ma Liangpu, 122, 128, 130
Manchukuo, 13; establishment, 12–13, 31,
    33–34; Japanese wartime identity and,
    26–27; recognition of, 14
Manchu Qing, 37; social Darwinism,
    impact of, 9
Manchuria, 11–12; invasion of, 84–85. *See
    also* Manchukuo
Manchurian Islamic Association, 52

Mao Zedong, 28; Suez Canal Crisis, 227
Ma Qianling, 39
March First Movement (1919), 64
Ma Ruitu, 38
Masayuki Yokoyama, 124–25, 187
Ma Shaoyun, 140
Ma Songting, 128
Massawa. *See* Eritrea
Mas' support for Nationalists, 40–41
Ma Tianying, 120
Matsuda Hisao, 50
Matsumuro Takayoshi, 175, 177
Ma Wanfu, 86
May Fourth Movement (1919), 87
Mei Cun, 62–63
Meiji era (1868–1912), 9, 14, 28, 33–35, 43,
    45–46, 63–64, 84, 170, 207, 214
Mesa, Yahia Abdul, 152–53
minorities: Chinese treatment of, 8, 17, 20,
    27–28, 61, 73–74, 78; Japanese treatment
    of, 21, 27, 35, 55, 63–66, 67, 83–85, 142, 190,
    223–24
minzu, concept of, 9, 56, 61, 76, 226
mobilization of Muslim leaders, 6, 72, 85,
    156–57, 200–201
Moros, 82, 111, 149–50
mosque construction, 70–72, 78. *See also*
    Tokyo Mosque
Mount Arafat, 137
Mughal empire, 60
Murata Shōzō, 215
Muslim Brotherhood, 49

Nationalist concerns regarding Japanese
    support for Chinese Muslims, 1–2, 6,
    73–75, 146–47, 186, 188–89; Nationalist
    reconnaissance missions to occupied
    China, 75–79
National Muslim Congress (1939), 75
National People's Army, 12
Nation of Islam, 44, 185, 193–94, 218
Nazi Germany, 12, 109; Aryan mythology,
    30, 185, 216–18; expansionism, 200–202;
    Japanese admiration for, 194–95, 200–
    203, 218–19; Japanese policy overlaps,
    29–30, 186–87, 224; Nazi propaganda,
    202, 217–18; racial categorizations, 202

networks of Sino-Muslims, 2–4; Japanese use of, 5–8
New Culture Movement, 87
Noda Shōtarō, 44
non-Han communities: data collection, 35; educational policies, 85; integration of, 8–9, 11, 21, 27, 90, 225; Mao Zedong, 28; Nationalists' policy, 73–74

occupied China, 13, 15–17, 28; collaboration, 19–20; collaboration of Sino-Muslims, 20–23; displacement of populations, 22; schools and educational reforms, 93–98; Sino-Muslim resistance, 49–50, 69, 70, 88–89, 93–98
Office of Strategic Services (OSS) (USA), 211; concern regarding Japanese overtures to Sino-Muslims, 221
Ōhara Takeyoshi, 44
oil concessions, 124–25, 166, 187
Okakura Kakuzō, 170–71
Ōkawa Shūmei, 56–57
Ōtani Kōzui, 207, 214
outreach campaigns, 2–3, 28–29, 31–32, 36, 50, 63, 66, 81, 121, 153, 202, 204; Afghanistan, 163; Buddhist networks compared, 55–56; Greater Japan Muslim League, 32–33; oil concessions, 124; tea trade, 163–69
overseas Chinese Muslims, 49, 61

pan-Asianism, concept of, 13–14, 54–55, 222; Afro-Asian solidarity, 222–23; Sun Yat-sen, 56; Suzuki Takeshi, 59; Tanaka Ippei, 57–59
Pang Shiqian, 128
People's Republic of China (PRC), 226; foreign policy, 226–27; forgetting as official policy, 6; integration of minorities, 28; Islamophobia, 228; repression of Uyghurs, 228
Philippines, 29, 109, 113, 145, 149, 154
postwar China: civil war, 19–20, 40–41, 221–22; exploitation of Sino-Muslim unease, 7–8
poverty and deprivation among Sino-Muslim communities, 35

Prince Hussein of Yemen, 113–15, 117
propaganda: Allied propaganda, 109; Greater Japan Muslim League, 197, 198; Japanese propaganda, 1, 3, 16–17, 18, 27, 66, 123, 145–46, 156–57, 193–94, 197, 198, 224; Muslim schools, 78–79, 88, 98–99; Nationalist propaganda, 30, 47–49, 61, 75, 90, 109, 120–21, 147, 213, 227–28; Nazi propaganda, 202, 217–18; Tokyo Mosque, 116–17
Prophet Muhammad, 11, 43, 58, 60, 158
publications for Sino-Muslims, 47, 50–53

Qing empire, 8–9, 62; ethnopolitics, 10–11; *hanzu*, concept of, 10–11
Quran: Japanese translations, 43–44; relation and state, relationship between, 48

reimagining history: construction of a Japanese Islamic history, 45–46, 59–63, 70–71
religion, concept of, 41–43
religious associations and Japanese expansionism, 51, 67
resistance to Japanese imperialism by Sino-Muslims, 49–50, 69, 70; educational reforms (Japanese reforms), 88–89, 93–98; educational reforms (Nationalist reforms), 88–89; lack of unity, 5–6; Malaya, 158–59; reporting on Japanese activities, 69–70
right to self-determination, 28, 149, 218
Russia, 190, 200–201, 204–7, 209, 215
Russian Revolution (1917–23), 64
Russo-Japanese War (1904–5), 12, 176, 191

Saudi Arabia, 124–25, 136, 139–40; oil concessions, 187
schools: curriculum changes for Muslim schools, 28–29; educating young Muslims, 98–105; Japan's expansionist use of, 70, 93–105. *See also* educational reforms to influence Sino-Muslims (Japanese reforms); educational reforms to influence Sino-Muslims (Nationalist reforms); language reforms

Islamic Civilization and Muslim Networks

Michael Muhammad Knight, *Muhammad's Body: Baraka Networks and the Prophetic Assemblage* (2020).

Kelly A. Hammond, *China's Muslims and Japan's Empire: Centering Islam in World War II* (2020).

Zachary Valentine Wright, *Realizing Islam: The Tijaniyya in North Africa and the Eighteenth-Century Muslim World* (2020).

Alex Dika Seggerman, *Modernism on the Nile: Art in Egypt Between the Islamic and the Contemporary* (2019).

Babak Rahimi and Peyman Eshaghi, *Muslim Pilgrimage in the Modern World* (2019)

Simon Wolfgang Fuchs, *In a Pure Muslim Land: Shi'ism between Pakistan and the Middle East* (2019).

Gary R. Bunt, *Hashtag Islam: How Cyber Islamic Environments Are Transforming Religious Authority* (2018).

Ahmad Dallal, *Islam without Europe: Traditions of Reform in Eighteenth-Century Islamic Thought* (2018).

Irfan Ahmad, *Religion as Critique: Islamic Critical Thinking from Mecca to the Marketplace* (2017).

Scott Kugle, *When Sun Meets Moon: Gender, Eros, and Ecstasy in Urdu Poetry* (2016).

Kishwar Rizvi, *The Transnational Mosque: Architecture, Historical Memory, and the Contemporary Middle East* (2015).

Ebrahim Moosa, *What Is a Madrasa?* (2015).

Bruce Lawrence, *Who Is Allah?* (2015).

Edward E. Curtis IV, *The Call of Bilal: Islam in the African Diaspora* (2014).

Sahar Amer, *What Is Veiling?* (2014).

Rudolph T. Ware III, *The Walking Qur'an: Islamic Education, Embodied Knowledge, and History in West Africa* (2014).

Sa'diyya Shaikh, *Sufi Narratives of Intimacy: Ibn 'Arabī, Gender, and Sexuality* (2012).

Karen G. Ruffle, *Gender, Sainthood, and Everyday Practice in South Asian Shi'ism* (2011).

Jonah Steinberg, *Isma'ili Modern: Globalization and Identity in a Muslim Community* (2011).

Iftikhar Dadi, *Modernism and the Art of Muslim South Asia* (2010).

Gary R. Bunt, *iMuslims: Rewiring the House of Islam* (2009).

Fatemeh Keshavarz, *Jasmine and Stars: Reading More Than "Lolita" in Tehran* (2007).

Scott Kugle, *Sufis and Saints' Bodies: Mysticism, Corporeality, and Sacred Power in Islam* (2007).

Roxani Eleni Margariti, *Aden and the Indian Ocean Trade: 150 Years in the Life of a Medieval Arabian Port* (2007).

Sufia M. Uddin, *Constructing Bangladesh: Religion, Ethnicity, and Language in an Islamic Nation* (2006).

Omid Safi, *The Politics of Knowledge in Premodern Islam: Negotiating Ideology and Religious Inquiry* (2006).

Ebrahim Moosa, *Ghazālī and the Poetics of Imagination* (2005).

miriam cooke and Bruce B. Lawrence, eds., *Muslim Networks from Hajj to Hip Hop* (2005).

Carl W. Ernst, *Following Muhammad: Rethinking Islam in the Contemporary World* (2003).

CPSIA information can be obtained
at www.ICGtesting.com
Printed in the USA
LVHW010038071020
668109LV00007B/764